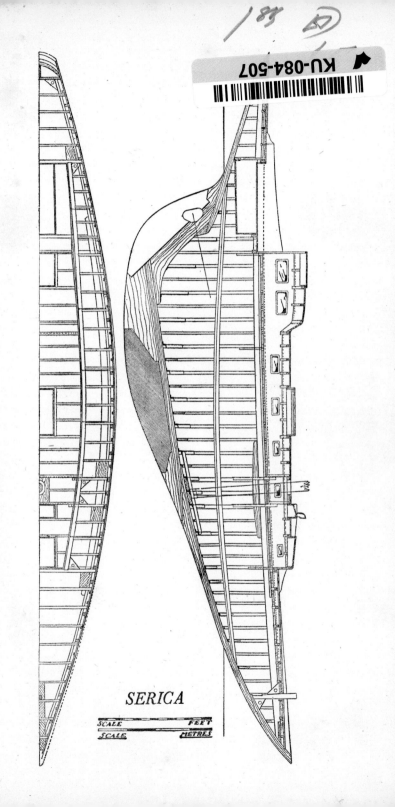

SERICA

SCALE        FEET
SCALE        METRES

# A WHITE BOAT
## FROM
# ENGLAND

❖

*SERICA* RACING AT COWES

GEORGE MILLAR

✧

# A WHITE BOAT
## FROM
# ENGLAND

WILLIAM HEINEMANN LTD
MELBOURNE :: LONDON :: TORONTO

FIRST PUBLISHED 1951

PRINTED IN GREAT BRITAIN
AT THE WINDMILL PRESS
KINGSWOOD, SURREY

To
Our Dear
Doña Maria Teresa

# CONTENTS

# ILLUSTRATIONS

# PREFACE

UNLIKE most others who have written on the sea and boats I know little about either, and this has advantages as well as disadvantages, since to describe some experiences on the sea in a manner understandable to landsmen may be easier for a novice like me than for one of the experts whom I so greatly admire. If I dare now to give an account of a journey by sea in a small boat from England to the Mediterranean it is because I enjoyed it and suffered it and wanted to share those feelings. What I must make clear is that I am not pretending to teach in describing so ordinary a journey. As a novice, my envy for those navigators who know —or seem to know—exactly what they are about is occasionally tempered by a suspicion that I get at least as much enjoyment out of our little promenades as they do out of their great ones. The reader will soon discern my method, for it is simple. After taking all reasonable precautions to see that hull, gear, sails, and crew are sound, I fling myself (and my wife) on the waters. Then we pick up the remains. The process is wonderfully stimulating.

The sea has really been very decent to us, and I like its smell, its unreliability, and its capacity for making the delights of the land seem desirable beyond the dreams of Alcibiades.

We have also been lucky with our boats. (I scarcely like, so early in my book, to write the Dutch word "yacht". Though I have no great dislike for the word, it is said to have an opulent sound, and I am a poor man living in proletarian days. I know that some yachtsmen would not have me call a yacht a boat—but what else? a ship, as many of them do? ridiculous!) We bought the first one soon after the end of the 1939–45 war, a thirty-one-ton ketch (with much auxiliary power) called *Truant*. We sailed her to Greece, where we sold her to a delightful cavalryman, the late General George Clark, who sailed her home again. *Truant* is in good hands today, as she deserves, and is much to be seen in English waters with a cheerful family crew. Our second boat, *Serica*, an exceptionally fast sixteen-ton sloop designed by Mr. Robert Clark, is an absolute contrast to our first. Where *Truant*, the converted Looe lugger, with her great beam, stumpy masts, straight stem, and transom with gilded dolphins, gives an impression of strength and great sea-worthiness, *Serica*, graceful, slender, tall-masted, and with long over-hangs for a modern boat, may look pretty rather than practical. *Truant* is a fine sea-boat, yet I have no hesitation in saying that *Serica* is the better in all weathers, and is the more comfortable cruiser. If I had to ride out a full gale in either I should choose the Bermudian sloop—for all her high mast—because when the sea runs high and the wind begins to whistle its threats she gives such a wonderful "feel", as a horseman says of his mount.

I have to thank Mr. Clark for the measured drawings which appear in this book. When I wrote asking for these I also asked what he had aimed at when he designed *Serica* (she was built in 1938 by the Sussex Yacht Building Company at Shoreham-by-Sea). He replied:

"I wanted to provide cruising accommodation with sufficient space and displacement for the comfort that is usually found in a twenty-tonner; to keep the boat as small as possible for economy and easy handling; and at the same time to design a hull form and rig that would give the boat a really good all round performance. I particularly wanted the boat to be fast to windward, a comfortable sea-boat, and a pleasure to steer, because a boat that does not possess these qualities cannot give the sort of pleasure that is the great delight of sailing. We have also built three other boats to the same design, *John Dory*, *Corinna*, and *Phantom Light*. These boats have demonstrated their ability to win ocean races against the best in Europe."

I must also thank my friend Mr. May of the Berthon Boat Co, Ltd. for giving me leave to publish the aerial photograph of the Lymington River,

We left England in *Serica*, not intending to break any records or to cover vast watery spaces, but merely to move about Europe economic-ally and in comfort, *great* comfort according to true standards. We sailed round the coasts of France, Spain, and Portugal, to the Mediter-ranean. I think we chose this route because we had taken *Truant* through the canals and rivers of France from Le Havre to Marseilles, and although we loved the inland waterways (and we often long to go back to them) we had both felt that that easy route was something of a cheat, and we wondered what it was like to sail round the outside.

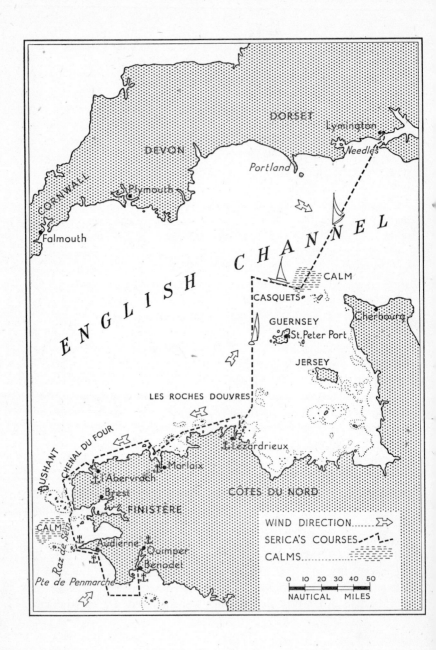

DORSET

Lymington

DEVON

*Needles*

*Portland*

Plymouth

CORNWALL

ENGLISH CHANNEL

CALM

Falmouth

CASQUETS

Cherbourg

GUERNSEY

St. Peter Port

JERSEY

LES ROCHES DOUVRES

CHENAL DU FOUR

L. Lezardrieux

USHANT

L.l'Abervrach

Morlaix

Brest

COTES DU NORD

FINISTÈRE

CALMS

Audierne

Quimper

*Raz de Sein*

Benodet

*Pte de Penmarche*

WIND DIRECTION........ ⊳

SERICA'S COURSES----

CALMS................

0  10  20  30  40  50

NAUTICAL   MILES

CHAPTER 1

## THE CHANNEL

Up the river the yachts lay that night with their flanks in nests of soft mud, deep mud said to be dangerous. The mud swallows everything; objects such as knives it devours, but lighter-density objects are sucked down slowly, slowly. Old men come to the yacht yard with metal cages on the ends of poles. They sift at the creamy edges of the mud and lift out carpet slippers and egg-whisks, which they regard with capricious interest before returning them to that smooth, all-consuming maw. How many yachtsmen have dismembered their mistresses and slid torsos, femurs, clavicles, and delicate, folded ears into the Lymington mud?

Beside the creek the agreeable town of Lymington slumbered with dignity, its sash windows reflecting the shining velvet of the night. An airless night, the sky clear of any shred of cloud, and unusually hot for June. The people of Lymington pushed down their all-wool blankets, and lay in the half-life of sleep, covered only by sheets.

At 4 a.m., when Isabel and I went on deck, the tide had whispered its moon-drawn saunter over the mud-banks, lifting the yachts, including ours, from their nests. The creek had become a river, wide, sullen, leaden, with the tide chuckling and the nervous yachts shivering against each other's fenders. Tall masts pricked a low sky that seemed to be a greater version of the river; some of the masts were painted white, but the majority, our own included, were varnished to display the golden wood that is known as silver spruce.

Aware of those who lay sleeping near us, we whispered, and stepped delicately on rubber soles as we set about the unfamiliar business of getting under way. It was a Saturday morning. Empty cars were herded in the yacht yard between the creosoted sheds. Week-enders were going sailing. An ocean race was to begin later that morning.

No wind. . . . our engine proved to be unusually silent. Soon we were moving downstream between two lines of moored boats, past the Isle of Wight ferry, past the Royal Lymington Yacht Club, whose balconies were empty, whose slips, clustered round with snub-nosed, short-bodied, broad-bosomed dinghies, were deserted. On the balconies

1

the telescopes on tripods stretched out their glinting eyes to the Solent and the mist-enshrouded island.

While, in the murmurous interior of the yacht, I was setting breakfast dishes on a tray I felt from a liberated swing of movement that we had cleared the river mouth. Isabel called from the cockpit: would I give her the bearing to pass the Needles? That landmark should have been visible, but we were brushing through a heat haze. Above us the sun was a sphere whiter than the surrounding whiteness, around us white tendrils were heaped on the smooth water. No wind. . . . Now and then the mists trembled to the bray of a big ship probing up to Southampton with pilot, echo-sounder, radar. On the radar screen we were visible as the smallest of small dots moving toward France. A forty-ton yawl came out from the coast of the Isle of Wight and crossed our bows, motoring. Her sails hung damply. Her professional skipper, perched behind the wheel, was rolling a cigarette. He gave us a nod, knowing, confident, neither friendly nor hostile. We saw no land after the sedgy mouth of the Lymington River (and were to see none for two days and a night). The red eggs of buoys, Trinity House spawn marking the channel between Hurst Point and the Needles, appeared out of the haze and vanished.

As the waking sun began to lick the haze off the water a flicker of wind came from the west. We hoisted the mainsail and the big Genoa. It was an unusual English Channel, flat, oily, hot. Even in the cockpit, under the sickle-shaped scoop of the mainsail, it was hot. Gently she sailed south, and while she sailed we felt her tiller and watched the ripples her form swept into the smooth water, and listened to her sailing noises. We lunched in the cockpit: omelette fines herbes, watercress salad, strawberries, Stilton, iced lager. . . . The light airs that were sending *Serica* along at four and five knots would scarcely have filled the mainsail of a slower type of boat.

At the end of May (twelve days before the night with which this book opens) we had determined to sail *Serica* to foreign waters. She had then been for twenty months in a shed on dry land. We hurried south from Sutherland (at the northern end of Britain) to Lymington (at the southern), lived aboard while the fitting-out was done—and now we were at sea, bound for the Mediterranean.

We had made no detailed plans before setting out, but had contemplated sailing down-Channel for Brest, or for the north-western corner of France. Now, with the Westerly fading and hot stillness all around, we chose to go to Guernsey, and began to study the Sailing Directions, charts, and Tide Tables, with a view to entering St. Peter Port. I was perplexed by the tidal data because, apart from a rushed crossing from the Hamble River to Le Havre in *Truant* (before thankfully squeezing the ketch into the canals of France), my navigating had been done in the all but tideless waters of the Mediterranean and the Ægean, or on the stones and grit of the Lybian desert. There is nothing complicated about navigating in tidal waters (I was soon to learn) once the navigator knows where to look for information in Admiralty or other publications. I was more seriously worried by my compasses, which differed by a margin that could only be termed enormous, namely eleven degrees. An experienced yachtsman (who writes *practical* books about yachting) had advised me to buy a hand-bearing compass of a type used by the Royal Air Force. I had mounted this instrument on a teak bracket inside the doghouse. By taking it out and sighting it along the yacht's centre line I could check the bearing on the big steering compass, mounted centrally at the forward end of the cockpit.

"The error will be in the big compass," I said.

"The big one looks the more reliable to me," Isabel said.

Although I had little respect for such reasons as she advanced for her preference, I decided to steer on a mean between the two compass readings, and at 8 p.m. we heard a fog signal booming ahead that we identified as the diaphone on the Casquets. We were therefore on our course for St. Peter Port.

The wind had died. Isabel suggested that since the weather was so remarkably peaceful we might go to bed. The last few days had been exhausting. . . . I took down the Genoa, double-reefed the mainsail (more to see if I knew how to do it than to accomplish any useful purpose), and lashed the tiller. The evening was so sultry that we felt the need of air, and we lowered the dinghy overboard in order to clear the saloon skylight. I hung the riding light on the forestay, and we were soon in bed and asleep.

A few hours later I woke. *Serica* was sailing herself in narrow circles, and at the same time was being carried by the powerful tide. Occasionally I would hear the cold beat of a ship's engines. I had convinced myself that the tides would take us north and west, and believed that there was no chance of our hitting land that night. But at 3 a.m., hearing more wind as well as tide, I could stay in bed no longer. Isabel, less nervous, slept on.

I eased the main sheet, hoisted the Genoa, and found myself sailing on a southerly course. When I had the feel of the yacht in the darkness —and very lively she was—I lashed the short tiller and shook out both reefs in the mainsail. The pram dinghy danced after me, pushing before its raised prow a boisterous moustachio of foam. (We had bought the dinghy at a London garage; it was the smallest yacht's tender available, being only six feet long. Although it was well built of silver spruce and mahogany, we were to agree that it had not been a wise purchase. . . . When we had fitted out *Truant* for a cruise to Greece I had acquired too much gear of every description, and had loaded the ketch with stores that we never used. On *Truant* I had insisted that we must carry a ten-foot sailing dinghy. *Serica's* baby pram, all of *Serica's* gear, and indeed *Serica* herself, represented the swing of the pendulum.)

When Isabel came on deck we hove to. We lifted the dinghy, lashing it to its chocks on the coach roof, and continued with mainsail and No. 3 jib. (*Serica* carried the following sails: mainsail, trysail, spinnaker, Nos. 1, 2, and 3 jibs—No. 1 being the Genoa, No. 2 a big jib, and No. 3 of more manageable proportions—and a storm jib of heavy oiled canvas.)

That day the south-east wind was gusty, and raised a short, grey sea. We sailed through morning, afternoon, and evening, at six or seven knots, close-hauled, and spent much of the time wondering where the devil we were. The horizon was banked with clouds that formed mirages, land and citadels and hamlets and the openings of mighty rivers.

Although the yacht had almost ceased to make water when on an even keel, she was now sluicing her white topsides, which had dried out and become porous during her long sleep ashore; she leaked so copiously that I had to pump every hour. (The bilge pump, excellent so far as its capacity for spewing forth water is concerned, is an exhausting contraption; the operator, kneeling on the floor under the doghouse, turns a brass handle in a horizontal clockwise movement.)

Wind and sea stiffened during the dark afternoon. The yacht increased her pace. Her decks were wet enough, since her sharp bows sliced through the tops of the seas and the wind flung the spray aft, but in the cockpit, protected by the curve of the doghouse and by the coamings, we were dry. Wondering about our landfall on a dangerous and unfamiliar coast in worsening weather, I was yet exhilarated by the lightness of the tiller in my fingers, the steadiness and drive of a balanced sailing machine, the long, tormented thread of our wake. Isabel dosed herself with a new medicine to prevent seasickness, and said that the effect was a kind of paralysis. She took her turns at the tiller, and between turns slumbered at my side.

In the evening I woke her and announced with distaste (since navies at sea are often a nuisance to yachts) that I had sighted ahead the combined fleets of the Russophobe powers. Those fleets, the B.B.C. had earlier informed us, were doing exercises off the coasts of France. Looking through the binoculars (which were encrusted with salt) I picked out the aircraft carrier H.M.S. *Implacable*, which was, I knew, flying the flag of Admiral Sir Rhoderick McGrigor.

We soon realised that the fleet, though we could see foam at the bows and sterns of all the units, was stationary, and when we had sailed a mile or two nearer we saw that it was no fleet but a collection of grey rocks upon the bases of which the sea rushed with a fury that, like aerial bombardment, was as terrifying as it was senseless. A Breton fishing-smack was working nets close to the rocks. She was about three times the size of *Serica*, but as she carried no sail she behaved stupidly, standing on end and rolling her scuppers under, while we, by comparison, were steady and nimble. We sailed close to her, and hailed.

"Où sommes nous?"

The dripping men on board answered in a chorus that came to us like the barking of sea lions. At length we made out:

"Les Roches Douvres."

We gybed *Serica* (for the first time) without difficulty save for a contretemps with the jib sheets, whose pull I had underestimated, and sailed with wind and sea on our port quarter, heading south-west. Now there was a flurry of charts and Sailing Directions. Where was the nearest anchorage? (With us in such circumstances the nearest is always the best.) A place called Lézardrieux situated some distance up the tidal Rivière de Pontrieux, of whose dangers the compilers of the Sailing Directions write in a tone even more tartly warning than usual. Lézardrieux it would have to be.

The light had slipped away; I was not sure of my compasses and had had no opportunity to test the patent log. What little was to be seen of the land to port more than confirmed the nightmarish outlines on the charts. Was this indeed the coast of Brittany, land of pink shrimps and cider, and butter white as Irish linen, this growling line of rocky defences so thick, so venomous?

I am of an inequable temperament, prone to sudden and foolish exaltation or despair. That evening I was low, miserable, puny, and afraid. Although Isabel always has a stouter heart, the anti-seasickness medicine seemed to be relaxing its druggy grip at the very moment when elements and circumstance were increasing their pressure. It was she who pulled us together . . . she made out a buoy which she identified on the chart, and that buoy was the key to the river.

Fate is a queer bird. The night before I had ordered my charts Mr. Adlard Coles had climbed down our ladder to have a look at us and *Serica*. He happened to mention the anchorage at Lézardrieux. So I had ordered, with some seventy charts covering the coasts between Lymington and Italy, a full-scale one of the Pontrieux River. On the chart the river looked small, but in the darkness (and we were entering at approximately high water) it proved to be vast. A sea writhed and in places boiled on the bar, but we buffeted through it. I had been so obsessed with navigation and so keen to get somewhere as quickly as possible that it had not occurred to me to reduce sail. Sailing at that speed with breakers audible and sometimes visible on either hand was too much for me, and I got down the mainsail. I had vaselined the track and the slides, and was agreeably surprised at the ease of handling a Bermudian sail. The engine started at the first touch of the button. We passed beacons, buoys, a cluster of wind-flattened islands, and then entered the land between hills. Leading lights guided us up the main channel. A bend, more leading lights, and the swell had changed to a ripple. The patent log showed ninety-five miles for the day's run. We dropped anchor in eight fathoms at the top of the last reach before the village.

How welcome, how precious the steadiness, the calm, the land-lockedness of the anchorage! Wind hissed through the trees on the slopes above us. Down-river roared the sea. And there we were alone, comfortable, suddenly hungry. No matter how rough the passage, you have but to find good anchorage and there, in the boat, are warmth, light, food, books, alcohol, tobacco, comfortable beds, violins, daggers. It is to enhance such contrasts with the sea and the wind that the truly wise yachtsman sails in the company of a beautiful or an intelligent woman—it may be his wife.

The yacht, now wind- now tide-rode, was uneasy at her anchor. She fretted with the cable as a blood mare that travels smoothly at any pace, and over any obstacle, may fret when held by the dismounted rider.

CHAPTER 2

## CHEATING THE CENTURY

A BRISK morning, gusty, with alternations of sun and swift shadow. . . .
The voluminous headsails had to be dried, folded, and squeezed each
into its canvas bag. I learned how best to do this by experience, and I
was slow that morning, indeed at moments the task seemed impossible.
We had left the hot weather in England. A few rusty trawlers chugged
out past us, their crews in faded berets, square men. It was a joy to
scrub *Serica's* teak deck, to see the water gushing off it and the wood
whitening as it dried. The wavelets of the river plopped against our
waterline. The yacht's bows rose and dipped, pointing downstream.
We were anchored at the end of a reach about a mile long and rounded
at either end. The river has there torn its way deep and wide into the
land. No houses were in sight, only a lighthouse, a few beacons, fields,
cattle, orchards, woods and a soft road—a stream of dust—with goats
tethered on its verges.

We beached the pram in the shingle, and carried it easily between us to
above the high water marks. Ashore the temperature was some fifteen
degrees warmer than on the boat. A grass snake squirmed away from
our feet as we followed a path through the woods, climbing.

We had the incomparable sensation—one that never stales—of being
behind the enemy lines, of having cheated the twentieth century. No
passports, no Customs, no fellow-travellers, no tickets, no time-
table, no preachers, no responsibilities. . . . I might have landed in
France in a dream. The sensation was deepened by the swing of balance
that long hours in a small boat induce; the land was *alive*, for it gently
pulsed as I trod it.

We found our way to the centre of Lézardrieux, to the bar of the
Hôtel Garibaldi, where the patronne made us a meal. She was helped
by her husband, who rolled thin wisps of smoked ham, and sliced
tomatoes with a razor.

For eighty francs we hired a tandem bicycle and rode into the
accidented interior. The south-east wind blew a rainstorm into our
faces. We perched the machine under the eaves of a café. Inside, on the

7

ground floor, there was only space for a kitchen and a dark narrow room with rectangular tables, marble-surfaced, iron-legged. A staircase with yellow linoleum on the treads mounted to the upper rooms. A girl came forward. The rain streamed over the windows and crept under the ragged edge of the door. For so small an establishment there was an unusual stock of drink behind the bar, champagnes, brandies, armagnacs. And why was the girl so well-dressed? Square pegs in round holes are, I think, rarer in France than in England. We heard noises upstairs, a man's voice and a woman's, then feet on the floor above our ceiling. The man whistled and called: "Thérèse!" The girl ran to him.

"Only two English people off a yacht at Lézardrieux," we heard her say.

"En ce cas . . ."

The girl reappeared and turned on the gramophone. *Sombreros et Mantillas* came storming out, and protected by that lively café noise, the couple negotiated the stairs. The woman wore a raincoat buttoned to the throat, and when she reached the last step she drew the hood over her black hair. A middle-aged woman, handsome enough, she gave us a look full of curiosity, and without a word stalked into the rain. Through the window I could see the water bouncing off her impermeable hood. The man was dressed in a dusty, blue, town suit of good cloth; his brown boots had been made in the country for the country. He ordered white wine, and went to the lavabo behind the café.

"A rich miller from . . ." the girl whispered to us, naming a small town fifteen miles away, "et un très bon client de la maison, gentil comme tout . . ."

Her description scarcely seemed to fit. The miller was corpulent, and the lines round nose, mouth, eyes, were deeply eaten in. He was short of breath; he gasped and puffed like Mr. Jogglebury Crowdy. He talked to us between puffs, attempting to shine before Thérèse.

"I envy you that life," he said. "I would give a million francs (if I had such a sum) to sail off in your yacht, to sail perhaps to Madagascar or some such romantic corner of the earth. Would you come with me to Madagascar, Mademoiselle Thérèse?"

"To the ends of the earth," she answered.

"We must drink to our adventure." He ordered a special bottle. While the girl was away he came to our table, and leaning both elbows on the marble, approached his face to mine, saying with an air of importance: "D'you know who she is, the little (puff)? She's the only daughter of (wheeze) the Colets."

"Who are they?"

He recoiled. Did we never read the newspapers? The Colets! They had been arrested at last, taken to Brest, and soon they would be on their way to an important trial in Paris.

"What have they done?"

What had they *not* done? They had embezzled millions from the insurance companies, millions. According to the miller the Colets had moved about France for years buying properties, insuring them, burning them. "God knows what their real name is, for I believe they've answered to thirty names in the last fifteen years," he said. "Thérèse says its Forbin, but how can you believe a word uttered by the child of such parents? . . . A wonderful girl," he said. "A perfect sample. It's my belief she knew all her parents were up to. She may have been the brains of the bunch. . . . And extremely (ex-trême-me-ment) well built."

She came with the bottle and four glasses. The rain had stopped. When we had drunk one glass with the miller we shook hands and left them. His hand was dry, hot, muscular, at odds with the fleshiness of his neck and his tormented breathing. He sounded as though he had swallowed an old bulldog.

"Well," the woman at the Garibaldi said when we returned the tandem, "I expected to see you both half-drowned."

We told her the name of the café where we had sheltered.

"And you met Thérèse? There's a clever minx. The richest miller for fifty kilometres round eats out of her hand. He'll marry her, for his wife lies dying at the mill. Thérèse is in no hurry; she's only nineteen."

"We thought her younger."

"I said she was clever."

"We met a miller at the café, a big man with heavy breathing . . ."

"That's him. Thérèse is lucky."

"She's unfortunate in her parents."

"Perhaps, but they haven't done much. A few permutations and combinations at the expense of the insurance companies. They'll go behind bars for a year or so, and when they come out Thérèse may be in a position to support them as a daughter should."

"The miller gave us to understand that the parents had embezzled millions."

"I keep on telling you that Thérèse is clever. She's also a considerate daughter. Which is it better to be, the daughter of the pickpocket who gets nabbed for pinching a lottery ticket, or the daughter of the burglar caught with the Rajah's diamond? She knows how to tell her story, our Thérèse, and sing! there's nobody like her. At Mass she can pipe the 'Agnus Dei' solo in a manner that brings tears to my eyes, and I assure you that when you've been in commerce as long as I have the tears are as stiff to draw as rusted nails from the oak. . . . In sum, Thérèse is a girl who'll end well."

The patronne exhorted us to tell all men of the excellence of her hotel. Les yachtsmen britanniques were the type of clients she wanted, she said. And her husband was a fine cook. "At one moment he was chef to Madame ——, the mistress of Monsieur ——, who was then Chef de Cabinet to Monsieur ——, who was then Minister of the Interior."

Hers is, yachtsmen britanniques, an excellent hotel. It has (or had) no bath, no inside lavatory flushed with pure water, no spring mattresses; it has no place to sit in except the bar, no telephone except the one behind the bar, no page boy, no lift. But the owner can cook, and his wife is lively.

After our excursion inland it was exciting to see the yacht again. We saw her first from the woods three hundred feet above the water. She was rolling her tall mast. There was a fierce little chop on the river.

We sailed at dawn. Conditions were quiet in the estuary, and there, with the large-scale chart and a score of landmarks to choose from, we were able to check our two compasses. The big steering compass proved, contrary to my expectations, to be accurate, even with the engine running, while the hand-bearing compass showed errors as outrageous as twelve degrees.

We turned west with the breeze aft, and when the sun came up there was all the wind we wanted with unreefed mainsail. When we picked up speed the propeller shaft, free-wheeling, revolved just audibly under the cockpit. We sailed on and off the coast, with a good deal of gybing. I took down the jib, continuing under mainsail alone. There was only a pleasant weight on the tiller, sailing like that, though I had expected the yacht to be nearly uncontrollable. We travelled fast, logging seventy miles from inside the Lézardrieux River to outside the entrance to Morlaix, and covering that distance in eight hours fifty-one minutes. Off Morlaix the sky darkened. When we came on the wind it was stronger than I had realised. We did not need the engine, and sailed in with the jib alone, so agile was the yacht, so quick on her helm. We found it difficult to distinguish the channel to Morlaix, a harbour that looks vast enough on the charts, where the water inlets form a bunch of tattered grapes dripping into the land. To the stranger and the novice the Brittany coast presents an astonishing plethora of feature; it is hard to identify the essential landmark from a multitude of landmarks. We entered on a compass bearing from Stolvezen, the buoy marking a rock off the entrance.

All the boats in the anchorage were wind-rode, and shuddering on their cables. Among them was a big British ketch of the Colin Archer type. We continued up-river, sounding, until I calculated that we should have three feet under our keel at low water. We felt the wind, but the water was restricted enough to be flat. Still higher up the river, we saw another Blue Ensign, on a small, workmanlike cutter. The anchorage was beautiful: an expanse of troubled water, sloping, buff-coloured land, red mooring buoys, white houses, a village appearing in the fold of the river bed, and another across the water, a profound impression of space and loneliness.

Had *Serica* drawn less water we should have spent the next day at Morlaix and tried to navigate round the bend of the river; but she is of a dangerous shape to go adventuring among tidal sandbanks and shallows.

Outside the harbour we had a stout breeze abeam, and made tremendous speed. Far ahead of us was an impressive vessel. She was at first only a white tower in the distance, but her outline grew clearer and we recognised her for the Colin Archer ketch.

When we turned to parallel the coast, making for l'Abervrac'h, the wind was nearly aft, and the jib would not draw. It seems incredible to me now, but I took down the jib, and carried on in a good weight of wind and with a high following sea, under mainsail alone. I can only suppose that I was nervous about getting down the mainsail, as even in those early days, when *Serica* was still a stranger, I must surely have realised that we should have gone at least equally well with a head-sail and no mainsail, and that there would not then have been the constant danger of an accidental gybe. However, the foolish sometimes profit from their foolishness, and we flew on, overhauling the ketch. A small French sloop, double-reefed and with a mere wisp of a jib, came out from the land and passed close under our counter in a smother of spindrift. She was very yachty: we could see the ropes coiled like table mats on her deck, the rigging screws of polished brass. The two young men in the cockpit were excited about something. They yelled at us and waved their arms, but we could not distinguish a word, and we were too busy to pay attention, for we were about to pass the big ketch, and at the same time were trying to edge to seaward of a buoy without gybing. The ketch carried reefed mainsail, staysail, and a raffee on her square-sail yard. She surged along, and judging by the foam and bother an onlooker might have thought her to have the greater speed, but we passed her as a swallow would pass a heron. Her decks were crowded with men and women passengers. When we were clear of her we took down the mainsail (no easy matter that day) and hoisted the No. 2 jib to turn for the rocky fangs guarding the entry to l'Abervrac'h. We had then logged thirty-seven miles at an average of 8.3 knots.

The weather was getting fierce. Inland, well on their way to harbour, we saw the lobster-boats chugging to shelter as fast as their screws would drive them, their earth-coloured mizzens full of wind.

We picked out the Libenter buoy. Isabel warned me twice that I was sailing too direct a course for Libenter, and she showed on the chart a series of underwater rocks. I was inclined to sneer at her warnings until a jolt from the keel shook the whole boat (and its occupants). Looking over the port quarter, we saw the rock below us, a mercifully-flat surface of ivory-coloured stone. I lost no time in steering seaward, and we did not touch again. Had we set fast on the rock we should have lost at least the yacht, for the sea had turned vicious, and was racing pell-mell at the jagged coastline, while the wind shrieked and buffeted. Greatly shaken by our "touch", we worked our way cautiously into a big and (that day) dismal natural harbour. We passed the jetty off the dark village of l'Abervrac'h, passed the lobster-boats, some twenty of them anchored in a companionable clump, high-bowed, squatting back on their counters, and dropped anchor in a sandy creek. Three men at once came rowing from the nearest smack. The holding ground in the creek was poor, they said, and the weather was very threatening. They advised us to anchor near the fishing-boats. We accepted their advice gratefully. *Serica* splashed around angrily in the lop, sawing at her cable.

Next morning saw the east wind tormenting the shore, pushing smoke down chimneys, pulling it from windows, tearing curtains, breaking flowers, whirling hats down the street. But how good the wind smelled as it rose to us off the white-capped sea! We managed to land in the dinghy without getting too wet. The jetty was long, and rather new and ill at ease. An old man was daubing the iron rings and bollards with black tar, another was sweeping sprays of dust into the wind. Below us, drawn up on the beach for repairs or scraping, lay five of the smacks, equally handsome out of the water as in it with their dashing flares, bold bows and practical buttocks. (And what a genius the French have for colours! Is there a minor God, some Winged Foreman, who makes it his business to look into every French paint pot? If so we should do all in our power to induce him to spend a few years in England, for which country he evidently has no natural liking.)

At the end of the windswept jetty a woman nervously approached us. Her brown eyes glistened in an unhealthy face, wrung, it seemed, by sleeplessness or sadness.

"Excuse me, but if you speak a little French I have a somewhat unusual request to make," she said. "My father is very, very ill. He once made a trip to your Folkestone, and when we showed him the yacht through the window, he said he would like to see the captain. Would you very much mind coming to see an old invalid? I know that you must be in a hurry. If you could spare only five minutes?"

The house, constructed of massive stone cubes, was one of three standing at a bend on the road to Brest. It was as though three dominoes had been laid end to end to form a right-angled Z. The walls were spread with thriving pear and cherry trees. Every door and window of the centre house was shut. Old newspapers (*Figaros*) were stacked on the stoves and in every corner of the interior. The atmosphere could have been sold as that strange perverted foodstuff of the white man—cheese. It seemed remarkable that human beings could live in that place, and God knows I am no believer in "fresh air"; I would usually rather have the window shut than open, the fire and the heating on than off, too many clothes on than too few, the sea too hot than too cold. . . . A fatty suggestion of simmering bouillon came from the back premises. We were conducted to a front room with a heliotrope wallpaper, an upright piano, framed photographs (one of Marshal Foch). On the tasselled woollen tablecloth lay the silver-mounted horn of a musk ox and a fretted box of pink coral. The woman told us that her father had been a lawyer in the town of Brest.

"Specialising in maritime cases, he was known for his great heart and for the volume and sweetness of his voice," she said. "He was successful (that it would be false for me to conceal), but he worked too long, and now he pays for those weary hours. His disease is extremely arduous . . . growths . . . vegetable-like growths all over the body. . . . I'm embarrassed to show him to strangers. I'd like you first to look at this photograph. Here is papa as he used to be, and here mama, and this is Monsieur Caproni, who was then of the Inscription Maritime . . ."

Her father stood in the coloured photograph a pace or two apart from his companions. He had struck a pose, with one hand thrust away from his body as though a falcon perched on the wrist and the other hand gripping with all but the little finger the carved handle of an umbrella. A bold-looking animal, stout, but well-built, with his daughter's dark eyes, a narrow forehead, full cheeks, a startling tie-pin edged with brilliants (which the photographer had coloured blue).

"Will Monsieur come upstairs," she said. "I must ask your forgiveness, Madame, but I think it wiser that you should wait here. It was 'the captain' that papa asked to see. He is precise by nature, and when he is ill I must humour him, you understand?"

She opened the door. An appalling stench of cigar smoke. The air was a milky blue. My eyes smarted and watered. The clean wind rattled angrily at the windows, but found no chink. The man in the bed picked up a lustre bowl, and after a few preliminaries of a loosening and menacing character, spat and voided his nose. He wore a bedshirt and a muffler was twisted round his throat. His face had vanished into the swellings or growths of which his daughter had spoken. The two dark eyes were preserved as in the photograph, as in his daughter. A small cigar or cheroot protruded from the mouth, and flared periodically to stinking combustion. From his bearded jowls hung a growth like a medium-sized parsnip tinged pink at the end. I stood by the bed, and lifted one of his heavy hands. When I released it it fell deep into the soft feather mattress. The woman talked to him brightly. I was sorry for him if she always treated him with such Christian brightness (preserve me from Christianity if I am ever sick or wounded—it's sometimes hard enough to bear when I'm well). He did not appear to listen to her as she rattled on about us and our "si beau yacht". His eyes would steal a glance at me, roguish as the eyes of a boar, and then flicker off into the past or the future.

The cigar began to swing like a turreted gun. Held in grooved tongue, it came forward from his mouth. It moved to the corner of the mouth, and was drawn securely in. Was he going to speak? The woman leaned forward apprehensively. After a few distant coughs and tunnel-like rumbles, he did speak.

"C'est bien un anglais."

The few words were followed by a torrent of guffaws. I dearly wanted to stand my ground until that disturbing laughter had stopped or given way to further speech, but his daughter hurried me from the room. She was full of apologies. I had liked the look of the old scamp in the bed.

*          *          *          *

There is a type of restaurant in France that sets itself out (in a French way) to look as forbidding as one of our grisly English tea-rooms filled with "cottage" furniture and with dark oaken beams across the ceilings. The French type (also mock-old and showing somewhat flimsier beams) can usually give you a decent meal, whereas the tea-room inevitably carries out the threatened assault on senses and digestion. Mock-old is the restaurant of the Hôtel de la Baie des Anges at l'Abervrac'h, but in it we fared well, and after the meal I bought from the chef three kilos of exquisite butter, which we carried back to the refrigerator on the yacht.

(Possibly it would not be out of place here to inform the reader that on this trip we had the intention of being economical, if not parsimonious, for we carried with us in Travellers' Cheques no more than the £100—£50 each—allowed us by the current British regulations for spending money abroad. We had loaded up at Lymington with a month's generous Board-of-Trade ration of ship's stores. But why eat bad butter made God knew how long ago in God knew what country by God knew what factory processes when fresh French butter was available? . . . Say what you like about Danes and other dairy farmers: the French, of all the peoples, understand how to make butter. . . . During a previous visit to France I sat—I must apologise for mentioning so rare an experience—beside a Duchess, whom I complimented on the excellence of her butter. She told me that she had taken a heavy truck and had driven the length of France to Normandy, where she had bargained with the farmers. She returned to her villa on the Mediterranean shore with two tons of butter, which she stored in a deep-freezing apparatus. . . . Yet some would have it that the upper classes are degenerate!)

I mentioned the refrigerator. . . . Our galley on *Serica* was a little unusual. We had done away with the bottled-gas cooker and had installed a paraffin-operated refrigerator in its stead. The only cooking apparatus on *Serica* was one Primus stove swung in gimballs on a shelf above the refrigerator. We had several gadgets for the primus, including a pyramidal toaster and a pressure cooker big enough for cooking a whole chicken. We had discovered on our trip to Greece that a galley fully-equipped with ovens and so forth was unnecessarily elaborate. Generally speaking, when I am afloat I like to consume wine and fruit in that order, being, so far as wine is concerned, quite typical of most Mediterranean sailors. Sometimes in France when it comes to ordering the wine the serveuse will say of me: "Un vrai marin, celui-là." I hold fast, dear reader, to that thread, for in no other respect (as you must discern if you know anything about the sea) am I anything of a sailor.

While on the subject of gadgets I might mention the "Tiny Tim". This pigmy charging motor was stowed in the forecastle and when needed for the batteries was screwed with two brass thumbscrews to the cockpit seat and connected to a plug inside the doghouse. The useful toy has a self-starter, charges at fifteen amps, will run for about three hours on a pint of petrol, and makes a good deal of noise. We only started it prior to making excursions ashore. Isabel detested the Tiny Tim; but I enjoyed it, and it proved to be a reliable servant.

*     *     *     *

We bought our tickets for the bus to Brest at a greengrocer's that was also a bar. The bus was overcrowded and smelled pleasantly of *Gauloises* cigarettes. We entered an undamaged part of Brest, and I noted the interesting name of a small bar near the Citroën factory, the *Six Cylindres Bar*. I began to recognise the streets, and to look for a restaurant where I had eaten almost supernaturally well as the guest of a French naval officer in 1939. But as we neared that site the town disintegrated; the pavé turned into beaten sand and clay, the stone buildings into huts made of boarding and paper. The old streets, sometimes sinuous as river beds on plains, had been replaced by roadways intersecting at right-angles and lined with impermanent shops selling impermanent goods. This new, temporary part of the town, although tawdry and unattractive, although combining the soullessness of a Great Exhibition with the dirt of a gypsy fair, seemed to suck the life from the old town. Here, within and around the hollow cubes of compressed cardboard, business was being done, money was being made. . . . We searched for linen hats of the type that sailing people wear in England and America. We were shown many hats, but could bring ourselves to buy none, though tempted by the black velvet men's "Homburgs", and also by the high-crowned "shooters' hats", wide-brimmed, and made of a quilted-khaki waterproof material, that were common to all the hat shops.

Enormous langoustes stretched out vermilion claws from the yellow stippled walls of the restaurant. The patronne came to ask if the steak was good, and I answered with unusual honesty that it had not quite come up to our expectations. She lowered her voice to tell us that things were going worse than they should in her restaurant because her husband had become erratic in his life. He was seldom in the kitchen.

"Politics, politics, and again politics," she said. "What business has a man who can cook to go meddling with politics?"

I disliked her, I am afraid, for the plaster lobsters, the expensive food, and the discontented faces of her maids.

"You and Madame are off a yacht at l'Abervrac'h," she said, and laughed at my surprise. "A client told me. Oh no, I haven't been to l'Abervrac'h for ten years, and doubt if I shall go again. . . . A client told me. They tell us all that goes on in the peninsula. Yes, we have a good business. That's why I keep impressing on my man that he should stick to his saucepans. Politics are not for those in commerce, politics are for men who can do nothing else; now if a man can cook as *he* can cook . . ."

I looked round the restaurant, recognised a face, and caught the man's eye. He bent over his fish. I had seen him in l'Abervrac'h. A thin man, anæmic, intelligent-looking, in a dark suit and a loud American tie. Secret police, I thought at once. Yes, he was drinking sparkling Vouvray; obviously a policeman. He had followed us to Brest, which was still an important naval arsenal. I shuddered, for I dislike policemen, particularly Latin ones, having seen something of their habits and of their stupendous capacity for error.

Returned to l'Abervrac'h, I determined to water the yacht, using the dinghy and two four-gallon cans. (*Serica's* water tank, moulded to the shape of the hull, is beneath the saloon floor; it holds forty-five gallons, and is filled from the deck.)

At the fountain in the street several women, foremost among them a very fat one, engaged me in talk when I had asked them if the water was drinkable, and they had answered that it was unreliable in its natural state.

"Bad weather," the fat woman said.

"Yes, Madame, too much wind."

"Ah! ça ne vous plaît pas, le vent?"

I thought that it would not please her either, if she lived at the foot of the high mast yawing beyond the fishing-boats.

"Our men think nothing of wind," she added. "But then they are well accustomed to it."

On my next trip ashore I was accosted by a drunk fisherman, a very young man.

"What do you make of l'Abervrac'h?" he asked in a somewhat truculent manner.

"Most agreeable," I hastened to answer, but he exploded at my tact, heaping all sorts of epithets on l'Abervrac'h, and telling me that he and all the other fishermen there came from a town where men could without shame live, marry, and rear families—namely, Audierne. The boat in which he crewed, the *Jean Jaurès*, was sailing for Audierne the next day. This interested me, for we had considered going there ourselves, but the Sailing Directions were particularly unenthusiastic regarding two tidal races, the Chenal du Four, and the Raz de Sein, which lay between us and Audierne. I mentioned the races, and he laughed at me.

"The Chenal du Four? nothing to it. The Raz de Sein? equally childish."

"Why, since you come from Audierne, do you fish at l'Abervrac'h?"

"Puisque les langoustes ne nous suivent pas—suivons les langoustes."

"And the men of l'Abervrac'h?"

"Neither the money to build stout boats nor the hearts to man them."

"Our sloop draws two metres; will she be able to lie afloat in Audierne harbour at low water?"

"Yes, the yachts anchor below the bridge and take stern warps to the bridge. Like that you can lie in a pool that has three metres when the rest is nearly dry. . . . Three in the morning, we leave. We should reach Audierne at high water in the evening. The weather will be good tomorrow," he said, swivelling an inflamed but positive eye at the mottled firmament. Then he began to tell me of his experiences ashore in England when he had served with the Gaulliste navy. . . .

The crew of a big smack were unloading their catch on the shingle below the pump. There were sixteen of them, and they formed a human chain, each man holding the handle of a basket in either hand. The baskets, brown in colour and overflowing with dark purple langoustes, were alternate links in the chain that shuffled diagonally across the stones and seaweed, negotiated the ramp mounting to the level where we stood, crossed the street, and awkwardly penetrated the passage leading into a tenement behind us. I asked the young man (who was talking about a fight in Liverpool) where they were taking the catch.

"To the entrepreneur, a Parisian. When they've weighed and graded the catch you'll see him go off to the bistro with the captain to fix the payment."

The fishermen came out, some of them silently on bare feet, massive feet and hard legs supporting the strongest, though far from the supplest, bodies in Europe, some in high, white, rubber boots made in England, some trailing sabots. Finally the captain, a hoary walrus, barnacle-encrusted, and following him the entrepreneur. The latter was the man I had taken for a secret policeman in the restaurant in Brest.

# CHAPTER 3

## FINISTERRE ADVENTURES

MIST lay on the land, though not on the water. There was no horizon. The sky drooped into the smoothly rolling sea.

I had thirty-three fathoms of chain out, but *Serica*'s windlass is light and speedy in operation, being of a type set low on deck, the gears turning in an oil bath, and the chain coming inboard on both movements of the lever. We carried a forty-three-pounds Danforth (a type of anchor that stows flat) forward of the windlass, a forty-pounds C.Q.R. aft of the cockpit, and a fifty-six-pounds Nicholson, stowed below against an emergency. We had only forty-five fathoms of chain (three-eighths of an inch), all on the Danforth. The chain locker was big enough to take more than double that amount, but we hesitated to put extra weight concentrated well forward in a craft so fine in the bows, and relied instead on two new forty-fathom warps of Italian hemp. I had intended to have a nylon warp for the second anchor, but had fought shy of the expense. In my own view (and anybody else's, I imagine) I had not enough chain, particularly for Mediterranean harbours where it is often necessary to drop two anchors and lie with the stern attached to a quay, an unnatural strain on the ground gear. On *Truant* we had carried 135 fathoms of chain, and had been glad of it; but then *Truant* had been a slow sailer, and speed in any sailing craft surely depends almost as much on the craft's power-weight ratio as on its shape and finish.

We motored out at the tail of a string of smacks. The string went to sea until it separated into dots tumbling somewhere between sea and sky, but the *Jean Jaurès* diverged and steadied on our westerly course. She had hoisted staysail, gaff mainsail, and leg-of-mutton mizzen; we could see no advantage in that, since her booms, dark, solid spars, jolted from side to side while the tanned sails hung empty. A great deal of marine traffic, now able to penetrate the Chenal du Four after some days of unsuitable weather, converged on the channel. It was coasting traffic, for the big ships go outside Ushant by some miles, shunning the island's reefs and races.

The tide was beginning to turn with us through the glistening channel.

*above*: Up the LYMINGTON RIVER (see page 1)

*below*: Isabel reads beside the PONTRIEUX RIVER (see page 7)

"Wider than the Thames."
Motoring up the River ODET from BENODET to QUIMPER (Isabel at the tiller)
(see page 31)

We noticed its speed whenever we passed one of the numerous buoys. The water was full of lumps, holes, and twists, and we found it necessary to steer carefully on marks in line. We were doing five knots through the water, the engine running easily. The *Jean Jaurès*, thumpety-bumping, went a shade faster. About the middle of the channel our engine missed for a time, and we saw sparks leap from the distributor (caused doubtless by humidity inside it). During those moments of doubt we knew fear of the Chenal du Four, even on so fine a day. When we had cleared the southern entry we saw most of the other craft turn to port for the harbours of Brest, while we continued south across the great bay called l'Iroise, making for a second race, the Raz de Sein. The *Jean Jaurès* had reduced speed, idling, we assumed, because the tide was setting through the Raz against us. My friend the drunk cooked on a charcoal deck stove. While the fishermen ate they passed from hand to hand pearly binoculars resembling grossly-swollen opera glasses. With the aid of that impressive optical device they made a close study of Isabel and *Serica*. We kept some distance astern of them, for we wondered what the captain would do at the entry to the Raz.

What he did was to veer to port into the cliff-hung Baie des Trépassés (which contains many submerged rocks). The race roared past at eight knots, carrying a brutal sea with it, and pushing a swell at an angle into the bay. The *Jean Jaurès* pottered about in zigzags. Isabel pushed *Serica* up close to them, and hanging on by our shrouds against the rolling, I asked them what they intended.

"We'll go through in an hour," the captain answered.

"But slack water won't be for another three hours," I said.

"Correct. . . . But I go my own way—through *there*." He pointed to a place where, between the headland and the off-lying rocks, we saw a strip of water forty to fifty yards wide, boiling and frothing. We thought he was joking. After anchoring in fifteen fathoms with the C.Q.R. and a warp, we ate. The sun was extremely hot. We wore sou'westers to protect our faces, which were getting badly scorched. When we had eaten we were so uncomfortable at anchor that we hauled in the C.Q.R. and followed the Breton slowly about the bay. He waved me to approach.

"You have a reliable bag of tricks down there?" he asked, referring to the engine.

"Yes."

"And you say you draw two metres? . . . The passage is narrow.

You'll have to keep your bows trained on my counter and at only ten metres distance, no more, mind, all the way to Audierne."

He stationed two look-outs in the bows and two amidships. He took hold of the tiller curving up from the deck, called for more speed to the man standing beside the oil engine, and headed for the channel between the point and the rocks. Being a Frenchman, he did all this with an air, and we, his audience, were tensely appreciative. In the orthodox channel, some half-mile further offshore, the tide was still running furiously, yet we noticed that there appeared to be less foam where he was leading us than there had been an hour earlier. Sightseers were standing high up on the cliffs of the Pointe du Raz, directly over the broken water for which we headed. They were standing on the most westerly part of the French mainland.

We expected the captain of the *Jean Jaurès* to rush the channel, for both boats were yawing in the stream, but he cut down his speed, and we of course had to do likewise until our engine, unused to such slow running, choked and stopped. Isabel darted at the instrument panel just inside the doghouse, and the engine restarted at once. Our guide was now waving us on. He was thrusting ahead to jump a wall of water at the *upper* end of the channel. (Here we could discern quite plainly that the sea was running downhill.) Isabel opened wide the throttle, our bows rose up, water surged along the deck, she struggled with the tiller for a second or two, and we were past and on the point of ramming the Frenchman. Being of sharper form, *Serica* had cut through the wall of water, while the French boat had leaped, after sinking on its counter as a clever hunter will go back on his hocks before negotiating a trappy obstacle. Isabel flicked the engine to "full astern", and saved our bows by inches. . . . It had been an exciting experience. (Later, when we reached Portugal, I told some knowing yachtsmen how we had been led through the Raz de Sein against the tide. A Scot who has sailed over most of the watered surfaces of the world said that he had heard of fishing-boats passing that inner way. "I suppose you're the only yacht that's been foolish enough to risk it," he added.)

By taking that unusual route through the Raz we had condemned ourselves to further worries, since we had, for the next ten miles, to keep to the "inshore channel" with rocks close on the port side, and surf on submerged reefs to starboard. Our guide would frequently, and without warning, shut off his engine, possibly to lessen the downward suck of his propeller, possibly to get his marks. At last this channel came to an end. The captain laid his not inconsiderable rump against the tiller, swung the *Jean Jaurès* into deep water, and, with a great wave of his two arms, let us know that we were clear of danger.

The crew of the smack now prepared for entering the home port of which they spoke so highly, lowering and roughly furling the still useless sails, folding nets, hoisting the Tricolor, sluicing down the tarry decks, throwing the cooking stove into the saloon, getting the anchor ready, coiling warps, and finally each going through his own pockets to see that they held no incriminating documents or articles (for women would be waiting on the quay at Audierne). Our own preparations were uncomplicated; there had been no breath of wind all day, and our decks were clear of sailing apparatus.

Audierne entrance is marked by a long quay wall. The port itself lies half a mile inland. We followed the *Jean Jaurès* close along the wall; a few twists and curves and we were in an overwhelmingly beautiful basin with the boat-building sheds of Poulgoazec to starboard and to port a sweep of quays packed with fishing-boats seen against a background of street, shops, houses, restaurants, bars. For a northern port the water below us was astonishing; it was limpid. As we swam along, a tall white swan, I could see little crabs scratching on the clean sand of the bottom. The clear water aroused suspicions. Using the lead repeatedly as we went in, I found that there would be at most two or three feet in that channel when the tide had ebbed. But several had spoken to us of Audierne's yacht anchorage, and now our proved guide, as he swung the bows of his ship towards one of the few vacant berths at the quay, shouted with a wave: "Allez par là! mouillez sous le pont! . . ."

The tide was already ebbing fast when we anchored as directed, and tried to take warps to the bridge. Our dinghy was a great deal too small to be ideal in such a cataract, but after several futile attempts I managed to get a warp out to the stern line of the Audierne lifeboat, which craft was made fast to the bridge. The structure of the bridge was all but concealed by a drapery of fishing nets, and I dared not burrow among their folds to make fast. I hauled *Serica's* stern round, using a block and one of our very powerful sheet winches. The Audierne lifeboat held firm, the bridge did not so much as tremble, but our warp (a length of stout-looking German rope, the only piece of rope still on *Serica* that had belonged to the former owner) broke with a report, and the yacht sheered violently, scarring her white counter against a mooring buoy in midstream. I made fast astern to the mooring buoy, wishing I had thought of that earlier. An elderly gentleman wearing a yachting cap, blue suit with black buttons, and buckskin shoes was ferried round us by a servant squeezing at the sculls of a smart dinghy. The elderly gentleman asked in nautical fashion whence we came and whither bound.

"You are in a pool," he assured me, seeing me fussing again with the lead. "The remainder of the harbour is already drying out, but you will be secure, my good sir, in three metres."

Soon after he had left us *Serica* had taken a pronounced tilt forward. (A glance at the yacht's profile will show that if she takes ground she first goes forward and down by the bows and then, if the water lowers still further, she lists to one side or the other.) The Tide Tables informed us that we had yet to endure three hours of falling tide. The list forward increased with startling rapidity and then she lay over on her port flank. After that her subsidence was more gradual. For two hours we crouched below while our boat and home assumed an ever more terrible angle. I happened to be sitting on the starboard, or upper, settee in the saloon, and Isabel was on our double berth, also on the starboard side. Separated by partitions and lockers, we could speak to, but could not see, each other. Through the skylight I watched an ever-slipping view: first clouds darkening for night, then smoke against cloud, then chimneys, then roofs, then windows, then the street, a café, oxen, people, a wine cart, then the sea wall. When I looked through the dead lights in the coach roof I was staring at the water or into our dinghy, which I had made fast to the port side (fortunately with plenty of scope on the painters) before the listing began. We dared not move from our perches for fear that the slightest alteration of weight might topple the yacht right over. The refrigerator filled the interior with black paraffin smoke. After consultation with Isabel, I risked climbing down the floors to put the lamp out. Isabel, being farther aft, could see the mast through the doghouse windows. She reported that it was bending throughout its entire length, and that the top spreaders were drooping. We did not think that the mast and its gear could survive such a terrible and unfair strain. Even if all held firm, would the yacht rise with the tide, or would it lie, held by suction, until water poured into the hull? One of the stranger aspects of our predicament (desperate as it seemed to us) was that the throng of people on shore did not appear to notice us, or to consider that we were in difficulties. There were hundreds, probably thousands, of fishermen on the quays. None seemed even to glance in our direction.

Promptly according to time-table (at 11 p.m.—I can never make up my mind which is the more wonderful, the moon or the Admiralty) the water began to rise. Taking careful alignments through the skylight, I made out that *Serica* was rising too. At first Isabel would not believe me. As the rise became a certainty we both dropped off to sleep, huddled on those sloping surfaces and exhausted by muscular effort as well as suspense.

We awoke with the yacht on a level keel, floating. Isabel washed her face and I drank some whisky. The mast looked none the worse. We examined all the gear that was examinable in the moonlight, and found nothing wrong. While we waited for high water (4 a.m.) we relit the refrigerator and cleaned up the mess it had made.

We moved downstream, sounding all over the harbour, which was supernaturally, tantalizingly beautiful. Nowhere, either in the harbour itself or in the long approach to it, could we find a berth that would have more than four feet at low water. The speed of the tide, we thought, had scoured the bottom flat and clean and had also silted up the deeper places, including, we supposed, the celebrated one below the bridge. Somewhat dazed by our experience, which, however silly it may sound, was certainly most agonising, we were eager to remain in a comfortable berth, but when all the scores of soundings had produced the same meagre figures we moved out and dropped anchor in the open Atlantic, where we breakfasted and studied the charts with but little enthusiasm, agreeing that we would have done better in Audierne to tie up to the lifeboat, and to remember that spring tides were running.

The next port (with plenty of water in it) seemed to be Benodet, some thirty miles to the east. We did not want to go there, for it meant cutting into the Bay of Biscay and we had (until the war scars of Brest and the fishermen's hosannas to Audierne made us alter our plan) intended to sail across the jaws of the Bay from Brest to Corunna. However, to put about and again negotiate the Raz de Sein was unthinkable. Benodet it would have to be.

At 7 a.m. an urbane wind, steady and warm, came from the northeast. In a few seconds our mainsail was catching sun and wind, the Genoa was sheeted in, and we slid off. Isabel took the tiller for the first two hours. When I relieved her we were making good progress through mist, sailing a compass bearing to clear the Pointe de Penmarche. I must have fallen asleep over the tiller, for I awoke to find the yacht plunging into a filthy sea where two tides met or separated. The Pointe de Penmarche, lit by shafts of sunlight on the port beam, showed a petrified forest of lighthouses, high rocks, beacon towers. We got the wind stronger, and began to race on with more splash, flinging out silver-gold cascades on either hand. We met an ugly Swedish motor yacht speeding in the other direction, and rolling hellishly. Penmarche was evidently her point of departure, for off it she sheered to port and belched out across the Bay. We were sorry for her occupants. To travel in her must have been like encasement in a drill vibrating in the waving hand of a drunk dentist who is attempting to gas himself while he works. (The yacht later earned fantastic charter money on the Côte d'Azur.)

The approaches to Benodet seem tricky enough on the chart, but the leading marks are excellently defined against the coastline, which at this point showed rich brown woodlands with crimson warmths in their depths. We turned north, then, and speedily closed the land, not expecting very much of the anchorage, although the compilers of the Sailing Directions write of it with unusual lack of chill. As we opened the mouth of the River Odet we were surprised to see many yachts within. We had soon passed the outer yacht, one of the bigger "Gauntlets", *Neon*, eighteen tons. We could tell from her rigging that she had been fitted out at Lymington. The touch of a good rigger is as distinguishable, as personal, as that of artist or architect. *Neon* was sensibly handsome: tanned Ratsey sails, dark blue topsides, pale blue boot top. (I am not sure about blue, though, as a colour for cruising in any warm places, because I have never yet seen wooden yachts of that colour that did not blister in any heat.) A man, one of the Ponsonby brothers, lifted a blue linen hat at the end of a long, wiry arm as we passed. We dropped anchor in eight fathoms of lively water. Benodet to starboard. The wide river leading the eye inland, reflecting the wooded banks. Here and there a belt of dazzling green or a château's mansard showing through the trees. A cove beyond Benodet with a big schooner yacht fitting out. Many French yachts, most of them small family cruisers, flimsy-looking, yet clumsy compared with *Serica* and *Neon*.

We went ashore in clean clothing to find a hot bath. . . . I am told that my face—cherubic enough despite a suspect ballooning of the lips— inspires confidence. When, after dining, I have turned out my pockets and have found no money to pay the bill the waiter has always trusted me to return the following day. Yet when I go with my wife to a hotel and ask for a bathroom the management frequently decides (as though such things matter) that we are up to no good. So it was in Benodet. The woman was determined to have no orgies in her hotel, and only when we produced passports allowed herself to be persuaded that a desire for cleanliness had driven us to her inhospitable doors. (When I am old let me be wistful for, but never envious of, the sensuous pleasures of youth and middle age.)

The hotel still reeked of German occupation. Nails protruded from the walls and the torn corners of German notices. Cockroaches moved, malodorous black tanks, across the grey deserts of dust.

Benodet was swollen with holidaymakers, mainly French with a spattering of Swiss, Belgians, and English. We held off until the hour was nearly decent, and went to get dinner at l'Océan, a small hotel, bar, and restaurant. The patronne, a splendid creature rippling as the corn, broad, capable, straight-nosed, full-chinned, waited on us. It was a pleasure to hear her rumbling, fruity voice, and she fed us well. We were the only non-pensioners in the restaurant, and the others, being on the prix-fixe, ate less well, and cast angry looks at our plates. One man of vast girth drank quantities of cider diluted with soda water, varying these drenches with smaller ones of red wine. He had a black-haired wife (her legs might have been covered in bearskin), and a black-haired poodle. While he ate and between sluices of cider and soda, he talked about the poodle, which was not allowed in the dining-room because of a former disgraceful incident. When he was not in the dining-room he shut his wife in the bedroom and went out to discuss her with the poodle. He demanded that evening three hard-boiled eggs en supplé-ment. The prix-fixe (though in post-war England it would have made four good meals) did not strike him as being sufficiently nourishing for a man of his splendid constitution. (Were I a female I should be attracted by vastly fat men. What secrets and surprises may not hide beneath those flaps and in those wrinkles?) A humming factory of an inside. A mill coping with torrents of cider, soda, and wine, truckloads of farine, protein, and roughage, with here and there a soothing rill of Dépuratif Richelet Intégral, and now and then a most necessary truncheon charge by the Bile Bean mounted police. The following day on the beach when I passed him, lying on his back in a pair of yellow pants, I could hear his mechanism gurgling and sloshing. By contrast his face was calm, his expression negatively sweet, yet shrewd. The poodle lay in his shade.

\*        \*        \*        \*

From raking bow to equally satisfying canoe stern *Neon* was exquisite, and we learned much of practical value from our observations of such beauty. The teakwork gleamed with the deep lustre of coat upon coat of good varnish skilfully laid on, daily washed with fresh water, and polished. Her stainless-steel (not a metal that appeals to me) deck fittings were covered with an invisible film of preserving gun oil. Her blue topsides were meticulously washed and cosseted with sponge and chamois leather. There was a lovely thick white cotton mat for your feet before you ventured in awe to set them on the still lovelier white teak deck. This superlative condition was maintained by the owners, Lieut.-Commander Nicholl and his wife, and Ponsonby, who was with them on that cruise. It is true that attaining such perfection left them little time for anything else, but at least they had more to show for their labours than most of us. *Neon's* layout below was all that I could desire: a big forecastle with one pipe cot, roomy, simple, and with good stowage space; a normal saloon (possibly rather dark, but *Neon* is flush-decked, and you can't have everything); a vestibule with oil-skin locker on one side, the washroom on the other, and the companion mounting to the deck; the owners' state-room, large and comfortable; and aft the small engine-room, entered separately from the cockpit. For her displacement *Neon* carried less canvas than *Serica*, and I should say that of the two on deck *Neon* would be the easier to handle, although *Serica* would be considerably the faster, even, I believe (though many would not agree with me), in heavy weather.

Another interesting, and very different, yacht was *Smew* 1, which sailed into Benodet while we were there, a boxy, extremely ancient, shallow-draft, gaff cutter, clinker-built and rough. Two Jerricans and two old tyres (fenders) lay on her narrow painted deck. Her owner and master, Brigadier Nott-Bower, tall, active, was at the tiller, and Mrs. Nott-Bower, an equally well-balanced and handsome figure, was forward by the anchor. (Most married couples who go sailing seem to reverse the duties that Isabel and I assume, but I think we have reason on our side, for I have more strength to deal with the ground gear, while she has the lighter touch and better judgment with the tiller and, if it be needed, the engine.) The Brigadier had bought *Smew* during the war when he had for a time to work in the War Office. He bought her as a "floating home" on the river at Richmond. When peace had been proclaimed (everybody was quite enthusiastic about peace for a time, you may recall) he and his wife set off on their first cruise, to the

Channel Islands, possibly the most difficult waters in the world. They next sailed from England across the Bay of Biscay, down to Gibraltar, up the Mediterranean to Sète, through the Canal du Midi to Bordeaux, and back to England again (most of this with an auxiliary engine that would not work).

By contrast with *Neon* and *Serica*, *Smew's* accommodation was of the roughest, consisting only of a saloon into which you had to crawl backwards, a small lavatory, and a forecastle without piped fresh water. But it was a delightful interior, painted white, and filled with books and the apparatus of living. The cabin is low, but roomy enough, for it has a wide floor that almost corresponds to the underwater shape of the hull. Being very aged, *Smew*, according to her owners, made a great deal of water, and generally when they were sailing the cabin floor was awash, and sea water slopped into the lee bunk. They had fitted a new bilge pump, the most modern thing on the boat, but the pump functioned much better with *Smew* on one tack than on the other. The Nott-Bowers on this occasion had left England when we did, and had intended to sail to Ireland, but they ran into heavy weather and sailing for Ireland put them on the wrong tack with regard to the pump. Accordingly they made for Finistèrre, and we had the good fortune to meet them.

*Smew's* stumpy "legs" were carried on deck. At Audierne *she* had squatted comfortably on the sand by the quay, and the Nott-Bowers had walked ashore over a plank stretched from the bows. They liked to take the ground frequently, for then they could pump plastic glue into the old boat's seams.

Which, then, is the best type of cruising yacht? An adaptation of the racing machine, like *Serica*, lively at sea, giving subtle pleasure by her balance and speed, yet comfortable and convenient below? The more solid *Neon*, still more comfortable, perfectly constructed in every detail and a creation of real beauty? Or *Smew*, the haystack, old, tarry, and lovable, able with her shallow draft to venture up almost any creek, to squat on the sand when the tide recedes, to find shelter when the faster yachts must roll outside, the kind of craft that scorns a few bumps, on which a mark or a graze does not matter, into which nails may be driven without spoiling the work of craftsmen, the sheen of paint and varnish?

\* \* \* \*

"Nine months ago," said the mechanic who had come on board at my request to examine the dynamo, "I was crushed by a Creasecraft . . . don't speak of speedboats to me . . ."

"I won't!"

"I was lying under the pestilential boat fixing a new propeller when the shoring timbers gave way, being rotten like every damned thing in France . . ."

"Come, you exaggerate."

"So they sentenced me to six months in hospital with slops to eat, no wine, and agony, agony. We haven't a doctor worth the name, not one. I assure you I'll never work again. I can't. I won't. Look at me, but for the love of God don't laugh at me when I tell you that I was once a powerful man. Since the affair of the Creasecraft I'm ten centimetres shorter on the left leg, fifteen centimetres on the right. . . . And now my wife has had to go to hospital to await our second child. What chance have we of rearing two brats with France on the verge of chaos, and the Americans, blast them, pouring wealth into Germany and succouring the Macaronis?"

When I had ferried the mechanic ashore, his work well done, I crossed to the other side of the river to get petrol, duty free, from the fishermen's bonded store. The Customs man stood by in uniform and gave us his advice. The young fishermen treated me as though I were a lily, taking the cans from me and filling them through rubber syphoning tubes from the big, dirty drums. French petrol has a vile smell, pungent and pervasive, far worse than English, Italian, Spanish, Portuguese, or Greek petrol; it is bad stuff to carry on a yacht. When all our cans were full we moved to the Customs office, which was also a bar, to sign declarations and to pay. I stood a round of drinks and they all chose to drink a dark beer, which they called affectionately "le stout". Three of them had been in England as sailors during the war. Two maintained silence regarding that period of service, but the third was enthusiastic, or pretended to be so. "Leeds, c'est charmant," he stated. "Maccles-field, c'est jolie. . . . À Brighton on est bien . . . Chouette, Sheffield . . ." The Anglophile was dark, with curly hair and a fierce profile. He was in partnership with his younger brother, a slighter, more ruminative youth. They showed me their open fishing-boat; not a shred of paint on it anywhere except on the engine, which was well cared for. . . . I remember that when I was eighteen I pulled the petals off a yellow rose (in some fit of wordless embarrassment), and old Madame d'Estournelles de Constant, looking down on my thoughtless fingers, said in her unforgettably liquid voice: "Mon cher Georges! tu n'as pas de respect pour les fleures?" Some Frenchmen of the younger generation might use almost the same tone of incredulous but philosophic disapprobation in saying: "Pas de respect pour les moteurs?"

The patronne at l'Océan was an exotic character. She had procured herself an unusual and romantic husband, a Spaniard. His French was fluent enough, if ultra-Southern in that part of France. He looked somewhat weak beside his beautifully strong wife, but we saw that he worked hard in the bar and carrying dishes across the back courtyard to the kitchen, where his mother-in-law and sister-in-law worked in black Breton costume, all rustle and bustle. I suppose his delicacy of line and bone structure appealed to his wife.

"He has the spirit of a tiger," she said. "It is difficult to make him rest, and we must all rest while we can, for in a week we'll be in the thick of the holiday season, every table, every bed, filled; every moment a mouth at the door demanding to be satisfied. That's real work, and you either work in our trade or you go under. Ah! how exhausting it can be! Fatigue catches us in different ways. My husband gets it in the back, whereas it attacks my voice, while the young person who comes from Paris to help me in the restaurant (she comes because she isn't strong, tuberculous in fact, and she needs the sea air), her it catches in the stomach. She was here last July and a good part of August. Yes, then she went back to her factory. She did her work magnificently, but she could hold nothing down, *nothing*. She was such a skeleton I didn't know whether to be glad or sorry to see her go. . . . She arrives next Monday, and doubtless it'll be the same story this year. Ah well, if we have a good season I've promised to take my husband to Madrid." She swung her splendid frame away to another table.

\* \* \* \*

At first the stream was rather wider than the Thames below Hampton Court, but deeper and more rapid, no river for punts. Seaweed like pale spinach cooked *en branches* floated up the river. The large houses on either hand were more countrified than their equivalents in the Thames valley. Pastures, bright with spring grass and meadow flowers, alternated with coverts on the river banks. Nannies and children were playing by a private boat-house, and a rich old gentleman sat on a basket chair behind three fishing rods held on forked rests and read a book that probably provided some contrast to his surroundings, for it was by (we were able to distinguish through the binoculars) Georges Simenon.

We had decided to venture up the Odet as far as Quimper, sixteen kilometres above Benodet. We started two hours before high water, doing five knots through the water and ten past the river banks.

Farther up, the river narrowed and the current became stronger, swirling on the corners. We had been advised to keep in midstream until the river widened. From that point the channel was shown by port and starboard marks on tall posts. We had moved into flatter agricultural country. In another narrow stretch we squeezed past a Dutch coaster of some 200 tons. She had a cheerful family group on her bridge deck.

We tied up to a stone quay in the lower outskirts of Quimper. A bridge ahead barred the way to us. Crowds came running to look at *Serica*, whose mast was visible from all parts of the town. We left her there alone and walked into the town, finding it most agreeable to be inland, for the sea anæsthetises the coastlines it bullies, and when you move inland you come almost to a new country, certainly to a very different one. At Quimper you might be 200 miles from the sea, and a very nice place, old, hot, and earthy, it seemed to us. As we were walking in the Rue Oudinot we witnessed a strange scene. A line of schoolgirls came down the street, two by two. They wore blue-and-white uniforms. One policeman walked ahead of them, another behind, and three on either flank. The policemen looked foolish, as champion sheep-dogs might look if called upon to herd a group of flamingos. The girls, on the other hand, were enraptured. Their eyes and teeth shone as they swivelled their heads from side to side, glossy hair a-swing under blue saucer hats. One mistress, tall and elderly, walked ahead, turning now and then to admonish the girls behind, and another, young, plump, and kind-looking, strove to accelerate the pace of the rear files. There were thirty-four girls in the "crocodile" and their ages would range, Isabel thought, from eleven to sixteen. They were silent enough, but their progress was far from peaceful, for groups of people, mainly women, growled at them or shouted insults. It was hard to see what anybody could hate in that defile of clean and handsome children. A café was conveniently placed. We took a table in the shade, ordered a Pernod and a citron pressé, and watched the crocodile out of sight. The waiter, a cloudy-faced individual with a grey moustache, and the emblem of an ex-serviceman's organisation in his buttonhole, stood near us, and I asked him the meaning of the police escort. He evidently felt strongly about it, for he turned to us with a torrent of words. . . . Those, he said, were daughters of the rich, even the very rich. They came from a school on the outskirts of the town. A Protestant school, not a convent.

"At this school," the waiter said, "the pupils arrive with trunks full of clothes, evening dresses, jewellery, riding breeches, German cameras, everything that wealth can provide. It would not be so bad if the headmistress had the decency to confine them to the school grounds, which are extensive enough in all conscience. But no! every day and sometimes twice a day, they come walking out as you have just seen in batches of thirty or forty."

"They make an agreeable sight."

"That may well be, and I can admit that they look fresh and delightful, but you don't know whose daughter is there . . ." He named a French politician who had been accused of collaborating with the Germans during the occupation, and had been condemned to a prison sentence. "When it became known that this girl was still at the school representations were made that she should be expelled, for we of Quimper were of one accord that it was a disgrace to have her in the region. But the headmistress refused, on the grounds that the sins of the father should not be visited on the daughter. So the child of the traitor continued to enjoy herself in that luxurious atmosphere. This was known in the town, for local men and women work at the school, and they reported that, far from being ostracised for her father's crimes, she was greatly loved and admired by the other girls, and was a pet of the mistresses. Presumably she has inherited an oily tongue and deceptive ways.

"A little further up this street, in an apartment over the rope merchant's store, there lives a certain Madame Valentin who is a patriot. The sons of this lady took a great part in our Resistance, which was particularly strong and resolute, as you may imagine. Madame Valentin was more outraged than most by the disgrace of this girl's connection with the town. When the girl herself passed down the street Madame Valentin would shout shame on her, and others would do likewise. Their anger was not lessened by the conduct of the other misses, who would crowd round the girl, if you please, as though to protect her, and would frown in a la-de-da fashion at those who shouted from windows, doorways, and pavements. In those days, of course, there was no police escort. . . .

"At length words seemed to Madame Valentin to be unequal to the task of expressing the depth of her feelings. She prepared a bucket, filling it to the brim with greasy dishwater and unappetising solids such as the parts of rabbits that are removed before they can be cooked, the rinds of old camemberts, the skins of tomatoes. The next time this girl passed under her window Madame Valentin emptied the bucket over her. The aim was good, but a certain amount spattered over the other girls, and the mistress walking in front may have received a drop or two. At any rate they turned and hurried back to the school, and the next we heard was that the headmistress had taken the matter up with the mayor and that Madame Valentin had been given a dressing down at the Mairie and even informed that legal action was pending. The news of this shabby treatment of Madame Valentin was very unpopular, you may be sure.

"But the next development came from an unexpected quarter. You saw that batch of girls coming along the street? Well, a week ago along came thirty or forty of them, just like these ones, and quiet as mice. But they were only waiting till they got opposite poor Madame Valentin's windows. There they all stopped, and I thought (I was serving a café-crème inside at that moment) there had been an accident. I ran out to the street here, and I saw all those blasted girls standing in a row facing the rope merchant's place. They were throwing things like mad, and screaming and laughing, and the two mistresses were nearly dotty what with wondering what the devil was happening, and trying to get those girls to move on in some sort of order. It seems that they'd left the school all ready for the attack. Each girl carried one heavy stone, and when they came to the rope merchant's they threw their stones at Madame Valentin's windows on the first floor. When that volley had made a proper job of breaking all the glass in the building they followed it with another, less dangerous but more insulting, for each girl had a second bomb consisting of something unwholesome. Some threw cods' heads, some bags of soot weighted with small stones, some stink bombs (bought, it was said, in Paris), and two or three threw (can you beat it?) rolls of toilet paper. Madame Valentin was out at the time, or the good woman might have been killed. If she had been there, though, and had survived the first salvo, I'll bet she'd have given them something to think about. Girls never can throw straight, as you doubtless know (something to do with their chests, no doubt), and the whole of the building received a pretty good peppering. The rope merchant's was the most terrible and disagreeable mess you ever saw in your life, what with soot and treacle and broken glass all over the goods and Monsieur Deprez himself taking cover under the counter and rendered ill by the smell of those bombs.

"Well, as you may imagine, the lawyers have been busy on all sides ever since, and nobody knows where the truth lies. It is said that the school sent its own carpenters and painters to repair the damages down the street, and it is said that the mayor has in some degree at any rate taken the side of the headmistress, and she in her turn is said to have omitted to punish the destroyers of property. It is likely that the mayor will feel the wind of all this at the next elections. Nobody can say more than that at this moment, for even Madame Valentin will not speak of the matter, since her lawyers have ordered her to keep silent until the day of reckoning when all, or nearly all, will be made clear.

"Now you know, Monsieur and Madame, why there was a police escort. The way things are in France today wrongdoers are protected and the righteous are attacked with impunity."

"What about the girl who was the unwilling cause of all this bother?" Isabel asked. "Was she in the crocodile that passed us just now?"

"*Her?* No, she hasn't been seen at all. It's said that she's been shamming ill ever since she received the baptism of Madame Valentin's slop pail."

But the tide was already on the ebb, and we had no wish to go aground again. . . .

We anchored six miles below Quimper. Near us blood horses were standing in rich grass and stretching themselves prior to eating the night away. Somebody was shooting in the woods, using the last of the daylight. A boy appeared in front of a yellow house just visible through the trees. Alert beside the boy's legs stood a liver-and-white pointer. The silence of the night formed a thick background to small noises, the splash of a fish, a ripple against the dinghy, the long sigh of a brood mare, a car's horn somewhere far away, the cry of a barn owl.

The following day was one of preparation for crossing the Bay of Biscay. Nicholl gave me a last word of advice about the crossing. "Heave-to at nights," he said, "and sleep soundly. Then you'll be quite all right, no matter what the weather may do. The only danger with a small crew in a good boat is the human factor."

# CHAPTER 4

## THE BAY

ON *Neon*, Ponsonby, desiccated, wiry as a hair-spring, salty as a shrimp, knowing as a hunting stoat, was already afoot, washing down. We were eager to make a good start under his politely alert eye, but for once I had difficulty in hoisting the mainsail, and it was not until we were well down-river, ghosting with the lightest of off-shore airs, that I discovered the small rope that had jammed in the track near the foot of the luff. The Genoa was filling and emptying, filling and emptying, but we sailed well enough to ripple through the last of the flood tide, and soon the ebb bustled under our counter to carry us out of Benodet Bay, where there was even less wind. We set the huge spinnaker, and for a time it drew us into the mist, but when we were seven miles from Benodet even that sail could attract no zephyrs and we lay rocking in the white, muffling thickness, the sea in our noses and the sun, filtered but already warm, on our cheeks. I had made up my mind, for no particular reason, that we would cross the Bay without recourse to our engine.

Scores of fishing-boats were working around us and, by some freak of the mist and the calm, the throbbing of their many engines joined in unison to give the sonic effect of the passage of one great steamship. Occasionally a boat would appear, dancing, in our small circle of visibility, the men piling lobster creels in the after end. They were startled by the sight of us, so white and ghostly and silent, and the comments came sharply over the steaming water.

"Yacht de course."

"Un anglais."

"Pas de moteur."

"Bête, ça."

For three hours and eight minutes we lay becalmed. Then a breeze from the north-west. The spinnaker came down, the Genoa was sheeted home, and we were off, curvetting over the swell. The log, which had been hanging like a dead arm, sang off the sea miles, nine, ten, eleven, twelve. We set a south-westerly course, aiming at the ramparts of Corunna, more than 300 miles distant, in the north-west corner of

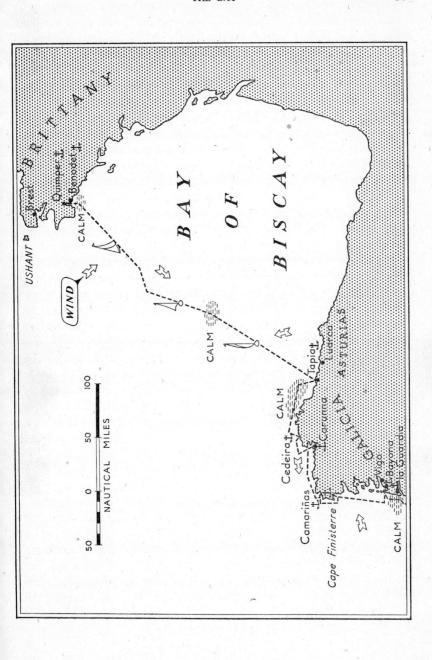

Spain. The reaching breeze held, and we profited from it, logging more than eight knots, hour upon hour. The sea gradually increased, and the prospect was dismal enough as night began to fall. But our speed was vastly cheering, and in the cockpit we were comfortable.

When it was dark we were still going so strongly that we could not bear to reduce sail, though I fixed the smallest working jib to the alternative forestay, ready to hoist. The glass was steady, the thermometer had fallen, and the sky looked greasy. However, when the stars appeared we thought we could look forward to a clear, fairly peaceful night. We were delighted with our neat electric navigation lights. Deep-sea yachtsmen are apt to disparage such lights, saying that they are vulnerable and are usually set too low to be easily visible from the decks or bridges of most ships, but, admitting those weaknesses, I still prefer them to their clumsier paraffin-burning alternatives. They were casting charming red and blue-green lights into the great headsail that hauled us along so powerfully.

When the log showed eighty-two miles the breeze, to our great disappointment, veered northward and slightly strengthened. The sea at once increased, and the Genoa had to be replaced by No. 3 jib. When Commander Nicholl advised us to heave-to at nights he advised a course of action for which both of us are unfitted; the moment we leave one place we are eager to arrive at the next. Only lack of wind or far too much wind would have made us heave-to, and we certainly did not intend to waste that or any other night of favourable wind.

We covered twenty miles on the new point of sailing, but neither of us cared for it, since it was taking us too much out into the Atlantic. We gybed. Isabel was seasick. I managed to persuade her to go to bed for a while. The gybing seemed to make her iller, and with this in mind I held on through the night to our new course, which was well east of the original.

The dawn (July 1st) was pale pink, and with it the wind vanished from that part of the Bay of Biscay. The sea was troubled. It surged under us in long rollers; it heaved suddenly as though turning over to scratch itself. We rolled and pitched. Checking my dead reckoning, I found we were a long way inside our direct course to Corunna. When I had done with the chart I made coffee. Isabel with an effort drank some. By contrast I was voraciously hungry. I left her at the tiller, and in the madly rocking saloon with the charts and instruments balancing on the swinging mahogany table I devoured a whole tin of bully beef, a loaf of

French bread, quarter of a pound of butter, 100 grams of saucisson, two litres of red wine, half a camembert, and four big pears. (Bully beef is one of the contrary points—perhaps the only one—of our marriage. . . . Isabel does not love me when I eat it. She cannot bear the stuff; the very smell of it revolts her. And her hatred seems to make it the more desirable to me. The canned, mottled remains of those miserable brutes that trail in weary hordes across the Andes, that smother themselves in the dust stabbed by their hoofs from the Pampas, are a *vice* with me [a vice contracted in an Italian prison camp, a former monastery]. As I should like to be more vicious than I am, and hope sincerely to become so as I grow older and wiser, those strangely shaped tins will always have a corner of my heart.)

We were becalmed for four hours, and then the wind came sighing from the east. We sailed south-west, Genoa and mainsail shooting us ahead. We had not long been moving in this godlike fashion when we met a pair of French fishing-boats painted white and royal blue, boats of some fifty tons with enormous rods stretching out on either side, like whiskers. They were bounding about, rolling their beamy bodies, creaming the sea in the most robust fashion, while we, under full sail, slipped past them steadily. This wonderful sailing continued all day, and as the hours passed we became rested and content.

Dusk looked more threatening than its predecessor, and the barometer showed a sharp drop. Should we hand the Genoa? A thousand times, No! We still had 100 miles to do to the north coast of Spain. Through the night we tore on, the spume hissing all around us, the breeze cold on our faces. We took turns of lying down, wrapped in blankets, on the cockpit gratings. We steered in short spells of an hour or so. The night before we had been tired, but now we were full of life. The one who lay down seldom slept, but usually talked to the one at the tiller. The big compass, electrically lit from below the card, gleamed knowingly—sometimes accusingly. At 3 a.m., with the barometer still falling, the Genoa became too pressing, and we changed it for the small jib. Dawn seeped through with an increasing sea and more weight in the wind. In the six hours of darkness we had logged fifty-three miles. The seas were immensely long (and therefore easy for a small boat) but there were intermediate, toppling waves between the big summits. We were carrying the absolute maximum of canvas, and I often considered the advisability of reefing. *Serica* remained steady and dry, despite her velocity through those troubled waters, and if the amount of sail we carried did make us a little wild on the summits, it helped to steady us in the troughs.

We had hoped at dawn to see a mountainous coastline. Instead we saw approaching us two Spanish fishing-boats belching black smoke from their funnels and carrying the giant whiskers of tunny rods that we had seen twenty-four hours previously. The whiskers constituted the only point of resemblance, for whereas the French boats had been beautiful and well maintained, and had been crewed by fat, lusty-looking men, the Spanish boats, with sharp bows and long, weak counters, were scrawny, pinched vessels with crews to match. We took the meeting as a sign that the coast might be near. I persuaded Isabel to snatch half an hour's sleep, and I steered in silence for a time. She awoke, looked at the log, which read 307, and then ahead.

"Mountains!" she said.

I had become so accustomed to "seeing" land that I had not been lifting my eyes except apprehensively to windward, but now indeed I saw the tremendous coastline, rugged, fantastically lofty, that had appeared as though by miracle out of the air and the water. At the same time we both viewed an open boat. We steered for it.

"Donde estamos?"

"Tapia . . . puerto de Tapia," answered the two men in the boat with waves of their arms towards the coast.

"Is there enough water for us there? we draw two metres."

"Ample. A Dutch yacht five times your size was in the harbour yesterday. You have charts of the vicinity?"

"No."

"Go round the island there, giving it a good berth. Watch for rocks on both sides of the entrance."

When we looked at a chart of the Spanish coast we saw Tapia marked in small letters to the east of Ribadeo and it was just there on our big chart of the Bay of Biscay (which did not name Tapia) that the line of my dead reckoning cut the coast. (Before we left England I had bought a yachtsman's sextant and a small book with some such title as, *There's Nothing to the Sextant*, together with a copy of Martelli's Tables. Had we got lost at sea I should only have had to read the book and teach myself how to use the sextant, an instrument in a highly-polished box that looked well on the saloon shelves, helping to give visitors to the yacht a false notion of the crew's efficiency.)

We remembered that the Nott-Bowers had been to Tapia in *Smew* 1,

and almost any port is an interesting port after two days and two nights
of sailing. When we were inside the island we saw a small boat coming
out to meet us. A boy rowed and a man stood in the stern sheets.

"Stop!" He held up an authoritative hand. "Pilot . . . com-
pulsory . . . no dues . . ." He climbed aboard, made fast his painter
aft, and took our tiller. "Start the motor," he said at once.

"Very well." I took down the sails.

He was a charming fellow, and despite bloodshot eyes, the night's
growth of ruddy beard, a stained shirt of striped cotton, and dirty bare
feet, he made an excellent impression.

"You want to go alongside a quay, Señora?"

"No, thank you."

"All right. With ships you know where you are: they all go alongside.
With yachts it's different: some do, some don't. Is the anchor ready?"

We entered a grey harbour, strangely Nordic. He told me to drop
anchor in the centre. The boy in the boat carried our warps to the outer
mole and to a dredger barge marked *Luarca*. We hauled astern, letting
out chain, and were comfortably moored. A demonstratively friendly
crowd of all ages and financial circumstances had assembled on the mole,
staring, chattering, laughing. The commandante del puerto arrived in a
heavy boat, and the pilot, who had learned our name, made the introductions. The official, in grey uniform with slanting gold stripes on the
sleeves and a peaked cap which he removed for an instant (because he
kept his cigarettes and matches in the lining), was very firm about seeing
all our papers. Apparently he had to know *exactly* how long we intended to stay in his harbour. He reverted to that question again and
again, and Isabel kept replying that we did not know; our departure
would depend on inclination and on the wind. Since we had an engine,
the official answered, what had the wind to do with it? But at length
he departed, and we were alone in another country.

We ate. The day was very hot. We put on dressing-gowns, lay on the
saloon settees, and slept. We had crossed the Bay of Biscay in forty-
seven hours, and had covered 308 miles under canvas at an average
speed of 6.55 knots, although for four hours we had been becalmed. I
don't remember ever sleeping better, or waking with a keener sense of
pleasure and physical wellbeing.

# CHAPTER 5

## SPANISH OFFICIALS AND LA LUZ

ONLY four hours after his first visit the harbour-master of Tapia returned with a burly man whom he introduced as a friend of his (which we hardly thought to be a sufficient reason for bringing him aboard, particularly as both men wore heavy boots which they had dipped in cinders).

"He's considering building a vessel for himself," the harbour-master explained, "so it will possibly be instructive for him to have a look at yours. . . . Made up your minds when you're going to leave us?"

"Depende del viento."

"Fear nothing, there will be no wind tomorrow. Now comes the good weather from the north-east, dry, warm, agreeable. Surely that delightful American engine works?"

"Yes, but we prefer the sails."

"All very fine for amusement," the official's friend said. "For men like me who earn—I mean *earn*—a living from the sea, engines are bad, but sails are worse."

I thought that both men regarded me with distaste amounting to nausea, and when they had gone I mentioned this to Isabel.

"I noticed it," she said, "and understood it, but thought I had better say nothing to you while they were still with us. . . . In Spain men don't powder their noses. . . ."

(Crossing the Bay of Biscay my nose—an organ that I had hitherto considered impervious to climate—had peeled for the third time since leaving Lymington. Isabel had prevented this in her own case by covering her nose with a preparation called *Shine-no-More* and then with powder. She had suggested, and finally tried, the same treatment on me.)

After her explanation I wished that I had been rude to our two self-invited guests, for if there is one characteristic that revolts me in a grown man it is brutish intolerance for other men whom he considers to be effeminate.

While I worked on deck I looked around me at the harbour. It reminded me of Troon harbour, in Ayrshire, with its men in cloth caps and its massive grey walls imprisoning the leaping sea. A flock of brown sheep was grazing on ground by the lighthouse that was prohibited to the public—secret ground. Two trawlers lay by an inner quay, disgorging cod. Posted at vantage points on the perimeter were some two hundred people, all of them watching us. When we launched the dinghy and descended into it there was a shout of laughter that was not wounding, but had applause and good-nature in it. The laughter continued as I sculled to an iron ladder near one of the trawlers. The spectators had never seen such a funny baby boat. Their own boats looked funny enough to us; at the inner end of the harbour were building ugly fishing-boats of the size, but not the power, of Loch Fyne drifters, while the smaller, undecked boats had hideous dragging sterns, like those of some river launches.

Tapia had the appearance of a man who has been wounded and has lost much blood but no courage. It is in the Asturias, the country of mines and violence, and its record had not been "good" during the Civil War. We saw no beggars, but we were frequently stopped in the streets, even by women, and asked for cigarettes. The people seemed grotesquely thin after the peasants of Brittany.

\* \* \* \*

We sailed next morning for Cedeira, fifty miles to the west. After twenty minutes of brisk movement with the offshore breeze we were becalmed. It was a morning of great heat. We lay panting for a while, tormented by the swell, then started the engine and motored on without help from the sails. We thus crossed, far out, the Bay of Foz, and rounded Punta de la Estaca, the northernmost corner of Spain. The day was tenebrous and, as often happens on such days, there was a glare from the water that drilled the eyeballs. The thermometer registered well up in the eighties, and the barometer had again fallen. We agreed that we should probably have more wind than we wanted before we reached Cedeira.

In the early evening the long-awaited wind came from the north-east with breath-taking suddenness. One moment the swell was smooth, the next spray was being whipped and waves were toppling. We ran on, over-canvased. Cedeira was only nine miles distant, and we hoped for a lee from the prominent Cabo Ortegal, round which we foamed at speed, rail awash and the sheets grunting. The wind seemed to pursue us round, and when the high land should have given us shelter it merely served to increase the force of the wind by funnelling it down on us. Off Cedeira we joined company with a steam trawler. She dawdled, creaking, to let us overtake, and then found that she could not keep pace with us. We were now sailing up the estuary of Río Cedeira. Charcoal burners were working near the top of the ridge that descends precipitously to the sea. Gusts of wind were signalled by the smoke from their fires as a magnetic field can be demonstrated with iron filings on a sheet of paper. It was disturbing, though useful enough, to see the smoke traces streak down, sometimes over our masthead, sometimes fretting the water inshore of us. Isabel had the tiller and I was forward unlashing the anchor and preparing to lower the jib. Her slender hands are "good hands", and when the gusts struck us I felt her delicately luff. Three motor-boats over-filled with excited passengers had come forth to watch our arrival. They approached us in line abreast and then suddenly scattered in panic as they got some notion of our speed, and saw our twisted course occasioned by the luffs. We raced through the narrows to drop anchor astern of a group of trawlers, dirty, sturdy animals squatting awkwardly on the choppy waters.

A boat came out to us bringing the harbour-master, two policemen with rifles, and a redundant interpreter, a Cuban. Isabel told the armed men that they would not be allowed on board if they had nails in their boots. One of them obediently subsided in the rowing-boat, his rifle wilting between his knees (and we instantly felt so sorry for him that we gave him a cigarette and some gingerbread), but the other, holding up his feet so that we could see, protested: "Goma, goma!"

We had to complete many forms and answer many absurd questions. The youthful Cuban interpreter, intelligent, but talkative and obsessed by his own charms (which were a little too obvious for my taste), was difficult to get rid of. A fish-canning factory on the beach belonged to him, he said. Next week his name was to be painted on the smooth white frontage in letters four metres high.

"The factory looks very well as it is," I said.

"Three months ago my grandfather's name was on it. Now it shall be my name. I want to see my name on my factory. So would you. I know you English: you have your names on everything, your towels, your match-boxes, your dogs. And as for your English towns," he said truthfully, "you can't even see the streets for the names on the shops."

The harbour-master wore civilian clothes, and was fairly agreeable in his dealings with us, but as they were leaving he took a firm grip of our teak ensign staff to pull his own boat close under our counter, and he hauled the staff's brass socket clean out of the deck. I refixed it at once, using longer screws and cursing shore officials who meddle with ships.

That night the wind from the north-east blew up very strong. Cedeira is not too comfortable an anchorage in such conditions. The holding ground seemed good, but one of the trawlers dragged past us with a great deal of harsh shouting that was still going on in the morning, although the ship was then well astern of us and, to our way of thinking, too close on a rocky lee shore for the crew to waste more time in apportioning the blame.

We sailed out with double-reefed mainsail and the No. 3 jib, breasting the compressed flood tide in magnificent fashion. Neither of us had ceased to be astonished at the way *Serica* sailed, at her power and steadiness, at the lightness of her balance on the helm. Just beyond the narrows, and under the great ridge that had bombarded us with gusts the previous evening, we were becalmed and were rapidly swept back towards the dangers. I waited until the last moment, and was about to start the engine, when a fierce gust, bringing whiffs of smoke from the high tops, shot us a mile out to sea, where we steadied in turn to a very strong north-easter. The sea had looked terrible from the harbour mouth, but once we were well offshore it proved, as it usually does, to be less uncomfortable than its appearance had suggested. The double-reefed mainsail set perfectly, and the yacht, though travelling at about her maximum speed, was steady, and only comfortably heeled. I doubt if any sailing could be better than it was with us that day in the hot sun and the fierce, but reliable, wind. We went six miles out, romping west, with a big following sea. Inshore we saw broken water. Charcoal smoke swirled in the chasms and coves. We met two British ships, one a dark, limping, romantic tramp, and the other a dandy of a banana boat. We got friendly signals from their bridges, but were too busy to pay much attention, too exhilarated by the rush of our progress. Now and then a lop from a diagonally-breaking sea would catch me across my bare back. I wanted to yell from pleasure, like a Cossack. I did.

When we could set a reaching course for Corunna we had an exciting gybe and then raced south across an emerald-and-ivory sea that grew smaller and shorter in a welter of white horses. We had the impression that we were sailing down the rapids—and now we were sailing south.

In Corunna's outer harbour we anchored beside a straight-stemmed

English yawl, *Debonair* (seventeen tons) of Falmouth, fitted out extremely deep-sea, with tanned elephant's-hide canvas, twin-boomed staysails, loose-footed gaff mainsail. A young man and his wife and two children came up from below to wave to us. We admired their sturdy good looks, and were sorry when they told us they hoped to sail that night for Gibraltar. They were bound for New Zealand.

Corunna seemed to be sending up a gas attack against us. We watched the grey clouds generating behind the quays and moving towards us at the slow rate at which clouds always seem to travel until they are overhead. When they arrived they proved to be composed mainly of cement dust. Three minutes later (considering our resistance to have been "softened" by the gas attack?) the first wave of authorities boarded, a naval officer and two ratings. When they had gone the Special Police arrived (only two of them). They found it suspect that Isabel should speak Spanish better than themselves, and that I should speak worse than none. What language did I speak, they asked Isabel. French! The policemen did not like that at all. (Italian or German would not have been nearly as dangerous as French, the language of Voltaire and other Reds.) And what was my profession? Escritor! They scowled as they turned their dark, normally amiable faces at me. Did I write newspaper articles? Ah, only books . . . books were fairly harmless, so long as they were not about Spain. They bundled themselves into their boat, carrying the dossier, and threatening to return that evening. In the meantime, they said, we should not move without advising their office. Then came the ordinary police. The sergeant hoisted himself on board, but the other two were made to stay in their boat because they had nails (not "goma") on their boots. Then came the Customs Police. When the fourth attacking wave had made good its retreat three rowing-boats, each containing one expressionless man in a dark suit, came out from the shore and slowly circled us, watching, making no sign. I wondered if it was a case of mistaken identity. Were they drug smugglers who had an assignation with some yacht? Were they waiting for a secret sign? Did they expect us to slip buoyant packets of hashish into the sea? Or did they expect us to auction our belongings, beginning with the yacht? British people at this time were regarded in certain other countries—mainly as a result of the wailings of the British "popular" press, and the much-publicised snarls of His Majesty's Opposition in and out of the House of Commons—as undesirable indigents. Undesirable I certainly am (I should hate to be considered anything else), but when we visited Corunna I was far from indigent (for we still had all of my tourist's allowance of £50, and thirty-six of Isabel's £50).

The naval authorities had asked us to berth in the Darsena de la Marina, off which we had anchored, but that basin, although attractive enough, was overcrowded and filthy. We declined their hospitality, and remained outside. As soon as our dinghy touched the steps there was a scuffling race, and a tattered young man who had once been harvesting in Canada, and who could speak some English, asked if he might look after our boat. Another man, of respectable appearance (belying his profession), approached us with a visiting card that proclaimed him a member of the editorial staff of *La Luz*.

We were bound for the British Consulate to collect our mail. How strange, the journalist said. He also was going there, for the Consul, an excellent, a truly most excellent, charming, distinguished, and intelligent person, a really beautiful man, was one whom he, *La Luz*, numbered in his special circle of friends.

"Here in General Franco's own city we have reason to be grateful for His benevolence and ability," *La Luz* said as we sauntered along at an easy pace designed to keep body temperatures down to a reasonable level in that hot air. "Spain is a poor country, yet year after year those great new buildings go up, and especially in La Coruña. Such buildings give work to many men. . . . And there are special vegetables for the poor. It is very democratic."

"If Franco's responsible for these monstrosities," I said to Isabel in English (referring to the new buildings), "he ought to be shot."

"You do not care for General Franco?" *La Luz* asked me in French.

"I don't care for politicians."

"But Franco is a soldier. You do not care for soldiers?"

"Yes, so long as they leave me alone."

"That is good: General Franco will not bother *you*," he said rather neatly.

We walked for a mile in the important street round the waterfront. On our right were the satisfactory buildings of a former age, whole elevations covered in a projecting web of window with smallish panes and sash-bars somewhat in the Georgian proportions. On our left were new buildings transcending in solid mass of horror British cinema architecture of the twentieth century.

When our business at the Consulate was finished the journalist still clung to us. I recognised that desperate, hangdog affability, for had I not at one time myself followed his pestilential calling? I knew what effort lay behind his offers of information and hospitality. My mind worked with his mind as it machined the phrases that editors regard as fragments of "human interest". Scores of questions he put to us, certain of them several times over, for the poor fellow asked so many that he lost himself in the labyrinth. I strove to humour Isabel, who did not like him at all; and to humour him, for whom I felt an inverted sympathy. The scoundrel in me leered at his efforts and strove to form the story that he would produce for the next day's earliest editions; my better nature remonstrated that even the vile should not revile the vile. . . . But where was the photographer?

The journalist led us into the narrow Calle Real. "The finest shops and cafés are here, and vehicles may not enter. See, the whole street is pavement, and so everyone who uses its amenities must walk, from the millionaire to the humblest beggar. We should do better perhaps to call it Calle de la Democracia, don't you agree? or are you royalists? . . ." He leaped to one side, and a photographer, hatless and ill-tempered, rushed from a doorway to take five or six pictures of us with a miniature camera.

"There was no need to take us by surprise," I said to La Luz in French.

"On ne sait jamais," he answered. "Il y en a qui sont rudement enmerdés l'instant qu'on ose leurs presenter un appareil photographique . . . Je m'excuse, mais il vallait mieux prendre ses précautions."

Many of the youths strolling in the Calle Real were army conscripts in the roughest of uniforms. Here and there the gaudy shops gave way to a dark café, a kind of hole or burrow from the narrow street, but a respectable burrow, with black leather upholstery all buttons and bulges, shining brass rims to the tables, thin waiters—studies in black and white, Aubrey Beardsley figures—the sheen of glasses, the tender glow of wine, the perversely appetising steam of strong coffee. Inside the cafés there were only men, of course, men with their eyes half closed, looking like the owls in the caverns of Battersea Park. The conscripts stared into shop windows with displays of everything unobtainable (for the poor) except by force, cigars, Dunhill cigarette-holders, Patum Peperium, Dundee marmalade, Canadian-Club whisky, Drambuie, gâteaux, les modes parisiennes, tinned frankfurters and sauerkraut, chowder from New Orleans, smoked hams, pâté from Alsace, crocodile-

leather shoes for men, onyx, ivory, silver, and gold cigarette cases. . . .
Ah! here was a shop where a soldier boy might buy—*Tickets for the
Lottery!* And here another—*Tickets for the Bull Fight!* And yet
another—*Tickets for the Cinema!*

The conscripts were an agreeable study. Their manners were distrait.
They seemed neither depressed nor amused, but somewhere in between.
Many were handsome. The rough uniforms, the cropped hair, became
them better than the padded and pinched suit (Hollywood influence)
that set off this typical young civilian, his hair fixatised and enmeshed
greasily in the hollow at the nape of his neck.

But the journalist was leading us now to a restaurant where he
promised to give the palates of even such experienced travellers as ourselves (he had to poke a little fun at us now and then if he was to keep his
sanity) an interesting surprise. Since the time was only 8 p.m., and
nobody would arrive to dine for at least two hours, the place was empty
save for an assistant barman and one waiter. Our host ordered his
special bottle and three glasses. It was a young, sour wine, closely
resembling in flavour and pale gooseberry colour the piquette that I
have drunk with peasants in France. When the bottle was half empty
*La Luz* summoned the waiter.

"There is a fly in this wine. Take it away, remove the fly, and bring
back the bottle."

Before the waiter had had time to carry out these instructions *La Luz*
dashed a coin to the tablecloth and hustled us out, wishing us a very
good night.

His article, which appeared the following day, fulfilled our anti-
cipations, being as full of lies and sentimentality as a plum pudding with
currants and brandy. As is the habit of many provincial journalists (and
not a few metropolitan ones) it was he, whatever his name was, who
took the centre of the article; more space and effort was given to a
recital of the intricate questions he claimed to have asked us than to the
replies (which he had also invented). Poor *Serica* was described
variously as a "frail embarkation", a "wisp of a yacht", and "scarce
worthy of the name of ship, though doubtless excellent enough in its
own way, and particularly to those practising, as all the English do, the
nautical sports". According ill with the above descriptions was *Serica's*
tonnage, which he had set down as sixty, instead of sixteen.

Corunna main post office, a Franco-sponsored pile, flaunted so much stained glass as to remind me of youthful wanderings in residential districts of Glasgow where red sandstone and stained glass predominate. The doors of the post office are in the wrong places. You have to hurry round sharp corners and along impregnable walls before you can get in. The letter-boxes are so positioned that it is difficult to find them and as difficult to persuade them to swallow a letter. Inside, under a market-garden acreage of stained glass ceiling, there are bronze guichets, coarse mouldings, granite facings, and pleasant employees who bring their knitting. The Banco de España is a trifle more practical and more religious (as well becomes a bank). The architecture (more Prudentialesque than that of the P.O.) includes sudden effects such as splashes of purple glass that throw their lights into the faces of the cashiers. Two soldiers with rifles were on guard in the customers' arena at the bank—a disconcerting sight, a psychological error; when Messrs. Lloyds adopt such practices I shall take my humble custom elsewhere. The cashier gave us all the petrol coupons we needed on condition that we cashed Travellers' Cheques to a minimum value of £2.

In the Calle Real we bought linen hats to protect our faces. The shop was owned by a beldame, lightly bearded, with black sequins and yellow egg-stains on her corsage. Among her choice of hats for women was laid a chorizo, the delicious red sausage of Spain. The sausage was not for sale; it was for her grandson, who was doing his military service in one of the Corunna barracks.

"Which reminds me," she said, taking a knife from a drawer in the counter. Forcing the blade with difficulty through the compressed cylinder, she cut it in two. An aroma of peppers and garlic was at once pleasantly distinguishable among the hats. "I'll give him only half this morning," she said to Isabel. "Then I'll have a chance of seeing him again after the parade tomorrow. At your age, Señorita, one can take one's pleasures; at my age one must scheme for them."

From this shop, which will doubtless make way for something "brighter" in a few years' time, we went to the market, a concrete structure showing more than a whiff of the Corbusier influence, and therefore, presumably, of pre-Franco erection. Within, at any rate on the ground floor, there was no provision for laying out the food, and peasant women were squatting in the dust surrounded by bundles of rancid-looking greenstuff. Behind the market was the black market, the only source of *white* bread, which was sold by women sitting on door-steps along one sun-drenched street. These women (because they were breaking the law?) were more smiling, buxom, healthy, than their scrawny sisters selling lettuces. The bread was expensive, even to us with our extremely favourable tourist rate of exchange; the complaint to be heard on all sides in Spain concerned the toil required to earn enough money to buy bread.

It appeared that the only petrol pump in that large and in some ways prosperous city was a mobile affair on wheels that was trundled daily to a triangular plaza near the British Consulate. (Don't imagine that I am criticising Corunna on that account.) It was for us a question of taking a taxi with the petrol cans or of moving *Serica* nearer to the pump. We thought pesetas too scarce to waste on taxis, so chose the second alternative. At a tourist bureau, a round beehive containing a queen bee answering the buzzings of a number of indigenous and foreign drones, we were given a pamphlet containing an excellent map of the town. With this on our knees in the cockpit we were able to sail *Serica* under jib alone into the main port, and to anchor her within 200 yards of the petrol pump. The commercial harbour we had thus penetrated was covered with a treacly scum of fuel oil and coal dust, and this, revolting though it was, helped to keep the water flat, for an east wind had suddenly whipped out of the blue hills around the wild, highland bay in which Corunna is set. (I had always imagined them hurrying Sir John Moore's body to the ramparts on the edge of a sandy plain, but the reality is romantic in a different fashion.)

The wind made a lee shore of all the steps in sight. A couple of intelligent boys discerned my problem in the dinghy, and came to my assistance, taking the painter and holding the dinghy safely off the stone steps with their bare feet, while they sat with their ragged little bottoms in oily spume. (Perhaps the greatest of all the great differences between a Latin and a Teuton is the size of *les fesses*. The first thing that always struck me about German soldiers, met in France during the Second World War, was the ponderous shape of their bottoms.) Thanking the boys in my ignoble Spanish (what a glorious, rumbling language it is! and so simple that I feel all kinds of an ass to speak it so ill), I hurried off with my cans. A crowd soon gathered round the wheeled pump, me, and my bona fide petrol coupons. I was embarrassed by the attention I seemed to arouse, and was by no means predisposed to listen, when a clear male voice asked, first in Spanish and then in English, from the region of my right hip: "The Señor sometimes goes to the circus in England?"

"Occasionally," I replied.

"Bimbo the Bottlesnatcher—you have seen his act? Fine!"

My interlocutor was a gentleman some four feet in height and pro-portionately well built to an unorthodox pattern. His blunt features were attractive; he had a good eye, gentle without softness, wide without dullness, fiery without temper; his teeth were creamy-white, large, and square. I scarcely like to say so about so agreeable a person-age, but his clothes showed that he did not, that day at any rate, belong to the richer income groups. He was well dressed, very, but there were patches and darns. His hat, though, a dark-blue affair of furry surface and with a black eagle's feather rising from the cord, had a Gascogne twist to the brim. . . . I told him I had never seen the performance of the Bottlesnatcher.

"But you will be able to find Bimbo when you return to England? You intend to return to England? Yes, I have Bimbo's address in Halifax. Tell me, they still have perpetual motion staircases in the Tubes? Piccadilly Circus, yes? Tell me, mister, will you do something for me with Bimbo? Please."

"Nothing illegal?"

"I am a barrister, mister. I know the law." He took me and my petrol cans into one of the dark cafés that I had noticed the previous day at the foot of the Calle Real.

"Spanish men, not polite," he said to me when he had ordered wine.

"No wonder they stare at my clothes. I'm disgracing you."

"I'll make speech with them," he said, gripping the brass edge of the table as though meditating a handspring. "Spanish I speak easily, for I have a Spanish wife."

"And you? are you British?"

"Not me! Born Hungary; father, Austrian; mother, Danish. . . . Many years I worked in England, as actor, and in a barrister's place. I played in films too, travelling each day to Ellis Tree. We lived in a hotel in Russell's Square, for we were rich then. A big hotel with good beds. Below the hotel, a Turkish bath: men couleur-de-rose, chairs like on a ship, tonic waters with ice and limones, masseurs like big animal fish, animal fish? . . ."

"Seals?"

"Seals. . . . They ask: 'Do you want for soap on the head, sir?' Then Turkish bed, with tea and Turkish bread with butter. Ah!" he cried. "Good! Good! Two times a week to the Turkish bath in

"Strong and shapely . . . full of life." Portuguese Sardiner (see page 108)

"Chose a berth among the river barges—sailing craft loaded with salt."  *SERICA* at SETUBAL
(see page 146)

Russell's Square, but never one fight. Englishmen are kind. Spaniards, not so kind. First wife," he said, tapping my arm delicately, "first wife Hungarian; small size, big heart. Second wife Spanish. But now of Bimbo, eh? Soon after I was married to Chiquita there was difficulty. Her papers were not so good. We must go to Spain to get better papers, but Spain from England is a long way and costs much money. My friend Bimbo gave some money for trains and ships. Bimbo is hot stuff," he said, handing me an addressed envelope. "Inside is a letter with the money for Bimbo. Back in England you will post it, please?"

"How much money?"

"Five pounds," he answered. "I bought them when I heard an English yacht was here, but the first yacht was no good, for the man was not going back to England."

"All right," I said, "but, between gentlemen, I must tell you that I'll have to examine the contents of the letter before I take it into England. We're afraid of our Customs, as you doubtless know. Under that condition I'll gladly take it and post it in England to Bimbo the Bottle-snatcher."

At that moment a blast of wind and dust rushed up the narrow street, reminding me of Isabel's predicament on the yacht, and bidding him adieu, I took my cans and hurried to the waterfront. He trotted at my side. *Serica* was jumping at her anchor; Isabel was on deck, shading her eyes and looking toward the shore. The two boys were still holding off the dinghy with their clever feet. I rewarded both, and turned to say good-bye to the barrister, but he had gone. A Guardia Civil stood on the top step, feet planted wide, shining hat forced down over puzzled brow.

I managed, with a great effort, to row back to the yacht. We lifted the dinghy, hoisted the mainsail, which was still, fortunately, double-reefed. Whenever the anchor was up I set the small jib, and we began to thrash out of the harbour. I went aft to discuss plans with Isabel, and found that we had both already decided to do the same thing, namely to beat across the bay and find shelter at the far side. Once outside the fort we felt the weight of a force-seven wind. We both went forward with cotton waste to clean the bottom of the dinghy before the water enfilading the yacht could carry the black oil of the port of Corunna to our deck. We saw as we beat across the bay that several fishing-boats had taken refuge inshore by a small village marked on our charts as Mera. It is not much of an anchorage, but it was sheltered that day, and we had more than enough of the wind in our hurried crossing. We anchored only at the third attempt. The first time I dropped too far out, and we fell astern close to two trawlers; the second I dropped over rock, and our anchor dragged so fast that it might not have been down at all. The yacht's topsides had been washed clean by our disagreeably stormy passage across the bay.

When we returned to England I fulfilled my obligation to the barrister in Corunna, and forwarded his letter to Bimbo the Bottlesnatcher, from whom—in Halifax—I obtained a receipt. I later had a gracious letter from Corunna—the barrister admitting in the first sentence that a professor of languages had helped with its compilation and orthography. The letter suggested that wind and waves had combined to force *Serica* into Corunna harbour so that a debt might be honourably discharged. And now it was so. . . . "Pray forgive my somewhat shaky hand," the letter continued. "In sooth, 'tis my left. The sun has not run his course since I had an alarming experience with a laughing hyena, an exhibit in the menagerie where I now work. The brute, disgusted by the meal I had just set before it, saw some prospect of a more variegated diet, and took a mouthful of my right arm."

I had enquired if we could send anything from England that would give him pleasure. All that he asked for—but then he would be determined not to put us to any great trouble or expense—was a tin of black boot polish of a widely-publicised brand.

# CHAPTER 6

## THE VIRGIN'S STONE

THE eucalyptus trees were swaying on the heights ashore. (What a delightful medicine eucalyptus oil was! or do I only think so now because I have not heard of it from the age of six, because it therefore represents love, shelter, warmth, for the helpless?) Eucalyptus trees can look very distressed and haglike in a wind.

Around us the Spanish boats, crusty, heavy, starved for paint, bobbed and tugged. The prospect of a day at anchor in that comparative shelter was agreeable.

When Isabel had finished her reorganisation below, which had been punctuated by such remarks as: "Your flags are now in the locker at the after end of the port berth," we landed on a gravel beach. Warm, marbled pebbles lay there in millions to form a carpet under grey cliffs rounded and folded like elephants' flanks. There we sand-papered the dinghy within and without. While we worked two young men came rowing across the bay to have a look at us (but disguising that intention, as they thought). One of them began to sing, and having sung not at all badly and very loudly, he stopped, and scrutinised the water. After unusually dramatic preliminaries he dived in. A long pause, then an arm appeared, followed by a blowing head; all was well. The sea was cold, and he was soon back, somewhat calmer, in the stern sheets. Then his friend began to show something of *his* prowess—as an oarsman. That exhibition soon took them out of sight, striking a very high rate.

From the deck of the yacht we had been able to distinguish the name of a restaurant in the village, *Café Bar La Perla*. To reach it we walked for a mile along paths and on powdery roads, brownish-yellow, the surfaces crumbling into dusty landslides. A pregnant woman met us in the bar, and said that she would cook us lunch. While she cooked we walked into the country. It was a green country with small granaries built high on stone legs, and each cottage with a line of smooth, raised plaster (about two feet wide) running round the edges of the front wall. Sometimes the wall would be pale blue or grey, and then the line round it would be white or chocolate; but more often the wall was white, and the line blue, or green, or grey, or red. The roofs, low-pitched, appeared to sink into the small buildings and the lines picked out the edges, making them bolder, as a draughtsman can emphasise his outline to give an easy, theatrical effect. Vines grew on the cottage walls, and there were gardens with flowers in prolific clumps, geraniums, roses, agapanthas, hydrangeas. Fields of grass, potatoes, and maize, chiefly maize, stretched over the horizon, but somehow gave little impression of food, of life. Below us the sea was still rushing away towards Corunna, which (thanks to General Franco) looked from that distance like San Francisco.

*La Perla's* floor, tiled, but covered with a few years' dust and debris, smelled badly. Unbelievably thin cats, their fur falling out in patches, prowled round the tables and jumped moaning to perch uneasily on chairs. We ate tortilla and then a risotto made with chorizo and pimentos. If we wanted to eat there the following day, the woman said kindly, she would make the journey by ferry-boat to Corunna to buy meat and fruit and better wine.

Two Guardias Civiles passed, overheated and jaded, carrying their coal-scuttle hats on the muzzles of their carbines. They looked into the restaurant, but did not stop until they were sixty yards down the road. Then we heard them discussing us, and one of them slowly returned to ask a few questions. He was ill at ease. He had felt it his duty to question us, but did not like doing it, and he told us so. The Spanish police have a bad name; many stories are heard of their cruelties and stupidities. It is only fair to say that, while they were a nuisance to us, they were personally (with one exception) agreeable enough.

France is the most civilised European country (I believe) for the cruising yachtsman, as indeed for the ordinary tourist. The authorities' Olympian attitude of trust makes France comfortable, but still more important is the attitude of the French people, who are normally un-interested in boats and their occupants, so that when you arrive in a French port or anchor off a French beach you can expect to exist, if you choose, in privacy. Not so in Spain, where life is made almost intolerable for the introvert yachtsman by the natural inquisitiveness, gregarious-ness, and talkativeness of the Spanish people. Most tiresome of all living things are the boys of Spain.

I have no liking for children; the females are uninteresting until the age of approximately thirteen, the males are apt to be intolerable until they are twenty. I suppose as boys go the Spanish ones are not unattractive. They are uninhibited (how agreeable it is to find inhibitions among the very young!), handsome, boisterous, and above all they are numerous. They are spoiled and trusted by their elders to such an extent that they seem bound to grow up into sloth and unstimulating dissipation. The girls are seldom to be seen; they are taught to work at home.

Boys of Mera were allowed to "play", no matter what the weather, with the boats in which their fathers earned a livelihood. In these boats they rowed out to *Serica*. They had not the dignity to hold off and regard us as so-called savages would; they grated alongside, they fingered everything, they begged, they exchanged obscenities far beyond their years, and shrieked with laughter at their own obscenities. Their impertinence was only matched by their watermanship.

The ferry from Corunna to Mera arrives at a narrow mole, a dangerous place, tidal and exposed, over which a horrible sea was breaking. When they were tired of bothering us, they would row off to the mole to bump father's boat and get a good ducking. For minutes on end I would turn my eyes in that direction, hoping to see a boat-load drown, or at least a broken leg or two, an eye hanging from its socket. Alas! their handling of the oars was too dexterous, their coolness and judgment unimpeachable. At the last flicker of the last moment one of them always did the right thing, and disaster was averted. I suppose that from time to time a brat or two goes permanently under at Mera, but the parents never seemed to bother about the antics on the sea, and possibly they feel, as I do, that there are too many boys in that place— in all places.

\*　　\*　　\*　　\*

A wet night was followed by a morning shivery, grey, and morose, but memories of our persecutors and of the smell of the floor at *La Perla* drove us out of sheltered water and soon we were plunging in the sea that swept the bay. We carried (for the first time) our trysail, a handy and confidence-inspiring triangle of heavy canvas. It is shaped like a burgee, and can be carried at any desired height on the mast; it has its own double sheets, and there is a chain kicking-strop to hold down the boom while the trysail is in use.

We had barely enough sail to carry us through the sea when we left Mera, so I handed the No. 3 jib, and set the powerful No. 2 instead. We then carried about the same area as with the double-reefed mainsail and

No. 3 jib, and the yacht sailed almost equally well (off the wind). No sooner had we cleared Punta Herminio—on which stands forth the magnificent light tower known as Torre de Hercules and behind which shelters the city of Corunna—than the wind came very strong and free. This was well for us, since there was an unusually high following sea, the legacy of two days of fiercer weather. We sailed one leg of twenty miles to clear the islets and reefs off Cabo de San Adrián. Rounding the Islas Sisargas, six miles out, we met four trawlers and one Spanish destroyer, all ploughing into the weather and flinging about a great deal of white water. It was interesting to see how much better the trawlers (poor though they were of their kind) rode the head sea than the destroyer. I would rather look at a trawler than at a battleship.

We now had a leg of twenty-two miles to clear Cabo Villano, but the wind was brought directly astern when we laid that course, so we had to increase the distance by gybing every five miles. Isabel, who likes to sail as fast as possible, looked disparagingly at the trysail, and would commit herself no more deeply in its favour than to call it "a strange object", or "rather small". I answered hotly in its defence, for I had no intention of coping with the boom that day. We were not half-way to Villano when the wind began to whistle, and then even she was satisfied that we were not under-canvased. The sea, mounting rapidly, broke in appalling confusion on the reefs of Lage, fairly close on our port hand. One sea, huge and green, lopped over the counter and filled the cockpit, quite submerging Isabel. She immediately broke her rule that she stays on deck in rough weather, and darted below for dry clothes. When she rejoined me she said that she was seasick. It was a worrying afternoon.

I was anxious to reduce our headsail area, but Isabel argued that we were travelling at just the right speed to prevent a repetition of the pooping incident. By that time we were within six miles of Cabo Villano, and once round that headland we only had to beat up into the landlocked bay of Camariñas to find (as we thought) complete shelter from all the ferocity around us. Her arguments against reducing sail were reinforced by the presence in the water of a shark some eight or nine feet long. He followed us for miles, and the sight of him disinclined me for journeys along the wet and narrow decks of a yacht that seemed to be as misguidedly sportive as a porpoise. At last the time came when we must gybe and reach into the lee of the cape, though giving it a wide berth, for Camariñas Bay is sewn with submerged horrors, particularly near its mouth. The wind's whistle had developed into a scream, and I feared that No. 2 jib would do itself a mischief. I hurried forward (the shark almost forgotten) to find that with all our gybing the two jibs had got themselves entangled. When I had handed the smaller one soon after leaving Mera I had not lashed it along the rail, as was my habit, for I had felt that lashing it was perhaps unnecessary. I had been proved wrong; No. 3 had done all manner of false things, even contriving to fix several of its piston hanks around No. 2's forestay. All I could do, and I was nearly blown away doing it, was to lower the big jib as far as possible, and then lash the two of them in an untidy bundle.

Whether it was the effect of closing the land and entering the lee of the cape, or whether at that stage the wind increased vastly, I cannot say. At all events it became so violent that I could not easily stand up in the cockpit, and the tops of the seas were cut off and flung across our decks. Pellets, balls of sea-water rattled and crashed on oilskins and sou'westers. The chart had to be pushed into a perspex holder, for the water beat on it with such fury that unprotected it would have disintegrated. These conditions were almost intolerably painful for the eyes. With trysail alone (it was fortunate that I had taken down the jib) we scorched along, heeled right over. But although we were making speed through the water, we had an ebbing tide against us, and we crawled in through rocks and reefs, searching (often vainly) for landmarks, and wondering if we should ever emerge from that situation of agonising, screaming discomfort. Once through the mouth of the bay, we had a beat of two miles into the harbour. The seas were now greatly reduced, but the wind continued to pick them up and throw them. The whole bay seemed to smoke. The trysail was strangely distended. When I looked up I saw tons of water stream from the sail and shoot to leeward in horizontal jets. It was disturbing for novices to find such conditions in the chosen refuge after a tiring day at sea.

Past the village of Camariñas, whose man-made harbour is too shoal for *Serica*, we pursued our course to the northernmost corner of the bay, and anchored as near to the shore as we could get. The anchor bit into sticky mud, and we lay in two fathoms with twenty fathoms of chain out. The yacht drummed in the wind. Too exhausted and drenched to do more on deck, we went below. The sea that had covered Isabel had managed to lick through the doghouse doors. Our bed was wet, but we were both asleep almost before our heads were down. The hymnals sometimes liken Heaven to a harbour gained in bad weather; I doubt if many of the various heavens can be as wonderful as that.

A fisherman sailing up the anchorage in the morning stopped to speak to us. He said he intended to net the mouth of the river and added: "The fish dislike the nord-este pardo as much as we do."

"The north-easterly gales (nord-este pardo or grey north-easter) are accompanied by much low cloud and dirty weather on the coast . . ." we read in the Sailing Directions.

Landing in a shallow bay was tricky, and for this reason Isabel, contrary to her custom, wore trousers. We went overland to Camariñas, three miles' walk. The wind pressed upon us, flattening the clothing on our bodies. The land's fringes trembled in dust clouds and the sun refused to shine. When we looked over an area of a few square miles we could count several hundred men and women working in fields that had been divided and subdivided until some of the divisions (carefully surrounded with walls made from jagged stones picked from the soil) were smaller than back gardens in Pimlico. The landscape constituted a strong argument for primogeniture. Impossible to look upon the country round Camariñas without concluding that in Spain there are too many Spaniards, and far too many of them seek their living in the same places and by doing the same work. It seemed unlikely that those fields could support even the people tilling them.

Camariñas' waterfront, on the inner edge of the tidal harbour, was crowded with fishermen disgruntled by the weather and aghast at the sight of Isabel's trousers. We had walked the length of the place looking for a bakery (and finding only bars) when we met a girl who said that it would be difficult if not impossible to find bread, but that she would guide us to the likeliest places. She led us uphill. The street, of no uniform width, was never wide. It climbed in a series of stone shelves. The household doors were open to the street, and women sat on the floors just inside the openings, making lace on frames, and talking to all but us who passed. Their comments on Isabel's trousers were acid, sometimes outraged, but it must be said in fairness that they did not imagine that their rudenesses would be understood. The news that two people off the white boat were coming up the street was carried ahead of us by urchins, electric particles flashing from one live terminal to the next. Our guide held open the door of a dark shop.

Two women came out from a curtained recess to stand behind the counter, an aged woman, toothless, with a face the colour of tobacco stain, and her daughter, little past the middle age, but already matronly. Although they had no superficial beauty, the pair were gay and their faces, battered though they were by a life of toil in Camariñas, were full of vigour and interest. Both wore heavy black dresses. Their legs were bare and their feet shuffled (as though receiving a confused hodge-podge of messages from the brain cells) in dirty white alpargatas. They thanked the girl for producing us, and laughed a good deal at the idea that we should have entered their shop, that we were really there. Soon the dark space behind us was filled with women and girls. The pair behind the counter put many questions. Were we brother and sister? Did we have beds, a fire, water to drink? Where did the water come from? Had we a telephone? Did the boat belong to us, or was it hired? How many sailors were there? Did we carry chickens? Had we come to trade, to fish, to escape from the communists in England? Isabel did the talking, and I stood there with a fixed smile. Behind me the shop was packed with shining faces almost the texture and shape of lemons, and with dark draperies. The earth floor was rustled by many bare feet. I felt little touches on the hollow of my back, my shoulders, my elbows. The talk revolved to our purchases. The older woman searched on a shelf beside a heap of new mouse-traps and pulled forth a cannon ball of bread, brown and dusty. She weighed it.

"One kilo: fifteen pesetas."

"Caro es."

The old woman nodded sadly. "What else can we find for you?"

"Lettuces?"

"There are no lettuces in the town, unless Maria Teresa's uncle has some in his garden."

"Spinach?"

"No spinach this year."

"Tomatoes?"

"None just now."

"Grapes?"

"Perhaps tomorrow there will be some fruit in the town. . . . Today we have onions and lentils and these few beans, but the beans are expensive."

When we had bought (to give them pleasure) a large bag of onions the girl led us further uphill. Her uncle was out in his fields, but she took us to the back of his house to look for lettuces. There were a few, but

c*

they were babies, carefully encased in meshed wire to preserve them from the pullets that had scaled the rubble wall to prospect for food in more promising places—a hopeless search. The girl was disappointed. . . . She had promised to carry a pitcher of drinking water to her grandmother, and she left us, advising us eloquently to make a pilgrimage out of Camariñas to a holy stone named la piedra de la Virgen. This stone was believed to move on certain days, and she said we should try to photograph it in movement.

Down on the waterfront we were told by the innkeeper that there was a man who spoke English.

"Ah! and here he is," said the innkeeper. "Don Fernando! Don Fernando!"

Don Fernando (an astonishing sight in that place and after all the evidences we had had of poverty) tall, supple, made apparently of ivory-backed hairbrushes, marzipan, and unsweetened chocolate of the best quality, came bending through the crowd to meet us. He was dressed (in clothes bought in Madrid) to play the fisherman. He wore sea-boots made of brown patent leather, trousers a pearly grey in colour, a shirt in browns and yellows like those of the fishermen but made of heavy silk, and a beret.

"What do you say of Camariñas?" Don Fernando asked.

"Delightful!"

"The fishing is wonderful here. I'll bet you've caught a ton of fish since you left England?"

"Not one fish."

"Bad luck."

"Cooking fish on a small boat makes too strong a smell."

"Ah, but no! Me, I adore the smell of grilling or frying fish. . . . I came here with my son because I have bought in Madrid a new outboard motor, but we had no boat in Madrid. And now we find that here also there is no suitable boat. They told me in the shop this outboard motor should push a boat at high speed; but here the boats are no good . . . too heavy, too long, too deep, too old, too rough. It is a grave disappointment for my boy. . . . You have eaten? You can eat at this man's inn, but unless you have the digestions of cockroaches you may pay for this meal more in pain than in pesetas. Perhaps I exaggerate. The fish is good here. I wish I could say as much for the wine. Meat, vegetables, and fruit scarcely exist. But I have a little house. One of the women will cook us something. Yes, yes, I insist. . . ."

We once more climbed up the narrow street, the brown sea-boots gleaming ahead of me like the seven-league boots of the fairy stories. Don Fernando's belt was of beaten silver from the American Indies, and on the fourth finger of his left hand he wore two heavy golden rings, scaled, like fishes or serpents. His person was fragile and attenuated, rather than powerful, and yet his walk was full of muscular grace and ease. I think I have seldom seen so handsome a man, or one better equipped by nature to wear brown patent-leather sea-boots. He should, of course, have worn a rapier from his silver belt. We noticed that all who met us in the street bowed to Don Fernando with deference. Now that we were in his company even Isabel's trousers occasioned no sneers; it seemed that they had been blessed by Don—I almost wrote San— Fernando.

He took us to a white house no different from scores of others. The ground floor was entirely kitchen and living space, unpartitioned save for six piers that supported the two main beams of the ceiling. It was a pleasant interior, clean enough and exceptionally neat. There was no cooking range or stove. The cooking was done with spits and cauldrons in an open fireplace big as *Serica's* saloon. In one corner of this ashy recess an oven had been built with bricks and cement. Five old women were there when we arrived. He gave a few orders and in a remarkably short space of time we sat down to a good meal. Wine, white and red, was poured from casks at one end of the kitchen into decanters with slender auxiliary spouts drawn from their necks. We ate grilled soles; then a kind of goulash made with chicken and pimento and onion; then goat cheese, white and bitter, figs and pears. Don Fernando spoke only English. He had no need to speak to the women, for they all fluttered around him like pigeons over a tray of grain, and seemed to divine his slightest whim. He kept saying how annoyed he was that his son had gone off with the outboard motor.

"I should like him to have met you both. He already speaks English, and is a boy of considerable promise. Mathematics and music are his strongest subjects. His mother is dead. During our Civil War she caught pneumonia and died for lack of proper nursing and medicine. I cannot think for her sake that her death was entirely sad, but for me it was disaster. It robbed me of her and it burdened me with my son. What a terrible responsibility! I fear it; it creates nightmares. . . ."

Around the rude walls were stacked Don Fernando's belongings, things that had been unloaded from the American-made motor-car that stood in the yard: pretty suitcases; rods and guns in strangely-shaped containers; the hide case for the outboard motor; a portable escritoire of leather.

"The nord-este is beginning to weaken," he said, leading us to the door. We sat round a table outside the house, and one of the women brought us coffee and cognac. "Tomorrow will be smoother weather. You will go; and I too."

"Where are you going?"

"Madrid, to leave my boy with his maternal grandparents, his only relatives, and then—Buenos Aires on business. Buenos Aires I don't like. Only three towns I like: Paris, Madrid, and Biarritz. Seville? yes sometimes, but not for long. The worst town on earth is Barcelona. The next worst is New Orleans. . . . The United States of America, they seethe godlessly, they steam and bubble with less purpose than a child's yelling, and they will evanuate with a hiss . . . but we shall all of us have trouble when that happens. . . ."

"What of Soviet Russia?"

"Ah, Russia? America I despise for her crassness and her bungling. America I envy for her virility and for her riches which should—had history not developed a humped back, a hare-lip, and a tendency to prostitution—have belonged to Spain. America I mistrust because she is an economy run by business interests, and not by a ruling caste or some other kind of astringent caucus. Russia I fear, and with fear rides respect. Do not misunderstand me: it is not communism that I fear, for I judge that to be more ridiculous and meaningless than dangerous. No, it is Russia, and behind her all the peoples of the East, and the pendulum of history slowly swinging. . . . We Westerners have had our play and botched it. It is soon to be the turn of the Easterners, and they will botch it too. But by that time and probably a lot sooner, you and I will be limes and phosphates. Oh, to have been born three hundred years ago! Oh, to have no son, no beloved son!"

"Do you often come here?"

"Never!" he cried. "In Madrid I live. This house and sixty-three hectares near-by I own because they belonged to my father. But I never come here. I'm a stranger here."

"Yet the people treat you with respect and affection."

"Have they no reason to respect me? I am rich by their standards, and they scarcely know me. . . . But affection, yes, that too, and I will tell you in a few words why for them I am a symbol. . . . They have so little outside their own imaginations. I mean something to them. I am a miracle to them—whatever I may be to myself. . . .

"I must explain to you then that my father cultivated the land and owned three fishing-boats. His first wife was of Camariñas, like himself, and by her he had five children, of whom I was the youngest. Toward the end of their married life my father had another woman, a woman of Segovia, and when my mother died of some internal disease that would probably today be called cancer he married the other, and by her had two children. Now my father had money, and the second wife wanted all for her own brats and none for the five older children. She created mischief, and there was much wrangling in this unhappy house. She it was—it is the kindest thing I can say of my own father—who drove him mad. One night in May, when all but he slept, he took a sharp axe and moved about the house, slaying his family. In the morning he went from the fields to one of his boats. He did not know what he had done, and he was covered in blood.

"The police came to this house, and as they were going from bed to bed, and in every bed but two there was a corpse, I entered behind them.

" 'Where have you been?' one of them asked me sternly.

"I could not answer (I tell you the truth) for at the time I was aged fifteen, and I had spent the night with a married woman whose husband was away at sea. I stammered that something had impelled me to go to watch the Virgin's Stone, and that I had sat watching it all night. I knew my story to be weak and silly, and was surprised to see the policemen's looks of wonder. They hurried me from the house lest I should see the blood-soaked beds and the bodies of my dear ones.

"My father was put in a madhouse, where he died only the year before last. And from far and near the people looked upon me as the symbol of a holy deliverance. The old money-box by the Virgin's Stone had never been so full of cash. As for me, I took all the money I could raise from the lawyer and cleared out, first to Toledo, then to Sheffield, in England, and now I am in Madrid, though I still have business in Toledo. I have passed examinations. I can speak English, German, French, and Arabic. The fishing-boats were sold long ago, though this house and the land still are mine—but I should never have come back if I had not bought that outboard motor; and the fishing is so wonderful at Camariñas.

"An act like my father's changes destiny. Today I could buy

Camariñas if I chose (excluding the fish factory—that would cost a pretty penny). But I hope I shall end my days in Paris, and I hope that my son may be a world-renowned engineer. . . . Now where has that boy got to with the accursed outboard motor? . . ."

One of the old women tapped him on the shoulder. Her neck hung over the collar of her black dress. He shook his beautiful head for a time, while she whispered in his ear.

"All right," he said to her, when he had teased her to distraction. He brought a case from his pocket. "Just one, now, no more than one."

She ran to the embers of the fire to light her cigarette. Don Fernando chuckled.

"I love them," he said to us. "I am as water in their hands. I can refuse them nothing, and the funny thing is that they are not even related to me, so far as I know. Just five poor old women of Camariñas. Their demands are so simple: this roof, a little bread, wine and water, a few fishes, the milk and the cheese of goats, a pinch or two of tobacco. I love them. . . . Where the devil is that boy? I tell you these five old women if they were five hundred would be less trouble than he alone. Would you believe me if I told you that now I have bought the outboard motor he has a fancy for a typewriter?" He put on his beret. "I'll walk to the sea with you. Supposing the motor has failed and he has been swept from the bay? The sea is bad off Villano tonight. No boats will be out."

# CHAPTER 7

## CORCUBIÓN, BAYONA, LA GUARDIA

AFTER an uncomfortable sail with a fluky north-easter and a high, confused sea, we came into a patch of dead calm beside the great cape of Finisterre. For an hour we rocked slowly, looking at Finisterre, which is held to be a weather-shed and a good place to be clear of. Every crevice in the dark stone, every bleached tuft of weed, was reflected in the water below. Near us lay a trading ketch of 150 tons, the *San Salvador* from Corcubión. She had been heading southward from her home port when the wind was sucked up into the dome of the sky, leaving her with her heavy booms crashing from side to side.

We started the engine, and moved into the lovely spaces of Corcubión Bay, dropping in three fathoms close inshore where the land is steep beyond the head of the fine beach known as Llagosteira. No sooner were we anchored than the north-easter whistled down on us. The holding ground was poor, but the Danforth must have found a grip among the smooth rocks, for we did not budge, and, as I said to Isabel, we could drag for a hundred miles or more without doing any damage. A shoal of fishing-boats approached rapidly, dousing their lateen sails when they were very close. After begging for this, that, and the other, the fishermen mentioned rope. I cut the German rope that had broken at Audierne into two-fathom lengths, and managed to supply nine boats in this way, but the tenth boat arrived when all the rope was gone. Its helmsman, a lanky man with tattooed arms and an engineer's cap worn on the back of his head, took it very amiss that I had no more rope to give away. Eyeing the other boats, in which the men were fixing the German rope round their cumbersome oars and tholepins, and jettisoning the yellow grass rope it replaced, the man in the cap made a vindictive speech about la Nacion and estranjeros. He had placed his own boat alongside *Serica*, and seeing two fine warps that I certainly could not spare, he shouted to the others that what I had given them was dross compared with what I had kept for my own use. He spoiled the scene, which had been amicable enough until then (although I always have to stifle an uncivilised distaste for beggars).

We longed for their departure, but they hung in the water, watching us, waiting. The man in the cap persisted with his spiteful grumbling until I wondered if he was trying to incite the others, friendly though they seemed, to an act of piracy.

Our tempers were not improved by a long swell that came up from the south. Caught between wind and swell, we rolled abominably. We looked without favour on two Guardias Civiles, who came hurrying along the road from the village of Finisterre, scrambled down the steep slopes, and took up a position perched among the scrub some twenty feet above the high water mark and some sixty yards from the yacht. Each carried a rifle, and they had a pair of binoculars, which they levelled at us frequently. Although Isabel asked in Castilian why they were there and what they wanted of us, she got no answer. We found this strange, for up to that evening the Spanish police had been loquacious. At any rate the presence of the policemen was apparently as distasteful to our bevy of fishing-boats as it was to us. They moved, sailing northward for the head of the bay.

It is very disagreeable to be watched while lying at anchor, fixedly watched, hour upon hour. As night drew on the two uncomfortable figures on shore seemed to loom larger and larger, and we were delighted when we saw that they were evidently having words about their further course of action. It was our turn to level binoculars at them. We supposed that they did not relish the idea of spending the whole night there without food or drink. One of them stood up, and shouted to us.

"Eh, *Serica*! How long do you wait here?"

We thought we might as well repay them for their former rudeness, and we both sat in the cockpit as though we were deaf. He shouted until he grew hoarse, even raising his rifle once in a threatening gesture. But in the end he subsided on the sharp stones, and as darkness dropped down over the hills we saw them still there, angry with us, enraged with each other.

We were roused shortly after 2 a.m. by a boat crashing into the timbers beside our heads. Jumping out of bed, I seized a heavy spanner from the engine-tools compartment, and darted into the cockpit, thoroughly frightened but almost equally infuriated in the bubbling and silly manner of the barnyard rooster. Beside *Serica* was a big open boat holding five men and the bodies of a million fishes. One man stood, knee-deep in silver corpses, holding the tarry mastodon of a boat so that it grated along our topside to the rhythm of the swell.

"Sardinas?" he enquired, as though that were a perfectly normal question to put to somebody you had wakened at 2 a.m., and whom you had probably intended to rob. He must have sensed my struggle for words. "No?" he said. "Adios." They rowed quickly away. From the shore came a flash of light as a policeman lit a scarcely-combustible Spanish cigarette. At dawn one of them was stretched out asleep, while the other kept a nodding watch on us. When we went on deck to make sail the sleeper was wakened. We sailed off south with the dreaminess and breath-catching delight of a gentle departure with a fair, sweet wind, and when we were a mile from the shore we saw the two watchers rise, sling their rifles, and climb stiffly to the road.

That evening we anchored at Puerto Bayona, near the mouth of Vigo Bay, after a perfect and easy run of seventy-eight miles in eleven hours, all of it a gentle reach. Vagaries of the wind had drawn us so far off-shore that unfortunately we had scarcely caught sight of what must be one of the noblest stretches of coastline in the world, that strange succession of great bays, Corcubión, Muros, Arosa, Montevedra, and Vigo.

We anchored among a bunch of steam trawlers at the end of the mole, where we knew fresh water was available. Two boys offered to fetch water for us in their cumbersome boat, and advised us to move deeper into the anchorage, saying that the thick weather would probably be cleared that night by "an explosion of the elements". A rising thermometer and very low barometer agreed with them. We soon moved and found ourselves under the fretted walls of the citadel and apart from the ruck of working boats, with good holding ground and any amount of clean water to swing in. This was our best and prettiest anchorage for a long time, and it came opportunely at the end of a successful day following on the heels of a period of comparative discomfort. We told ourselves, in that warm, sticky, evening air, that with Finisterre astern we could expect more favourable weather and more sunshine. There was fiesta in the small town rising from the water, well aware of its own robustly common charms. A German band was playing. Tram-cars from Vigo crawled along the edge of Bayona like ladybirds with bells. The people raised a din of song and shout. Beyond the fish market a game of football was being played and watched on a dusty slope. Wagons drawn by lean mules and leaner black horses waited to take the fish away. The beaches were dotted with bathers of all ages, the women in costumes with heavy skirts that seemed to call for wheeled bathing boxes and whalebone corsets hanging on the hooks within.

When the boys had made several trips with our water-cans we invited them on board and gave them a feed. They declared that if they had such a boat they would instantly sail in it for South America. They looked wonderingly at my bare feet. Could a shoeless, tieless man really be the owner of such a boat? They were natural and cheerful boys except that now and then they would remember that they were on a foreign craft and accepting the hospitality of foreigners; then they would trot out the patriotic phrases taught them at school, and their faces would become superior.

At the top of the beach we sat on a fish barrel and put on our shoes. The boys had asked us if they might look after the dinghy; they stood, staring down at the little boat as though they would never grow tired of its strangeness. We walked through the fish market. The stacks of flat boxes were filled with one kind of fish and one only, a fish with a tape-like body anything from six inches to a yard long, headed and tailed like a pike. The land smelled of wine, with under-smells of fish, dust, scent, and frying onions. This was a Sunday evening, and Bayona was filled with Galicians from Vigo. The band, having had its limit of marching in the heat, had stopped outside the Café Real, and after drinking wine and beer, beer and wine, had formed a circle. The man with the drums was smoking a cheroot. The throat and chest of his scarlet tunic were open and his brown skin, sewn with black hairs, showed through the gap. Now tangos, rhumbas, sambas, and foxtrots were played, and the people made a black, white, and olive palisade around the inner red and brassy circle of the band. Some danced, buffeting their way through the crowd, woman often dancing with woman. For a while I watched the conductor, a fat man so constricted in his uniform that the buttons heaved to his breathing. Unlike his musicians, he did not look into the crowd. His eyes saw only the score and the players. They were magnificent eyes, dark, compassionate, mysterious. His plump hands wrung out the pulpy music, his small left foot tapped. By contrast the musicians, with their mechanical efforts and straying interests, were dull. The concerted noise may have been only brass-cum-saliva, but it was triumphantly right at that time and place. Behind the lively water-front lay dark streets where the buildings, leaning slightly forward and liberally studded with terra-cotta balconies that looked like plasticene models, shut in yet more closely the acrid smell of red wine. Pale walls stained in prudent corners with urine. Streets paved with smooth, almost black, old stones. Shops were dark gaps, the mouths of caves, and old hags had been left to guard the mouths on that evening of fiesta. We bought eggs at ten shillings the dozen and vegetables for almost nothing, then walked up the hill to look at the cathedral. On its outer wall was a strangely impressive memorial, unlaboured as memorials should be and seldom are. The Falange sign above, then a big Christian cross and the names of the fallen, the first name Primo de Rivera. Words and signs, printed on the rough wall surface, were inexpressibly delicate and touching, even to me, who had been taught to regard the Falange as wicked and retrograde. German memorials on the battlefields of the two German wars sometimes catch me with the same twist of the emotional poignard, reminding me that we are all men born of women, we fools who fight and who kill.

Outside the town the lane narrowed to a footpath lest the odd centimetre be lost to the vineyards. One small field, highly walled, had been saved from the claims of the cultivators, and was piled high with corpses, stacked in an arrangement that may, for all I know, be a common enough form of cemetery, but that struck us as gruesomely bizarre. The perimeter wall of the cemetery was honeycombed on its inner sides, each cell of the comb designed to take a coffin. When the coffin had been pushed in, the outer end was closed with a slab decorated according to the fancies or fantasies of the dead person's relatives still breathing Bayona's wine-impregnated air. There might be a fragment of verse or a bunch of enamelled metal flowers, a small case displaying the dead man's medals, a coloured photograph of him when young, or a lock of his hair. Between those thick walls pitted with decay was the usual dry turf, humped, sewn with cheap crosses. We took it that a berth in the honeycomb cost more than the common sod. The crosses were intersewn with bushes of kitchen roses.

From the cemetery (such is life) we went to a restaurant where the proprietor had contracted to give us dinner as early as 9.30 p.m. A marble counter stretched the length of the narrow space. That part of the counter nearest the door was the domain of the proprietor himself, a capable, lusty, young fellow, wearing a striped shirt, tight black trousers, a pencil behind the ear. Further in, the space behind the counter constituted the kitchen, ruled over by a stout, exceedingly handsome woman called Maria. There was a tall youth, aged perhaps

sixteen, dressed as chef, and most determined, it seemed, to help Maria
and to keep her in a sweet or sweetish mood, and also to learn from her
masterly treatment of the dishes (masterly, that is, from the point of
view of manual dexterity and unhurried speed). Lastly there was the
dishwasher, a small woman from the mountains, withered, bowed,
reddened, gnarled, everybody's butt, and a good hand at washing
dishes and sluicing the counter. The Red Indian features of the dishwasher remained imperturbable when turned to volatile Maria, con-
vulsed with rubbery merriment when turned to us. Maria, a tremendous
figure with breasts fit to nourish Romulus and Remus, had chestnut hair
pulled tight round her head and secured at the neck in a shining globe.
Her arms were the colour of white ivory billiard balls, and the general
colour of the restaurant was the aggressive green of a billiard table when
the lights are lit. Maria emptied vats of red shell-fish to the marble
counter. The shell-fish looked like turtles' legs seen through the wrong
end of a telescope. The fish had to be drawn from the shells, and there
was a prolonged noise of sucking all over the restaurant. Nobody else
was dining, but many people were demolishing the shell-fish, or slabs of
tortilla, or sardines. There was a noise of rushing feet on the road, and
all the other clients hurled themselves from the restaurant. Isabel
thought that some bulls must be passing on their way to the bull-
ring; but it was a tram-car, the last one back to Vigo, a single-decked
conveyance made up of four coaches. The people fought their way in,
and when the men had gained a foothold in the oscillating interior they
hauled their women after them. Young children and babies were passed
up through the windows. The ride to Vigo must have made a hot
climax to the day. From the windows tendrils of dust and heated air
rose, and the rumbling sound of spoken Spanish, a snatch of song, a
bubble of female laughter, the raucous cry of an infuriated boy whose
foot had been trodden on or whose ear had been burned by a cigarette.

The proprietor was busy with sums. He whispered figures and made
squealing noises on the marble with a broad-leaded pencil. At the
kitchen end they were in a frenzy of last-minute preparations. Load
after load of boiled shell-fish was rattled to the counter. Corks were
drawn, tables laid, lettuce washed. We ate fried octopuses, beef-
steak, and green figs. The bill with a bottle of white wine and a bottle
of red, came to only fifty-four pesetas, then about ten shillings. The
food was coarse. We told the proprietor what we had eaten and
drunk, and he did a pencilled sum on the marble. The counter at that

end was covered with the attractive arabesques of his additions. When we left the restaurant we saw that there was a commotion on the surface of the harbour. The two imps were rowing our dinghy, both seated on the centre thwart, pursued by some fifty boys in ten heavy boats. Rather slower, but less heavily-laden and much faster on the turns than its enemies, the dinghy made a fair show at eluding them. When the two oarsmen saw us they summoned an effort, spurted away from the others, and beached the dinghy at our feet. Most of the varnish we had laid on so carefully at Mera had been knocked off, and the boat was nearly full of water, sand, and dirt. But the pair were so delighted with their performance that anger was impossible. They helped us to wash the dinghy at the edge of the sea and then, enviously, watched us row out to the yacht. While we rowed the storm began.

We sat in the doghouse to watch the lightning playing round the peaks, Monte Parada, Picos de Galiñeiro, Monte Nuestra Señora del Alba, Monte Corujo, Pico Sansón, Monte Facho, Monte la Greba. Rain lashed on the yacht and wind beat at her in gusts that sent her scurrying in her usual silly fashion round her cable. Yet when day broke the storm seemed to have expended itself, and there was just enough breeze to move us gently from the anchorage.

The light airs failed us when we had cleared Vigo Bay, and were off Cabo Silleiro. Puffs only strong enough to flicker the burgee came at intervals from all directions. We were disappointed, for we had expected to have a fair breeze, like that of the preceding day, and had intended to make for the Portuguese harbour of Leixões, at the mouth of the Douro. We did not feel inclined to motor the sixty-two miles to Leixões, and elected to motor instead the ten miles to la Guardia, on the Spanish side of the frontier. This so-called port promised little comfort, for it is a mere inlet completely open to the north-west; we reasoned that we were only going there to wait for wind, and that the moment wind came we should be off. We entered la Guardia on a compass bearing, and it was not until we were at anchor that we distinguished the two leading lights, for they were "camouflaged" (better than anything the experts did during the war), blending into the background of white, blue and yellow houses, some of them checkered with thick bands of black pitch instead of (or covering) mortar. La Guardia was ahead and to port; to starboard was the straight mole that gives some shelter from southerlies; astern was the open sea, with a swell rolling straight in at us. Monte de Santa Tecla hung her brush-covered skirts over the town and us. Where the background to the houses was not mountain it was a sloping carpet of cultivation, a net of stone walls holding the tamed earth.

Every boat in the harbour turned beam-on to the swell and rolled. Isabel lay down with a book, and I sat in the cockpit, asking the marauding boys, who in that place must be among the most persecutorial in Spain, to try to avoid smashing into our sides; and watching the shore where, as the tide fell, the mussel-hung rocks emerged like giant hippopotami. The fishermen's houses grew in irregular outlines from the rocks, and the natural terraces were hung with nets, saffron-coloured blankets, and seaweed that old women collected in dark brown baskets and then exposed on the rocks to wither. Through the day the town seethed with men and the harbour with boys, who came out in all sorts of waterborne objects, including round washtubs, each tub holding a babe who sculled with fantastic dexterity through a groove cut in the side, and who nonchalantly baled his fast-leaking tub with swift flips of his fins. Even the harbour-master, who came aboard at tea-time, could not drive away the boys, though he tried with all his might. When he had laboriously copied out most of the foreign words on our ship's papers, he began in his own fashion to persuade us that Spain had the government she wanted. We tried to arrest his eloquence by telling him that the Spanish Government was Spain's affair, and not ours.

"Now we have a true prosperity at last," he said, pulling from his pocket a leather note-case and showing us first a photograph of his wife and eight children, then a photograph of his house, and lastly a bundle of insanitary banknotes. "Look now! These are one-hundred peseta notes, and these fifties. Let us count it. One thousand, two hundred, and eighty pesetas, seventy-eight centavos. I, mark you, am, when all is said and done, only a government officer; others are immeasurably wealthier. And I show you the money in no spirit of boastfulness, but merely to prove that everybody in Spain has money to spend, except the communists, who work for the rest of us in concentration camps. Now I don't like the idea of concentration camps any more than you do. But where you have communists you must have concentration camps, for how else are you to turn communists into good citizens? You may laugh, Señora, you may sneer, but I have seen many a loafer go off for a period of training and discipline in a camp, and come back to this very town a good worker and a good Spaniard. . . . I bear England no ill-will," he added, "except in so far as her former ambassador in Madrid is concerned. That gentleman was well treated in Spain and had every opportunity, so we are told, to learn the truth about us. Yet he went back to his own country, your country, and wrote a book of pestilential rudeness. He let it be understood that we were poor, downtrodden, illiterate, and had ill-feeling toward our Government. Ah, you can shake your heads, but there was not in the book that warmth of tone that we expect from foreigners who leave Spain. However you may deny it there was a note of criticism that fell harshly on Spanish ears. The B.B.C. had the bad taste to broadcast some of the passages I refer to. I shall never forget it, *never*!"

" 'Never' is a big word, Señor Commandante."

"For us Spaniards, I can assure you definitely, 'never' is a small word."

Following the shadows of night, fishermen began to drift to the harbour with the purposeful yet sad air of men going to work that is hard and too familiar, and for which, they doubt, the recompense will be too small. Some of them in batches of six to twenty puffed out to sea in noisy motor-boats, but most, in pairs, rowed out in scow-like boats, flat-sided, flat-ended, yet with a beautiful curve to their bellies. The boats moved well, skimming the water (though I hardly think they would be so kindly in a sharp head sea), and each of them had, lashed along the gunwale, a long, slightly curved mast, sometimes with the bark still on it. They hurried out, shouting to us cheerfully enough, past the crumbling end of the breakwater to a sea of smooth rollers coloured indigo and palest blue, with a wedge of dark maroon to the southwest.

We were ready to leave, and eager, but there was no wind, so we sat in the cockpit talking quietly, for as the light dies the voice falls. Two girls were practising rowing for a regatta that was to to be the event of the following week at la Guardia. They rowed round and round, managing the four ponderous oars with no skill but great energy. A crowded boatful of boys put out to mock at and insult the girls, and when they tired of that they made for us, unloading themselves of a score of obscenities from a range of five yards, each obscenity accompanied by squawks of satisfaction. Isabel told them quietly that it was a pity their manners were so bad. They hung there in their boat, silent and still, and as astonished as we should be if the voice of Madame Melba surged from the throat of a goldfinch. They moved a few yards further away as the boy sculling over the transom slowly wagged his oar, and then they began to sing a repetitive song concerning a railway that was building along a pier. They sang in voices half-falsetto, half-true, now deep and pure, now treble, now an insanely touching quaver. The lights were shining from the town in yellow pathways. A few fishermen who had not gone to sea and who had just shaved off the day's beards leaned from their windows in clean white shirts. Some of them joined their bass voices to the boys' song. From quarter to ten until quarter past clocks were chiming ten o'clock. The song went on and on, and the splashing of the girls' boat as they rowed in the darkness, wearing themselves out in the cause of sport. They tugged so hard at the oars that at each stroke they lifted their bodies from the thwarts.

At 4 a.m. we heard a part of the fishing sortie returning. The crews looked exhausted and their catches were meagre. We weighed anchor and sailed with an offshore breeze. Outside we found a light wind from the south, a head wind. A mile from the mole we sailed through a group of boats, all of them running back to la Guardia, their sheets free. The men greeted us genially, one of them declaring that we were "valiant". We looked at the dark mat of cloud ahead, where the wind came from, and wondered exactly what he meant by the adjective. We now had the Portuguese coast abeam, and very dismal it looked, swept by rainstorms and shadowed by thunderclouds.

CHAPTER 8

## FIGURES ON A WINDSWEPT BEACH

WE had not left the Spanish fishermen far astern when we knew that we were in for a strong "dead-noser". We beat out on a ten-mile leg to seaward, then inshore on an equal leg at the end of which we identified the Rio Lima and the entrance to Pôrto de Viana do Castelo, which was some distance ahead, although by my dead reckoning it should have been abeam. Unfortunately I did not take warning from this error.

Isabel, owing to our jolting progress through that steep head sea, was nearly prostrated with seasickness. She suggested entering Viana do Castelo, but I allowed myself to be frightened off it by the dangers listed in the Sailing Directions, and in any case I was interested (selfishly) in the prospect of a sail to windward, and was obsessed by the obvious necessity for reefing without delay, for we were dashing into the sea at a wild and awful speed. While Isabel steered close to the wind I lowered the mainsail to the deck. After putting one tyer round the belly of the sail I reefed it easily enough. I was delighted, and had encountered no difficulty except that I had not hardened the main sheets enough, and had nearly been catapulted into the sea as I hung across the boom. *Serica* now forged on with a more comfortable movement, but when the wind, instead of strengthening as I had anticipated, weakened slightly, I was too lethargic to shake out a reef and forgo the security of the smaller mainsail. In any event the wind came in fierce squalls from time to time, always from the south. Rain fell on us in torrents, but I soon thrust aside my oilskins. The heat was stifling. For some hours this dreary sailing persisted, and then the rain clouds, blown away to the north, gave place to a dazzling sun. Although I wore a hat and dark glasses, I began to feel eye-strain from peering at the misty coastline. . . . The Sailing Directions identified places by mountains—but there were mountains everywhere; by churches—but I had never seen so many churches; by sandy beaches—but the coast was fronted by one magnificent rim of pale sand. I kept a scrupulous dead reckoning, allowing one degree for leeway.

Late in the evening when, by my calculations, we should have been

77

approaching the great lighthouse of Leça on Ponta Boa Nova, immediately to the north of the port of Leixões, I thought that I had picked up landmarks to correspond with my chart work. There, surely, was the long beach with pine trees mentioned in the Directions, and there the mouth of the Rio Ave entering the sea from the north-east and showing two leading lights for fishing craft. Good! Only another ten miles to go. But where the devil was the Leça lighthouse? The Sailing Directions showed an excellent silhouette of it, a brobdingnagian candle in a candlestick to match. We beat out to sea once more, then in, while I glared through salted binoculars at the long, flat coastline backed by mountains.

Isabel came to life with her usual resilience in any emergency, and she also tried to identify the coast. (But for her seasickness we should have been in no such fix, since she has a considerable talent for chart work, and she enjoys coasting, whereas I prefer to be out of sight of land and am worried by frequent references to books and charts.)

Could *that*, on the port bow, be a place called Pôrto de Póvoa de Varzim, she asked. No, I answered firmly, we had passed Póvoa an hour earlier; the place must be Leixões. Then where, she asked, was the lighthouse on Ponta Boa Nova. Where indeed? Never mind; it was 8 p.m. and high water. Whatever the place might be it was a considerable harbour. We would go in and have a look. The drawback was that the entry was open to the southerly weather. I started the engine, which missed badly. When I had fitted new plugs it ran better.

Seas broke foaming on either side of the narrow central channel, revealing shoals or rocks, and in the channel the waves increased so hellishly at the entry that we knew we were crossing a bar.

Hundreds of fishing-boats were drawn clear of the water on a golden, curving slope of sand that formed the natural sides of the harbour, and the high moles, dark and grey, were swept clear of weed and dirt by the waves that hissed against them. Sounding as we entered, I found my depths disturbingly small, and lost no time in anchoring. A crowd in violent movement had gathered on the end of the mole nearest the town, and another crowd, equally excited, on the beach. Their cries could not reach us upwind. A mass of concrete, steel, and glass was marked *Casino*, and the town, such of it as we could see, was a mixture of raw new buildings and squat old Aztec-looking ones, dark and sly. A boat fought its way out to us, rowed by a man in a checked shirt and a lean boy in oilskins.

We trusted them from the start, but it was difficult to communicate. We tried Spanish, French, English, Italian, German, with indifferent result, but as the Portuguese words flowed Isabel caught their similarity to Spanish and understood that Checked Shirt was telling us we must anchor a little further offshore in a place he would indicate, the only place in the harbour where a boat of *Serica's* draught might lie in such weather. We moved, following his boat, and laid out two anchors. Isabel had to lie down in the cockpit, and I managed to explain to the man that she must be got ashore at all costs. He said that he would go and seek from the police and other authorities permission for us to land. I showed him our Portuguese visas, obtained in London, but he was unimpressed.

"Donde estamos?" I asked him (using a Spanish phrase that, the reader may have discerned, comes readily to my lips).

"Póvoa de Varzim."

It is always helpful to know which port you are in. . . . I picked up the wet Sailing Directions and read: "Póvoa de Varzim.—A small but important fishing harbour, consists of a cove entered southward . . . depths of 2 fathoms in the fairway leading between reefs into the cove, and of one fathom in the northern part . . . bottom is mainly sand over rock. The cove affords no shelter from onshore winds. . . ."

While the Good Samaritan in the checked shirt was ashore pleading on our behalf I gathered a few things together in a battered German despatch case that is one of our oldest friends. When he returned he jumped aboard with the eagerness of the politician who believes he has signed a treaty that will bring prosperity to his own country and peace to the world; he made it clear that he had obtained permission for us to land, subject to police supervision. He would watch the yacht for us through the night and the lean boy would put us ashore. We shook him by the hand and asked him (hoping that he understood) to make himself comfortable and help himself to food, wine, and tobacco. Although *Serica* was standing on end in the seas she was riding well to her two anchors, and I had few (perhaps too few) fears for her.

A score of hands seized the heavy rowing-boat and dragged it through the surf. We were able from the bows to jump clear of the water to soft, damp sand. A black line of people had formed on the pale beach. Behind them lighted windows, a darkening and stormy sky. Four important figures waited in front of the rest, like officers at a review, three policemen in Japanesey uniforms, grey with high narrow caps, and one burly man in civilian clothes and a hat of broad-brimmed American shape. He belonged to the Customs Police, and in case we should underestimate his authority he at once showed us his identity card. Standing there within a few feet of the wild water, with the south wind blowing through our clothes and whisking the words from our mouths, they put us to the test of a hundred questions. I could scarcely identify one word in ten, but Isabel, quickly recovering with land under foot, was able to understand the Portuguese.

Both of us were elated. . . . There was drama in the windy scene, all darkness and shadows save for the almost luminous sand, in the eastern uniforms, the dark suspicious faces, the strange language, full of twangings and the deeper note of the bassoon and the plashings of water-falls. After much consultation among the police it was agreed that we might spend the night in the Hotel Superbo provided a policeman sat in the hall to keep some check on our activities until "Lisbon" had sanctioned our presence in Póvoa de Varzim. All four policemen ploughed with us up the sandy slope, making for the esplanade behind which rose the precipitous outlines of the casino and the Superbo. The crowd fell in behind us. We advanced like Napoleon's splendid Old Guard, in a solid wedge. The wind beat upon us; we advanced with steady élan through its fiercest blasts. More uniforms waited ahead upon the esplanade. Some were ordinary policemen waving truncheons at urchins who ran to see us and to join our Legion; others, even more impressive, proved to be the ground-floor staff of the casino. We shook hands with each of the four major policemen and turned into the door-way of the "modern" hotel. The concierge said that he spoke French, and repeated the words: "Chambre où manger? Manger où chambre?"

"Les deux."

The dining-room was a forest of glazed blue columns. Empty tables faced us in rows, glasses upside down beside each cover, the tables being laid in the Anglo-Saxon manner. One party was dining, a family party numbering about a dozen. They were dressed in city clothes, the women's ears and necks alight with jewellery. They must have thought that we cut odd figures in our garments stained with salt water. Coldly the waiters gathered around us, clean and efficient. The head waiter wore a dinner-jacket, his lieutenants tail-coats, and the rank and file brown coats with gold braid on shoulders and sleeves. There was only a table d'hôte menu, and the atmosphere among the cold blue columns without capitals was one of uniforms, cleanliness, and dirigisme. Hungry, and grateful for our release from discomfort, we admired everything, and enjoyed the way the columns and the springy floor rocked gently to the rhythm of the salt sea. The host at the next table was summoned to answer a telephone call from Rio de Janeiro. We were impressed, but his family and friends seemed to make an effort to regard as ordinary (glancing at us) the miracle of the submarine cable and the tiny Portuguese words darting under the Atlantic beyond the plate-glass windows, flickering across the depths at fantastic speed.

Those people who have one or two hot baths every day of their adult lives can have no conception of the delights of hot baths, since those are delights that stale even more completely than most others when subjected to constant repetition. I seldom lower myself into the steaming water without thinking of Napoleon, who liked to plan his battle order, his schemes of reserves, pivots, and corps-de-chasses while the water slowly cooled and the orderly appeared from time to time with another cauldron freshly boiled. I often think of Dr. Crippen, and his method, perhaps the most subtly cruel means of murdering yet devised. And sometimes I wonder at the courage of those who have committed suicide by piercing an artery and dying in the reddening water. (Looking at my diary, I see that my first hot bath after leaving Lymington on June 18th was at Benodet on June 26th, and this, the second, was at Póvoa de Varzim on July 12th. It is easy enough to keep your body clean on a boat, and I have an idea that the body is better and stronger without hot baths, or at least without too many of them. I do remember, though, that when I was a prisoner in Italy, and was allowed one hot shower per week, my whole system was indescribably toned up for some hours after the shower, probably because of the additional oxygenation of the skin. I remember too that when I was young and enjoyed subjecting myself to physical tests of endurance I was discouraged by the training experts from taking more than one hot bath a week—though many cold ones.) In any event, a hot bath is most wonderful when the wind howls round the house, and so it was that evening at Póvoa de Varzim. Landsmen can, because wind does not affect them in all they do, come to a state of ignoring all winds less strong than gales. But he who lives on the water is in tune with the wind, reacting to it both waking and sleeping so that it becomes a part of him, a part that he both loves and fears. Of course different men react differently to wind. I was interested, for example, to find so much

of it in the autobiographical monuments of Sir Osbert Sitwell. It was
natural to find wind in those books, since the author spent much of his
childhood at Scarborough, but what particularly interested me was his
reaction to the gulls, the "cruel" gulls. The gulls to me are solid fragments of the wind, and I identify them with my feelings for wind, my
love and my fear. If I could move from my already ageing body into
another I would be a gull. Yesterday we were riding through the winter
scene in Dorset, and in a sheltered valley near the small, shut-in village
of Hilton with its many evocative tombstones showing the immutability
of life and the stream, strong, thick, and red, of those families who go on
and on and on working, generation to generation, we suddenly saw a
patrol of herring gulls gliding over the wet green fields. They brought
the sea to us, and as the horses stamped, and jingled their bits, and blew
their steam into the bitter air, we thought of the sea and judged that
there would be a very strong south-westerly in the channel. The gulls
had brought the sea to us in that sheltered place.

Outside our bedroom window the wind almost drowned the noises of
loudspeaker music and of baby boats with one-cylinder engines that
sped about within the confines of a rectangular pond outlined with blue
strip-lighting. The esplanade below, with its rifle-ranges and sideshows, was ready for thousands on the spree. But the south wind blew
upon these small things, as over all the mountainous coastline from
Trafalgar to Ushant, and the humans huddled indoors.

Waking, I wondered where I could be, for my eye lit on a door with
no proportion in its forms, its mouldings, its chromium-plated handle,
its notice stating that the management would not be responsible . . .

We walked to the mole to look at *Serica*, still bounding in the harbour
with the watchman's boat attached to her beautiful counter like an ox
attached to a racehorse. We turned back to the town. Adult pedestrians
showed a tendency to chase away the small boys who pestered us,
begging, but the worst nuisances until we had cleared the esplanade were
the sharp-shooting photographers who had set up cameras on shaky
tripods round the restless statue (most Portuguese statues are restless,
you feel they want to bash you in the eye, or stand you a drink, or make
you a political speech) of a Romantic Hero scanning the Atlantic. The
fishing-boats, hauled out on the beach, impressed us, newcomers to
Portugal, most forcibly by their elegance and their superiority in every
way to the boats in Spain. Beamy, well-shaped boats, double-ended,

and painted from bows to sterns with names, stars, flags, crosses, angels, and other devices, all in faded colours, rusts, yellows, blues, oranges, browns, greens. Their names were chiefly those of the Catholic saints, but we saw among them Sea (Mar), Adored Country, and My Father's Only Sister. The fishermen looked fit to man such boats, for emphasising their dark, Phœnician looks, half-bawdy, half-handsome, they were dressed in woollen large-check shirts coloured somewhat similarly to the boats and equally faded by exposure, blue trousers rolled below the knees, and cloth caps set tightly on. Their legs and feet were bare, the toes gripping the sand of the shore or the stones of the pavement.

The inner streets, after those of France and Spain, struck us as being almost grotesquely unattractive, as though, in material things, Portugal had sifted the ugliness from other countries. The core of Póvoa de Varzim showed us English telephone-kiosks and letter-boxes, German Hitlerian architecture of the cafeteria-cum-stadium type, French between-the-wars "modern" furniture, glossy, bulbous, crude, and unfunctional. By contrast a member of our police reception committee was an agreeable sight in his Japanesey uniform. (Possibly the Japanese wear Portuguese uniform?) His small, dark face was creased with his welcome, and showed a line of chipped teeth. He conducted us to a bank, and was very abrupt with any small boys who came near, though they seemed rather well-behaved after our experience of Spanish urchins.

The hotel bill amounted to 265 escudos (then nearly £3). We walked to the beach, carrying our single, insignificant piece of luggage. Another policeman, who was waiting for us beside the water, with the single word "Komm!" led us to the jail in the old fort standing at the corner of the cove, taking us up a ramp so covered with fine sand as to be all but pedestrian-proof, and through a strange Roman archway of black stone into a courtyard surrounded by doors painted purple. The centre of the courtyard was cultivated with potatoes, runner beans, and green peas. The crops were languishing.

Four policemen waited to question us inside a cell-like room fitted with a deal table, two benches, and two notices, one recording a saying of Dr. Salazar's concerning the warm, natural, and praiseworthy love of the Portuguese people for their country, the other a memorandum that a policeman should keep silence regarding all details of his service. . . . The accusation was not grave: we were told that I had not signed the

Traveller's Cheque I had cashed that morning. An argument ensued, for I was able to point out that the cashier certainly would not have given me money for an unsigned cheque. At length the argument was settled when the bank manager was brought in with the cheque. I had signed it correctly, but they required (for some reason best known to themselves) another signature on the back. We returned to the beach accompanied, in the most friendly manner, by all the policemen in the jail excepting one who was watching three prisoners swill out the latrines.

A woman in garments of weeping black helped us into the boat. She had a saintly face framed in black hair marked with white.

"Husband or brother?" she asked Isabel.

"Husband."

"Then God's blessing on the pretty married ones and carry them safely home."

Isabel shaded her eyes and looked with no approval at the sea, which had not moderated since our arrival.

As they pushed out the boat and the boy's oar-blades scraped at a mixture of foam and sand there was a further commotion among those volatile policemen, and shouts that we must put back for interrogation.

"They aren't trying to be disagreeable," we enjoined each other. "Smile!" We were bustled across the esplanade and up a staircase to the offices of the Captain of the Port. That naval officer castigated the police by departments for not informing him of the arrival of the foreign vessel. He was, however, extremely affable to us, and on learning that the police had every possible detail of the yacht, including all the ports she had touched at since leaving England, he forgave them handsomely.

"You see, this is not a port where passengers are supposed to land," one of the policemen said as he accompanied us to the beach. "This is a fishing port. The tourist side of it is separate. We get Portuguese yachtsmen from Leixões and Oporto, but the tourists come by land. . . . Leixões, though, is a commercial port; there you will be made welcome, I should think. They'll probably allow you to land there straight away. . . ." He made a defiant gesture at the offices of the Captain of the Port, and said: "You'd have thought *they*'d have seen your yacht, since they have an unobstructed view of the harbour from their windows. But the Navy are like that—so busy peering into the fog that they stumble over their own feet. Fortunately your countrymen have perfected this device known as radar. Already we fit radar to our ships; when we fit it to each individual naval officer those gentry may be able to direct themselves better. Is it true," he asked with a severe change of tone, "can it be true that you British have sold radar to the Bolsheviks?"

"Very likely."

"It reminds me of the saying: 'The pig will eat its young,' and the Englishman will sell you his country but charge you the earth. I see," he added, with a touch of malice, "that the pound sterling is down another point."

"The cheaper the pound the cheaper our goods, and the more you rich Portuguese will buy," Isabel said, sensing that my Spanish was unequal to the strain put on it.

"Once we were rich, but where Portugal has sown others have reaped. We ought to have done well out of remaining neutral in this last war. But the money seems to be all gone. Would you like me to give you a clearance?"

"Thank you, no," Isabel said, and added to me in English: "I expect he'd charge us for it; he seems to be financially alert."

We boarded *Serica* with no more than a severe wetting, and hanging on for life with the spare hand, each of us saluted the guardian, who proceeded to help me with the anchors while the engine was warming up. I hoisted the mainsail and the small jib, for I hated the look of the sea in the harbour mouth, and did not incline to put all my trust in sparking plugs, distributor, and carburettor. When we were nearly ready to move, the man in the checked shirt made two expressive gestures. First, he opened his right eye widely with his left hand, and with the right hand pretended to prop the eyelid with a matchstick. (Not a wink of sleep all night.) Then, holding one hand out at chest level, palm up, he rubbed the ball of the thumb over the ends of the index and second fingers.

I gave him a 100-escudos note, and he was delighted, so delighted that he forgot to hold on, and *Serica*, choosing her moment to buck, pitched him clean over her rail, cap-first into the seas. He clambered quickly over the gunwale of his rowing-boat, clutching the cap in one hand and the banknote in the other.

He and his companion, the thin boy, were honest and honourable. We had left the interior of the boat in disorder, and nothing had been touched in our absence. For example, my gold watch (I must not be blamed for the metal, the watch was presented to me), was propped on the shelf beside our bunk. Although there were signs that they had eaten on board they had provided their own food, for none of ours had gone.

I had greater difficulty than ever before or since in getting the bower anchor on board. Isabel pushed *Serica* dead into sea and wind with the engine, and when we were well across the bar she turned off the wind until we were sailing. She stopped the engine and lay down. Her pills against seasickness were finally having a bad rather than a good effect.

After some reflection on my faulty navigation from la Guardia to Póvoa de Varzim I had concluded that my error had been caused by excessive leeway. Since I knew this could be no fault of *Serica's*, I judged that it had been mine in pinching too near the wind, and in sailing her a shade under-canvased. I lashed the tiller, therefore, and shook out the reefs in the mainsail, before settling in the cockpit to sail her for all she was worth. I must admit that in such conditions and driven hard to windward *Serica* is not a dry boat. But it was a warm day, and I enjoyed the spray that crossed the decks while the free-wheeling propeller shaft revolved oilily and the outlets of the self-draining cockpit gurgled by my bare feet. I now really got the feel of the yacht to windward. We sailed out to sea for nine miles and then on the other tack, closing the land, for eleven—and there stood the entry beacon of Leixões harbour, dead on the bows. On this occasion, though the distance covered was trifling, my reckoning was as accurate as it had been crossing the Bay of Biscay (when again I had simply concentrated on keeping the yacht moving at or near her maximum speed and had let the navigation follow suit). From this day on nicety of direction on the chart took second place with both of us to speed through the water. Between Póvoa and Leixões, beating into a stiff sea and with some unfavourable tide our average worked out at 6.4 knots.

The entry to Leixões, a big man-made port at the mouth of the Douro, was peculiar, even dangerous. The long mole running out to the entry beacon had not been completed, and was submerged at anything approaching high water. (We had been sufficiently warned of this by the Sailing Directions and by every harbour-master for many miles north.) There was a bad sea in the entry, and I did not relish the possibility of an accidental gybe. Isabel took the tiller while I furled the mainsail. I noticed her stagger, and I hurried to the cockpit. She told me after-wards that she had nearly fainted, but at the time she insisted on steering in, and did so with her usual precision. The swell surged into the great square outer harbour, but we had noticed on our chart a small basin dug out of the north-easternmost corner, and since we saw a yacht's high mast there, we made for it, bowling along under jib alone. We found the basin to be overcrowded with small craft and with big sardiners, fine ships, which occupied most of the space round the quays. Standing on one quay was a building marked in large letters *Club de Vela Atlantico*. We approached the white sloop whose mast we had spied from outside. The anchor went down in three fathoms, the engine frothed us astern until the club's yacht hand, who had put off in a dinghy, could make our stern warps fast to the buoy of the pilot boat. Almost instantly another dinghy came from the club. The President, Senhor Calem Holzer, in admirable English (interspersed occasionally with such words as *immer* or *toujours*, for he plainly had several languages at his disposal) made us welcome and begged us to make use of all the facilities of his club. This charming man had reached us even before the first onrush of police, and when they came (in boats, for Portuguese policemen are quite amphibious) he was able to persuade them that it would be sufficient if we called at the office of the International Police the following morning.

Senhor Holzer had not been five minutes gone when we witnessed an unusual scene that seemed all the stranger by contrast with his urbanity and the civilised messages he had delivered in so polished a manner. . . .

Ahead of us as we lay at anchor was a long quay stretching out from the mainland far enough to make one of the jaws of our small harbour. The sardiners were about to put to sea, their fishy cargoes discharged, their nets overhauled. The crews, extremely large crews of boisterous men (drink is good, cheap, and plentiful in Portugal) were crowding back on board. All this friendly bustle was in an instant transformed to melodrama.

At a moment when the quay was clear of people a young man came running at top speed along it, pursued by another young man, who was followed by some fifty fishermen with a spattering of naval or dock-yard police dressed in grey with pistol holsters, leggings, and flat caps. The quarry's clothing was torn and dusty, as though he had been pounded on the cobbled highway to Oporto. The leading pursuer wore a blue suit with a pale stripe in the cloth, and possibly he was impeded by his tight clothing, for the man ahead gained appreciably at each desperate stride until, at the very end of the quay, he paused, looking over the broad, watery scene. Then he vaulted the iron rail, and fell some twenty feet into the water. Blue suit hung over the rail, howling threats. The man swimming clumsily in clothes and shoes looked up into the face of his enemy, who had now been joined by a naval police-man. Three naval ratings in a launch were called to the scene. The ratings were impassive, and possibly sympathetic; the swimmer allowed one of them to catch him under the arms and haul him from the water. A figure to inspire pity, one would have thought in any breast, he sat dripping in the stern, watching the quay, where the naval policeman, who now had his pistol in his hand, was embarking in a rowing-boat. The man in the blue suit also intended to embark, but the policeman turned on him furiously, and gave him such a thrust in the ribs that for a long second the blue suit was in danger of total immersion. These actions occurred in such a tumult of shout and counter-shout that the attention of the whole harbour was attracted. Yacht club members had hurried from the club house, or from the cabins to the decks of their boats. On *Serica* we were in the front row of the stalls. We saw the splash of foam on the mouth of the naval policeman, the oil on the indigo barrel of his pistol, the slightly protruding tongue of the fugitive and the terror in his eyes. He cowered as the bulky form of the police-man drew nearer, and when it was but a yard or two away, reverting to nature again, he flung himself into the water. The policeman, with hoarse cries, urged his oarsman to pursue the swimmer, and when they got the bows over the timid water-rat the policeman picked up a heavy oar and, raising it high in the air for each stroke, crashed it down. Again and again he struck. Now the crowd growled with anger and the growls enraged the bully, who fortunately missed as often as not. At last the launch came over the wretch, and he was lifted in and laid across a thwart. His head, bloody and limp, dropped down, swinging. The policeman had transferred himself to the launch, and he stood over the poor slimy figure, his pistol directed menacingly at that dangerous enemy of society. The motor-boat headed for some big ship in the harbour, and the crowds dispersed, muttering and arguing. Two young officers, one of whom had spoken to us in English, stood on the deck of the sloop near us. I asked him for some explanation of the scene we had witnessed, but he could only suggest that the fugitive might have been a naval deserter.

"This was an unusual happening in Portugal," he told us seriously. "But no country should be judged by its ports. I could tell you things about Portsmouth and Plymouth. Very lawless things."

"That's interesting," I answered. "For all the outcry in our newspapers against brigandage and ruffianism, England is apt to seem a little tame to those who live there, we sometimes wonder if we are not too bovine in our comings and goings. We were not always so— certainly not in Shakespeare's time, or in Dickens's. . . ."

I had to pay for this stupid remark for the officer disappeared below decks, and in no time he was aboard *Serica* with a book entitled *Shakespeare—The Whole Works*.

"Why do they praise this writer so?" he asked. "I want you to explain me this, for according to my observation he is never true to life. His characters, while they make many long speeches, do not stand out as human beings each with his own strengths, weaknesses, and mannerisms. Now I open the book at random, and I ask you candidly . . . here is a nobleman who speaks, and what does he say? . . .

> " 'If music be the food of love, play on . . .
> Give me excess of it that surfeiting
> The appetite may sicken and so die . . .' "

CHAPTER 9

## "HERE LIES WILLIAM SQUID"

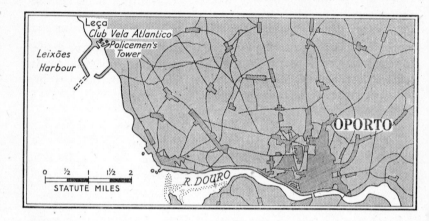

CURTAINS of drizzle, grey and cold, draped over the gorge of the Douro, were slowly pushed toward the stone box in which we lay. The sun had vanished and, muffled by the wet, thick air, we heard the rumble of the southerly swell against the moles. We pulled oilskins over town clothing, and landed at the club steps.

The Atlantico Sailing Club had recently been opened as an off-shoot from, and adventurous child of, the Sport Club de Porto, which had (and has) premises on the bank of the Douro River. The new club showed promise of developing into a flourishing concern. It consisted of a long shed with boats ranged down either side of the interior, a bar at one end, showers and changing rooms for the sexes in the middle. A derrick on the quay outside could deposit members' boats in the water and pluck them out. Moored in the basin astern of *Serica* were pleasure boats too heavy for the derrick, mainly American speedboats, bulbous roarers that powerfully appeal (alas!) to the Portuguese temperament.

Passing through the club, we made our way to the offices of the International Police, a corps that would seem to incline more to

90

xenophobia than to internationalism. Many Portuguese refer to them as the "Foreign Police", and it is true that they take a keen interest in foreigners, both visiting and resident in Portugal, chivvying them energetically through all the coverts of town and country and generally instilling into them a "wholesome" fear of the pack. Those International Policemen whom we met wore plain clothes, and were sometimes mousy, sometimes loudly tweedy, in appearance. The tower that they inhabited at Leixões was near the entrance to the club. They worked (if policemen, busy though they sometimes are, can ever be said to work) in one of the top storeys. When we pressed the bell at the bottom of the tower the door flew open in the most uncanny manner imaginable, one of the Internationals having pulled a string that was trained down the spiral staircase. The two men in the office upstairs spoke Spanish with some fluency, but with obvious distaste. (While the Spanish as a race seem to aim at forgetting for long periods that Portugal exists, the Portuguese readily show antipathy to Spain and Spaniards; it is well, therefore, when speaking Spanish in Portugal to make it clear from the start that you only do so because you cannot speak Portuguese.) The senior policeman took our passports from us, and gave us yellow cards in their stead. Behind his desk was hung an advertisement in which a photographically reproduced young woman presented her scarlet and orange bosom, a repulsive sight. I was horrified that the monstrosity had been designed and issued to advertise a British-manufactured article. At the base of the policemen's dark tower we caught the tram-car for Oporto.

What a delightful means of locomotion is a tram! A strictly fore-and-aft movement, plenty of solid seats and, if the seats be occupied, a solid platform to stand on, large windows, strong brakes, tinkling bells, potent acceleration, interesting advertisements (mainly, here, for patent medicines and port wine), interesting passengers. Many of my memories jingle along in tram-cars, for when I was first beginning to stir alone, a tentative fugitive from the close skein of a Scottish family, I travelled through Glasgow in the double-decked trams of that rich and heterogeneous city. I remember the trams with excitement: the Red Car that occasionally whirled me out to the grain fields and gas works, canals, golf courses, and sheep-dotted hills, on the perimeter of the town; the Green that travelled down Great Western Road and over the romantic River Kelvin to St. George's Cross, near which the riding school squatted in its never-forgotten atmosphere of ammonia; the Yellow, that serpented down Byres Road past the shop that sold water-pistols and pea-shooters, pink celluloid windmills, football cards, sporting newspapers (one of them pink), catapults and potato-guns, sticks of liquorice and cinammon, and stink bombs; past Colquhoun's the bakers where I would see hundred-weight cubes of virgin chocolate standing by the side door in the lane, waiting for the metamorphosing hand of the confectioner; then more twists and turns, past the building where the later editions of Hengler's Circus appeared and after them the Motor Show, then into dignified terraces housing men who smelled of formaldehyde, precincts that would be passed in earnest thankfulness that today was not the day for doctor or dentist; and so into Sauchiehall Street, with its fur coats, its Moorish-Doric cinemas, its picture and carpet shops, its strange dark inns from which furtive figures emerged. . . . It was on the upper deck of a Green Car travelling west past the Glasgow Academy that at the age of eleven I smoked my first cigarette (a Chesterfield—so superior a foreign brand!) through a tortoiseshell holder tipped with gold that my mother had once used and then laid aside in the drawer where I had found it. And on Friday evenings (before I was banished to a boarding school), I used to catch the Yellow Car for the Grosvenor Cinema (the name Grosvenor then seemed to me opulent, *English*, and romantic) or another smaller cinema whose name is forgotten although it showed for a time an unforgettable "serial" called *The Tin Man*. The "serial" I remember at the Grosvenor was *The Three Musketeers*. Cinema organs had just been invented (even in those days I hated them) and the favourite tune of the Grosvenor organist was called *Drift With Me Along the Shores of Minnetonka*.

A busy town is Oporto, beautiful where it is cut by the tawny Douro, jostling between dun rocks. By afternoon the drizzle had gone and the air was stifling. Down on the river delicately-shaped boats with long, long steering oars and spritsails patched with grey, or pale ochre, or Chinese white, were sailing. They navigate the Douro up to a point some fifty miles above Oporto. They sail only with favourable winds, but then with exquisite effect.

On another tram-car, making a circular tour of the town, we were engaged in conversation by a tall man who showed me a card on which the first name was Antonio and the second was so complicated that I instantly forgot it. Isabel made me ask him if there was in the town or near it a cool garden where she might drink chocolate.

"Sartinlay," he answered. "We have the best cafés you'll see any-where, right here in Porto."

"I really meant some place with a garden," she said, "and not a café." She had noticed that the many cafés were filled with men, all wearing their hats as they sat closely packed round the tables, apparently breathing through their gills. No women were tolerated in those dark interiors.

"Then I'd like to take you to the establishment of a friend of mine, where you will sartinlay imagine yourself in England."

He drove us along before him. He was a conspicuous figure, tall, with a pouchy face, unshaven of course, because the inhabitants of Spain and Portugal generally have themselves shaved in the late evening instead of the early morning. "Otherwise," as a young Spaniard said to me recently in London, "it would be inconvenient for us, since we have much sprout on our chins, to make love at night." I asked him what happened if he wanted to make love in the afternoon. "Afternoon!" he answered. "Afternoon is for premeditated love—*l'amour à la française*." But to return to Antonio. . . . He pushed us into a stuffy tea-shop, and it takes a good deal of force to get me into one of those places. He loaded our table with liquid chocolate and sticky cakes of large pro-portions. I was interested in him. His hands were impeccable, at odds with his otherwise rather flashy appearance, which was further denied by his hat of black velvet, and his black tie. Was he then some kind of servant? His fluent English suggested that he might be a guide or a waiter, or a ship's steward (though a steward might have been expected to be dirtier, particularly about the hands). I wondered what his game was. He did not eat himself, yet he insisted on paying the bill. Then he began to talk, importantly. . . . Had just been on a trip to France with his "boss". Yes, Paris and so on. But he did not like France, no, not at all. He had been pleased to return to Portugal. "Because in Portugal we sartinlay have everything." On Sunday (his day off) he would come down to Leixões in a big car driven by a chauffeur and would take us to the northern frontier, stopping for lunch at a place called Póvoa de Varzim: "They have everything in that town, I tell you." He would send down a few cases of wine to our yacht. . . . I had decided by this time that he was no rogue; worse, infinitely less interesting, he was a patriot. At a loss to know how to pass a free hour, he had decided to impress two foreigners.

On leaving the tea-shop (how good the air smelled outside!) we

D*

walked a mile downhill at his command to goggle into a window containing beaten silver; half a mile's hot toil uphill to look at an even more hideous display of china. Now where would he take us? He can hardly have considered the cathedral or the Gothic church of Cedofeita. The next call was a vast café. We struggled along the waiters' aisle, with hatted men sitting in solid wedges, like ruminant frogs or stout fishes, on either hand, and so upstairs to a billiards room with eighteen tables. Antonio kept us standing there for ten minutes to let the spectacle seep in. The players were young, and the play poor. Next he led us to an empty cinema. (Clever Dr. Salazar, making the drought and the consequent shortage of electricity his excuse, had had the excellent idea —Portugal, like England, was deluged with American films—of shutting every cinema for several days in the week.) Our guide rattled at the box-office window until a caretaker had given him a key, and then he marched us into the sombre interior, which was indeed unusually spacious. Standing in the front row of the dress circle, he pointed out the various amenities of the house, not omitting to translate the different notices that were set over the doors. Then he took us to see his "boss".

"Where is he?" Antonio asked the maid who let us through the heavy portico.

"Hacking away."

We passed through a series of dark but otherwise comfortable rooms to the garden, and then to a shed, where an elderly man of correct and intellectual aspect *was* working with chisel and mallet at a graveyard monument in the shape of a rugged cross some five feet high. He had not taken off his coat to work, and his fine grey suit was white with dust. The chisel bit fiercely into the stone, cutting out the lettering already pencilled on the plinth, which read as follows:

Here Lie
The Mortal Remains of
WILLIAM SQUID
Murdered 14th July, 1949,
by the Fisherman
Joachin Bisbao
REST IN PEACE

"Well, what is it now?" shouted the gentleman with the chisel, wheeling round. "Oh, it's you, Antonio. You're late! What's that?

English people. Delighted, delighted. . . . But take them away now. They can see I'm busy. They certainly won't grudge me a few moments to get on with my work. Give them some curaçao, Antonio, there's a good fellow, and explain the situation to them. *Now look what you've made me do, you infernal ass.* I've hit my thumb again and spoiled the four. Oh dear, I shall have to change the 14th to the 18th now. *Go away, Antonio.*"

Antonio gave us liqueurs in one of the dark rooms. "The boss won't come now," he said. "But at any rate you've seen him, and he's a great gentleman and a genius. Once he finds his true outlet the whole world will sartinlay know of him. He'll be cutting at that monument all night, and tomorrow I'll have to pay six men to carry it down to the graveyard and help the boss set it up." He explained that his employer, once a successful exporter, had retired to this large villa and had taken up gardening for a while. . . . "Then marine photography," Antonio said, "then stage scenery, then medieval French poetry, then the history of the donkey. Now it's monuments. The whole of the foot of the garden he's turning into his own private cemetery."

"Who was William Squid?"

"That was him—that jelly-looking thing in the big glass box beside the new monument. The boss bought him yesterday in the fish market."

\* \* \* \*

There was some difficulty when I asked for the tickets on a No. 1 tram-car because we had not understood that the Portuguese pro-nunciation of "Leixões" is something like "Leshoinge". The men passengers were unusually polite, we noticed. They rose to their feet to allow women to sit (I did not see this elsewhere in Portugal, only in Oporto). Most of the men wore dark glasses, and their soft hats had bows at the back and not on the right side, giving the wearers something of the whimsical appearance of Italian hurdy-gurdy men. An English-man sat in front of us in the tram, a little Englishman, very neat, with expensive spectacles, a summer overcoat, brown boots, and the *Sunday Express*. He got out at a desolate place half-way from Oporto to Leixões, a place where we saw nothing but shacks and inferior hen-runs.

Isabel (we were both heavy-laden with melons, pineapples, and other ponderous fruits) left her crocodile-leather bag in the tram-car. The bag contained money, our yellow passes from the police, and some semi-valuables, but we both believed that we should get it back intact, for if we had seen little of the Portuguese poor we had seen enough to decide that they were both kind and honest, and although the richer Portuguese are perhaps not at first sight quite so prepossessing, the middle classes in any country are usually honest in the small things that don't matter. I told Calem Holzer of our loss, and that we intended if the weather seemed more favourable to leave the following morning. He was worried about the yellow cards, but seemed hopeful about recovering the bag from the tramway's lost property office.

We went into the poor, companionable streets round the harbour to bargain for ordinary provisions in shops where there was little enough to buy and where old women, dear old scratchy hens, did the selling. Different prices were quoted in every shop. I led Isabel down some steps into a catacomb of a bar, to buy wine for the yacht, but the fishermen and sailors spat so obtrusively that before I had found a wine to my liking she asked me to take her out. Spitting is a background to public life in Portugal. In no other country with the exception of the United States of America is there such widespread and noisy indulgence in this vile, dangerous, and unnecessary habit.

Down on the beach between the port and the great lighthouse of Leça on Ponta Boa Nova the south wind had bowled over row upon row of bathing tents. A few enormous bathing attendants, female versions of the popular conception of a eunuch, were securing the wooden frames and pinning down the blue-striped canvas with big stones. The women ploughed through the sand on steady bare feet surmounted by thin ankles and thick calves—John Leech legs, beefily seductive.

The thermometer below decks registered eighty-seven (F) although the evening seemed cool enough outside, and the ventilators were driving a strong draught through the accommodation.

We had long been asleep when there was a tap on the side. It was Calem Holzer, a man whose kindness knows no bounds. He had brought us Isabel's bag, recovered from the tramway authorities complete with all its contents. He also brought several bottles of an interesting, extra-dry port, two loaves of Viennese bread, and our passports, which we had forgotten to retrieve from the eyrie of the International Police.

# CHAPTER 10

## NORTH WIND

As though eager to learn from our erratic movements, the yacht hand of the Club de Vela Atlantico watched us prepare for sea. His moustachioed face was respectfully serious, but perhaps he was inwardly ashake with laughter. When the anchor was under foot I hoisted the Genoa. Isabel sheeted it in with a clickety-clacketing of ratchets in the winch, and *Serica* scudded off like a racing dinghy. But when we were outside the harbour the wind ceased, and we rolled in the fairway.

After the engine had run for twenty minutes it was red-hot, and presented a disagreeable appearance. Full of gloom, and saying that we would have to put back to Leixões for repairs, I waited for the glowing metal to cool. Removing the water pump severely taxed my abilities as a contortionist and as a mechanic, and when I had removed it I could find no fault in it. I merely cleaned, greased, and replaced it. The engine then ran normally, and Isabel, who, mechanically speaking, is the greater greenhorn, said that I had been clever. We were both relieved when the wind came again, and from the north.

We sailed with the sheets free, our movement, a loose, swinging one, gradually sweeping us out from the long, straight coastline. In later days I should have set the spinnaker for that wind, but at this time I was still remarkably pusillanimous and lazy, and had not realised the full capabilities of the boat, which, dear thing, ambled along all day with a light wind on the quarter and a heavy beam swell, seldom dropping her speed below six knots. Darkness came at 9.20, following a spell of faster sailing, and the patent log showed that we had covered eighty sea miles, or about half the distance from the Douro to the Tagus.

On we blew, under mainsail and Genoa, through a lurid night with great cloudbanks and sudden squirts of lightning high to the west and the north. Isabel relieved me frequently, and that night it was she who did most of the steering. When we distinguished the seven-league arms of the great light on the Ilha Berlenga (Burling Island), we gybed and headed inshore—a stupid move, for on nearing Berlenga and the off-lying dangers of the Os Farilhões we ran into the steamer lane. Our

powerful electric torch, useful for shining into the mainsail when a big
ship was approaching, had been battered to fragments when it was
swung from its hook during the rough beat from la Guardia to Póvoa de
Varzim, while our navigation lights, set low on the coach-roof, were
always liable to be obscured from an oncoming vessel by the mass of the
Genoa.

There was nearly a disaster. . . . I was asleep in the bottom of the
cockpit, and Isabel, sitting on the starboard seat, would have had to
stand up to see that our port light was out. We were on the port tack,
and a liner was rushing at us as though intent on slicing us from the port
bow to the starboard quarter. Isabel wakened me with her foot, and I
ran forward through the darkness along the deck. The lead from plug
to lamp had been shorn off by the wire sheets of the Genoa during our
last gybe. After a *very* brief consultation we put about, presenting our
undamaged starboard light to the liner, and getting slowly (all too slowly
it seemed) clear of her course. She passed, a surging metal mountain,
humming, a purposeful and dreadful sight.

Dawn was thundery. Cursing the fitful breeze, we sailed into the
huge bay north of the mouth of the Tagus. Now, with daylight, and the
approaching hours of tide favourable for mounting the river, we saw
ships everywhere, as though it had been war-time and a convoy were
gathering or dispersing. We stood in for twenty miles and more, until
we could distinguish the grass stalks on the bluffs of Estramadura. Then
we gybed, setting course to clear Cabo da Roca, twenty-five miles
distant, at the head of the bay. With the appearance of a fierce sun the
breeze had dropped almost to nothing. The sea was in a nervous
condition, presaging wind. The heat was so intolerable that at midday
Isabel would eat nothing. I went below and ate about a pound of
smoked ham washed down with a pint of Calem Holzer's port, a wine
that I thought tasted of brandy (and I am interested in almost anything
that tastes of brandy).

Within five miles of Cabo da Roca we were completely becalmed.
The engine was brought on again, and we motored with the sails hanging
limp. The cliffy cape, backed by the corrugated ridge of the Sintra hills,
seemed to recede as we motored on. The glare from the sea was pitiless.
*Serica* is not the same boat to steer when motoring as under her natural
power, and my arm began to ache from the pull of the tiller in the swell.
At last we crawled (or seemed to crawl) round Roca, the westernmost
point of the Continent of Europe, and round the next cape, Cabo Raso.

Yet another stretched ahead, Ponta da Alpendurada, a low promontory sneaking from the hills. The mouth of the Tagus (we could not see the far bank) was a desert of hot glitter and tide-tormented water.

But near Alpendurada we heeled to a strong north wind, and immediately began to sail at full speed, easily cutting through the tide, which now set against us. No more rolling, no more fumes from the exhaust, no more tugging at the tiller; only the hiss of our passage, the bite of the wind from our mainsail crinkling the water to leeward and spilling its blessed coolness over our heads and shoulders. Fatigue, ill-humours, discomforts were dispersed and only recalled to increase the wonders of the moment, the paradise of sailing movement.

It was Sunday. Hundreds of motor-cars were ranging the coast road to windward. As we raced along, close in, we studied and discussed the "detached residences" standing in their little gardens behind the road and staring with their ill-shaped, glassy eyes across the incomprehensible sea. One of them—though we did not know it then—housed the King of Italy.

We had intended to sail up-river to the yacht harbour of Lisbon, Belém Dock, but at the last moment we could not face the prospect of a hot, and possibly dirty, harbour, so we whirled round into Cascais Bay and dropped anchor between a fleet of sardiners of the Three Seas class and a white yacht, an old yawl of about *Serica's* tonnage. The yawl, chartered for the week-end, carried some thirty people, as against our two. We had hardly begun to straighten up on deck (for this was a breezy, yachty place, and it behoved us to make a good appearance) when a tender came alongside with two hands and a correct gentleman in a white-covered yachting cap (something I could not emulate). He was the secretary of the Club Naval de Cascais, and he brought both oral and written invitations to us to make use of the club, a handsome white building stepped, with its long quay and its sheds, on the rock below the fort of Cascais.

Two Dutch-built yachts anchored astern of us. One was *Falcao*, a comfortable motor-cruiser with many windows; the other, *Saltillo*, a ketch, had at her wheel Don Juan, King of Spain (then officially known as the Count of Barcelona). While we watched the King's efficient sailing of the solid craft (he had four Spanish yacht hands on board), *Serica* was struck a most foul blow in her midriff by an undecked fishing-boat got up with salmon pink lateen sail, yellow spars, black topsides, and two great eyes painted on the bows. She was crewed by four fat young men, well-to-do burgesses. I had noticed them bearing down on us, and had thought nothing of it, but at the last moment the helmsman and owner lost his head, put the helm up instead of down, and rammed us. The wind then carried them aft, scraping all the way and tearing off our starboard lifebuoy. After several attempts the helmsman picked up the lifebuoy and came back with it. While tossing it to me he rammed us again, this time in the quarter. All the apology I got from him was the sometimes inadequate English word, "Sorry".

\*      \*      \*      \*

Originating from the small resort-cum-port in Scotland of which I may be said to be a native, Alasdair went young to work in Spain and Portugal and, consciously or unconsciously, adopted with well-merited prosperity the bearing of a Spanish grandee. He is some few years my senior, is powerful and exceptionally well preserved, and has the benefit of a handsome face, curling moustache, and smiling eyes that send out their glints from attractively worldly folds. He could break me across his knee. . . . His hobby has always been sailing, and he has sailed his own boats in many waters. It was accordingly with some inner trembling that I answered his resonant "*Serica* ahoy!" as I was cleaning the brass sheet-winches on our first morning at anchor off Cascais. He sailed up to us (very adept, no suspicion of *his* ramming us) in a half-decked boat with an ochre sail.

"Good gracious!" was his first word, "somebody's hit you a dreadful dunt on this topside. Where did that happen?"

I told him of the man in the black boat.

"The father's a first-class fellow and worth a lot of money. But I'll tell the son what I think of him, and I'll bring him out to you to apologise."

"Please don't, Alasdair, I never want to see him again."

"And tomorrow I'll bring some safety-razor blades (no, you must have blades of your own on board, haven't you?) and I'll show you how to get rid of those foul black marks. Beautiful enamel, by the way. Did they put that on for you at Lymington? . . . Did you get my letter before you left England? You didn't? I wrote advising you never to come. Someone in England, I forget who, told me *Serica* was an utter pig, full of tricks and vices—but I must say she looks well. Don't know that I ever saw a yacht looking better after the trip out. You must have been damned lucky with your weather. . . . You've come to a rotten place for sailing: either too much wind or none at all. But a paradise in every other way. Perfect climate, decent people, the comforts of civilisation. . . . Lord Almighty! what a number of encumbrances you've got hanging round your mast. Is that your topping lift? You should change that. I have mine to the end of my boom—far simpler and more efficient. . . . Don't think anything of your dinghy; I always carry a ten-footer, and that's plenty small enough. Can I go below? Delightful. Very well installed engine, but have you no engine temperature gauge, George? I'd never be without one. . . . Let's have another look on deck. A fine teak deck. Did you scrape it this season? Ah, I thought so. Remember every time you scrape you weaken your ship. . . . I'll give you a tip to avoid getting fuel oil on your nice fenders: wrap a bit of old canvas round each fender when you're in a dirty port. . . . I expect your mast was scraped too? a fine spar, but I prefer a painted mast myself, more practical, the Americans all do it now. . . . I like her lines; she should sail like an eight-metre. I'd forgotten she was so fine a boat, but of course in England you see such numbers of yachts and each one sinks into the mass. . . . She's light, though; far too lightly-timbered for a trip like this, I would say. And for sailing in these parts and the Mediterranean you'd be far better off with ketch rig and two engines. . . ."

"We tried ketch rig and two engines and we don't agree with you," Isabel said. "You say this one's too light? our last boat was a heavily-timbered ketch with two engines, and it took half a gale of wind from the right quarter to make her sail at all. This boat is wonderful. . . . Where's Helen?" she asked, referring to Alasdair's wife, and changing the conversation, for being of a fiercely loyal nature, Isabel does not easily accept criticism of people, beasts, or even things, of which she is fond.

"She's jumping her stallion, practising for the Concurso Hypico next week. Come and see her and have lunch with us afterwards. I'll ring our cook from the club and see if she can scratch something together for the sake of auld lang syne. Life gets very expensive here. Rents are rather higher in Estoril than in Mayfair, and food goes up every day. Still, we stumble along, and we're always happy to share our crust with you both."

He landed us at the Club Naval, and drove us in his aged but ever-youthful Hispano-Suiza up suburban roads to a house with an arid garden at one end of which a number of jumps had been set up. The house was empty, and the garden had been loaned to a riding school.

Helen was on Belshazzar, a splendidly muscled Spanish barb stallion, full of condition, his lean sides all gory from her spurs. He jumped cleanly, with adroit lifts of his hinds. His iron shoes beat the ground, drawing from that hard, sunbaked substance the booming of a drum in the jungle. Two Portuguese horsemasters, standing in the centre of the rectangle, leaning forward from distended waistlines, sweated as they taught or admonished with harsh cries and much mime. They were concentrating on teaching the rider to hollow her back and give impulsion as the grey stretched his neck before each fence—though indeed her performance left little to be desired. The two instructors wore breeches cut in the baggy Italian manner, small hats like those of youths at Welwyn Garden City, shirts, soft riding boots, spurs. They taught in a mixture of Portuguese, English, French, and Spanish. Dust from the hoofs formed a mist in the arena, entering noses, mouths, ears. Helen stopped to talk to us, and while she talked the stallion bit Isabel's hand. She withdrew it just as his teeth clashed, and he only snatched skin and a small piece of flesh which he swallowed with apparent relish. The riding teachers (Helen was their star pupil) were impatient at the delay. The fences standing there so dumbly with the dust tendrils waving around them were a challenge. On! on! They put Helen on a new horse from Ireland, a big bay. He was heavy on his forehand, and he jumped less well than Belshazzar. The ground reverberated, the hoarse cries grew fiercer, the dust thickened, the sun burned hotter. The scene was savage, the more so because of its setting of cactus and sand, its sense of the Church of England just around the corner, and the Roman Catholic Church behind that.

\*      \*      \*      \*

The sun was brilliant and the club attendants were panting as they lowered Stars and Sharpies with an electric crane from the high quay into the water. Maria, the wife of one of the attendants, lived in a dark apartment at the end of the main shed. She was bare-footed, strong, brown, and amiable. She took our mainsail bag, filled with linen, and said she would have a few shirts washed and ironed for me within the hour. The secretary came up while I was with Maria, and engaged me in what was to be the first of many talks. He spoke English more fluently than most Englishmen.

"When the whale lives he owns the sea," the secretary said, his eyes hot in a face gouged by suffering. "And when the whale is dead he is a blot on the sea. Now I am dead, but it was not always so. At one time the world was mine; now I am the world's, like a strand of Sargasso weed swaying to the ripple of the water, not (so far as I know) edible, not useful, just litter at the whim of elements that obey a scheme set out in millions of light years, a scheme with no bearing on the human span. . . . I am a scientist. I speak besides my own native tongue English, French, German, and Spanish. As a young man I worked for years in England" (there followed a string of names of towns, factories, universities, individuals), "then in America" (more names), "South Africa, Colombia, Canada, England again, and then Germany. When I went to work in Germany I thought I could ask no more of life. My mother was with me, I was well paid, and most important of all, I loved my work. Germany was the best country for the scientist, and I had an excellent position, something experimental and urgent. . . . I was doing film research work on living organs and tissues. But the war came. We were chased by bombs. British bombs, Canadian bombs, American bombs, Russian bombs. My mother was killed horribly, horribly. My apparatus and all the records of my work were destroyed. My notebooks were burned in the great fires of Berlin. Eventually I became a fugitive, suffering from exposure and hunger, terrible hunger, bestial and degrading. My digestion is ruined. If I eat olive oil now I am ill, nearly to death, for days. I eat little, and I am wasting. Look at this suit, which was made for me in Berlin. Today it would hold three of me.

"I have come back to Portugal," he said. "Very fine! very nice place. Yes, but no place for a scientist. Here we do not recognise our need of science. Here the Church is strong, science weak. In Germany it was the other way round. Here there is religion (quite good), sun (good), plenty of meat and wine and bread, nice people, big houses, yes, even yachts . . . but for me it is no good. I am a mis*fit*, yes, a mis*fit*. What are my languages?" he cried, pulling at my arm. "What am I? . . . Nothing without my work. . . . I want to go back to Germany, but am not allowed to go. And how can I start again there when all my savings and all my equipment are gone, gone, gone, with my digestion? . . . But what is left of me is entirely at your service."

A fat man passed along the quay, through the boats perched on trestles. He towed by one hand a young boy of astounding fatness.

"Bonjour," the man said.

"Bonjour, monsieur," the secretary answered with a saturnine glance at me. "Don't imagine that *he*'s French," he said when they were gone. "Most of them like to show off such languages as they possess, and of course I am here to humour their fancies. Now you had better let me show you over the club. It's very convenient and agreeable, though you mustn't expect a Royal Yacht Squadron. For one thing, we have women too, you know. Women mix with the men. If it were not so perhaps we should have very few members." When I gave him my card he said he would pin it at once to the notice board. "It will make the members feel cosmopolitan," he said.

He disliked England, and would get in a dig at her whenever he could. We believed, however, that he reciprocated our liking for him. Yet he persisted in being evasive and mysterious. Time and again he promised to visit us on the yacht. Others whom we knew less well came and went, but the secretary never came. At midday he would go off to his home; his was a figure that seemed to melt away, and I never even saw which direction he took. Once I asked him where he lived, and all he answered was: "A small house and a housekeeper to look after me. No family, no fuss." And once when he returned to the club in the afternoon he said: "I ate a little oil with my salad, Mr. Millar. I'll pay dearly for that folly." For four or five days we did not see him, and we were told that he was very ill. But he returned as bitterly voluble as ever. One day when I went to ask him for the key of the shower-room I found him sitting in his office separated from the main club-room only by a partition of ornamented glass. His expression was miserable, and his dry-skinned hands covered his ears. In the club-room a gramophone was playing popular jingle, and some of the members were dancing.

"Music!" he said. "Music is one thing I desperately miss. Here, men are interested in women; what other interests are they educated to enjoy? They listen to such noises as you hear now. They go to the cinemas. They do not read, no: they buy the pornographic American magazines you will see thick on all the Lisbon bookstalls—for with one hand America most kindly gives us gold for our material rehabilitation, and with the other spiritual poison to rot the children and turn the world into a vulgarian zoo. . . . *If I could only get back to Germany.* There will be music among the ruins. What does food matter to me? I could be happy in Germany. I must get back to Berlin. . . . Often I ask the rich members to help me in this, but they *laugh* at me as though I were a baby, and say: 'My dear fellow! why on earth should you go there? You are far better off in Portugal.' " Then he suddenly lowered his voice and asked me: "Have you noticed how a rich man is apt to talk to a poor man? It is like a man talking to a child. I suppose that I have been guilty of that myself. Once, in my strength, in my prosperity, I was arrogant."

&ast;    &ast;    &ast;    &ast;

The terraces of the restaurant known as the Casa Laura were cool, and isolated above the dust of the streets, the whirring of the motor-cars, the genial shouts of the fishermen. We sat looking out over the bay and admiring *Serica*, her Ensign standing out stiffly in the north wind. Being hungry, we disregarded the rule that in the more expensive type of Portuguese restaurant it is wiser to order "One (helping) for two (people)", since the helpings are as generously proportioned as many of the customers. Where else (unless perhaps in North America) have you the privilege of seeing so many hugely fat people as among the richer classes of Portugal?

When we staggered down the steps of Casa Laura, carrying with pleasurable difficulty (because, whatever anybody may say to the contrary, it is agreeable and even beneficial for a healthy body to be gorged and surfeited from time to time) a French-named cargo of langouste à l'americaine, tournedos poivré, pommes frites, asperges, ananas, café turque, deux bouteilles de Dão, et une fine maison, we set a slow course for the shopping streets of Cascais, pleasant places enough. Father, mother, and daughter talked hard and worked jerkily in the dark fruit-and-vegetable shop. The daughter (a head on her shoulders) ran the shop and was engaged to be married to the baker down on the corner (who ran the bakery for *his* father). If we return to Cascais in ten years we shall expect this couple to have eight children and a motor-car. And they will remember us; for if the fruit might have been better considering that powerfully sunny climate, the people who sold it could not have been. The bread, on the other hand, was very good, and the wine was the best and cheapest we had found in Europe since the end of the second German war. Two five-litre flasks (more than a gallon in each) of drinkable and potent *clarete* cost us less than ten shillings.

&ast;    &ast;    &ast;    &ast;

A glance at Cascais on the map will show that it can lay small claim to being a secure anchorage, for it offers shelter only from northerly winds. Yet instead of staying there for one night, as had been our intention, we

stayed there happily for a month. In the heats of July and August
Cascais offered the freshest anchorage on the Tagus. Up-river, both air
and water might be odorous, but down at Cascais, with the expanse of
the open sea to southward, the north wind kept the air salty, almost cool.
"At Lisbon," according to the Sailing Directions, "winds from between
north-west and north-east attain a frequency of about sixty per cent in
winter and seventy per cent in summer." From our experience that
summer the percentage would be nearer 100, for night after night the
north wind roared down at us from the Sintra Hills, and frequently he,
he and no other wind, blew strongly through the glaring day as well.

  During the first nights I survived nervous crises occasioned by the
strength of the wind. Often it seemed certain that we should be blown
from our anchor. *Serica* would swivel and heel and jerk at her cable.
The wind, entering the yacht through the large ventilators forward of the
mast, rushed past us and into the cockpit. Outside was the slap of
water against our dinghy, trailing astern, and the dark beauty of the
open sea soaking up in places the lights of Cascais, of the Club Naval,
the riding lights of *Falcao* and *Saltillo*, and, far beyond them, the lights
of the pilot boat, ready to do its duty if needed, even at that hour. If I
pumped the "Baby Blake" (w.c.) the inrushing water lit up the wash-
room with its phosphorescent glow. When we woke in the morning with
the sun's first bright fingers in the doghouse the wind would generally
have dropped, the water would be smooth, clear, and friendly, but cold.

  The north wind brought many advantages; we never saw a fly or a
mosquito on board, and though the weather ashore was hot, the interior
of the boat remained cool and wholesome. (The ventilation on *Serica*,
as is the common practice on modern yachts, runs from the bows
through every part of the interior, including the bilges and all the cup-
boards. To my mind this system of ventilation is the biggest step forward
yet seen in the construction of cruising yachts; it makes a remarkable
difference to the comfort, and even the health, of the crew, and [the
experts say] to the life and freedom from rot of the vessel.)

*          *          *          *

  An engrossing study, one that might well be pursued for ten years by
any writer, is that of the British Colony in and round Lisbon. How
varied were the houses we visited, and how varied their occupants!
from dear Alice, an intellectual who works in hourly but unstaining
contact with the happenings of the world, and who was living in a

tumbledown little farmhouse in a vineyard behind Cascais, to the stiffly lovely old lady still living in the days of waltzes in her stiff, cool, old house in the Rua Sacramento da Lapa; from Alasdair's comfortable villa near the Estoril golf course to the romantic house of the Gains-boroughs, separated by its gardens, terraces, lagoons, and high, spiked railings from a dark grove of factory chimneys where communism flourishes succulently, like trompettes-de-mort, in the darkness, among the dank smells of rot, and with the murmur of the river always moving among the reeds.

It would be ungrateful in me to say a word against Estoril, for we had many kindnesses from people who live there and enjoy sanitation, fresh air, and a scrupulously guarded public propriety. Nobody, for example, was allowed to walk the Estoril pavements barefoot, whereas in Cascais the fishermen (and some others, including myself) seldom bothered with shoes. In Cascais, too, you might appear in a sarong or even a solar topee, whereas these, and particularly the latter, might draw down the wrath of the police force either in Lisbon or in Estoril-the-respectable, because a solar topee is regarded as a colonialism, in Portugal, and the height of bad form, the most outrageous of bad manners. It may be admitted, I suppose, that Estoril, like Madrid, Chicago, Bourne-mouth, and Regent Street, was built at an unfortunate time. It certainly lacks architectural charm. We heard of a sensitive Englishman working in the pleasant old town of Lisbon who, to save himself from acute melancholia, closed his eyes whenever his chauffeur was driving him through the clean streets of Estoril to some destination beyond. In case this example (and it would never be consistent with my temperament to emulate it) would seem to be born of national arrogance, I hasten to remark that a large number of my compatriots live permanently in Estoril, thinking it perfect, or at any rate one of the most comfortable places on earth; and many others, who trek there for their holidays, are of the same opinion. . . .

What of Cascais? We liked it, finding it a satisfactory base for our vague and unambitious explorations of Portugal, a country whose fascination and strangeness we had not realised until the wind took us there.

It seemed that in Portugal there was a peculiarly sharp dividing line between rich and poor, the rich being unattractive, the poor perhaps the most charming people in the world, hard-working yet happy-go-lucky, full of music, hospitable and merry with each other and more so with

strangers, amusing to look at and gifted with a sense of costume that is
lacking in the richer crust. As we lay at anchor in the north wind, our
bows pointed at two beaches, one long, the other a small, rocky cove.
The long beach, the popular bathing place for both Estoril and Cascais,
was flanked by two houses belonging to a distinguished Portuguese
family and built, it is claimed (and it must be admitted with some truth),
in the "English domestic" style (as exemplified, let us say, at Bognor
Regis or North Berwick). The smaller beach was used for bathing by
prosperous families who left their shooting brakes at the top of the steps
and sat on the sand under striped parasols, and was also used as a
latrine by the less prosperous families who lived in the tenements above
it, picturesque tenements. To port, a line of delightful, white, fishermen's cottages, clamped to the rocks, had been converted unit by unit to
the use of richer people, some of the occupants being English or
American. Then the bay swept round to a third beach flanked by the
town sewer, a Stygian version of the St. Gotthard tunnel, and backed by
the more interesting but equally pungent fish market. Between us and the
Club Naval was the recognised anchorage for sardiners, strong and
shapely motor fishing-boats, well maintained, full of life. Each boat had
its mongrel dog. The dog, a true sailor, never went ashore. He was left
to guard the sardiner when the bipeds landed, and he sustained his rôle
so fiercely that if we had a bone for him we would have to throw it from
the dinghy, for he might readily have seized the hand that held the bone.
The crews (including the dogs) lived off three staples: bread, wine, and
grilled sardines, all most excellent in their way. The wine containers,
five-litre flasks covered with straw webbing, were hung in the sea to keep
the contents fresh while the boats were at anchor; the bread was bought
daily ashore; the sardines, grilling on small charcoal stoves set on deck,
sent their appetising smell hurrying south on the wind. The fishermen
were immensely friendly. If they were eating, and they usually were,
when we passed in the dinghy, they seldom failed to invite us to share
their food, and what could be better than a fresh sardine freshly grilled
in the open air with new bread and half a pint of strong red wine?

I wrote down the names of a few of the sardiners sheltering at Cascais
from the northerly blow on the evening of July 19th: *Primorosa*,
*Bairrista*, *Perol Adacosta*, *Ruilino*, *Zita*, *Cristouão*, *Primeira de Setubal*,
*Augusta Maria*, *Lilaz*, *Deus Contigo*, *Troiana*, *Flor de Peniche*, and
*Morro Peixe*. The last named was always at Cascais, for she was the
mother duck of the local fishing. On fine evenings she would gather up a

brood of large open boats, each with its sail and mast stowed flat beside the rowers, and would tow them out in two strings for the night's work. By dawn the *Morro Peixe* would be at anchor again, deserted except for her dog, and the boats she had towed would be rubbing gunwales in a line tightly moored near the fishermen's beach while their crews dragged the catch across the sands.

The fishermen, padding barefoot through the streets, make Cascais a living and beautiful place, but like so many fishing ports Cascais is being swallowed and digested by people unconnected with the sea who are yet eager to pay high rents in order to live among such outwardly vaga-bondish (though hard-working) specimens. A new station, terminus of the electrified railway running up the north bank of the Tagus through Estoril to Lisbon, had recently been completed at Cascais, and the authorities had made it particularly spacious and grandiose. "Quite out of keeping with Cascais—we used to have such a dear, quaint, little station," complain those people who have expelled the fishermen from the best houses and installed themselves together with plumbing, gin, and American magazines.

# CHAPTER 11

TAGUS

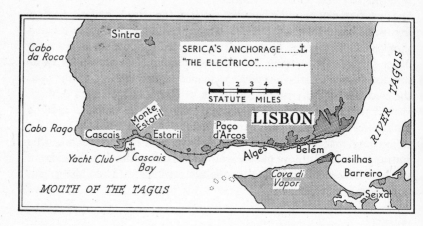

BARON OLEDO kissed the women's hands. One half of his face dwelt in permanent shadow, for it had been riddled with shot from a twelve-bore gun. My neighbour at the luncheon table told me that the baron was a great sportsman, and president of this and that. He was a slender man, carefully dressed in dark town clothes cut after the English manner. "Extremely wealthy," my neighbour whispered, "a dead shot, walks or climbs tirelessly all day, and is one of the finest horsemen in Europe. A private life without blemish. To show you how very admirable the baron is, he remains on terms of the closest friendship with the Conde de X" (the man who accidentally shot the baron in the face). "The Conde de X., another capital fellow, is apt when shooting to prolong his swing."

The baron was silent, speaking only when spoken to, and then in a voice so muted that not a vestige of sound carried across the table. He did not participate when the talk, becoming general, turned to royalty. The Kings of Italy, Spain, and Rumania, all of whom happened at that time to be staying in Estoril, were discussed. We could not help wondering why, with nearly half the world to choose from, the Kings should choose Estoril. Had their choices been made for practical reasons?

110

Had Estoril merely seemed a safe, or clean, or respectable place to live in? I had always tended to take the romantic view of those beings who see their first dawns in palaces, imagining that they would scorn the unimportant comforts with which the middle classes pad their existences; I had evoked for myself an idea of royalty which seemed to suggest that if a king were stripped of all but his title, his past, and a comfortable income, he would prefer life on a barge, or on a farm, or in a cave, to life in a convenient villa set in a row with its garage alongside, and new shops in frigid clusters, travel agencies, banks, at the corner of the well-drained, thoroughly-washed, electrically-lit street. It would seem that I was wrong, and that the deposed king chooses the trivialities, the golf, the card tables of the middle classes.

We walked to the Concurso Hypico, which was staged near Alasdair's house. Many jumps had been fitted into the narrow rectangle. The riding master—cylindrical hat and baggy breeches—carried a leather cutting whip in his hand, and the tan was making his brown boots dirty. He was the centre: all those nags, all those cavalry officers, yes, even the King and Queen, had been organised by him. For he was not only a riding master, no sir! he was a colonel who had fought in Spain during the civil war. Yes, although he was Portuguese he had felt impelled to have a pot at those "Reds" (the swine!). A great horseman, he was not riding that day, only seeing that things happened in their proper order. His eye continually darted to the small raised box draped with scarlet cloth in which the King and Queen (the Count and Countess of Barcelona) were taking their seats, looking, as kings and queens generally do, very much like anybody else, but more composed. We sat in a bigger structure, a grandstand for relatives or friends of competitors (and for any others who had the strength to push their way in).

Apart from Helen, a picture of practical Anglo-Saxon beauty, the civilian competitors were showily and flimsily clothed. This one wore a tweed coat and a white stock with a diamond pin in it; that one eye-blistering scarlet and a stock loose at the ends and blowing in the north wind. The cavalry officers looked like bus-conductors. A Russian woman in a golden shirt and golden breeches stood behind us, commenting on the performers. She damned every horse; this one was mad, mad! that one would never face timber—a worm! the one over there was hopelessly unsound—a dropped stifle, fit only for the knacker. If there was a refusal at any fence the animal was spurred into turning pirouettes and then was flogged by the rider over the head, always the head. The

Russian behind us would cry then: "The whip! that's right!" After such treatment the horse usually faced the obstacle, preferring any supposed risk to further persuasiveness from the beast on his back.

Helen's stallion, Belshazzar, had either enjoyed too liberal a ration of oats, or, as stallions do, he was allowing his mind to stray down voluptuous paths. Although he got round the course he performed in an offhand manner, doing most of his jumping between fences, and going through the fences as often as over them. At the end of this spectacular exhibition he bit a gelding on the neck, and was led away trumpeting. The King and Queen were going to a cocktail party at the riding school and Helen had promised to help there with the drinks, but Alasdair thought it was about tea-time, so we returned with him to the house and drank tea with solemnity and pleasure, eating Scotch scones (baked by a Portuguese) with fresh butter and strawberry jam from Essex. Later Alasdair drove us to the riding school. The crowd was disintegrating from the bar in the corner of the balcony. The King and Queen had already gone and Baron Oledo, taking his leave, was kissing hands by the score. Portuguese, Russian, French, Hungarian, Spanish hands flew to his lips like butterflies; but the hands of English and American women had to be pulled up with swift jerks, much more exciting work.

*          *          *          *

Sailing on the Tagus. . . .

We spent the early morning hours cleaning the boat and marketing. At 10.30 a.m. we saw our party approaching in the club tender. They were six, and we had expected only three. They disposed themselves and their bags, towels, bathing costumes, and smoking apparatus about the cockpit and the decks. Accustomed to sailing with but one companion, I felt that the yacht would turn over and deposit us in the sea; but it showed no such inclination. We motored demurely up the glassy Tagus.

Alasdair issued loud orders—occasionally reminding me that I was the captain and must run my own ship and tell them all what to do. (I had no wish to be captain; I never have any such wish.) We were to lunch and bathe in the Cova di Vapor, an anchorage praised by Tagus yachtsmen (though not by Alasdair, who thinks the Tagus pretty poor cruising water compared with the Clyde, and I suppose he is right). As we approached the cove there was a breath of wind. Alasdair took the tiller and we sailed in on the rising tide until our keel touched the soft, shelving sand. The cove was marred by a grouping of tarry shacks, and by a long iron quay. A few boats were moored at the inner end, but our deep keel would not allow us to get near them. Alasdair was the first ashore in a perfectly legal black bathing costume (in Portugal it is a punishable offence for a man to bare his chest in public) and a soft hat. He stalked alone round the edge of the water, a magnificent and proud figure occasionally pompomming a few bars of Gilbert and Sullivan. The others swam hard to keep out the water's icy chill. Down in the galley Isabel and I cooked, nearly swooning in the heat, and envying the bathers.

Somebody shouted that the north wind was rising. Somebody? Alasdair of course. "*Now* we're going to have a sail," he cried. "And the sooner we clear out of here the better, for we're nearly aground on a lee shore."

We sailed very fast up-river. The tide was still with us. The nice English girl from Stockholm steered ably, weaving in and out of the shipping. Mara, a Hungarian, lay in the saloon. Her small daughter lay on the floor beside her. When I went below to try to make them comfortable they asked why the boat was leaning over in such a peculiar manner. Mara's fine dark eyes were staring, staring at the deckhead, and her long fingers damply clutched at a handkerchief.

The north wind came sizzling from the hot hills, from Lisbon, rising, a back-drop of indeterminate architecture, pale blue shadows, tawny surfaces, from the waterfront with its trumpeting derricks, from the piazza known to the English colony as Black Horse Square (and to the Portuguese as Plaza de Commercio).

The shipping on the wide river was impressive. Dark barges with painted beaks, slender jibs, and great loose-footed mainsails with short, curved gaffs, lovely sails made of flax that was the colour of a pigeon's downy breast. Grey warships, destroyers and corvettes. Here and there a visiting steam yacht. Alasdair knew the English yachts, and he hailed them as we fled past. The Portuguese freighters lay turning to the current, almost-new motor ships from the yards of the Clyde and the Tyne. Portugal, rich in sterling from war profits, had placed big orders in the British shipyards, hoping to become again one of the leading maritime nations. But the balance of trade was shivering, pale, uneasy, and bipartisan, so the new ships, the beauties, lay empty, swinging to anchor on the Tagus while they longed to track the great oceans, and we, a white butterfly, slid past them unfettered (though I cannot say un-affected) by the balance of Portuguese and other trades.

Our temples ached and our skins crackled while the hot, heavy wind rushed eddying round our bodies.

We put about and sailed downstream, breasting the three-knot incoming tide for the first half-hour. Helen was now at the tiller of the far-heeled yacht. She stood, a splendid figure, steadying herself with a white cotton tiller line, and steering with her bare knee. Alasdair offered advice from time to time, for he, being an old inhabitant, knew every landmark before he could see it. The north wind, since the shadows were lengthening, increased in strength. Had we reefed we should have sailed faster and drier, but reefing with all those people on board and under the expert scrutiny of Alasdair did not appeal to me.

We sailed into the heart of Cascais Bay forty-five minutes earlier than Alasdair had prognosticated off Black Horse Square. When I went forward to unlash the anchor the deck was almost vertical. The jib came down, the anchor cable rattled out, the mainsail shivered as it divided the powerful wind. The guests departed, and I was left to dry the sails, bag them, clear the decks, collect the things that people had forgotten, hang up the anchor light, stream the dinghy. Isabel was at work below decks. My skin was burning. I was very tired. The yacht seemed still to be whispering, as though all those people, even the brave and silent Hungarian, had left whispering ghosts behind them. . . .

*     *     *     *

Skunderthorpe boarded the *electrico* at Cascais, having driven there in a racing car from his quinta somewhere in the hills. He was dressed as usual in desert boots, dark trousers, and a rather seedy linen coat. From his excited manner, the emphasis of his gestures, we deduced that he had been on the tiles the night before. His eyes neither smouldered nor sparkled; they *burned*, they flamed, in crucibles of acid and pitch. His voice rasped with an unnatural loudness. He filled the sedate carriage with his account of the experiences of the night, an account full of gaps and sudden laughter.

"Had a business disappointment yesterday afternoon. Just failed to bring off a deal. So called on Robert and had a few with him at the Vim do Mundo—always a fatal move. All Lisbon was there (floor space twelve foot square) including the English dancing girls from the Casino, who arrived with a nasty bit of work, a Brazilian. A few of the livelier parties present, Yanks I believe, threw the Brazilian out. Then we all went on to Palm Beach and stayed there till five this morning, when there was a bit of a schemozzle because the band suddenly decided to stop working. . . ."

All the sunblinds were down over the windows on the southern side of the carriage, the river side. The morning was blisteringly hot. Pale palm trees whisked past the windows on the landward side, palms, villas, quarries, level-crossings, forts. We had gone first class because the train was crowded. Overdressed elderly women with purple beards and black gloves were going to Lisbon to play cards. They trembled amusingly to the shake of the train. They eyed our party closely but without concupiscence. (Lust on a Portuguese countenance is usually frank.) How delightful was the *electrico*! we never tired of it. And that morning we had the agreeable sensation of being carried to Lisbon and far beyond at somebody else's volition. Skunderthorpe's volition; the outing was his idea. Even in his alcoholic frénésie he exuded confidence. A delightful fellow. I admire alcoholics, and intend to be one myself some day.

At the Lisbon terminus we waited on a tessellated pavement for the English girl who was to complete our party. She was tall, thin, and exquisitely dressed. Skunderthorpe is the type of man who is meticulous about having equal numbers of the opposite sexes on any planned occasion. He bundled us into the ferry that crossed the Tagus to Casilhas, telling us exactly where we must sit on the upper deck. In all the long years that I had known him I had often been surprised at his successes in the business world, but now, feeling the warmth of his planning around me, basking in the friendship I had done so little to deserve, I recognised his genius. A car waited at Casilhas with newspapers hung over windscreen and windows to keep out the hot sun. Skunderthorpe darted off "to buy cigarettes" and I saw him toss a glassful of beer into the fiery aperture of his gullet. After an extremely long and hot drive that was made tolerable by the inextinguishable vitality of our leader, and by two stops to sample wine at estaminets, we arrived at our destination, the quinta of Giorgio, a house containing every modern convenience and—much more important—every unmodern convenience. Giorgio was making gin in the cellar, surrounded by oak casks each holding more than a thousand litres. Two menservants, white cotton gloves held in dark, hairy hands, hovered behind him, unable to understand why he wanted to make the gin himself. Giorgio's daughter rode into the dining-room, clattering on the red-tiled floor. A boy with bare feet came to take the horse away. The horse was called Jupiter. Before lunch we were offered drinks under a vine pergola. Skunderthorpe, now that luncheon was at hand, the arid spaces of the morning nearly past, looked younger, cheerfully handsome with his dark head, short black beard, and long, wagging nose. He asked for beer to begin with, and followed the beer with dry Martinis. Poulet-en-casserole and other good things were provided for lunch. It was very hot outside the house. The dogs lay panting on the tiles at the barred edges of the sunlight.

We were going to bathe. . . . The horse Jupiter again entered the dining-room, saddled, bridled, and wearing a straw hat of the Mexican type, with two holes cut in it for his ears. The English girl also wore a Mexican hat (bought in Cannes). They put her on Jupiter with a towel to protect her knees from the hot saddle. We set out to walk to the beach, pausing to admire Giorgio's stack of wine bottles, all clean and glistening, a stack as big as a ten-ton hayrick. Giorgio picked two big water-melons out of the melon patch. The earth was like brown face-powder, serrated with dry ditches, tormented by hoes, a rich man's farm in Portugal. We climbed a ridge, the seaward lip of the Portuguese saucer. At the top, Giorgio launched one of his melons down the slope; the polished green ball broke into pink fragments. The horse devoured all that we did not eat. Before us lay the sea. Giorgio said that the sea was sucking away the land, but that the land was not valuable enough to matter. We were warned not to go out of our depths because of the currents. The sea was warm, entirely different from the water in the Tagus, not many miles to the north. There was a persistent current pulling to the south (a current that has its counterpart in many of us northerners). The horse Jupiter also bathed. He scooped water over himself in the shallows and then waded through the rollers until he stood with only head, neck, and wither above the highest crests. But when he emerged he looked very bad-tempered. He lay down on the sand with a groan, his coat steaming, his damp straw hat on one side. Giorgio organised cricket with a home-made bat. I discovered, neither jubilantly nor otherwise, that Isabel played cricket well, and I remembered that she had had a childhood not unlike my own. When we had eaten the second water-melon, we began the hot trek back to the quinta. I walked on ahead with Giorgio. We were followed by his daughter, riding Jupiter. The other three were soon lost behind.

Piloto Eugenio, a decent man full of unselfishness
(see page 168)

"Milk?...Cheese?..."
Joachin Fernão de Silva and Isabel go shopping at MILFONTES
(see page 164)

Giorgio began to speak of Piccadilly. He said that the prostitutes should be cleared from the London streets, that if prostitution was inevitable it would be more seemly to have brothels. He was angry and serious about the matter, even when I suggested that English women were so accommodating and accomplished that there was little call for prostitution in London except to cater for strangers and for a few men with odd desires. "It's no joke," Giorgio insisted. "All those women with their death masks!"

The powdery earth burned my bare feet. Near the front door of the quinta Giorgio showed me a wine cask filled to the brim with cold water. Climbing in, I sank my head down, down, expelling the air from my lungs. A tea-coloured world, floating in a tub between earth and sky. Suddenly weak and sleepy, I sat on the doorstep, listening to the cicadas. Giorgio's pretty daughter brought me mulberries from the tree. Her two coloured birds were making love on their stand below the pergola. A baby white turkey pecked gently at my toes.

Skunderthorpe arrived with Isabel and the English girl, dusty and weary. Skunderthorpe had been carrying all the bathing things and the cricket bat. Feeling tired, he had put his load on the back of the ass an old woman was driving home from the beach. Following in the steps of the donkey, they had lost their way, and had walked three miles instead of one. They climbed into the tub, one after the other. I was glad I had been first.

After nearly causing us to miss the ferry-boat from Casilhas while he gave us beers in a café, Skunderthorpe persuaded us to drink more beer in the station at Lisbon. We healthy ones were pleasantly exhausted by the fresh air, salt water, and sun, but the fires were still banked in Skunderthorpe, generating energy, forbidding relaxation. He wanted to take us all to the feira at Algés, to have dinner "and then a stab at the sideshows". The young Englishwoman went with him, but we remained on the train until it reached Cascais. A north wind was raging, and we had difficulty in rowing out to the yacht. But once there all was so lonely and clean and cool that we were well satisfied with our choice, and happy at so fine an ending to a memorable day.

*     *     *     *

We anchored off the yacht harbour at Belém, and Nelson climbed aboard from his dinghy, clutching his chest, for one of his lungs was temporarily deflated and was extremely painful. His wife, Irene,

14                             E

followed. Nelson, an important business man, is a member of the
British colony, knowing Portugal as well as his own country, and
thoroughly loyal to both. A powerful swimmer, he had deflated his lung
only a week or two earlier by diving into the river and swimming at top
speed in that cold water. He wore a yachting cap, shirt, khaki shorts,
and had the appearance of a genial Captain Kettle. He piloted us (he is
one of the most enthusiastic and expert of the Tagus yachtsmen) to
Seixal, pointing out on the way a hundred sights: the factory Alasdair
once owned; the ferry-boats; the new ships that sail away for months
and come back laden with Arctic codfish to be dried and made into the
bacalhao of which the Portuguese are so fond. We stole into the creek
leading to Seixal. It was morning, and the breeze was feathery. Irene,
full of poetry and music, asked us if we did not think Seixal was like a
French village. We agreed a little doubtfully. There was a strong whiff
from the cod factory. A big dredger was pumping sand. Hundreds of
acres of mud banks sewn with oyster shells rose from the sludgy, copper-
coloured water. Nelson advised me, since there was no room to swing,
to let out only three fathoms of cable.

While we were below, eating lunch, I felt a slight jar, and pushing my
head out through the hatch, soon saw what had happened to us. The
rising tide had held us stern on to the wind, but the wind, strengthening,
had pushed us, bows first, down the creek. The jar had been the signal
that our anchor had fished one of the massive mooring chains of the
sand dredger. We appeared to be firmly caught. Nelson hailed the
captain of the dredger, and that worthy was rowed over to us by two of
his crew. The captain was in shirt-sleeves, braces, soft hat, checked
trousers, and open-work shoes. His chivalry took our breath away.

"We'll move the dredger," he said at once.

Nelson, in his admirably polished Portuguese, began to apologise on
behalf of all of us, but the captain cut him short.

"With a few hours of work we can move the dredger," he said,
"whereas if we don't move you'll either have to cut or slip your cable,
or stay here, possibly for days. Don't worry!"

The dredger was moored with six anchors laid out across the creek
and with several hawsers to points on the land. It was also attached by
giant bolted flanges to the pipe through which it pumped sand ashore.
The crew were already beginning to uncouple the flanges when, using
every trick I have learned about freeing an anchor from an encumbrance,
I gradually began to work our anchor along the chain, and finally set us

free. There were cheers and counter-cheers from both vessels; Nelson made a handsome speech of thanks to the captain, and seemed pleased when I told him how dumbfounded I had been by the captain's kindness to strangers, a kindness that we never saw surpassed in any other place or country.

After an afternoon of sailing we dropped them at Belém. Nelson had done far too much work himself, considering the state of his lung, and had been full of nautical cries such as "lee-oh!", sounds that we can never encompass and that make us want to laugh. By contrast Irene was calm and untechnical. We enjoyed their company.

The north wind grew so strong on our return down-river to Cascais that I furled the mainsail and sailed on with No. 2 jib alone. With that one sail *Serica* went well enough to edge fairly close to the wind up to her anchorage.

We were both in bed and asleep when shouts outside drew me quickly into the cockpit. It was a black night, and the yacht was digging her nose into a hard chop. The north wind was blowing furiously. Two men in a rowing-boat were hanging on to our accommodation ladder, and before I could see who they were, one climbed aboard. It was Skunderthorpe, his arms full of packages and bottles. He told the fisherman to go away and return in half an hour, but it seemed to me unlikely that the man would have either the strength or the will to return. I pulled Skunderthorpe below, for he was swaying dangerously on deck.

"A stormy passage," he kept saying. "A stormy passage, and the trouble was I was none too sober. Never mind; I'll have steadied down for the return."

He had brought two bottles of red wine with him, a paper bag of sliced smoked ham, and a bag of enormous and juicy prawns. When we had eaten and drunk I began to make up a berth in the saloon.

"What on earth are you scuffling about with those beastly blankets for?" Skunderthorpe said, as though the sight of them annoyed him. (I believe he is one of those men who have a constitutional hatred for beds; certainly he will go to any lengths of invention or expense to avoid going to bed.)

"You're marooned here for the night," I explained. "The fisherman won't face another journey like the last, and it wouldn't be safe to take you in our dinghy, for the wind might blow us right out to sea or the dinghy might swamp. You must make the best of it."

"Have you any whisky?"

"No. Brandy or gin, though."

"I don't like brandy, dangerous stuff, and it's too late for gin," he said despondently. "I've bored you long enough. I'm going ashore."

"How?" I asked. "Listen to the wind. You'd much better stay the night here, and we're delighted to have you on board."

"Look here, George," he said, raising his voice and looking me straight in the eye in the most Kiplingesque manner imaginable, "I . . . am . . . going . . . ashore . . . now. I won't be put off by a drop of wind," he added. "I'll swim."

"Don't be silly. We're a long way from the beach, it's a head wind, and you know how infernally cold the water is. You'd have cramp before you were half-way there."

Our argument became furious. Isabel rose from her bed and added her pleas to mine. Skunderthorpe was enjoying himself; his black beard stabbed from side to side, his eyes flamed redly. At last he said he would listen to no more arguments. He rose, shook hands with both of us, and removed his linen coat. I followed him up on deck to see what he would do. The scene was very wild. The north wind was boisterous and the yacht was yawing in it. Skunderthorpe walked unsteadily to the bows, and began to climb over the rail. I caught him by the shoulders and hauled him back. I had no idea how he swam, but it would have taken a powerful (and sober) swimmer to reach the shore that night. We struggled for a while on the deck. He was a much stronger man than I, but I had the advantage of knowing intimately the complicated and lively surface upon which we fought. At length he was still.

"Look here," he said. "Aren't you making rather an ass of yourself? You can't hold me here all night, you know. At this moment I'm regrouping my forces, and at some not undistant point in time I'll leap from your arms and disappear into the sea."

"How's your swimming?" I asked.

"Pretty putrid."

"Then I tell you what I'll do, I'll try to get you ashore in the dinghy, but you must promise to sit absolutely still, and balance as well as your cargo of alcohol allows."

"Land-ho!" he yelled, and followed me aft. I put sculls, rowlocks, and bailer in the dinghy, and lowered myself in carefully. Isabel helped Skunderthorpe from the deck. He did his best, and the luck of the drunk was on his side. After some terrible wobblings and a good deal of water-shipping, he was sitting facing me. Then began my ordeal. I could not hope to pull straight into the wind, but thought I might manage the trip to the nearest beach, the small, central one, by rowing in two diagonals, the first taking me into the lee of the cliffs. Four or five times I had to bail. I could not let Skunderthorpe do it, for each time he moved we shipped water. He encouraged me by singing a dreadful song (for such he called it) in which each refrain ended with the words: "Follow up, follow up, follow up, follow up, follow *UP!*" We were within thirty yards of the beach when that which I had feared happened. Skunderthorpe swayed to one side. Over we went, and both of us were spluttering in the water. I had hold of both sculls, and rowlocks and bailer were tied to the boat. I swam, pushing the dinghy, while Skunderthorpe, singing no longer, splashed alongside me. He helped me to haul the dinghy up on the sand and we climbed the steps to the street, which was busy and fairly well lit.

"Come and have a drink," he said. Water was spouting from the point of his beard and his black hair hung over his bony face. When I made my excuses he shook my hand, and apologised most charmingly for all the trouble he had given us. His hand was warm and his voice steady, though my teeth were chattering, and I could scarce open my jaws to speak. I watched him stroll up the street, a two-legged watering cart, and enter the prosperous portals of the Vim do Mundo. I could not think that, in his unusually damp condition, even he would be welcome in that intimate bar. I would dearly have loved to watch his entry, but I had neither the courage nor the stamina. The row back seemed childishly easy, and Isabel was glad to see me.

*          *          *          *

"My dear, you must on no account do that," Mrs. Luke said.

"Why not?" Isabel asked. She had made up her mind (a singularly unwavering one) to see a Portuguese bull-fight, and there was to be a bull-fight that evening in Setubal, some miles to the south and, from our point of view, on the wrong side of the Tagus.

"Because we don't travel in Portuguese buses. Thé *electrico* to Lisbon is all right. But don't risk the buses. . . ." She walked with us to the station, still telling us that we were mad, and when she returned to her own cool house she immediately telephoned her friends about our trip. We walked very, very slowly. An excursion in the heat demands control of will and muscles. No movement must be brusque. The leather seats of the *electrico* were burning. I took off my coat and my tie, and sat forward to prevent a wet patch from forming on my shirt. The drawn blinds were like sun-penetrated eyelids.

Having landed from the ferry at Casilhas, we walked slowly to the line of buses drawn up beyond the fruit stalls, and found that we could reserve seats in what looked to be a hygienic and speedy vehicle. There was time to have lunch in a big restaurant with several storeys over-looking the Tagus. The floors were tiled, the tables close-set in ranks, the waiters overworked. The central figure at one neighbouring table was a female child with a festered mouth, an evil disposition, doting parents, an exhausted nursemaid. Our other neighbours were two loving couples, like four barrage balloons joined in pairs, and a middle-aged chaperone, a powdered vulture. We managed to persuade the waiter to bring us melon (melão), grilled sardines, salad, fruit, and white wine, before it was time to catch our bus. (The sardines were something of a triumph, for Lisbon restaurants do not often include them on the menu, holding them to be common fishes, and the staple diet of the working classes; also, by the summer of 1949 sardines were becoming scarce, since they showed signs of leaving Portuguese waters for the coasts of Africa, having, it was said, had about enough of being fished up in their billions, interred in cans, and resurrected in hors d'œuvres.)

The atmosphere in the bus trembled with heat. However, it cooled perceptibly as the driver engaged his gears and attacked the road. We travelled at great speed. The passengers, doped by the heat, allowed their heads to loll forward, and awoke from time to time with jerks.

Setubal, though only some twenty kilometres to the south, is in-finitely more southern than Lisbon or Cascais. The houses contrive to have a more enigmatic appearance, for they are flatter-fronted, scorning the subterfugical decoration of heavy moulding, more drawn into their shadowed selves, balconied, shuttered. By contrast the cafés overflow copiously with tables, chairs, and relays of waiters, to the pavements. The sea front is bare and quiet. Men were crying in the streets and cafés that they could (and would) sell tickets for the bull-fight, but an old man in uniform saw us listening to those cries, and guided us to the official ticket office, where we obtained without difficulty (despite warnings to the contrary before we had left our base) two sombra seats for the market price of seventy escudos (then 14s.) each. As we could find no vacant table in or outside any of the cafés, we went to the Club Naval de Setubal, which proved to be a lucky choice. The Club Naval, as it was then called, was club, hotel, and restaurant combined. There we washed away the dust of our journey and refreshed ourselves with *foie-gras* sandwiches and iced white wine in a shuttered room, lulled by the peaceful dronings of flies and the noises of the street, faintly percolating in. We wakened the waiter to pay our score.

Walking very slowly to the bull-ring, we just kept pace with a turgid current of pedestrians. Women and children stood in their doorways watching the passing flow. The bull-ring, a somewhat shoddy arena, is at the top of a rise dominating the town. As we took our seats and bought cushions the shade crept round the amphitheatre to cover us soothingly just before the opening fanfare, which ushered in the procession led by two of the great mounted bull-fighters of Portugal, Nuncio and Simon de Varga. They wore medieval costume, Nuncio in a silk coat of hard blue colour, the other in hard green; three-cornered hats plumed with ostrich feathers; white breeches fitting so close as to outline the reproductive organs (something that would be frowned on in the British hunting field); high riding boots reaching above the knee, with long, silver spurs. The stirrups box-shaped, of black patent leather decorated with silver. Both rode admirable barb stallions, handy animals standing about 15.3, showy yet so docile in the hands of the masters that they danced tangoes and waltzes, walked backwards on hinds alone, and curtsied. This remarkable exhibition won mild applause. Simon de Varga took the first bull. He rode long, sitting close in his heavy saddle, controlling the stallion with his legs, a short banderilla appearing from the lace that drooped over his right hand. Man and horse enticed the bull to charge, the man with teasing gestures of the banderilla and small mocking sounds, the horse with snorts, tosses of the head, and beckoning pawings of a forefoot. At the last moment of the charge the horse darted to one side, the rider planting the banderilla. When he had done this three times Simon knotted his reins and let them lie on the stallion's crest. He took a banderilla in each hand, galloped round the bull in narrowing circles, and when the maddened animal charged, both banderillas were planted simultaneously.

Eight men dressed as rogues now entered the arena. They wore woollen hats made like old-fashioned night-caps for men, voluminous white shirts, scarlet breeches, thick white stockings. While they had been near us, awaiting their turn, the air had smelled of brandy. They formed up in a tight row, back to front, and the line orientated at the bull, so that he saw only the front man. When the bull charged, this man, who had his hands clasped in the small of his back, whipped them round, took one horn under either armpit, clamped his chest to the heaving poll, and gripped the bull round the gullet. The other seven flung themselves on the animal, the heaviest man running round to seize the tail. When they had immobilised him they let him go. Two more men in approximately the same costume drove a bunch of steers with belled necks into the arena. When these inferior animals had run round a few times they ran out, the bull in their midst, for at Portuguese bull-fights the bulls are not killed. The second horsed bull-fighter, Nuncio, was less lucky with his bull, but being the darling of the crowd his every movement was lustily applauded with voice and hand and whistle and flying hat. The third bull was taken by a Mexican matador, a slender young man with an Indian face, who fought orthodoxly, on foot. He was brave, if a little clumsy. The fourth man on the bill, a Portuguese, was big, bold-looking, and very bad. The crowd yelled at him ever more jeeringly until he had been goaded into such a rage that he could make no attempt to do his work.

During the interval an Englishwoman picked her way round the terraces to give us an invitation to dine with Mrs. Gainsborough; she had been told of our "plight" at Setubal by the friend in Cascais who had gone to the telephone after we caught the *electrico*. The crowd drank lemonade from small bottles peddled by boys, ate chocolate-coated ice-cream, or relieved itself in the dark tunnels through which we should presently have to pass to the comparatively bull-less outer world. Policemen crowded every corner and passage whence they might see the ring (for they could enter without paying a cent).

The second half seemed long-drawn to us. Nuncio's horse (a fresh one) was slightly gored in the flank and became bull-shy, but the artist on his back managed to coax him near enough to plant all the banderillas. The crowd threw more than a hundred hats into the ring. The Mexican Indian became drunk with danger, took great and yet greater risks, and received as many hats as the great Nuncio. The Portuguese matador, feeling that he had much to emulate as well as his past failure to atone, stood up before us and indicated with grandiloquent gesture that he, and not the agile youths who darted on long, thin, white-stockinged legs across the red, watered sand, would plant the first banderillas. Perhaps that had, in the days of his youthful slimness, been his speciality. But alas! he had grown too ponderous and too conceited. When he had made several lumbering runs (what a footman he would have made! his calves were tremendous) without getting near the bull, one of the boys, alarmed by the menacing howls of the now tired crowd, leaped in and planted the banderillas with the cruel ease of youth. The matador was again blinded by his own rage. At the bull's first charge down went the beautiful big man, and lay a motionless hulk, shamming dead, while the bull pricked him, snorted over him, booted him, and then (to the jeering applause of the crowd) left him as trash.

Two friends from the British Embassy in Lisbon drove us in their car through darkening country to the quinta of the Gainsboroughs. We came to the gates, spear-shaped uprights pleasingly awry and standing dramatically against the grey-black night clouds. A guard or servant opened the gates and we drove into the estate with its lagoons and its thick foliage. Gainsborough himself came from the house and led us in. He was dressed as though for the south of France, and indeed the night was overpoweringly hot, and the smell of water was heady in the air. I remember a shaded, wonderfully comfortable house, with an American voice and English voices. I remember that it was difficult to move my face, which was held in a plaster cast of fine dust that no ordinary washing could remove. I remember with deep gratitude how we were fed and entertained after the hot excursion of the day. Gainsborough, putting us on the last ferry across the Tagus, advised us to travel on the top deck for the view, which was indeed lavish, all purple water and golden lights. We caught the last train to Cascais, and did not see the yacht until 2.30 a.m., when we carried the dinghy down the slipway of the Club Naval. *Serica* looked lonely and fragile, far out there on the sea. It was a good night, with less wind than usual, and all the fishing-boats were working. Several miles off Ponta da Salmodo we saw a line of dots. That was the broody motor fishing-boat, *Morro Peixe*, with her string of ducklings.

E*

# CHAPTER 12

## HIBERNATION

EARLY on a cold, wet Monday in February the alarm clock roused us. I pushed my feet into clammy rubber boots in the stone-paved hall, and, wearing a coat over my dressing-gown, groped my way to the stables. Roosky Lad, the big gelding, rose as I entered from his nest in the warm straw. He is a horse who likes his box, and knows how to be comfortable provided the humans play their reasonable part. He roared for his breakfast. The brown mare, Prudence, whinnied in a cracked and wheezy voice. *Our* breakfast was ready when I got back to bed.

At 7.30 a.m. Isabel and I were both in the stable. The big horse arched his shining, mouse-coloured neck, and nipped at me when the body brush pressed over the ticklish parts of his skin. Occasionally, knowing it to be a hunting morning, he would swing back one forefoot and swing it forward to crash into the side of his box. In the next box old Prudence stood impassive while Isabel groomed her.

The meet was at Frome Whitfield, near Dorchester (Hardy's Dorchester), that morning, and we had decided that Isabel would go on by car while I rode Roosky Lad and led Prudence, because we feared that the long hack of eleven miles in addition to a hard day's hunting might overstrain the mare.

Before 9 a.m. I was in the saddle, my whip tied across my back, wearing a raincoat that I would discard at the meet. The rain-clouds showed signs of thinning; their blackness was already mottled with pale grey. The horses, still digesting their breakfast, and feeling the chill of the morning after their warm rugs and the dry stable, were uneasy in their movements, now skittering forward, now drooping along, stumbling, or pretending to stumble, on the rough surface of the drive. The elms drenched all three of us as we crunched under their knotted black branches.

Osbert Buckle, a local groom, waited for me by the Eagle Gates, a wet figure draped over one wet horse and leading another. His bowler hat dripped rainwater and his coat collar was turned up high so that only a small segment of pink, chilled face showed between hat-brim and collar. He was then new to the country, and I was to act as his pilot to the meet. At that time I did not know Osbert, and he was not then the lusty fellow he has since become, with the names of all coverts, hills, and hamlets, all farms, farmers, and subscribers to the hunt, listed in his head and his muscles trimmed by grooming, exercising, and digging, from the autumn to the spring, and harvesting in the summer. I noticed at once, however, that here was a manly fellow who did not spoil the morning with too much talk. He fell in behind me with his charges, and after exchanging a few remarks about the filthiness of the morning, the scenting possibilities of the day, and the distance to the meet, we rode on steadily with plenty of opportunity to look around us. Before Bramblecombe Farm, a dark series of buildings pushing backwards into a fold of the downs, we turned into the fields, steering south through a series of gates familiar to me and to Roosky Lad, who was capable of opening these obstacles unaided. Prudence, feeling turf under foot, wanted to scamper on, but he, sagacious animal, still ruminated over his breakfast; an occasional clap of mellow thunder from his vast inside signalled the processes of digestion, while he watched carefully where he placed his feet among the rabbit holes, and also noted which route across country we were taking, deciding, no doubt, where the meet was likely to be that day. So we creaked and jogged and walked across the bare countryside, horses and riders, noting here a gap that had been wired up by its owning farmer, here a new gate, and here a hunt jump with its sliprail and T-shaped lower section. The rain began to overflow the brim of my tall hat, and wetness found its way through the knees of my breeches and between my neck and my stock. Cheselbourne village appeared below us on our right, the church slightly aloof, its massive square tower overdominating the nave. We crossed the tarmacadam Puddletown-Cheselbourne road, and the big horse suddenly cantered on to leap the ford, while the mare beside us, unused to his tricks, splashed through. We worked our way up the stiff hill beyond, hoofs slipping on the wet clay of the track, and found ourselves in a sudden shaft of white daylight looking southward over the downs. The foxhunter is always looking into the past. Now, as I saw the downs, lovely in their spread of waxy, teapot-brown plough and pale, bristling stubble, I longed to see them turned back again to the folds of turf kept healthy by flocks of sheep. . . . We remarked that the day was warming up, and opened our steaming raincoats. I remember reflecting that I was lucky to be there, on my strong horse, and happy to be there. Hacking to the meet need not be the least enjoyable movement in the symphony of the foxhunter's day.

"Hold up, 'oss!" Osbert exclaimed as he fumbled with his pipe and tobacco pouch. To the keen scent of the damp winter's morning was now added that of burning nut-brown shag. We advanced down a "drove", a narrow track with cut-and-laid hedges on either side leading over a wide stretch of country unsullied by traffic. The droves were the old tracks for pack ponies, and at one time were much used by the smugglers of Dorsetshire. With the great expanse of farming during and after the second German war, and the cultivation and enclosure of what were formerly sheep downs, the droves were again proving their usefulness. The surface of our drove was of grass and clover churned to mud in places by the fat tyres of tractors or the chisel-like feet of cattle. The four horses stepped out freely, as delighted as we that the day had cleared. Sometimes Roosky Lad, an amorous beast (probably gelded too late), would press his nose against the jaw or neck of the led mare, leaving a trace of soapy foam on her skin. I looked down at the muscles sliding in his neck and shoulder, felt the thrust of loin and quarter, the lift of pastern and thigh, and thought of all the pleasure he had given me. By contrast the mare, Prudence, was almost a stranger, for she had been loaned to Isabel by a friend who had married a naval officer in the hunting season, and had had to follow her husband to a region where there was no foxhunting. Prudence, an aged mare standing under fifteen hands, was a good performer, keen and clever, though we were a little uncertain about the soundness of her forefeet.

Down into the hollow by Doles Hill Plantation we rode, passed through mud and under the leafy arcade on the lower edge of the wood, and then, taking the overgrown drove (which put many scratches on the surface of my hat) leading behind Bourne Farm, worked our way over to the Piddlehinton-Dorchester road, a road "hard as steel and surfaced with glass". We walked on steadily. It was 10 a.m., and we had covered nearly seven miles of our journey.

"They was telling me you were away last summer on a sailing-boat, sir," Osbert said, knocking out his pipe on his boot. "I've never done any of that myself. Are you and Mrs. Millar for abroad again this summer?"

"We'll be off in the early spring. We left our boat at Lisbon."

"Not before the end of the (hunting) season, then, sir?"

"No."

"And where would you be going from Portugal?"

"To the Mediterranean."

"I saw Naples during the war," Osbert observed. "It was a fairly crumby place. Rome seemed a bit better, but they whistled us past there quickly. . . . How d'you manage to leave a boat in Portugal?"

"We left it in a yacht dock, and I pay a Portuguese sailor a pound a week (that's quite a lot of money there) to wet the decks every day and look after the warps and anchors when the weather's bad, as it has been lately."

"Will there be any boat left when you get out there again?"

"We think so. The Portuguese are honest people."

"Are they now?" Osbert said. "They're not like the Eyeties then. . . . How much further, sir?"

"Another two miles on this road and then a mile of private road. We'd better jog on. . . ."

"If you don't mind, sir. I wouldn't like to keep Mr. Dick waiting."

Isabel was waiting for us at the edge of the crowd of horses, dismounted riders, grooms, and foot followers.

"He means to draw Pigeon House first," she said, when she was in the saddle.

"The wind's south-west; a good run downwind from there would take us somewhere near home." (An advantage of hacking one's own horse to and from hunting is that in addition to the pleasures, varieties, and excitements of the hunt itself, the day develops into an interesting lottery—"Where shall I end up? Will it be near my stable? or shall I have a ten-mile hack with a tired horse, perhaps in the darkness?")

Now the field moved off, a field of about fifty men and women, the majority of the men prosperous farmers in black coats and hunting-caps, most of them well-mounted and eager to go. Soon a fox, ruddy and mysterious, was away from the Pigeon House covert, and among us all was bustle and scramble.

The strange thing about my present (and possibly lasting) absorption in foxhunting is that when I was a boy I hunted for a good many seasons (in another country, it is true) without greatly enjoying it, but then, after an interval of some sixteen years, hunting imprisoned me in a net of pleasure and longing from which I hope I shall never escape so long as foxhunting exists and I can throw a leg over some kind of a horse.

This fox ran strongly downwind. We were hard put to it to stay with hounds, for that is a hilly country and there were bottle-necks at fences and hunt jumps. Where there was turf it was springy, and my big horse pounded on, much more sagacious than his excited and scarlet-faced rider. After a couple of welcome checks, the fox turned upwind towards Dorchester. Isabel had been ahead of me to this point, but her mare was less strong on the hills than the big horse, and she was behind me as we galloped south. They hunted him right into the back gardens of Dorchester, and viewed him negotiating the hen-runs where, doubtless, he had often prowled by night and reconnoitred by day. Draggled, but still full of heart, he turned from the town and us and made off down-wind, through pastures holding flocks of fat, square-shaped sheep. Hounds found the line fouled, and while the huntsman made his cast we stopped on a knoll, and I slid off Roosky to ease him. Steam rose thickly from us.

The admiral rode up to me.

"Have you seen Isabel?" he asked. "She was down at that post and rails where we crossed the lane soon after the turn upwind."

"Was she all right?"

"Yes, I thought so," the admiral answered, watching hounds carefully, and ready to be off any second, "but there's Liza Mann. I saw her catching Isabel's mare, and she should be able to tell us all about it."

Mrs. Mann was reassuring. She said that the mare had apparently failed to rise at a solid rail, and that horse and rider had come down on the far side.

"I asked Mrs. Millar if she was hurt," she said, "and she said she was perfectly all right, and begged me to go on. So I did. The last I saw of her she was standing beside the mare, holding her."

"Then I wonder where she is," I said.

"Perhaps she can't find us, or more likely she discovered that the mare was lame, and decided to go home."

Our talk was interrupted because hounds were on the line again and running. Three hours later Mrs. Dent from Godmanstone came up on her husband's big bay.

"I've been looking for you for hours," she said. "I'm afraid Isabel's been hurt, but she should be all right now. She was in a car when I last saw her, and she asked me to tell you that her mare had been taken to Higher Burton Farm. She won't be able to ride home. I think it's her arm. . . ."

We were then at the edge of a covert above Piddlehinton. I was on a tired horse, and Higher Burton Farm was a good many miles away across-country. Thinking that Isabel would already be at home, I decided to hack straight there and make other arrangements about Prudence. It was raining again. The cold drizzle of early morning had returned. We splashed back through the droves, the horse jogging along happily enough, knowing his head was toward his stable, with its thick, dry bed of wheat straw, its hay net, its rugs, its chilled water, and its warm linseed mash. I made him walk up and down hills. He started at every sound, for his nerves, like mine, were strung up. At long last, in the darkness, we clumped through the gates. Mrs. Gilroy came running out when she heard the hoofs to tell me that Isabel was waiting for me at the Manor House in Midford Pastures. Leaving the horse rugged and feeding, I got the car and drove the seven miles to Midford Pastures, still in my wet clothes and muddy boots and spurs.

She was lying on a sofa in the morning-room when I arrived, and our friends, Robert and Ann Scott, were sitting with her. Shortly before my arrival the doctor had examined her, and she had fainted. Robert and I carried her carefully to the car. When we got home I had to carry her up the spiral staircase—no easy matter, for one of her legs was stretched out straight and was hurting even more than her obviously broken arm. The doctor had given her morphia and a sleeping draught. Before the merciful drugs floated her away down the dark moonshine canal of sleep she told me how she had found herself with a broken arm and a useless leg standing in the middle of a bare bit of country holding a restive horse and listening to the receding music of hounds, the dying note of the horn. Then some friends had materialised in a car.

The following morning I fetched Prudence (lame in both forefeet) from Higher Burton Farm, and then drove Isabel to Sherborne Hospital. Her leg was only bruised and jarred, but her left forearm and wrist were badly smashed, and she came out of the hospital with that forearm encased in a formidable lump of white plaster. When the season was ending and the point-to-points beginning, we turned our horses out on the hill, and departed for Portugal with her arm still in plaster and still painful.

# CHAPTER 13

## BELÉM ELEGANTE

WE landed at Lisbon on Monday, May 1st, 1950, after a fast passage from Southampton in smooth weather that suddenly grew remarkably hotter and brighter on the second day out. How droll it was to see the Tagus from the wide teak decks of the liner, to see Irene Nelson's house nestling (there could be no other word for it) in its bougainvillæa, to see the mast of *Serica*, which was tall enough to show over the warehouses separating the yacht dock of Belém from the quay at which our leviathan had berthed! A great many people had assembled on the quay below us, and many were known to us at least by sight.

I looked down on them with feelings of joy spiced with mild apprehension, for we had the Customs to negotiate and many organisational details concerning *Serica* were tramping, trotting, darting, through my mind. We had not failed to think of the yacht during the winter, and much correspondence had flown between Dorset and Portugal on her account. Alasdair—I could see him below there, splendid as ever, in grey flannel, the usual Jermyn-Street hat, exquisite brown shoes (St. James's? Burlington Arcade? Dover Street? Oxford Street?)—had very kindly organised the antifouling of the yacht in February. He and the sailor, João, with three other men, had propped her on the grid at one end of the yacht dock, and (between tides) had given her two coats of Kobe Green. All the movable gear and furniture of the yacht had been stored with Alasdair in Estoril, and, because he was himself returning to Britain for the months of summer sport, he had taken the trouble to move the gear in about six Hispano-Suiza loads to his cousin's house in the Rua Sacramento da Lapa. When we (later) went to collect the gear we found it to be in immaculate condition, and beautifully packed. Dear Alasdair! I suspected that his opening remarks would be as pointed as his conduct in our absence had been kind, and I was not deceived. He greeted us in a fashion that from anyone else might have seemed surly, saying: "*Well!* It's about time you two showed up, I must say; and God knows what kind of a state you're going to think your yacht's in. . . . I've got all the gear safe and

dry in my cousin's house, sails included; and while we're on that subject
I may as well say that I couldn't follow your august wishes and send the
sails off to be treated (this isn't England or Scotland, you know), but I
washed them all with my own lily-white hands and the garage hose-
pipe on my own lawn, and there were some infernal black spots on them
that wouldn't come out even with petrol. . . ."

We were shunted away from the other passengers and taken to a long
shed where, beside the resplendent baggage of a Spanish ambassador
"in transit", our uncouth collection of kit-bags was labelled "Re-
Exportation".

João, who had been having words with Alasdair over the state in
which that perfectionist had found *Serica* shortly before our arrival,
greeted us warily, and ferried out our baggage to *Serica* while the fiscal
policeman stood by to see that everything really was "re-exported". I
gave the policeman a reward of ten escudos, and that operation was
satisfactorily over, thanks to the unobtrusive help we had had from
several of our English friends in Portugal.

My first intention had been to fit *Serica* out completely at Belém and
start the second leg of our voyage in proper trim. Quantities of gear had
been prepared to my orders by the yacht yard at Lymington, and had
been packed in three stout cases. I had sent lists of the contents (paints,
hanks, ropes, steel wire, canvas, etc.) to the Portuguese authorities, but
it seemed likely that I would be charged heavy duty, and even if yacht
stores of that quality had been obtainable in Portugal, I could not afford
to lay out foreign currency on them. Alasdair had settled our minds on
this matter not long before we sailed for Lisbon.

"There are so many difficulties with the Portuguese Customs," he
wrote, "that if I were you I would seriously consider doing the minimum
in Portugal, and fitting out in a seamanlike manner when you get to
Gibraltar. You should blow down to Gib. in two or three days with so
fast a craft," he added characteristically, "and there I'm sure you'll find
the best of workmanship and materials, and you'll be allowed to pay for
them with your own money, in sterling."

Remembering the prevalence of the north wind (the "Portuguese
Trades") I had agreed with him that it would be easy to make a swift
passage to Gibraltar.

\*      \*      \*      \*

In the first flash of recognition poor *Serica* after her winter à la belle étoile looked small, naked, and dirty. She had been jolted about, for although Belém is fairly well sheltered, the gales on the Portuguese coasts in the early months of 1950 were unusually severe. Her white topsides were stained with oil and covered with dirty grazes. Her deck was suspiciously dark, although the last words we had exchanged with João had been employed in extracting from him a promise that he would wash down or wet the deck twice each day that we were absent. But we had no time to look at the yacht, for we had promised to go to the house of a friend in the Embassy, and later to dine with Nelson and Irene.

Almost straight from the wilds of the English countryside, where, except in the hunting field, we seldom see or speak to anybody but each other, we found ourselves for two hours with many beautiful and at least superficially amusing people—Frenchwomen, Danes, Norwegians, Dutchmen, Swedes, Belgians, Spaniards, Portuguese, English men and women, and Americans of the cosmopolitan sort with military or diplomatic titles, longish hair, and some tolerance for Europe. I do not know if any of those people would have deserted that type of house, with its flowers, its painted walls, its careful pictures, for the discomforts that we had chosen for ourselves. . . . After dining with the Nelsons, who already seemed old friends, we walked to the dock and rowed ourselves out to the yacht in one of Nelson's dinghies (which he had kindly loaned us until our own should be ready for the water). Alasdair had described *Serica's* interior as "filthy". The cabins were a little dusty, but João had scrubbed the floors, and the yacht had been well aired. I had to clear a space, moving much baggage and the charging motor, before we could get to bed. Isabel, being one-armed, could not help with such work except with skilful advice (for any situation calling for clearing and organisation challenges one of the most potent sides of her nature as inevitably as it discourages me).

Early next morning we put on denims and set to work. The interior of the boat after months of absence seemed constricted and unfamiliar. It was a day of bruises from corners that had been forgotten.

João had told us that the pumps from the fresh-water tank would not work. . . . I spent most of that day dismantling the teak floors, unbolting the manhole covers and examining the tank, which I found to be clean and sweet. (The pumps sucked air because João had not put in enough water to cover the outlets.) At midday, agreeably tired, we went in search of a restaurant (a more testing search than might be imagined, since Belém, on the industrial outskirts of Lisbon, is no tourist centre, and Portugal is not profusely restauranted like France). But in the Restaurante Belém Elegante we struck gold. It was a small place, and unpretentious. The white panelling, Empire style, had been inlaid with tier upon tier of shelves holding bottles of wines, vermouths, brandies, sugared liqueurs, gins and whiskies. A glazed partition separated the restaurant from a bar, and the former was furnished with some ten tables, a wash-basin with a towel and a pear-shaped glass holding liquid soap.

At the table nearest the wash-basin sat a stout young man, who rose ponderously to his feet, and asked in English if he might translate the menu for us. There was no need, for we had previously fathomed such mysteries as may exist in the Portuguese orthography, and the dark waiter at the Elegante was a Spaniard, but we accepted his offer politely, and he then said he would sit with us and smoke a cigarette. He intended to improve his English. Following the grammar-book layout, his talk was of material things presented in short, sharp sentences (although he did tell us that he had been to Rome with his mother, and had there had audience of the Pope—and while some might call *that* material too, I know that most people would put it in the spiritual credits column).

Despite the young smoker's presence, and his watchful examination of every forkload raised from the plates to our molars and incisors, lunch was a great success, partly because we both were tired and hungry, partly because after seven months in England followed by a few days of the anæsthetised, refrigerated, woolly food of an ocean liner, the Portuguese food, and particularly that in Belém Elegante, tasted robustly excellent.

Rested, fed, and more adjusted to our surroundings, we walked out into the brightness of a Portuguese spring day, an astonishing brightness in which everything seemed to dance (after the half-lights and shadows of winter Dorset), and an astonishing warmth, too, for arriving by good fortune at the end of a period of rain and cold weather, we had stepped into a week of heat and unpercolated sunshine.

By the next morning the yacht was becoming serene below decks, thanks to Isabel's hard work. I left her polishing the floors with her feet wrapped in cloths, and went myself to the Rua Sacramento da Lapa because Alasdair had offered to bring some of our gear to the yacht if I would help him to load the car. I had promised to arrive punctually at 8 a.m. I did arrive punctually, and followed the old, grumbling maid upstairs to the salon. It is an ancient house, utterly delightful, looking out through shutters into a secretive street of embassies and chancelleries. The salons run, with uninterrupted sheen of parquet, through double doors into the dining-room. Seeing Alasdair at the breakfast table, I moved across the intervening parquet towards him, but as I approached he rose from the table and shut the double doors in my face. For a moment I stood there. Through the doors I heard the clink of china as he continued with his breakfast, alone. I went downstairs, chuckling, to the room where our gear was stored. There *are* some men who set great value on "having their breakfast in peace". When Alasdair joined me, some ten minutes later (he had been at the toast-and-marmalade stage when I so nearly interrupted him), neither of us referred to our earlier glimpse of each other. Helen appeared with her whip, and dressed for her last ride on the stallion. I managed to get all the sails and the navigational instruments into the back of their car, and travelled to the dock sitting in front with them.

\*     \*     \*     \*

A little boy with a strong Scots accent swam out to the yacht while I was at work on the running rigging. I gave him about one-third of my attention, and allowed him to babble, and romp freely over the boat. He was a hardy specimen, aged about nine, and well-travelled in the wake of his father, who, he explained, was an engineer. After a while, finding the child's flow of questions oppressive, I rowed him ashore and exchanged a few words with his father, a gaunt young man who said that he was on the point of returning to his native town, Glasgow, for a holiday. "But they tell me it's hard to get whisky in Glasgow now," he said. "Is that the truth? There's plenty of whisky here, though it's an awful like price. The thing that's cheap here is their vinho, but that's poison; so long as you keep clear of that you're all right. . . ."

\*     \*     \*     \*

We had settled into our fitting-out rhythm, were enjoying ourselves, and were working well . . . 6 a.m., tea with lemon; 12.30 p.m., lunch at Belém Elegante; 5 p.m., tea with lemon; 9.30 p.m., Nescafé without milk (there were no cows at hand); then bed. After three days of this régime I was in good health, and quite recovered from the liverishness induced by life on a big ship with nothing to do but fatten myself and kill time.

João turned up on Thursday morning, saying he had come to clean out our water tanks. Isabel told him (he could not understand my vile Spanish-cum-Portuguese) that he was three days too late, but gave him plenty of work to do, and from that moment we got on famously with João, who, having overcome his mistrust of us had decided that we were harmlessly insane, and proved himself to be useful.

Isabel now had nothing further to do below decks, so I landed her with brushes, paints, and all the rusty objects on board such as petrol cans and Primuses. She painted happily all morning, sitting on the sun-drenched quay, her sleeves rolled up and her plastered arm resting in its sling (a horse's tail-bandage). João and I (he up the mast in the bosun's chair) completed the work on the rigging.

The stout young drawback to the Restaurante Belém Elegante found himself in a dither that morning because while he was sitting with us another English couple entered the restaurant. At length he asked if we would excuse him for a few minutes while he translated the menu for them ("This is sheep with butter sauce, beans, and brains; this is pig cooked on the fire; and this is the feet of small cows with cabbages . . ."). He then settled himself on them like a large bluebottle, savouring their vocabularies, which were unusually extensive. I liked the look of them. . . . The man had long fuzzy hair and a brown linen hat. He and his young wife both carried haversacks. When the bluebottle had buzzed himself away to the cake shop at the corner we spoke to his latest victims, and invited them down to the boat. They were adventurous people, and had come to Portugal intending to spend a month there and then hitch-hike back to England across Spain and France. They lived in a caravan near Oxford, and they were both (understandably) doubtful if they could forgo for so long a holiday the pleasures and delights of Oxfordshire in the summer-time. When we had shown them what there is to see on a small boat like *Serica* the man asked me straight out if we would take them both with us to Gibraltar. He seemed to understand my halting and shamefaced refusal. I felt myself to be a selfish fraud as I stumbled and fumbled with the truth. There are times when English is a devilishly awkward language.

By that evening I had bent on the mainsail, and had overhauled and stowed all the other sails. Only two small problems remained to worry us: the wire of our handrails was red with rust, and had to be discarded; and the Portuguese mechanic who had overhauled the engine just prior to our arrival had had the bad sense to use the long brass handle of the bilge pump as a hammer, and in so doing had dislodged from it the protruding tooth that engaged in a socket and revolved the pump—that most vital part of our equipment. Three times that day the fool had taken the handle away, and three times when I tried it the tooth he had braised in refused to stay in place. As for the handrails, I had always hated the things anyway, and would have liked to do without them, but Isabel, who remained at the tiller while I went forward alone and sometimes feared that I would be washed overboard, did not share my low opinion of their usefulness, and in any event, as she pointed out, the boat looked silly with the stanchions sticking up and no rail.

Next morning I improvised rails, using, instead of wire, manilla rope that had formerly been on our main halyards and had been discarded as unsound. The rope looked well, but otherwise proved to be a most unsatisfactory substitute as it continually had to be tightened. I took, from the neighbouring Shell depot, supplies of petrol and high-grade paraffin. Those who go abroad with paraffin-operated refrigerators must beware of using the paraffin sold in ordinary shops (even when the vendor claims indignantly that it is the best American kerosene). English paraffin (like most simple things, if the truth be admitted) is of higher quality than that sold for domestic consumption on the Continent unless the purchaser takes the trouble to seek out the extra-refined product. I took four gallons, which would, I calculated, give the refrigerator an ample reserve until I could tap English stocks at Gibraltar. The Electrolux people in England had sold me a new burner for the refrigerator, and this burner was already proving its superiority. The hammering mechanic had not returned the pump handle. Otherwise we should have left Belém that morning, but at least his negligence gave us one last opportunity for eating in Belém Elegante.

The bluebottle, alas! was there in his corner by the wash-basin, and was hurrying through his *flan* (caramel custard, the only sweet offered by the Elegante, and very good too) in order to join us. We were sick of him and his smoke, which he blew into our faces as we ate, and then scooped away from under our noses with two-handed gestures that made us blink. On this occasion he went too far, for when he had dropped a pile of ash on the clean tablecloth he put a cigarette-end into the salad bowl. (Incidentally, the lettuce at that time in Portugal was the best I have ever seen or eaten.) Isabel was goaded by these performances into asking him if he would smoke *after* we had eaten. He agreed humbly, and, afraid that we had hurt his feelings, we abased ourselves before him in a welter of politenesses which he was quick to take advantage of. He said that since this was our last day (the Spanish waiter had betrayed us to him) he would ask for the afternoon off, would borrow his cousin's Dodge, and would drive us round Estoril. We swiftly counter-attacked over Estoril. He was chagrined by our remarks, but agreed rather stiffly that Estoril was perhaps a little cosmopolitan, and not very Portuguese. Then he said he would take us to the Coach Museum, which is just across the street from the Elegante. We owe him a debt of gratitude. The Coach Museum is fascinating, and lets one see how much beauty and elegance has been sacrificed to the internal combustion engine. They were comfortable, the old lumbering coaches, their massive, bending springs so sensitive that a finger on the door-handle set the creation of paint and gilt and plate-glass and velvet bobbing between its four great wheels. The Portuguese coaches shown are florid; the French graceful and with the most chastely seductive upholstery; the Spanish sinister, of squarish shape and with panels of dark leather outlined with brass nailheads; and the English models light and rakish by comparison with any others, and although in themselves so lovely, searching forward, it would seem, into the age of speed, gadgets, and unmitigated vulgarity. At the door of the museum we said good-bye to the stout vocabularian, and I wish him well wherever he may be. Sometimes even now I think of him lunching at Belém Elegante, eating his pork (he loved pork) and his *flan*, and then waddling to the pastellaria at the corner for his cup of coffee and two or three sugared cakes. He must already, God save the mark! be more rotund than when we, and the Pope, last laid eyes on him.

From the museum we boarded another fascinating coach, one of the older trams of Lisbon, an open-sided vehicle, deliciously prim in its stiff cast-iron curves fabricated in an America still influenced by the graces of Victorian England. Even the electric-light bulbs and holders were show pieces. These trams are swiftly being replaced by more "stream-styled" models, for it is the belief of the New World that everything from a washing machine to a street car should be manufactured to look as though it will travel at 100 miles per hour, a domestic comet all a-glisten with chromium—and Portugal, determined to be up-to-date, will gladly lap up new uglinesses. The afternoon excursion (successful in that I managed to buy from a chandler a 1950 edition of the British *Admiralty Tide Tables*), ended at the quiet house in the Rua Sacramento da Lapa. Alasdair and Helen had sailed for England and the rumble of their departure still hung in that fragile ambiance, while the old lady lay ill in bed upstairs and the maids slid over the tiles and the parquet in their rope-soled, heel-less slippers. There is a garden behind the house. The beds were spilling over with rampant geraniums, sweet-scented stocks, and thickets of sweet peas. In one corner, by the dripping water tap, a dog's grave with a black Celtic cross and the name CARLO. The dog had been cremated, but it had seemed kinder to bury his ashes in an urn than to scatter them in the peaceful Lisbon garden where he had died.

*　　　*　　　*　　　*

On Saturday, the sixth day after our arrival, we began to set *Serica* free. The six days had passed like six minutes.

Belém Dock is in the form of a rectangle, and *Serica* had been moored at one of the shorter ends, with forty fathoms of her own cable out to her own C.Q.R. No fewer than four other yachts had subsequently been moored with their cables over hers, so, as can readily be imagined, we had much work to do in getting our anchor. All dodges had to be tried: slacking other yachts' chains; bouncing the bows; getting warps under other chains by manpower (João's and mine) or by submerging a wooden bucket; unshackling our own cable inboard and passing it through. . . . When all that had been done we had missed our tide. Indeed the morning and part of the afternoon had gone by. I was annoyed by the sight of our excellent chain all rusty from its long immersion, for I had hoped that the boat would lie on a mooring through the winter. The foredeck was covered with rust stains and mud, and my person was in a similar condition. I paid off João after we had dropped the C.Q.R. again, outside the harbour mouth and with strong old Tagus pulsing under us. There was no wind, and we judged it best to wait for the ebb and the north wind that would surely come in the evening. João offered to wash down and to help with the sails, but we knew that he had other work to do, and firmly said good-bye. We were glad to be out of the dock, agreeable though it is of its kind, and to feel the surge of the river after the dead water inside.

That evening, with the turn of the tide, the wind came very strongly. We fairly hurtled towards the sea with the mainsail double-reefed and the smallest jib. Once past the Tower of Belém, in the open reach, we began to take spray, and had to put on oilskins. So fast did we travel that we kept our place ahead of a 3,000-ton freighter that was close

astern of us at Belém. It was cold in the cockpit and the scene was grey
and brutal. The pace was too hot for an inaugural sail. We were glad,
after little more than an hour's reaching, to beat up into Cascais Bay.
It was getting dark, but our landmarks (so familiar) were distinct
enough, particularly the white strip of the Club Naval. We anchored
close in to the smallest beach and, although it was late, put ashore in the
dinghy to see our friend the secretary. But we met with grave disappointment, for he was no longer at the club, and nobody could say
where he had gone. We hoped that he was in Berlin, because we knew
that was where he would want to be (at any rate until he got there). We
decided to telephone Skunderthorpe, and invite him to dine with us at
Casa Laura. But the maître d'hotel at the quinta told us that his master
had flown to the Argentine on business. We rowed back to *Serica* and
put extra blankets on the bed, for the air was suddenly unaccountably
cold, rocking there on the edge of the open sea.

*       *       *       *

Then the north wind blew such a gale that for some days we were
stormbound, a concourse of shipping gathered in the bay, and the sea
rolled away from us, toppling, to the south. We attended a good many
hospitable entertainments which, however enjoyable they might be,
tired out Isabel, whose arm was still hurting, and reduced me to a jelly,
for roomfuls of people have that effect on me. One evening we met the
King and Queen of Spain, to whom the diplomats and then the rest of us
were presented in order of precedence, with bows and curtseys. Don
Juan, who still bears the stamp of our Royal Navy, discussed *Serica*
approvingly with me, and ended our talk with the (as they were to
prove) appropriate words: "If you meet a real levante in or near the
Straits of Gibraltar, don't beat into it; I've tried, and mark my words, it
never pays. . . ."

Turning from this breezy Royal advice, I enmeshed myself timorously
among the diplomats and ladies-in-waiting, a wooden cog in a purring
hum of steel. Trays of drinks floated round me, caught in this eddy or
that, trays of strawberries, of little pinky-winky shrimps protruding on
sticks from the sides of a baby marrow hollowed out and filled with the
stiffest of mayonnaise; trays of sausages, of caviare, of cucumber sandwiches. What should be done with the stick when shrimp or sausage has
been despatched? The duchess hid hers in the orchids. Young Thisby
used his as a toothpick. Lady Thatford walked right across the room,

hurled the stick out of the window, and returned to her conversational partner of that moment. The elderly German who had told me that you needed £4,000 a year these days to *exist* as an undergraduate at Oxford pushed stick after stick into his pocket.

Life aboard *Serica* was almost intolerable while the north wind so madly swept the deck. We spent our time ashore in the Lukes' house or on the small rockgirt beach nearest to *Serica*. The wind was too strong to allow us to row to the Club Naval, and since our friend the secretary had departed we did not feel inclined to go there. The small beach is, as I remarked before, the most chic of those at Cascais, but the bathing season had not begun, and there was nothing chic about it at the blustery beginning of that May. The striped parasols and the fatherly and motherly beach caretakers of the summer months were not in evidence. The purposes for which the people living in the old houses around used the beach, and especially its rocky fringes, were soon forcibly brought home to us, and we sometimes preferred to spend the whole day in the Lukes' house, either sitting in the tiled patio or in one of the dust-sheeted sitting-rooms. The owners were in Paris, and the old house was interestingly empty and sad. The housekeeper, an elderly woman whose husband was a Customs official up the coast at Guincho, occupied a bedroom on the ground floor, and it was necessary (since the main door from the patio was locked) to pass through the bedroom to reach the rooms upstairs. The housekeeper's husband was able to stay with her from time to time; his best uniform was suspended behind the door and a bottle of liquid vaseline for his hair stood on his wife's dressing-table. When the fascination of the picture became too strong for me, I would steal along the passages to the main bedroom of the house. Behind the bed hung a picture showing a Moor, all teeth and sinew, seizing in his arms a Circassian slave girl of a voluptuousness seldom, alas! achieved in life, and displaying an even rarer alarm at the prospect of her impending experience. . . . It was strange to sit in the hooded rooms and imagine them, later that summer, boisterous with the life that Emma Luke would bring to them. I could feel that the voices of the summer before still had their places in the air, and the wind licking through an open window would rustle the newspapers covering cushions or books, giving the illusion that somebody who had been there, and was supposed to have gone, was sitting with me, turning pages.

Our last evening was a sunny one, and was spent on the small beach. I was worried by the sea, for, as I pointed out to Isabel, although the

north wind had blown its hardest for five days, the swell was beginning
to roll in from the *south*, presaging, I surmised, a complete (and for us
disastrous) change of wind.

An old man ruminatively (Ah, another!) came down to the beach.
He shambled off to the rocks under a new, yellow villa (with a party
playing canasta on its terrace).

The Town Authority has built a new retaining wall round the back
of this beach, also a new series of steps, with a flat stone balustraded
coping down which the children slide all day long from a height of some
thirty feet. They sprinkle a little sand on the bare stone, then boys and
girls slide down, sometimes on their rumps, feet in air, sometimes on
their backs, sometimes on their bellies with arms outstretched like the
skeletons of wings. It is a dangerous sport, and sore on clothing. The
noise it makes is highly disagreeable.

Another man came down to the beach, and crossed to the rocks, a
strong, young man, known to us, the captain of the sardiner called
*Costa da Gale*, and a Setubalense with relations in Cascais. The captain
is quicker than the old man. Then he crosses the beach, and as he walks
sends out a cry that leaps the waters and electrifies all the men and the
boy and the dog on board the *Costa da Gale*. The boy jumps into the
long-boat bobbing astern, and rows for our beach, while the captain
poises himself on a rock, ready to leap.

How handsome the *Costa da Gale* is! A bright-blue hull with a
white line on the bulwarks to emphasise her sheer; two narrow white
rings round the top of the blue funnel; the foremast-cum-derrick
(stayed only on one side) painted a dull yellow ochre, and the main-
mast black with a white truck.

The captain makes his spring. He helps the boy with the heavy
oars, pushing with all his great body as the boy pulls, twisting his
thin back. The captain throws the boy up to the deck of the sardiner.
He tells ten men to haul the long-boat on deck, another ten to go
to the anchor warp. He himself enters the small wheelhouse forward
of the funnel. The throb of the engine is heard, a steady, pulsing,
solid beat, bop, bop, bop, bop, bop. . . . Forward, they haul swiftly
in unison, singing, and he gives two or three kicks ahead with the
engine to help them. The man leaning over the bow yells. The black
grapnel, eight feet long, has appeared with a cork anchor buoy attached
to one of the prongs (a seamanlike precaution). He who yelled has
thrown a noose over the grapnel, and now a smaller team hauls in

unison. Then full speed ahead, and *Costa da Gale* bustles out to sea, sliding her great beam diagonally in the swells, her black pomeranian barking, barking.

"They're off," I said to Isabel. "We'll leave at dawn."

CHAPTER 14

## THE UNFORESEEN

THE pilot boat, which we were accustomed to see at anchor a mile or two astern of us, had moved to lead up the Tagus a steely assortment of American men-of-war. They steamed in a slow queue, and we, sailing still slower (there was little wind, and that from the south), pierced their line. We were not yet unduly worried by the contrary wind, for we assured each other that it was fluky, and would soon give way to its opposite, the north wind that was to blow us down to Gibraltar "in two or three days". When we rounded Cape Espichel we turned east, planning to have lunch at anchor off Sesimbra, a lovely village set in the flanks of the Serra da Arrabida. A southerly swell was piling on the shallows. We anchored near a new breakwater behind which a few fishing-boats were lying in comfort. Isabel wanted to move into the shelter, and so did I, but our chart (according to my reading of it), indicated only three-quarters of a fathom there, and the water looked suspiciously bright and sandy. *Serica* pounded into the short seas as we had never heard her do before, and at high water I agreed to explore with the yacht behind the breakwater. We found three fathoms, so we stayed inside. Many of the sardiners moved from their exposed anchorage off the village to that more sheltered place, which soon became overcrowded. We passed the night disturbed by yells, laughter, and singing from the fishing-boats, by hissing acetylene flares, barking dogs, the bop-bopping of their engines, and the bumps they gave us. And as the night wore tediously through, the sea, increasing after more than twelve hours of south wind, began to curve round the jetty, catching us broadside. Then the noises from the other boats were as nothing to the splashes of our rolling.

At dawn we sailed out on a stiff mainsail breeze from the south. *Serica* was lively, and Isabel had difficulty in moving about safely with her injured arm. It was weather that demanded "one hand for the ship and one for yourself". We set course for the port of Setubal and had a rip-roaring sail, reaching for ten miles along an upright coastline with the colouring of a golden eagle.

145

We passed a white boat, high-ended and made from a hollowed-out log. It carried a brown, balanced lug amidships. An old man and a boy crouched aft behind what appeared to be a not very considerable cargo of brushwood, the man steering with an oar. This boat, which might have come out of the pre-Christian era, sailed like a fleet and frenzied ghost. We, in all the nobility of *Serica's* modern, shapely power, passed it when the helmsman was easing it through a squall, letting the sheet run through his fingers, but although we raced on until it was no more than a dancing white blob astern, it slipped, more ghostlike than ever, into the dock at Setubal soon after we had tied up. An hour later the pair, having disposed of their cargo, put off, and we watched them beat out across the lagoon and through the white, smoking walls of surf over the bar.

Setubal's lagoon is magnificent, and that day it was superlatively so, with the tawny water frothing in the wind and the tawny southern town veiled in dust and blown sand. We eschewed the small basin normally used by yachts, for it seemed to offer little shelter from the sea running in the lagoon, and we furled our sails to motor into the commercial dock, a narrow strip paralleling the water front, and with an entrance in the middle of the outer breakwater. We nosed around in there. The wind was gusty and there was barely *Serica's* length to turn between the double lines of moored vessels. At length we chose a berth among the river barges, sailing craft loaded with salt until the decks were nearly at water level. We lashed alongside one of them, putting out all our fenders, and taking warps in many directions.

The captain and owner of the barge to which we had secured introduced himself as José do Nascimento Paulino, from the town of Alcacer do Sals. Senhor Paulino made us free of the sardines he was grilling on deck (and there was certainly no shortage of salt, for he had about 100 tons of it lying within hand's grasp of the iron stove). As we were peckish after our sail, and knew by now the spirit of Portuguese hospitality, we made free with the sardines, and brought out one of our decanters of Clarete Sanghuinal. Another man, younger, Julio Luiz Rodriguez by name, took part in this feast, and later in good fellowship came aboard *Serica* to help straighten the tangle of warps on deck. When this was done we would fain have been quit of Rodriguez, but he stayed as though he considered himself to be our man for life, so saying good-bye to him we went off to the town, being ferried to the quay by Paulino's young assistant, Antonio Luiz Battista, a broth of a boy, barrel-shaped and chubbily handsome.

I led Isabel to one of the best restaurants in Portugal, and perhaps in Europe. It was the place where we had rested before going to the bull-fight, but now it seemed to have changed its name, calling itself Restaurante Naval Setubalense. What hors d'œuvres! they consisted of almost everything that comes fresh out of the sea, and other stamina-creating and piquant foods such as radishes, croquetas, and curried rice. Then we ate grilled red mullet with a thin lobster sauce, chateaubriand, haricots verts, strawberries.

Setubal is listed as the third town in Portugal. A very unusual place, it gives the impression that it was laid out to be of immense importance, and that the inhabitants then found a truer, less worldly, sense of values. The squares seem to be dissolving into sand. The sunken gardens are solariums and feast-chambers for lizards. The yellow churches are dreamlike structures compounded of sun and heat; their spiritual beauty does not go uncontradicted, for they are liberally counterpoised by barracks, prisons of the spirit and the flesh.

In the evening I stole out on deck to untwist the main halyards. Rodriguez, who had been watching us, at once came on board and tried to help. Flustered by his unwanted presence, I let the shackle go, and it sailed up to the masthead. I put Rodriguez in the bosun's chair, and hoisted him on the spinnaker halyard. He had to shin up the last ten feet of mast, pulling himself out of the chair, and although he did not like it at all, he accomplished it safely. I could not breathe until he was back on deck. The people around were laughing, but they would scarcely have laughed had they been as unsure as I was about the strength of the spinnaker halyard. While he was aloft I kept thinking that our teak deck would never recover if he fell and splashed blood all over it.

José do Nascimento Paulino visited us that night in a merry but lachrymose condition. He tried to persuade us to take the yacht up the Rio Sado, on the estuary of which Setubal lies. He would pilot us to his home, twenty-seven miles up-river. I wish now that we had gone, but at the time we did not feel inclined to expend petrol on the trip, and we found Paulino rather too much for us. He gave us three battered and greasy little pictures of She whom men call Our Lady, and told us with tears of his religiosity. His breath was pungent. But I believe his heart was good. From religion he turned swiftly to business discussions. His barge, and the others around us, some fifty in all, had come down the

Sado and were waiting for the ship that was to load their salt. Paulino had been waiting for fifteen days, and he was bitter about the financial loss thus incurred.

During the night an east wind of fearful strength began to batter us against Paulino's barge. He was unwakeable, but his barrel-shaped boyo turned out briskly and helped me to lay an anchor off the port quarter. This was most necessary, since with the change of wind a sea came slanting in at the harbour mouth and made us roll against our neighbour. By morning all our yacht fenders (some of which had been impeccable) were in pieces, and one of our bow warps had been sawn nearly through where it had chafed against a barge. Heavy rain curtained the lagoon with the east wind, but at dawn the wind dropped and veered back to the south, and the rain stopped. The bargees followed our example and part-hoisted their sails to dry them out. I was interested to see that the sails were well-shaped and in fair condition. The barges were cutter-rigged, and by no means under-canvased. Like their more magnificent cousins on the Thames, they were handled by small crews, usually a man and a boy.

The southerly weather continued. . . . After our fourth successive luncheon at the Restaurante Naval Setubalense we were finding the food too rich for our health, if not for our appetites, since at home in England our diet is from choice easily digestible and adequate rather than heavy. As we left the restaurant we chose to believe that we saw signs of the wind changing from south to west. Back on the yacht, we found that the barometer had risen sharply. That was enough. Paulino and Rodriguez were absent, but the stocky and humorous boy, Antonio, cast off our many warps with such vigour that in a moment we were hanging precariously on one of them.

We motored over the lagoon to the bar, which, in a passage only 260 yards wide, was marked by breakers of Grand National height, for the tide was ebbing with us against the wind. We crossed the bar in company with five sardiners of the Three Seas class, each with forty-two able-bodied men aboard. The big crews carried (the overall length of a Three Seas boat is about the same as that of *Serica*) constitute a danger, for to have so many individualists on so small a vessel militates against order and clear thinking.

The bar astern, Isabel turned to beat into the wind, which proved to be uncompromisingly from the south. We sailed our first long leg into the bight between Setubal and the Cape of Sines, punching into a steep

*left:*

"Antonio Luiz Battista—a broth of a boy" (see page 146). Note the improvised rope rail fitted to *SERICA* at LISBON

*right:*

José Cartillo Torrecillar— "reminded me of my dear Berger" (see page 181)

*above:*

The four at LARACHE.
SPANISH MOROCCO
—from left to right—
Mariano, Manolo, Julio
and José
(see page 184)

*right:*

Joachin and Isabel at
MILFONTES
(note Isabel's arm in
plaster)
(see page 164)

sea with spindrift flying off the tops. Darkness closed on us while we were still on that tack.

I was disturbed to find myself ill. I have never known seasickness, and my illness was surely occasioned by a surfeit of shell-fish and other rich foods. I tried to settle myself at the tiller and forget my body apart from drawing deep breaths of clean, wet air into it. But as the bitter night wore on I began to fear that something was seriously wrong with me, and to wonder what the devil we were to do. The sensible decision (I now realise) would have been to put back to Setubal, but neither of us even thought of putting back. Our progress was poor, for as the head seas grew steeper and the wind stronger I had to gather all my forces and tie in a reef. Isabel's plastered arm, soaked through and through with salt water, was causing her great pain, and she obviously could not sail the yacht one-handed in such weather. The only port (and that a dangerous one to enter) was Milfontes, and I knew that I could not hold out until we reached Milfontes because when I tumbled back into the cockpit after reefing I was soaked with sweat, yet my teeth were rattling in my head, and my hand shook so violently that I could scarcely keep it on the tiller.

We were now beating out to sea to clear the dangers off Cabo de Sines. I went below, rubbed myself down, changed my clothes, and drank some brandy. When I got on deck I was again miserably ill. I doubted if I should be half alive in the morning. . . . Somehow I managed it, and at dawn we scooted into Sines Bay, an admirable anchorage when the *north* wind blows, but in a south wind an unwholesome, not to say dangerous, lee shore. I drank a little more brandy to give me strength to lay out two anchors and to get the sails down and secured. We dropped near two sardiners lying off the town in four and a half fathoms, on sand. The chain of the bower anchor chose that of all mornings to leap off the windlass, and as the anchor bit and the yacht, rounding to wind and sea, put her weight on it, the chain ran wild with nothing but my weak self to arrest it. I stamped on it, I flung myself on it and was dragged along the watery deck to the bows. At last I secured a hold and yelled to Isabel. Braving a fall, she ran forward and took two turns round the chain with the end of a jib downhaul purchase. Then I was able to secure it properly. Our damage list at Sines was to be heavy, but here already was the first of it: two bruised knees, four bruised and skinned fingers, and one nail torn nearly off.

From the shelter of the doghouse I watched to see if we were dragging.

The movement was appalling, and the sea was certainly too fierce for our dinghy. Astern was the sickle of rock-bestrewn sandy beach and on the starboard beam were the walls of the small-boat harbour that unfortunately dries out. For an hour I was at peace, for I either dozed or lost consciousness. I came to with Isabel pulling at my sleeve. She made me go below. She herself was seasick, but much the stronger of the two.

Below was a dismal scene. The floors soaking, the berths soaking, the settees soaking, the galley adrip, the forecastle a haystack of wet clothing. I lay down thankfully on a squelching settee, put an aching head that felt eight times its normal size on a wet pillow, and pulled a wet blanket over body and face. But the yacht was snubbing. I went on deck and fixed a spring from both cables to the mast. Up there in the spray and wind I was seized by a fit of the shivers that seemed likely to shake the life out of me. I collapsed on the coach-roof and from there rolled to the deck. Isabel, with her one sound hand, dragged me to the cockpit. The two sardiners now got their anchors and motored round our counter, shouting to us that we should be in peril of shipwreck if we stayed there longer. They plunged off into the head sea. I watched our position carefully, and before they were out of sight thought I noticed an easing of the wind. Leaving Isabel on anchor watch in the dog-house, I lay down again below.

In the evening she roused me, saying that the weather had abated and the fishing-boats were returning. Determined to get me to a dry bed ashore, she had packed a small sail bag with clothes, books, and other necessities. We managed between us to launch the dinghy, and she helped me into it. She sat in the stern sheets and rowed with her one hand, while with both hands I just managed to pull the other scull. It was a long row, and the seas were still uncomfortable. Ill as I was, I could not help laughing at her, crouched there in her sodden reefer coat, her face pinched in, her hair wet around it, her bad arm in its ludicrous encasement held gingerly in front of her. Fishermen waved at us from the harbour, trying to make us understand that we must keep more out to sea because there was a current setting inshore across the entry. Safely within, we made for some steps. Two men lifted me out, a third lifted Isabel, another took the sail bag, another the dinghy, and there we were, standing dripping at the end of the breakwater in the middle of a gathering of two hundred fishermen. A policeman, who was on duty there, appeared to order a tall, unshaven fisherman to accompany us to an hotel (or the hotel). It was all that I could do to walk after him up the ramp and through the town. His feet, long and shapely, were bare. He padded ahead, carrying the sail bag and saying to all whom we met: "Now I am a porter!" Narrow streets, low white houses, cobbles.

"Bonito es," I said of Sines, hoping that I could slow his advance to suit my ebbing strength. He turned his dark, weather-stained face on me until I became hypnotically influenced by a small clearing in the forest, a bare patch on one side of the hairy chin, and I wondered if he were a good man or a bad one, and if he had ringworm.

He took us past the ugly new post office, past the Café Clemente, and so to a squat building like any other in the street save for its sign, *Pensão Clemente*.

Clemente met us at the door, a small, hunched man, grey-headed, with an apple of a face, and strong, clever hands dangling low. He had a quick way with him and a voice that was both husky and penetrating. We were to learn that the huskiness came from continual use, and not vain use either. We were taken to a bedroom, and I collapsed, the last of my strength gone with a gasp. When I came to I had been washed and put to bed. The room contained a double iron bed, a table incorporating a looking-glass, and a washing arrangement consisting of an enamel basin on a metal stand. The floor was of bare wood, the ceiling of painted wood; the walls, whitewashed, were criss-crossed with electric wires mounted on studs. I lay there in a high fever. The white room revolved around me. Night was the same as day. Rain beat on the pantiles outside the window, and sometimes the breezes from the south stirred the tender plants that grew among the tiles.

Isabel spent most of those hours flapping a Portuguese newspaper over me to keep the flies from settling to bite, but on the afternoon of the second day she went to the yacht to dry some of the wet bedding and to see how things were on board. She was rowed out from the harbour by the tall, unshaven man, who had constituted himself guardian of the yacht, and by his partner, a youth of lowering aspect. The two men left her alone on board, and while she worked there a strange man joined her, a man with a face flour-white, and with features continually on the move, like shifting sands. His face was not improved by his narrow tweed cap, which he wore with the scoop turned up. Unlike the other fishermen, he did not seem to understand her Spanish, and she did not understand him until she grasped that he was trying to speak Italian.

He hung over her while she worked in a manner that she at first found exasperating, and then alarming. She was desperately wondering how to be quit of him when she saw sculling slowly past *Serica* a young man with spectacles, a round head, an American leather jerkin, and canvas shoes (shoes were an unusual sight in that place). She had earlier seen him outside the Café Clemente, the stamping ground of the younger blades of Sines, for he had walked past her several times so that he might show off his knowledge of the English language (favourite phrase: "Don't mention it"). She invited him on board, and when he saw the man with the shifting features he angrily drove him away, screaming insults at him. Eduardo Luiz, the man in the shoes, then informed Isabel that she had spent the last hour with a lunatic.

She gave her new companion a glass of Madeira, and asked him to pump out the bilges, a task that she could not perform one-handed. When he had done it he was overcome by seasickness, and darted up on deck, where he stirred himself to get things ready for departure, deluging her with half-dried sheets, blankets, and clothing. He did not rest until he had jumped into his own rowing-boat, whose movement was more to his liking. He took her ashore, sculling from the stern with long, beautiful strokes of the flat oar. He spoke of the fishing industry, saying that, through the partial disappearance of the sardine shoals, it had fallen on hard times. The sardiner in which he had a share was "broken in the engine", and nobody could or would pay to have it repaired. They walked up the ramp to the town together, and passing the fountain Isabel heard a "Pssst!"

"My wife," Luiz explained, pointing to a black, hooded figure hurrying down the road overhead. "She fat now," he continued. "Have baby next month."

"Congratulations."

"Not good. Very bad, when boat is broken and no money," he answered sourly. He did not introduce his wife, a handsome woman. Isabel took her hand, and spoke to her in Spanish. The woman would not look at Isabel then, but later stole glances from behind and side-ways as she followed them up the streets like a well-trained and mute working dog.

On the third morning I determined to return to the boat although I was still fevered. When we got up at 4.30 a.m. I was doubtful if I would be able to leave. However, we packed the sail bag, put on our sailing clothes, and tiptoed from the dark hotel. (We had paid our bill the night before, and our burglarious exit was occasioned by the presence of sleeping men on the landings.)

The streets of Sines were not over-sweet, being impregnated with urine, but at that dark hour, and after my frowsty time in the Pensão, they smelled to me like the walks of paradise. I had not gone far, though, when I was overcome, and running to the battlements, I endured a prolonged and agonising attack of sickness. When I had in part recovered we walked down nearer to the yacht. *Serica* lay with all the cabin lights burning, and the anchor light hanging correctly on the forestay. We turned sadly for the Pensão, where I was just able to lever my body back on to the bed, moaning with relief. When the shops opened Isabel bought me another bottle of castor oil, and that day passed for me in the almost agreeable state of illness and fever that is part waking, part sleeping, part floating, part falling, part hope, part self-pity, part interest, part shame.

During the afternoon Isabel got the unshaven one and his partner to put her aboard. She told me when she returned that she had had the impression that the two fishermen were nervously watching her while she was in the saloon, as though they feared that she might discover some delinquency. We agreed that they had probably been drinking our wine. Shortly after she returned to the sickroom there was a knock. It was the unshaven fisherman, clutching the little chambermaid by the arm. The maid, he announced somewhat dramatically, knew where he lived, and he had commanded her that if there should be anything the Senhora wanted she (the maid) was to run instantly and fetch him.

Fifteen minutes later there was another knock. This time our visitors were the unshaven one, his dark-browed partner, and the English-speaking Eduardo Luiz. I looked at them out of my hot haze, and listened. . . .

EDUARDO LUIZ: These boys say they want money for two nights on boat.

ISABEL (going forward resolutely to the door as though to shield her sick husband): How much do they want?

E. LUIZ (after whispered promptings): Two hundred escudos. Fifty each boy each night.

ISABEL: Tell them to go away. They are disturbing my husband, who has a high fever.

E. LUIZ (after more prompting): Hundred and twenty?

ISABEL: They have destroyed any confidence we had in them.

E. LUIZ: I tell them.

ISABEL: The big man knows that I told him after he had pestered me (and Senhor Clemente can witness this, for he was present) that *he*, and he alone, might keep an eye on our boat. Tell the big man we know that he is fishing all night, and only his accomplice is aboard. Also tell them that we saw the yacht early this morning, and all the lights were burning, wasting the batteries. Tell them that, please.

E. LUIZ: Sure, I tell them.

ISABEL: Now I'm going to give them forty escudos between them, and if they come here again while my husband is ill they won't get another centavo.

They cheerfully took the money, a fifth of the extortionate sum they had demanded.

That night I was restless, and although I could not eat I accompanied Isabel to the dining-room, which Clemente had had decorated with three-ply panelling. The plates were turned upside down so that the sticky-legged flies might not walk on them. An enamel basin of potato soup with olive oil floating on the surface was brought to Isabel, then taken on its rounds. After the soup came a hodge-podge of fried fishes, then steaks, potatoes, and beans, then fruit. It was a heavy, and to me unappetising, meal, but I was diverted from the fatty smells by the behaviour of three commercial gentlemen who sat near us. One tucked his napkin into his throat. He was thin, decisive, small, and bossy, inclined to talk business, and he shot the victuals into his mouth with the knife rather than the fork. I believe he was one of the leading knife manipulators in the world (and I have watched many such experts), for he would cut his meat or fish up very small, and then either catapult each segment to its destination or jab it up with movements so rapid that the eye could scarcely follow the blade—and talking all the while. A remarkable performance. . . . His companion was of another type, and though probably the small man's inferior in business, he considered himself superior in life and etiquette. He (chevalier preux) allowed his napkin to lie across his knees, and let his tie, shirt, and coat, take their chances. He scorned his knife except as purveyor and conveyor to the fork. He talked more about the outside world than of office sales sheets and business wrangles. A dismal-looking cove. . . . At the neighbouring table was a little man all ringlets and crinkles, chubby, vulgar, and sure of himself. He talked much to the other two, although it was plain that neither of them liked him as well as I did. At the other side of the room a uniformed policeman was dining, and flirting with the comely waitress, who showed a grave interest in him, as in every man in the room. The policeman was somewhat put out by the arrival of two dusty travellers who climbed from a small Ford car outside the dining-room window and then entered, loudly demanding food and divesting themselves of Germanic outer garments made of black leather—two members of the International Police from Lisbon. When they had made some telephone calls they settled down to eat, champing philosophically at all that was set before them, and studying a map showing the roads leading to Lagos. Their sharp faces were frequently turned to look at us, but it was clear that they were after other game. . . . Later that night, lying sleepless, I heard a hubbub. The telephone rang again and again. Then the two International Policemen drove away in their little car.

Next morning, Friday, May 19th, we awoke to the dreaded noise of wind from the south. I assured Isabel that I needed fresh air, and at 5 a.m. we were standing on the ramparts. There was no light on *Serica*, not even a riding light. The sea was beginning to rise. Isabel said that at midnight she had dreamed that the yacht was in great danger.

I was convinced that if only I could breathe in enough salty air I should recover my lost strength, and I insisted on walking out of Sines on the Lagos road, mysterious and (while it passed between the grey-white and blue houses) Utrilloesque. Groups of dairy cows (resembling Ayrshires) were being herded to their grazing by men or boys, each with a crooked stick, a soft hat, a striped blanket folded over one shoulder, bare feet, a dark, unbelievably dirty face. The allowance (in that unfenced country) seemed to be one herd to three cows. The landscape opened before us, and the wheat crops, pale and heavy, stood against a background of baked red hills. We rested in a eucalyptus grove, but the stumps on which we sat were sodden with rain, and the wind was cold. Where the Lagos road runs into Sines, in the seedy Square of the Republic, there were banks of magnificent carnations, and in the gardens of those houses that bothered with flowers the waxy Madonna lilies grew in sophisticated profusion, like squads of slumming princesses.

I managed to eat one of Clemente's buttered rolls (we ordered bread, butter, and coffee for breakfast, but he was too canny to give us butter in a dish), and lay down again on the bed.

A boy came running with the message that our dinghy had been lost in an accident. We both hurried out. Eduardo Luiz shadowed us through the streets. There was silence as we walked downhill, past the men examining or repairing nets on the wall, to the sunken hole of a harbour where, as usual, there was a great gathering of fishermen. They closed round us. The unshaven man's partner (or accomplice) cleaved a way through until he stood before us. One glance at his face was enough to tell that he was drunk. He shouted at us. His story was that he had spent the night on *Serica* and that as he left the yacht in the morning the dinghy had turned over, spilling him into the sea. He had lost many belongings, and would expect us to pay for them.

"What time did this happen?" Isabel asked.

"Just before six, this morning."

"You are lying. My husband and I were watching the yacht from five till six. The sea was calm then, and there was no sign of anybody on board: nor was the dinghy to be seen."

The unshaven man now appeared, contriving to look very worried. He was sober. At my request he showed us the dinghy, which was intact, though it had survived a severe battering and scraping. He swore that he had the oars and rowlocks at his house, and that they were undamaged. His accomplice was still bellowing. I hated him with the hatred of the weak. I wanted to tear his throat out, to fling him on the stones and trample on his nose, to gouge out his inflamed eyes with my thumb-nails, to flog him with a jagged steel rope. But I had to keep all my energies for the task of regaining the hotel, where once more I fell panting on the bed, useless.

The drunk appeared almost immediately at our bedroom door, shouting for his "rights". We must pay for his clothes or he would have us jailed. Isabel walked straight at him.

"Get out of here, you sodden fool," she said in her aristocratic Spanish. "And don't dare to come back. Whine about your 'rights' to your own police or to the British Vice-Consul. Either will know what weight to put on your miserable lies. . . ." She slammed the door so that it struck him hard in the face.

Fifteen minutes later the maid brought us a note written on a dirty scrap of paper. "Please give something to the man who saved your boat," Isabel read. Clenching this missive in her one hand, she hurried below, and immediately I heard her voice in the street among the crowd of loafers outside the Café Clemente. Hammer and tongs she was assaulted by a drunken voice, one that we had not heard before, and hammer and tongs she replied. Little, stooped Clemente (God bless him!) darted out of one of his twin lairs to protect her. This time the protagonist was a man who claimed to have saved our dinghy at great risk to his person and damage to his clothes. Clemente was wonderful. With Isabel at his left shoulder he outshouted and outdamned the drunk, and drove him away down the sloping street.

After this scene Eduardo Luiz came stealing up to Isabel, and told her that both the men who now demanded money because of the dinghy's "accident" had been drinking until midnight in a bar beneath his house. It was his impression that they had then decided to go to the yacht to drink some more, and that as they were together leaving the beach in our dinghy they had overturned it.

Meanwhile the south wind was rising. From my bed I listened to it, and watched the trembling weeds lying flat on the roof-tops. At 10 a.m. Luiz knocked gently. Isabel, reading beside me, started up to the attack, but sat down when she saw it was he. Luiz said he was worried for the safety of the yacht. He had been to the harbour-master's office, and the barometer was not rising (which, according to him, was in our favour). Perhaps the south wind would ease; perhaps it would worsen. Any easement should be apparent by midday, any worsening by 2 p.m. But, he concluded, he had eyes in his head, and he would watch carefully. If the boat showed signs of dragging he would let us know at once.

*    *    *    *

Luiz knocked again at 1 p.m.
"Mas viento!"
Now we were for it. . . . I was still shivering. Isabel dressed me in three jerseys, two pairs of trousers, sea-boots, oilskin. We went to the harbour, Eduardo Luiz carrying our sail bag. I was beginning to feel better. Anything was preferable to waiting in that bedroom.

A quartermaster from the harbour office was there, a smart uniform in the centre of a wild crowd, their voices dulled by the clamour of sea and wind. The quartermaster had been called down by the man who claimed to have saved our dinghy. Isabel stated our case (I don't know how we should have got through the events at Sines without her fluent Spanish), speaking out boldly in the face of the crowd, which seemed to be hostile. At the word *borrachos* there came a shout of laughter from most of the audience, and rumbles of anger from the two drunk men. The quartermaster wavered and almost took our side.

"I advise you to give this man something, say ten escudos," he said. "Nobody can prove that he saved the little boat; but nobody can disprove it."

The man took his money and disappeared. Then the case of the unshaven man and his accomplice was argued, but the unshaven one, who, I am still inclined to believe, was a good man, pressed no claim, and the young drunk, roaring and frothing in the most disagreeable manner imaginable, condemned himself. The official advised us to give them nothing. Then the imbecile who had frightened Isabel on *Serica* came whining to us, begging, but all shouted at him so furiously, poor man, that he pulled his wet cap over his ears and walked off, glaring from side to side and kicking his bare toes against the walls.

Next came the problem of getting to the yacht. We asked the quartermaster to find us a big rowing-boat with two strong men for the oars.

"You know a little of the fishermen's ways now," he said, not unhumorously, "and you must realise that they'll expect money for such a service. . . . Well, here are three men who say they'll put you on your yacht for thirty escudos. Too much, Senhora?"

"Far too much."

"All right, then, twenty."

"They should charge us Portuguese prices—not special prices invented for foreigners. But never mind, twenty will do."

"There's this to be said for them," the quartermaster argued. "If they don't row you out you'll lose your yacht, and they know your yacht to be worth more money than any one of them earns in a lifetime of hard work."

They put both of us in the stern sheets and the dinghy was lashed across the gunwales, between us and the rowers. Eduardo Luiz leaped into the bows. We had a crazy passage to the yacht. Each time a wave broke over us one of the oarsmen, an elderly man, giggled with a high squeak. Neither of us was in a giggling mood. We jumped aboard *Serica* one by one, choosing our moments. Luiz helped me to set the dinghy on its chocks and lash it down. We gave him a present of money as well as our best thanks. He had been a great help to us.

My first thought was for the anchors, and I saw at once that we had lost the C.Q.R., which I had let go on thirty fathoms of two-and-a-half-inches Italian hemp with a six-fathom chain tail. The warp had parted near the join with the chain. Thinking that this loss (in foreign waters) would be irreplaceable, I hailed the boat, which put back. Luiz said that if the weather improved fairly quickly they might be able to fish up the anchor with grapnels.

I then received a worse shock. . . . On going below I could see no anchor chain rising from the chain locker to the deckhead. The chain locker was empty. Were we adrift then? I raced to the bows. The chain was holding, and the mystery was soon solved. . . . The men "looking after" *Serica* while I was ill had undone the spring I had fixed from both cables to the mast. The chain of the bower had then jumped off the windlass in some particularly heavy snub, and had run out until the full weight of the yacht came suddenly on the rope leading to the second anchor. This (already frayed on the sandy bottom) had parted, and the weight reverted to the chain, which ran out and tore away its inboard end, shackled to a small brass plate screwed down on the oak keel in the chain locker. The screws were torn out as though set in putty, instead of healthy oak, and the plate had flown up to the navel, where, by some amazing and blessed fluke, it had jammed lengthwise across the under edge of the hole (instead of slipping through, as it might easily have done). This small plate, hitched perilously under the deck, was all that held us off the rocks astern. I righted matters, telling Isabel of our miraculous escape, and promising the plate that one day I would have it covered with gold filigree or any other decoration it might prefer.

We soon discovered that the sombre young man who had guarded *Serica* during my illness had not been forgetful of his own comfort. He had drunk more than ten litres of the strong red wine I had bought in Cascais, as well as a litre of good Madeira. He had taken all our cigarettes, which we kept to offer to people like him, and which Isabel had told the unshaven one to smoke whenever he felt so inclined. He had emptied the bread locker, consumed about three pounds of palatable and expensive Portuguese cheese, and had made away with most of our store of tinned food. After these discoveries I felt sure he would not trouble us that night (I had thought of freeing one of the cockpit winch-handles, eighteen inches of steel, nicely balanced and terminating in a round steel ball, with which to say hullo to him), and I also knew why the unshaven man had looked so ashamed, and had asked for no more money.

But all was well; I was feeling astonishingly stronger, and we were quit of them. . . . I settled in the doghouse to rest on anchor watch, and read E. M. Forster's engrossing *Aspects of the Novel* from cover to cover. Rain fell steadily, and I sat in a series of drips. In the evening I summoned enough energy to set the trysail and the small jib, ready for instant departure in the night, should that be necessary. I found that the guardians had exhausted our batteries, but I managed to start the engine by hand, and it seemed to be running well despite its outwardly damp condition.

The yacht was pitching and taking seas over the bows; the movement no longer disturbed me. I lit the oil lamp and read Balzac all night. Outside our bounding walls the wind neither worsened nor improved. Rain beat down on the rough waters. The deck, in need of caulking after its winter in the sun, leaked badly.

It was a repulsive dawn, grey streaked with dull yellow; wind due south; heavy rain. Isabel was surviving the pounding well, but her arm was giving her trouble, for the plaster was again waterlogged, like everything else on board. While we breakfasted, cursing the man who had stolen our bread, we looked at the chart and discussed our next move. From Sines to Cape St. Vincent is a distance of only fifty-five miles, but it seemed unlikely that either of us would yet be strong enough for so long a beat into that weather, and once round the Cape—the quartermaster from the harbour office had assured us, and common sense supported him—we should have little chance of better conditions. There was one other possibility—Milfontes. We took the volume marked *West Coasts of Spain and Portugal* from the many damp Sailing Directions on the shelf, and read as follows:

"*Rio Mira.—Light.—Anchorages.*—Rio Mira flows into the sea through the middle of a beach; the mouth can be identified by the lighthouse and also by a fort near the northern entrance point. . . . The entrance to the river is about one cable wide, but is fronted by sand banks between which there is a shifting channel which had a least depth in 1927 of three feet (Om9) and the river should not be entered without a pilot. Vessels of light draught can reach Vila de Odemira, about twelve miles up-river. The village of Vila Nova de Milfontes is situated on the northern bank about half a mile within the entrance. . . ."

The tide tables told us that high water at Milfontes would be at 5.46 that evening. We should have to time our arrival carefully.

"We won't go well enough to windward with the trysail," I said. "I'm going to take it off, and double-reef the mainsail. We'll have a go at Milfontes, and if we can't get in there we'll lash the tiller and let her beat on towards Cape St. Vincent."

Getting the anchor was not easy. The deck, forward, seemed to be rising and falling some ten feet, and I was sometimes under water. My left hand gripping a stanchion, I kneeled beside the windlass and worked the lever with my right, easing off as the chain was stretched when we rose on a wave, winding in the moment we had passed the crest and were sliding down. Isabel helped with the engine. When the anchor was lashed I put on a wet duffle coat and settled down at the tiller. It was a tricky beat out of Sines Bay between the tunny nets that stretched for a mile seaward from either point. Both wind and sea were fierce. The barometer was rising. The sun was out and the sky had cleared save for some queer yellow puff balls hanging to the south and a ridge of dark cumulus to the east. Even the double-reefed mainsail and the smallest jib constituted too much canvas, and the sailing was the wettest we had known as the yacht drove on powerfully. We were making a lot more water than we liked, and I pumped regularly, though never for long at a time, for I feared that my newly found strength might ebb. We kept the yacht sailing as fast as she would go in those conditions. Identification of the Rio Mira was not easy, but identify it we did just ten minutes before high water on the bar. I had hoisted the pilot flag, and we beat up to and off the pilot station for a time, but as there was no sign of a boat putting out to us we decided jointly to risk the bar before the ebbing tide made conditions impossible. I went forward on hands and knees, like a baboon, and got the mainsail down easily enough. We turned, with the wind on our starboard quarter.

What a relief to have the wind there! How silent! The small jib pulling like an express engine, we raced for the bar, assuring each other that it was easy enough in that following sea to distinguish the narrow channel from the shoal water on either side.

More difficult to distinguish, however, were the breakers on the bar itself. I was on my way forward to keep a look-out when I felt the yacht lurch. The first of the big waves over the bar had put such force on the rudder that the tiller had knocked Isabel off her feet. A dash aft, and I fought with the tiller myself. Two hands and all my strength for a mad instant, and then we were sizzling along in smoother water. People standing outside the pilot station waved to us. A bend in the river. We swept round it at racing speed. A rowing-boat flying the pilot flag was approaching in midstream. The man in the bows held up his hand, signalling that we must stop. Stop? I ran forward to the jib, which collapsed obediently on the deck. Then aft to swing the engine. The pilot boat laboured far astern.

Two men in uniform came aboard and showed me where to drop anchor. We lay in fifteen feet of water between two other craft, *Maria Isabel*, of Sines, a sardiner, and *Rio Mira*, of Lisbon, a coasting schooner. Flat water. Brown hills land-locking us and the white village of Milfontes. The wind now able to do **no** more than scream at us. Safe! That was a happy night.

CHAPTER 15

## JOACHIN AND THE PILOTO

IT occurs to me that our experiences at Sines were particularly illustrative of life, for I remember how in the first moments there I loved the white town, the cobbled streets, the burrow-like security of the Pensao Clemente, yet today, because we suffered there and were robbed, and were lucky to escape with *Serica* from the lee shore, today I cannot think of Sines without the skin shrinking on my back, drawing my shoulder-blades together like the touch of an assassin's steel. I must go back there one summer day, and see the holiday people lying sun-bathing, enjoying the beach that was only a menace to us; and yachts and fishing-boats lying to their anchors, their bows pointing into the bay that offers them fine shelter from the Portuguese Trades. I should like to meet Clemente again, and Eduardo Luiz. I would shake hands with the unshaven man, tell his dark-skinned partner that I bear him no malice and hope he did not catch ptomaine poisoning from such of our tins as he sampled, and I would give a bottle of whisky to the man with the upturned cap scoop. Yes, I ought to have another look at Sines.

Our memories of the Milfontes anchorage are full of pleasure, and I advise any yachtsman who passes down that coast to brave the bar (which indeed must be easy enough at high water, in fine weather, and with a pilot) and enter the Rio Mira, for there can be few more peaceful anchorages in the whole world. The holding ground (sand, stones, and weed) is excellent; fresh water can be had either from Vila Nova de Milfontes or from springs on the opposite bank; the tides are fast, but not too fast for a dinghy; provisions are cheap, and come fresh out of the agricultural countryside; and there is the boy, Joachin Fernão de Silva.

We met him on our first day in the anchorage. He came rowing out in the rain and presented us with (of all surprising gifts in that out-of-the-way place) *Yachting World* of January, 1950. On the front of the magazine was a picture of the fine English yacht, *Dyarchy*, and above was written "Adams—Please Return". We gave him a copy of *Country Life*, and studying the pictures of houses, old silver, and china, he was enchanted (though he could neither speak nor read English). Joachin promised to meet us at nine o'clock the following morning, since that day we were too tired to go ashore and had more than enough work to do on board.

Our next caller was the captain of the *Maria Isabel*. He seemed to know all about our stay in Sines (his native port), and said that we had been unlucky there. He made us a present of two spider crabs. These were still living, and when the donor had gone we slipped them into the running tide, for the very sight of them made me wonder if I had really recovered.

The third caller was the senior of the two pilots who had met us when we arrived, Piloto Eugenio, a plump, serious fellow with a gentle, rather sad, eye, and good manners. He said that the wind the previous day had been a cyclone (surely a romantic exaggeration?) and that it had done much damage to the vines.

Joachin was a little puzzled by us when we landed. He had preconceived notions, it was soon clear, regarding foreigners, and particularly English people. He had known the crews of two English yachts, and he believed, for example, that all English women craved tobacco. Although Isabel told him that she did not smoke, it took him some time to get used to that idea. Also, as he led us through the sinuous streets with their one-storeyed cottages forming white walls on either hand, he kept uttering the English words "milk" and "cheese", which found small response from us. These words he had learned, we gathered, from the lips of Vice-Admiral Sir Lennon Goldsmith, Commodore of the Royal Cruising Club, who had sailed into the Rio Mira a month earlier in his new cutter, *Diotima*, and had spent more than a week there. The admiral had been very good to Joachin, and had seen much of him in his perambulations on shore. Contact with that distinguished, yet at times boyish, figure had made Joachin expect much from any people of the same race. We therefore had a standard to live up to and, if I may say so, Joachin, a Portuguese boy who had never been away from his native village, was a good advertisement for the Royal Navy. A quiet, stringy boy of sixteen, but younger in appearance, and extremely cheerful, a ready laugher, he helped us at every turn, and he did it not for lucre or for any favour but the pleasure of our company and of being allowed to slake his interest in the yacht and its appurtenances. We do not know his parents, for in all our explorations with him and visits paid in his company he never, so far as we knew, took us to his own home, but whoever they may be they also are to be congratulated.

Without Joachin's help we should have found few of the supplies we wanted, for vegetables, eggs, wine, bread, and honey were bought in the dark interiors of what outwardly were ordinary private dwellings, the main room in each of them no bigger than a small cloakroom in an English country house. Our drinking water was drawn from the well of Piloto Eugenio at the end of the garden behind his house, a garden that was an intertwining mass of vines, hydrangeas, lilies, and nasturtiums. Water was scarce at that time, and in giving it liberally to us Eugenio was being very generous. Honey we bought in a wine bottle (twenty-five escudos the litre, expensive, but the man at Sines had swiped all our jam and marmalade) from an old woman who lived by herself at the foot of the village. The step up to her front door was nearly three feet high, but she took a few hops and jumped it without offering a view of her bare legs under the thick black skirts. She was nimble, if she had no teeth. She led us into her house, square, whitewashed within and without, and the size of a small loose-box. She darted round to the back places and from among the piles of brushwood that she had dragged there for her own warmth and cooking she picked out the stone jar of honey collected by herself from a tree and dripped through a cloth into the jar. In such places the old, when they are left alone, work to keep themselves alive. With age comes no leaning back; on the contrary, the struggle grows the more bitter, the more vital as the end is viewed and ignored. On three occasions in my own life I have known myself to be near death by violence, and at those moments I found in myself a determination to live, a passion, a force, infinitely outswelling any normal forces. How well they work, the old in Milfontes who fend for themselves! how active they are! how *alive* they are!

She was very shy. When the sale was completed, the bargain struck (very much in her favour, I suspect, though Joachin did beat her down a little), we sat talking with her and she kept drawing the black hood over her face and then peering out, carefully, as though we were a swarm of bees. We saw more of her, for she also sold eggs, and we enjoyed watching her stow each egg separately in our basket, the miraculous globe held so gently in the ends of her knobbly, yellow fingers, freckled and warted and resembling those edible twigs that are made for eating with apéritifs. Once, however, I saw her killing a chicken, one of her own chickens—and that spoiled her for me in a way, for I thought I detected a cruel relish in her wrinkled features.

The turreted Moorish fort at Milfontes has been converted into a rich man's house, but so tactfully that you can, if you prefer, imagine the Moors still in arrogant occupation. The fort dominates the anchorage. I wonder how the Moorish vessels negotiated the bar. They could sail in, as we did. But how did they get out? With oars, I suppose, and in fine weather only. The cobbled and paved alleys were clean and sweet-smelling, possibly as a result of the frequent, and unseasonal, rain-storms. The low houses were clean too, and showed no lack of paint. The people have reason to be proud of their village.

The wind continued to come, sometimes at gale strength, from the south. We could see the bar itself only by walking some distance on shore. But when the ebb was on we saw, rising high above the pro-montory that sheltered us, a wall of spouting spray.

There was no restaurant in Milfontes or within ten miles of it. We ate simple food on board, mainly fresh vegetables steamed in the pressure cooker, and I made a complete recovery from the illness of Sines. Twice each day we landed and walked both for health and for pleasure. During the first part of our stay I made efforts to start the charging motor, which had been uncovered by the yacht's guardians at Sines and had been waterlogged. I took the whole engine to pieces and soaked different parts in petrol to dry them—all to no avail. Had I had an oven in the galley I should have been successful. As it was we made do without electric light, and to keep the discharged batteries from collapse I had to run the big engine for a little each day, which meant a serious drain on our petrol reserve. The failure of the charging motor was but another reminder that there was much to be done to the yacht in Gibraltar. I had learned at Sines that she was making water almost dangerously in bad weather. The British Naval Attaché at Lisbon had explained to me that many of the smugglers operating in Mediterranean waters since the second German war were pretending to be British yachts, and that accordingly it had become difficult for any bona fide yacht to enter the Naval Dockyard at Gibraltar without special cre-dentials. I had obtained such credentials (or at least a guarantee that I was not a smuggler) in the shape of a letter from a mutual friend to Vice-Admiral Brooking, then Flag Officer at Gibraltar. But we knew that Admiral Brooking was due any day to be posted elsewhere, and feared that our letter of introduction might then be useless.

The Rio Mira is about 400 yards wide at the anchorage. On the

south bank, opposite the village, we found a countrified antidote to the
salt sea that kills growing things. There, on a height over the river, stand
farm buildings large and complex by local standards. The stock consisted of a herd of forty brown steers, long-horned as Highland cattle,
each with a tape attached to his left horn tip and with a deep-toned bell
on his neck, a herd of 200 goats, a mare with her foal, a donkey, and
fifty-eight swine, muscular, yellow, and healthy, that lived in pigsties
cunningly built with barricades of pine saplings. The steers loved to
descend to the deep sand of the beach. There they would rest their
heavy bodies, gazing for hour upon hour at the waving rushes and the
restless, whispering water. The steers were attended by a boy herdsman
with striped blanket, felt hat, stick, and slung wineskin. The goatherd
was a more agile boy, one given to hurling stones and abuse at his all-
devouring charges.

In the deep cuts around the farm there are fresh-water springs,
rivulets, and thick vegetation, but if you follow the plateau on the edge
of which it stands the paths through the cork oaks will lead you to a
prairie where, during our stay, Indian corn was breaking the sandy
surfaces with damp green lances, and the thin wheat and thinner oats
waved despairingly in the wind. Sheltered grooves in the face of the
prairie were peopled with cork trees, stripped of bark so that the bared
trunks, dark and squirmy, looked like the legs of elderly actresses in
tights. The drinking troughs are made of the hollowed trunks of cork
trees, and these, stranded pirogues, are set round wells that are wide,
and built of masonry. We walked in sand, always sand, except when we
went to the place below the farm, where there is a different life, thick and
jungly. The springs are permitted to run unpiped through beds of velvet
moss, grasses, and shining boulders red and black; at the bottom
behind the beach they fill a mere, rush-bordered and full of clamorous
frogs that dive cheerfully under the duckweed at the approach of man.
Keeping the mere on your right, a path leads to a one-room building,
the windows shuttered but unglazed, where a family of eight live when
they are not working outdoors. They keep pigs, and cultivate vegetables
in three patches surrounded by cement-and-stone walls of great solidity
(constructed so that the ground, combed out and pomaded with pig
manure, may be flooded in times of drought, or protected against
flooding when the rains are heavy). A path, eaten deep by the feet of
pack mules and asses, leads through the vegetable plots into the thick-
nesses of the wood.

After the rain-showers the wood closed over us, glistening, breathing, dripping. Barbary oaks, ilexes, magnolias, cypresses, maples, and even elms, grow there to no great height by English standards but in an extraordinary density of greenness under which the rivulets tumble. Below leaf level the tree ferns are rampant. This was indeed another world; the air seemed thicker, and the sounds were strangely at variance with the noises of the sea so close by, for the nightingales sang there by day and by night and the dragonfly wooed his mate over the sweet water.

Piloto Eugenio visited us every day. Once he came in his best uniform to show us how smart he could be. He told us a good deal of Admiral Goldsmith (whom the reader will meet later). He insisted that the admiral's yacht was "inferior" to *Serica*, from which we rightly surmised that *Diotima* was firstly smaller, and secondly less showy, less yachty. "The admiral's cabin," Eugenio said, "is not built like this one in the manner of a piece of fine furniture and of expensive hardwoods, but is only painted, and part of the interior is occupied by a gigantic water tank. Yes, I assure you, the admiral eats off the tank, for his table lies on top of it. . . . You would never catch a Portuguese admiral behaving like Admiral Goldsmith, travelling all over the world in a boat even smaller than yours, cooking his own meals. . . . I tell you, it's insane. Does any man in his senses *choose* to peel potatoes? . . . But this I will say," he declared, "everybody in Milfontes treated your admiral as though he had been a millionaire in a steam yacht with twenty sailors, three officers, and six stewards in his pay."

"Why do you and your husband spend so much time in the wood?" he asked Isabel one day.

"Because the wood is a wonderful change after the sea."

"Then why do you sail on the sea?"

He understood Isabel's Spanish, but seemed to believe that she was speaking English (and therefore that the latter bore a strong resemblance to his own language). When we met any stranger in his company Piloto Eugenio would explain: "Husband and wife. English. I can understand her almost word for word, but he speaks too fast and swallows his vowels."

One thing that pleased us about the pilot was that he took pains to be as polite to the boy Joachin as he was to us. He was a decent man full of friendliness and unselfishness.

On Thursday, May 25th, we had made an excursion up the north bank of the river and were watching a man clearing with his sickle a piece of rough land that he intended to farm when he had enlarged the cabin there and married a widow from Odemira. We suddenly noticed that the hissing of the blade through the weeds was the only sound in the air. The south wind had stopped blowing, and cloud-banks were piling to the north. We hurried back to Milfontes, Joachin leading us by the shortest route behind the village to the house of Eugenio, who took us to the post office. He picked up the telephone somewhat gingerly, and after repeating fortissimo several times: "Here at the apparatus is Eugenio Barreto, Cobo de Mar e Piloto do Rio e Barra de Milfontes," he obtained a weather forecast.

"If go you must, tomorrow morning at high water will be a good time," he said. "I'll come with Joachin at ten o'clock to pilot you over the bar. Yes, yes, you must allow me to do you this small favour."

They were late, the next morning, and came with Eugenio's co-pilot, whom we had not seen since the night we arrived. Joachin told us that the co-pilot had insisted on coming, despite Eugenio's arguments. That was why they were late. Just before they arrived I started the engine by hand. It backfired, and the starting handle caught me across the upper lip. No teeth were broken or even loosened, but my face was smothered in gore, and as fast as I stanched it the crimson stream gushed out. I tied a kind of gag round the lower half of my face, for I was afraid of spotting the deck with blood.

Joachin, ecstatic at the thought of a trip on the yacht, no matter how short, yet sad at the thought that it was going far away from him, helped with the anchor. Eugenio took the tiller and we moved downstream under power. Crossing the few sharp waves on the bar (it was a windless morning) there was a scene in the saloon. The second pilot demanded from us money, money, and more money. Joachin stood on deck with a frozen face, pretending not to hear. Eugenio made frantic gestures at us from the cockpit, and cried down to his colleague that *he* wanted no money, and was doing for friendship what we could easily have done for ourselves.

"More than that, come on," the other man said. "There are two pilots and the two oarsmen in our boat. The boy doesn't count. That's not enough, not nearly enough. Pilotage is an expensive matter. . . ."

"Pay no attention to him," Eugenio cried, almost in tears. "What's he done for you that he should make such demands? I'll report him for

this, I assure you. I'll never speak to him again. Give him nothing,
nothing."

To be ended with the embarrassing scene we gave him 200 escudos,
which was over-generous, but only half what he demanded. Then the
rogue, having done his best to poison our departure, had the effrontery
to hold out his hand and wish us both bon voyage.

Eugenio embraced me, flinging his arms around me and squeezing,
and pouring out a lot of navigational advice. The three of them
jumped into the rowing-boat that we had towed out. As we made sail
we watched them dropping away astern. Joachin and Eugenio looked
fixedly after us, but the other pilot sat facing the rowers, looking
toward Milfontes.

*          *          *          *

I had been warned by Eugenio that the north wind would come in the
afternoon, and that I must be careful not to be caught with too much
canvas up. It came at 3 p.m., and we flew before it with a sea on our
quarter. Now the miles tripped away easily. Cape St. Vincent, bold and
bare, was booming and whistling as the seas dashed into the caves
pitting its base. The log read 45 as we weathered the cape. An American
Export Lines steamship, paying not the slightest heed to the rule
of the road, did her best to run us down, but failed narrowly. Two
grinning negroes were watching us from the shelter of her forecastle
head. A big British motor yacht came round the cape astern of us and
steadied at once on a course for the Straits of Gibraltar (*en route* for
Cannes, as we later discovered). Through the binoculars I watched a
steward carry a tray with glasses and a bottle to the well-lit wheelhouse. I almost envied those he served, for in our cockpit the wind was
cold and salty.

Three miles south-east of Cape St. Vincent we turned into the small
horned bay at the head of which is the village of Sagres. The anchorage,
admirable on the chart, was disappointing in reality. It is forbidding
like all the surroundings of the cape. It afforded good shelter, though,
close to the beach in water whipped flat by the north wind.

A band of fishermen with uncouth shouts hauled a boat down
the beach and put off to us. Their spokesman was almost incomprehensible, for he spoke in a vernacular and his voice seemed to change
key as he continually took off and put on a dirty beret with a hole in the
top. At length we made out that we had anchored where they wanted to

lay nets that night, so we moved to a less comfortable place of their choosing.

We were glad to get under way at dawn, sailing slowly out of the bay with light airs from the north-east. We knew that the safest and best way to make for the Straits of Gibraltar would be the longer route, clinging more or less to the southern coast of Portugal and the south-western coast of Spain, but despite the fickle breeze we were at first able to make such good progress on a reach with mainsail and Genoa that we set course direct for Gibraltar, 180 miles away, a foolhardy decision, since we had cause to know that the yacht was not tight and that we might expect a change of wind on leaving the coast of Portugal, and bad weather from the east as we neared the Straits of Gibraltar. It was a decision that we were bitterly to regret.

From 9.30 a.m. for nearly twelve hours we were sailing through calms. Sometimes our speed fell as low as one knot, and that with mainsail, spinnaker, and the Genoa boomed out. We managed to cover fifty-eight miles thus, but only at the expense of much chafe and hard work, sail-changing. We had little petrol left, and our batteries were all but flat. At 9.10 p.m. with the night there came a good steady breeze from the north-east, and we felt handsomely repaid for the minor irritations of the hot day when we darted on, reaching at seven or eight knots on our chosen course. I steered through the early part of the night. The breeze had stiffened, though we could still carry the Genoa. During Isabel's first night trick at the helm I had to hand the Genoa and set the small jib. I thought seriously then of setting the trysail, but the mainsail was doing such fine service and we so badly wanted the speed and the distance that I hesitated (and was lost). The barometer was steady, but the wind was getting more easterly and tending to push us south toward the steamer lane, which I had been carefully avoiding (there was so much lighted shipping on it that it showed up like the Great North Road at night). The only light we carried was our paraffin-burning riding light. I told myself that I was unnecessarily nervous. We could always switch on the electric navigation lights in any emergency or near-emergency; we were travelling at rather more than seven knots despite a lumpy sea; the decks were dry; and I was not having to do much pumping; at that rate we should reach Gibraltar before lunch-time.

After eating a sandwich I lay down in our berth under the dog-house. The sounds of the water rushing past the yacht's skin beside my head, of the main sheets creaking, of Isabel clearing her throat, of the wind, could not keep me awake.

I woke with a jump. There had been a noise like a cannon shot or a clap of thunder inside my pillow. The yacht was lying right over on her side. Part of a sea came splashing through the doghouse. All round was blackness and a ghastly shrieking of wind. Still dazed with sleep, and inclined to feel that somebody had played me a filthy trick, I fumbled my way into the cockpit.

# Chapter 16

## LEVANTE

THE scene in that wild darkness will exist in the palpitating vacuum of memory at any rate until I am dead. As I sit writing this embalmed in the slumbering peace of a Dorsetshire garden in winter sunshine, the creaking of the big elm, the sighing breeze in the Wellingtonia, the noise of a tractor from the field over the hedge, the tapping of a great tit on the coconut, these and a hundred other distinguishable sounds merge into the frenzy of the levante that hurled itself down the Straits of Gibraltar to strike us with (to be exact) the impact of a gunshot or a bomb. That impact, lashing out of the darkness without warning, had blown out our mainsail, parts of which hung in sodden tatters over the deck and the cockpit where Isabel crouched up to the waist in water, still gripping the tiller with her one hand and trying to right the yacht. The "explosion" that wakened me had been the sound of the mainsail's demolition. In those early moments I had the impression that the strong and healthy cotton had been blown entirely into shreds and wisps. . . . There was urgent work to be done.

The small jib was holding us flat in a steep sea that came from two directions. I freed the sheet, and, as the deck regained a more normal angle, went cautiously forward to take down the sail and secure it. Isabel told me later that this simple task (one normally done in a few seconds) took me twenty minutes. The jib fought in my hands and arms like a python. I then turned my attention to the mainsail. The sodden mass was heavy; bit by bit I got it to the boom and lashed it. We were now scudding before the gale, our mast and rigging giving the drive of a spinnaker in a full breeze, but this was a perilous movement for us in the cockpit, since *Serica* yawed before the toppling seas, which frequently pooped her with thunderous crash and rushing torrent.

After dragging the reefed trysail through the interior, I chose my moment and got it to the cockpit, then forward to the mast. That strong little sail felt good in my hands, but there was heavy work in getting it over the boom to fit the slides into the track. When that was done and the trysail well sheeted in, the yacht turned until she was

173

sailing herself slightly into the still-increasing gale. Then the cockpit drained itself, and although waves still broke on deck, they broke over the port bow and amidships, crashing on the upturned dinghy, secure on its chocks. I sent Isabel below. She called up to me that water was several inches deep over the cabin floors. I watched the behaviour of the yacht; with the tiller unlashed she sailed herself better, slightly into sea and weather, than she had done under my guidance, so I left her to her arduous task, and went below, battening down. What a heavenly relief to be out of that wind with its hideous pressure and shriek, to be sheltered from the fierce lashing of the spray!

I found that I had next to no voice left, and my wounded mouth was smarting as though it had been held against red-hot metal.

Isabel, worn out to beyond the reach of seasickness, beyond the pain in her broken arm, lay on the lower (starboard) settee. I put a pillow under her head and two wet blankets over her, then I turned to the pump. Water was more than ankle-deep on the floor (and beneath the floor *Serica* has very deep bilges). I had to pump hard for an hour (with several rests) before at last I heard the machine suck dry. I lay down on the weather settee, back aching, arms aching, head aching, longing for rest.

I expected then to have to pump every half-hour for a minute or two, and that seemed a reasonable prospect. But the weather was getting worse rather than better, and I had not realised how much water could come through when the deck (badly in need of caulking and marine glue) was constantly awash and frequently had tons of sea pounding on it. Most of the water was coming through forward of the mast, not through recognised openings such as the hatch or the navel—these I could deal with—but through the deck itself. I wish that João from Belém could have been with me to see how the deck had dried out during the winter months—and to help me with the pump. I had not lain long when I felt it necessary to look into the bilges again, and when I looked in I had to pump.

We should have been almost comfortable, and certainly without any shadow of fear, had the yacht been watertight, for, although at times the trysail vibrated like a heavy machine-gun firing bursts, she was sailing herself perfectly, and when I watched her at it through the streaming doghouse windows I felt that she was aware of every tremor in the weather, every gust, and that she was playing the terrible wind against the equally terrible sea. I loved her in those moments as I never loved

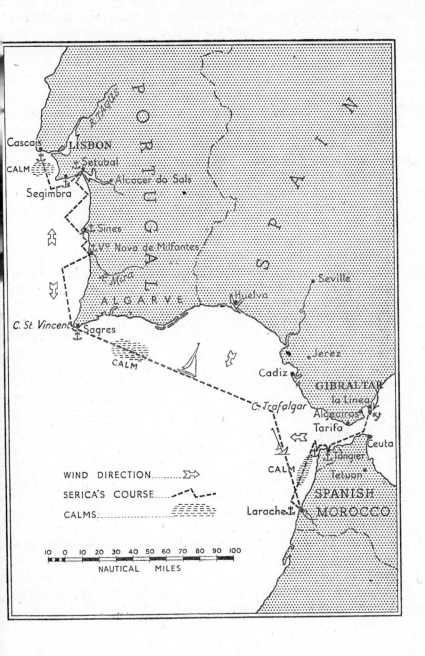

WIND   DIRECTION..........▷▷

SERICA'S   COURSE.....▬  ▬  ▬

CALMS.................

10   0   10   20  30  40  50  60  70  80  90  100
NAUTICAL   MILES

her before and (I hope) will never love her again. But though her balance and skill and strength were apparently unbeatable there was this seeping disease in her entrails. When I picked up the teak grating and looked into the bilges I saw water streaming in.

My pumping took on a dreadful routine: I would pump for 500 revolutions, then lie down for ten minutes' rest, then another 500 or more.    If my strength held out I thought I could keep the water down. But would my strength hold out? The work was strenuous.  At the end of 500 turns I would be sweating and panting and would stagger from my sore knees to my feet, unfitted to bear the yacht's jerking and plunging.  Could I hold out?  How long would the levante continue? After the first two hours it brought heavy rain with it, and I found in the rain some hope that the gale might moderate.  The Sailing Directions for once contrived to make me feel optimistic, for they state that the levante usually falls at night.

Between my ordeals at the pump I tried to eat and drink in order to maintain my strength.  I usually managed to suck some condensed milk from a tin or to drink a little wine, but I only craved rest, and above all the luxury, the supreme luxury, of sleep.

"Where are we?" Isabel asked, and I answered that according to my reckoning the wind had struck us when we were thirty miles west of the entry to the Straits of Gibraltar; the yacht was sailing herself south by east, and I thought therefore that we should be closing the African coastline, which shelves out a little to the west as it drops from Cape Spartel at the entry to the Straits. But as we had never contemplated cruising down that coast of Africa, we had neither charts nor Sailing Directions for the area.

2 p.m.: I had been pumping for nine hours with ten-minute breaks when the weather eased enough to allow me to reduce my efforts to 400 turns every twenty minutes.  For the first time in nine hours I raised my head up above the doghouse hatch.  The scene without was so intolerably desolate, so inhumanly majestic, that I hastily withdrew my head and closed and bolted the hatch.

3 p.m.: The levante came back more fiercely than ever, its first gust again laying the yacht flat on the sea.  I was hard at it, with scarcely any rest from the pump, until from 5 p.m. to 6.30 the water was gaining despite my utmost efforts.  I began to fear that the trysail might be blown out, for at times it drummed terribly.

6.30 p.m.: I drank half a glass of undiluted brandy, stripped myself to the waist, and kneeled to the brass handle, promising that I would empty the bilges or burst a blood vessel. The alcohol pulsing in my veins and exuding through my skin, I had about emptied the water when we heard the blast of a siren close by. I put on a jersey and went to the hatch.

A whaler (of what nationality I do not know, for she flew no flag) was hove-to near us. Her slow-turning propeller showed in the air each time her bows plunged. Her numerous crew was gathered on and under the main bridge, watching *Serica*. Perhaps they had thought her to be deserted. I put my head out of the hatch, ducking each time a sea came over, and waved to them. A few waved back, but they continued to watch in what I judged to be a curious manner. Did they expect us to ask for help, I wondered angrily, watching their antics; now they seemed to be 100 feet above me, now their hull was hidden and I looked at a wooden box clustered with wet men.

Human pride is a strange force. I realised that our situation was one of danger. On the vagaries of the levante and on my ability to pump out as much water as found its way in depended not only my own life but that of Isabel. Yet I would never have hailed them. And it was with ungenerous pleasure that I noticed that the whaler's thin funnel had been damaged by the gale so that her smoke issued almost at deck level. She was a good little ship, handsome and practical, with a catwalk running from the bridge to the harpoon-gun platform high on the forecastle head. . . . The rain had stopped and a great fan of fragile white cloud was beginning to break up over the cruel dome of the sky. I returned to the pump.

When dusk came I took the anchor light on deck. I could get no farther forward with it than the main rigging on the weather side. Soaked and with all the breath blown out of me, I was thankful to get below. I had seen the whaler, still hove-to, and now about a mile to windward and slightly astern. I had also seen, up there by the shrouds, that despite the extremely high and irregular seas the yacht was sailing at surprising speed.

I lit the oil lamp in the saloon. The atmosphere was steamy. We were warm enough, though wet; indeed I was too warm while I pumped. But I seemed to have found a new reserve of stamina (possibly the air on deck had done me good), for I pumped so steadily that I got her dry for the first time in four hours.

Then I nearly spoiled everything by falling asleep sprawled over the weather settee. I was wakened in the most agonising fashion. A particularly sharp pitch of the yacht flung my body up till it struck the deckhead hard, and then I smashed down over the sharp corners of the table, which wounded one shoulder and one thigh muscle.

Back to the pump. But I had stiffened while I slept, and was not strong enough to pump her dry. Rest . . . pump . . . rest . . . 400 turns . . . wine . . . 600 . . . condensed milk . . . 450. . . . At 11.48 p.m. I put my head up through the hatch and saw (oh miracle!) a light ahead, flashing just below the horizon. I returned to the pump, then looked again. There it was! I counted the flashes. Two every fifteen seconds. Back to the pump. Isabel was asleep, poor little thing. The plaster on her arm was so waterlogged that I could push a finger into it. She moaned in her sleep. I tried to identify the flashes from the Admiralty List of Lights, but failed. My brain was scarcely working, my head ached so. Back to the pump.

12.30 a.m.: I woke Isabel and told her that *Serica* was sailing herself for a lighthouse that was probably about twelve miles away. I could also make out the lights of a trawler working between us and the light-house. Even more important, the wind had moderated to half a gale. She did not appear to believe me. I fell asleep on the floor beside the pump.

She roused me gently at 3 a.m. She said the wind had dropped to cat's-paws, and the lights of the trawler were quite close. I began to pump, for the water was again over the floor, but at first I could not turn the handle fast enough. When I had done 1,000 revolutions I went on deck and hoisted the jib (the waterlogged Genoa was too heavy for me). We sailed slowly up to the stern of the trawler. Men were grouped aft, eating in the light of two swaying electric bulbs.

"Hablan español?" Isabel cried.

"Si, si."

"Donde estamos?"

"Africa."

"And the lighthouse?"

"Larache, Spanish Morocco."

"Larache is a port?"

"A good port."

Under the great occidenting light of the lighthouse shimmered hundreds of smaller lights carried by a fleet of fishing-boats. We sailed on slowly with the most fitful of onshore and offshore puffs. At dawn I worked for a while on the engine, but I soon saw that it would remain inert and sparkless until distributor, coil, and so on, had been baked dry.

Isabel made me lie down and I slept like the dead for two hours. When I woke we were crawling through the fishing-boats, and the town ahead was hidden in fog. Fish were jumping around us and diving under us, and we saw that all the fishermen were making huge catches. We hailed several, imploring them to give us a tow into harbour, but none would pay any heed to us. They never seemed to look at us, those strange, dark men, though we surely presented an unusual sight in that place.

Hours later we slowly approached the land. We had no idea what to expect. The town was sited on the southern bank of a fairly wide estuary, and the port was evidently some way upstream. Jutting from the north bank was a sea wall with a beacon at the seaward end. The water was shoal and clear, the bottom sandy. We sailed in with try-sail and Genoa, just moving on the glassy surface.

Men fishing with bending rods from the sea wall shouted and beckoned us over to that side, but no sooner had we obeyed than men in a fishing-boat beckoned us away from the wall. Evidently, I said to Isabel, it was a twisting, silted channel, and we were lucky to be entering with the flood. Then there was a jar from the keel and the yacht tottered stupidly as she lost her free balance. We were firmly aground, and the tide ran past us with eddies and bubbles.

\*    \*    \*    \*

Neither of us was greatly upset by our plight, which we saw to be fairly grave since the tide was running much faster than we had suspected before we grounded, and instead of lifting us it was bumping us more and more into the shallows. The reason for our calm was that having just come from danger in deep waters our unlethal predicament in those sunlit shallows seemed puerile.

A small harbour launch (built in Britain and bought in Gibraltar) cruised round us with a tall, Moorish-looking man at the rudder and two other rough-looking customers, Europeans, on board. The tall man said nothing, but threw me a grass warp which I made fast to the samson post. After clever manœuvring and much frothing of the water he dragged us jerk by jerk into the channel. They towed us upstream to a filthy quay where many fishing-boats and schooners from Seville and

other Spanish ports were unloading or loading. Isabel called to the
pinnace that we did not want to go alongside there, and the small sailor,
after consultation with the tall man at the rudder, said that they would
tow us across to the river, the Wad Lekkus, but that we should find
malarial mosquitoes there and a swift current.

When we had dropped anchor in water running faster than at Benodet
or Milfontes the pinnace came alongside and we realised why the big
helmsman had not spoken to us. He had no voice, but could make
himself understood at close quarters, mouthing his words with a queer
hissing and clicking. From a range of three to six feet anybody (even
myself) could understand that epiglottal Spanish. Cancer of the throat
had almost gagged him, and he was tubed like a horse. Instead of collar
and tie he wore a striped scarf that formed a tight St. Andrew's cross on
his upper chest between the lapels of his worn denim jacket. The tube
lay under the centre of the cross, and the ingoing and outgoing breath
made a harrowing noise: "Ah-horff! ah-horff! ah-horff!"

His name? José Cartillo Torrecillar. He was married, we immediately learned, with many children. The sailor, Manolo Garcia
Trastallino, and the mechanic, Julio Rodriguez Bejerano, lost little time
in telling us of José's cancer. At any rate he showed no sign of re-
linquishing his authority over them, and this was fortunate for us. We
both guessed from the start that the tall, dark-skinned José was our
good friend, but that Manolo, small and waspish, and Julio, plump,
sensuous, and pouting under his small moustache, looked on us with a
somewhat cold curiosity that might become hostile.

At José's clicked and hissed command Julio came aboard *Serica* and
dismantled the engine parts vulnerable to damp. They all exclaimed in
horror when we opened the floor to take out the batteries, revealing the
bilges full of sea water. José told us that they were employed by the
Ministry of Works. At 6 p.m., when their normal work for the day
was ended, they would return. Meanwhile the harbour authorities and
the police came aboard to question us, but they saw our extreme fatigue
and were remarkably sympathetic and ungarrulous.

On the sandy shore near us, dotted with the hovels and reed fences of
poor natives, red sows wandered, bathing their trotters and teats in the
brine. A ferry service in rowing-boats connected that shore with the
white town of Larache (formerly El Araish) across the swift river. The
boats were packed with long-nosed Moors and blunter-faced and somewhat darker Jews. Up a shallow creek a new fish-canning factory blew

forth its mysterious and unattractive odours. Upstream were fields of
grain and expanses of scrubby estuary land where goats and turkeys fed
in herds.

We ate a little when I had pumped *Serica* dry, changed our clothes
(both of us were covered with bruises and Isabel had developed salt-
water sores under the plaster on her arm) and slept until six, when the
pinnace made fast to our side.

While Julio dismantled the carburettor, the little sailor, Manolo,
bathed the whole engine in a mixture of petrol and oil. They could not
work fast, for the air was heavy and they seemed to breathe with
difficulty, being malarial and undernourished.

José reminded me of my dear Berger, the big, strong, and gentle
Francomptois who had been my servant and bodyguard in the maquis
toward the end of the second German war. Here were the same broad
shoulders, the dark, muscular face, the wide, craftsman's hands, the
slow, unobvious, rewarding smile. All that was missing in José was
Berger's bull-like voice. We could not but trust José's lined face, yet
were he an actor I suppose he would be cast in the parts of villain or
gangster, murderer or devil.

A fog, white and choking, closed down at night. The clammy
darkness held as though in cotton wool the specimen sounds of mosquitoes, Moorish singing, oars, coughing, sneezing, and the rushing of
the tides.

# Chapter 17

## AFRICA

A MORNING of make and mend. The levante had broken our temporary handrails in seven places, the Genoa and No. 3 jib needed repairs, and I stitched the mainsail temporarily to hold it together on the boom until I could get it into a sail loft in Gibraltar. The damage to the mainsail was not so serious, however, as we had feared. One long panel had been blown to pieces, and would have to be replaced. It was useless weather for sail-drying; the air was as steamy as it was hot. José often cruised round us in the course of his duties, asking if he could help us. He would not allow us to go ashore in our dinghy, which, he said, would be unsafe in the currents.

The waterfront at which José landed us from the pinnace at midday was alive, prosperous, raucous. Larache exports grain, eggs, beans, figs, and wool, and it seemed that all the fishes in the sea (including the sardines from Portugal) had gathered off this dank, steaming coastline. The bigger fishing-boats were ponderous double-ended craft, high out of the water. Each was manned by one or two Spaniards and twenty to forty Moors. Grabs hauled the catches from the holds. Tunny-fish were unloaded at one section of the quay; their twin-bladed tails noosed with chain, they were hoisted two or three at a time and lowered into trucks. All the tunny were heavy but some were bigger than bulls, and all gushed dark, thick blood over boat, crew, quay, and truck. The mackerels and the red mullets were twice the size of members of their species in other places. The quay was one vast, heaped sea morgue, representing millions of deaths an hour.

"Spain must be glad of all this food," Isabel said to Manolo, a Spaniard from Huelva.

"Spain?" he answered in his hoarse voice. "None of this fish goes to Spain. First it's canned in the factory, and then it goes to Italy. We are told that the Italians pay for it with money sent them by America."

We asked José, Julio, and Manolo to recommend a restaurant. They had difficulty in thinking of a name, for they were poor men, and restaurants were outside their orbits. Julio said we might try the

182

Cocodrilo and José, solicitous for our wellbeing, sent a boy with us. He warned us that we should give the boy nothing since he happened to be the son of a gentleman.

The son of a gentleman led us up a street six feet wide, the paving rising layer upon layer, past shops that sold a little of every kind of eatable, including bread in small loaves of cement-like consistency, shops that sold shoes without heels, bazaars that sold trinkets, tobacco, nougat, and all manner of secret things. Here was a barrel-vaulted cavern in the walls where men squatted on the stone floor sipping at coffee and talking an undistinguishable but obviously friendly language, like so many dark pigeons conferring in a loft. We passed through the Moorish market, set out in a narrow plaza. The vendors displayed their goods on the ground, and each crouched among his fruit or vegetables or sweetmeats or trussed livestock, sheltered by a wattle screen propped up with a stick so that a wedge of shadow fell over him and his wares. Their fingers were always busy, darting here and there, arranging over-ripe apricots, small miry eggs, in rows or phalanxes, circles, diamonds, or swastikas. Parsley, glistening French parsley, seemed to be the eatable most widely purchased. Swifts scythed the air, finding their food just over our heads so that our ears were full of their squeaking and the brush of their daring passage. Moors strode about in their heavy, creamy robes and yellow slippers dangling at the heels. It was surprising to see them sucking in the smoke of American cigarettes, and carrying bunches of parsley in their hands. With their giant frames and secretive, bony, politely arrogant faces, their feet outstriding ours, their air of controlled power and of belief in something beyond comfort, beyond death, they made us remember that they had once all but mastered Europe, they made us wonder if it would not have been better if Charles the Hammer had lost instead of won the battle for Christendom at Tours in A.D. 732. His victory was won because the Moors, grown rapacious with years of conquest in Persia, Syria, Africa, Egypt, Spain, and lastly the southern half of France, were too confident and were laden with booty and with women; yet seeing those present-day Moors, subjects of a Christian race and without power in the world, one could not but contrast them favourably with the white men who still perch albeit shiftily and querulously on the top of the world.

There were Moors at the café; they sat inside, drinking coffee and gazing calmly out from the shadow of their hoods. The white men, irked by the heat, sat outside on the shaded terrace, fortifying themselves with alcohol. Many varieties of excellent sherry were available, but beer was the most expensive drink in Larache, more expensive than brandy, more so than wine. Most of the people, and particularly the wives and female friends of the garrison officers, drank beer. To drink beer was a gesture, an extravagance.

Pedestrians moved past our table in a thick, jostling stream, Spaniards, Moors, French tourists, soldiers of the Spanish Foreign Legion, very smart in their pale uniforms, well-polished brown boots, side-arms, and small forage caps with tassels hanging forward over clenched brows. Larache is one of the garrison centres for this impressive unit. Among those on the pavements darted bootblacks, pimps, and sellers of American cigarettes, which were smuggled across the border of the International Zone of Tangier (only forty-five miles N.N.E. of Larache). The urchin salesmen all mistook our nationality, since Spanish Morocco, like Spain, was crowded with the most astute of tourists and the most demanding (the French).

We walked through the bar to the blue-painted restaurant of the Cocodrilo, and while we ate a heavy and indifferent meal Spaniards who would not lunch before 3 p.m. leaned on the bar drinking, dicing, and glancing through the blotched newspapers, frowning in the humid heat and waving the flies away from their temples.

That evening the pinnace came to us and four men boarded with all the parts for the engine. The newcomer was the senior mechanic of the Ministry of Works, one Mariano Ruiz Avila from Granada, a man of delicate, pale, and temperamental appearance. He and the other mechanic, Julio, worked on the engine in short spells interrupted by storms of coughing and by the rolling of Rubio cigarettes that spilled their powdery tobacco before they could be induced to burn. They worked under difficulties, for the temperature below decks was intolerable. José hissed and clicked his stern orders. The others, even Mariano, were afraid of him; they did everything as he said they must, and this was well for us.

It was a clear night without wind, and José had brought us from his own store sufficient petrol to motor up to Tangier, some sixty miles away by sea. He told us we should aim to clear Cape Spartel before dawn, keeping at least five miles off the African coast to avoid the many steel tunny nets that were set at right-angles to the shore. We must not turn directly west for Tangier or Gibraltar, he said, but must carry on out

into the Straits so that, in the likely event of a levante, we should have
sea-room to beat into Tangier harbour. Sound advice. . . .

The mechanics were full of praises for our engine. By 9 p.m. it was
reassembled, and after a short trial trip up-river we anchored and sat
down to await the rising tide that would allow us to cross the bar. We
sat in the well-lighted saloon and drank Portuguese red wine, which
they said was very strong. They were abstemious. Each drank exactly
a tumbler and a half, and then would drink no more. At 10.30 José said
we might go. He stayed on board, steering through the whispering
night, and the others followed in the pinnace. When we came to the
outer beacon he warned us again of the tunny nets, and jumped into his
own boat. We said good-bye to him with the warmest feelings of
friendship and admiration. We had tried to reward them all generously,
but money should not be spoken of, since they had asked for no reward
but our thanks, and perhaps had expected none.

For two hours we motored north in a moonlit calm, trysail and
Genoa hanging dripping. To starboard we could just distinguish the
coastline. Decks, hands, clothing were wet. Curtains of dew clung to
our eyelashes. The sea was alive with fishing-boats, some working with
dazzling fans of acetylene light. Then I saw clouds of steam coming
from the exhaust. I switched off the ignition; the engine continued to
turn, the cylinder head glowing red-hot. With the petrol tank sited
above the engine this was an unhealthy state of affairs. We took down
the Genoa, sheeted in the trysail, hoisted the riding light, and went to
bed.

\*　　　\*　　　\*　　　\*

At 7 a.m. we rose and looked out over a hot, glassy sea disturbed only
by the passage of big fish or fretted by shoals of small ones as though the
gods were dropping handfuls of peas. Four flying fishes had killed
themselves on our deck. Despite Isabel's remonstrances, I cooked the
pretty things, and very good they were in the eating. Still not a breath
of wind, but the currents were carrying us back down the coast. Isabel
suggested that since we had covered twelve of the thirty-five miles to
Cape Spartel we should kedge and wait for a breeze, but I was eager to
meet José again, and argued that he and his men would soon put the
engine to rights. We entered Larache unpiloted, running the engine for
seven minutes, which was not long enough to make it boil. On the way
out with José at the helm both of us had taken note of the channel (in

order to see why we had run aground on arrival) and those observations now served us well.

We anchored in the same part of the river as before, and within five minutes José was alongside with his pinnace. Greetings were warm. They all came aboard that evening and worked till dark, overhauling the water system. The work would be completed, they said, the next day. But the next day we had bad news.

We saw the pinnace moving about the harbour, and strangely altered it was, for the towering figure of José was no longer in the stern and the birdy, slightly malevolent little Manolo was there instead. After several vain signals from us, Manolo and Julio took us into the pinnace and landed us. Where was José, Isabel asked, was he ill?

"Cartillo?" Julio answered casually. "He's gone. Gone to Tetuan for electrical treatment of the throat. He'll be away two months, perhaps longer."

Now there was a certain lethargy in their friendliness; the dynamic, supplied by José, had given way to the languor of that malarial river. Had José known the previous night that he was to leave for Tetuan early in the morning? Manolo and Julio said that he had, but we did not believe them.

We felt that we must get more money (the bourgeois answer to difficulties). We also needed petrol. A boy carried our twenty-litre can up into the town. The petrol pump was in the main street, but we could not pay the Moor in the office until we had cashed a Traveller's Cheque. Here we met with unexpected difficulty. Four banks refused our cheques. We came to a fifth and asked for the manager. In those banks the manager does not, as in Britain, occupy a separate frosty sanctum, aloof from the cash though responsible for it. The manager sat at one of the many tables behind the counter, and soon we were sitting opposite him, a Spaniard of pleasing exterior and most gloriously deep and fruity speech, and Isabel, with the merciful grace that absolute knowledge of a language alone can give, put our case to him. Although subordinates were continually approaching him with papers to be initialled (for there is much paperasserie in all Latin banks), he was affable, and brought deliberate consideration to our small problem.

"By our present law," he said, "I am only allowed to give you thirty pesetas to the pound for Traveller's Cheques; but that is an absurd exchange. It would break my heart to rob you, and I think it would be most unjust and inhospitable, particularly since bad weather caused you to take refuge in our harbour, and since in Tangier the present exchange for the pound is, let me see . . ." (consulting a newspaper), "just over 140 pesetas. The only way I can envisage to get you a reasonable exchange is an illegal one, but I think, under the special circumstances, that it should be tried. I can send one of my assistants to find a Moor who will perhaps buy your cheques. The Moor I have in mind is a customer, and I think that in front of me he will quote you a reasonable figure." He called an assistant.

"Is el Moro in Larache today?"

"I think I saw him at his office."

"Ask him to be good enough to step over here."

Well over six feet in height, grey-bearded, and with a superbly dignified presence, the Moor swept into the bank, dwarfing all of us. He sat down with us before the manager's desk. He too looked at quotations in the Tangier paper, and said that he would change us any sum from five to five hundred pounds at 130 pesetas to the pound. He took our cheque, handed us the pesetas without more ado, and swept from the bank after polite, though somewhat distant, salutations.

"There's no need to be so grateful to him about it," the manager said. "He's making a profit out of the deal, and the Moors are keen on the pound sterling just now, believing it to be undervalued in relation to the American dollar."

This agreeable and unusual bank manager then did us another good turn by advising us to eat "downstairs at the Café Central".

The heads of four fighting bulls jutted out over the tables. Even taxidermists cannot stifle the power and the glory in the head of a Miura bull. The heads were only an incidental to the decorative scheme, for the whole restaurant was a chapel to the memory of a great, sad bull-fighter, Manolete. Under the heads of the bulls were scores of brilliantly taken photographs of Manolete fighting, and in the middle of one wall there was an oil painting of the bull that killed him. The painting was framed in laurel leaves, and below it was a photograph of Manolete lying dead while the crowd wept, stunned by their irreparable loss. At the end wall by the wash-basin were several lurid posters advertising the coming appearances at Ceuta of the foremost applicants for the adoration given Manolete, two youngsters, Aparicio and Litri. The other end of the room held a long bar presided over by a man who had been in some way, great or small, connected with bull-fighting. The man made play in a hearty manner with all the drinkers who stood before him, recounting some of the exploits of the matador whose sombre grace was better explained by the photographs on the walls and by the heads of the fine animals he had killed with unforgettable artistry.

In this place we ate superbly. Even the bread was bread. The waiter was good enough to tell me where we could buy such bread for the yacht, and he explained that we must ask for "pan frances".

The engine was failing and weak when we started it to move out on the evening tide. I went ashore in the dinghy to find Mariano. Julio, the junior of the two mechanics, was on the quay. He brought Mariano forth from a shed where he had been smoking. Mariano came slowly to the water's edge; he stood there glumly, looking in my direction, but not at me. Julio came out to the yacht. He refused to risk his skin in the dinghy, but hoisted the little boat into the pinnace. He brought only one screwdriver with him in the way of tools, and with this he merely retarded the ignition a little before assuring us that all was well. We did not believe him, but what were we to do? We were unwanted.

It had been blowing a hard onshore breeze all day. Now there was an onshore sea, and no wind. We agreed, however, that if the engine would only give us a safe offing we should do well to wait at sea until we got wind, any wind.

The sea was horrible at the mouth of the channel, and when we were little more than half a mile out the engine began to exude water from the cylinder head and seemed to be on the point of either stopping or exploding. We were in an extremely difficult position, and could see only one solution—to beg a tow back into the port. One of the big fishing-boats took a warp from me and began to tow. But *Serica* carried her way so easily that we ran up to the fishing-boat on the swells more than the captain relished, and at the mouth of the river, in the very worst place to do such a thing, he cast off the tow. I let go the Danforth on twenty fathoms of cable, but the holding ground was of the poorest and the seas and eddies were hurling us about. I let out another ten fathoms, and still could not be sure that we were not dragging. As he cast off the captain had yelled that he would inform the practico, but the hour was getting late, and we had seen enough of the harbour authorities to be fairly sure that no help would come from them. Our situation was desperate, for if the wind blew up from the west, as we half expected, we would not have sea-room to beat clear of the dangers around us. We hailed other fishing-boats, but their crews turned deaf ears as they hurried in, skidding alarmingly on the seas building up ever higher on the bar. The movement where we were was indescribably savage. We waited one hour, two, hoping against hope that the pilot launch, or Manoló and Julio in the pinnace, would take pity on us and come to tow us clear or tow us in. The water in the channel was nearing that point of lowness when entry would be impossible.

The solution suddenly came to me. The engine had had time to cool off. Without explaining what I was doing to Isabel, I went below and shut the cooling water entry. With that shut I thought that the engine would take us through the channel. I got the anchor on deck, started the engine, and we ran the gauntlet. It was hard work at the tiller, for the breakers were vicious. We were helped to keep in the centre of the channel by a Moor (fertility to his loins!) who, standing silhouetted on the breakwater, guided us with signals. At length we were safely within, the panting engine switched off but still turning with its heat. A lurid, greasy twilight with gathering mists.

\*        \*        \*        \*

We rowed ashore with the morning ebb (reminding each other that José had not allowed us to "risk" using the dinghy in those waters), and had a cool interview with Mariano, Julio, and Manolo. I told Mariano that I was sure the main gasket had gone. He answered that they would visit us in the middle of the morning.

The morning dragged past. We did not bother to eat. Our stock of food was low, and we had no inclination to go ashore.

At 2 p.m. Manolo came with Julio (no Mariano, and he was the important one). They were lethargic, and I knew what was the matter, having had experience of men of their temper during the war, men who will work brilliantly for a time but who are easily sickened by apparent lack of success. They needed cajoling, I knew, and during the war it would have been my duty to flatter them. But now I was my own master and I did not feel ready to draw out their grievances with the wet dressings of soft, warm words. Had the matter been left to me we should have parted then, and sourly. But Isabel applied a blister instead of a poultice.

"You're tired of us and tired of the engine you at first praised so highly," she declared. "You won't help us any more. It was all right when things were easy. The first difficulty—and your friendship pales."

G\*

This drew a flood of protestation and assurance. They would do anything to help us, anything. But unfortunately the ayudante de Obras Publicas had come to Larache from Tetuan, and they could not let him imagine that they were neglecting their own work, even in our favour. They therefore would not be able to attempt to put the engine to rights before Sunday (this was Friday) and then it was doubtful if Mariano would feel strong enough to work for us. Manolo here attempted a diversion by cursing Larache's climate and telling us that he had just parted from his oldest son, whom he had packed off to Huelva to breathe a cleaner atmosphere "free from malaria or cancer or both". But they had given Isabel an idea. Who was the ayudante, she asked, where was he?

In less than an hour she and I were asking for Don Antonio Delmas de León at the Hotel de España in the upper part of the town. A polished gentleman, he took us into his hotel bedroom, gave us the two chairs and himself sat on the bed. He listened to our story and drove us in his car to the waterfront, where he spoke firmly to the mechanics, ordering them to set to work on our engine. They did not look pleased at the order, but next morning they were alongside when the hooters sounded.

Mariano agreed that the trouble came from the gasket, and had I carried a spare (as I normally do) all might have been well. Mariano said at once that he would make another gasket. I was puzzled by such brilliance, but took his word for it that the task was possible, and gave him money to buy the necessary material (copper and asbestos, I thought). We walked with him into the town and on the way he showed us a bazaar where he said we ought to get a fair exchange for a British cheque.

The bazaar was small, and was suffocatingly overcrowded with the tawdry goods on sale. A figure of death stood behind the counter, a tall white-skinned Jew expensively dressed in European clothes. His right shirt-sleeve was rolled up to reveal the flabbiest arm imaginable, and a medical probationer (something between a student and a doctor) was giving him an injection of a calcium fluid exported by an English firm of manufacturing chemists. We had to wait an interminable time while the fluid was slowly, slowly pumped into that ghastly white arm tinged with purple. He would not talk business while the injection continued, but made heavy conversation with us while I, wobbling and sick on the other side of the counter, looked from the scented cigarettes to the cigarette lighters and ash-trays, from the ash-trays to the tartan dolls, from the dolls to the Spanish combs. When the needle was at last withdrawn, the shirt-sleeve rolled down, the gold cuff-links adjusted, he asked us our business—and offered us only 115 pesetas to the pound. We refused. Walking through the streets, we saw the superbly dignified Moor who had obliged us before. We approached him and asked him, after polite preliminaries, if he would change us a further five pounds at 130. He looked at us closely, weighed the matter up—and offered 115. Greatly deceived, we went back to our friend the bank manager, and he at once produced a dark man in a tarbush who gave us 130 to the pound. The moral seemed to be that bankers are better than stray amateurs at such illegal transactions.

We had ourselves ferried back to the yacht in one of the rowing-boats that made the passage from shore to shore. Our fellow passengers were Moorish girls with tattooed lips, painted eyelids, and teeth symmetrically capped with gold adornment. We thought them very lovely and very dirty. The pinnace was alongside *Serica* and the two mechanics had just refitted the cylinder head when we arrived. They started the engine, which ran correctly for ten minutes. Then there were howls of anguish and hate. They cursed the engine, the boat, the heat, their cigarettes that refused to burn. The new gasket had blown immediately, and when they had removed the head I understood, for their gasket had been cut out of a fibrous compound that looked like linoleum. (Mariano said angrily that it did its work well in all the fishing-boat engines.)

They now replaced the original gasket, smearing it liberally with some chocolate-coloured paste that Julio carried with him in a small bottle. They did not finish until the light had faded, and then only with despair, groaning, and coughing. When Isabel asked for news of José, Manolo answered disparagingly: "Cartillo? What should we want with news of him? He's as good as dead, anyway. . . ."

She spoke hotly in praise of the absent man, saying he was the most undead being we had met on our travels. We gave the three men 400 pesetas and bundled them off the boat, refusing to allow them even to test the engine. We had lost confidence in them, and they in us. How humbling are human relations, even good ones, when they are lived out to the dregs!

# CHAPTER 18

## DANGEROUS WATERS

WHITE fog, layer upon layer of blindness, hid the upper buildings of Larache from us at 6.15 a.m. and began to spill down into the river. I failed to get the anchor aboard before the fog reached the channel. But this was one tide that we were not going to miss, and since it was high water we felt justified in nosing our way out. We crept ahead on the engine; I stood forward prodding with the long boat-hook and ringing the hand-bell. We now felt that we knew the Larache channel, and this was proved by the entry beacon, which sprang out of the fog only thirty feet off the starboard bow. As soon as we were clear of the shore we stopped the engine, which was going dot-and-carry-one, and ghosted on the lightest of onshore airs. I streamed the patent log and saw that although we seemed to be stationary the apparatus was just turning. So, with trysail and Genoa, we slowly edged north, the yacht steering herself while I lay in the cockpit under an awning improvised over the boom, sheltering from the clammy heat. Isabel, whose balancing tubes were troubled by the swing of the beam swell, lay below. Fish leaped round us all day, making us nervous with their mighty splashing. One of Isabel's visits to the cockpit was enlivened by a giant swordfish that propelled itself into the air at what seemed dangerously close quarters. We saw the water fly from his fearful weapon and the splash of his return gave us a shower bath. To pass the time I hung a mackerel line over the stern, and before long had taken four outsize fish, shimmering in fantastic striped beauty. I filleted them, salted and peppered them, sprinkled them with chopped herbs, and spread them out in the sun to kipper, promising Isabel that we should have a good supper. Alas! the butter was lacking. We had tried to buy butter in Larache, but had found only a Dutch tinned variety which sold for about ten shillings the pound. We had bought Dutch margarine instead, and this proved to be such a vile frying medium that I was quite discouraged from fishing any more, and wished that I had left the big mackerels sporting and prospering in that phosphorescent sea.

At 5 p.m. (after nearly eleven hours sailing in our fast yacht) only ten miles showed on the log, but I believed that we had gone a good deal farther, and my calculations were triumphantly confirmed when darkness came, for we saw ahead the light on Cape Spartel (thirty-five miles from Larache) while the ever-to-be-blessed Larache light that had drawn us out of the levante's rage into life again was not to be seen astern. Through the night the four beats every twenty seconds of the Spartel light were to me like the beating of my heart.

I stayed on deck. Not a respectable puff of wind did we get all night. I never worked harder to coax a boat along. I changed headsails. I hoisted the spinnaker as a mainsail. I boomed the Genoa. I changed Genoa and boom from side to side. . . . And when the dawn came the lighthouse on Cape Spartel was for one instant of glory in plain view.

Then the fog closed on it and on us. The air became still and soporific. We lost steerage way. I fell asleep, happy because I had achieved something during the night hours. Thirty-five miles made good can mean more than 350.

I awoke stiff, damp, and hunched stupidly over the tiller. We lay rolling and clattering in a hot, milky fog. My coat was a wet poultice, my temples were burning, my throat was dry. Somewhere not very close the diaphone on Cape Spartel was sending into the fog its four booms every two minutes. A turtle some two feet long was floating beside the yacht. Half-doped, I watched it, longing to pull it from the sea to caress its little feet, its innocent silly face, its glorious shell. When I leaned over the turtle submerged, but remained near. I put my hand in the water to splash my hot head, and the turtle went down, down until it was only a pale blob and my waking world was revolving in giddy whirls.

After another hour of calm, delicate airs similar to those of the previous day and night gave us steerage way, but we were pushed dangerously inshore by currents until the booming sounded over our heads and to port instead of starboard. Gradually, painstakingly, we beat our way round that weirdly brontosaural noise, and then suddenly conditions completely altered, the fog disintegrated, and there was the Cape to starboard, half a mile away.

In my preoccupation with the task of getting to Gibraltar without delay I had (stupidly enough) omitted to consider the complicated and fierce streams running up and down the Straits, and we had mistimed our arrival, for as we began to round Cape Spartel we found a strong current running against us and (even more serious) a towering sea. We were not to be halted however until every card had been played, so we started the engine and plunged into the sea, which came green over the bows. We had some wind to help the engine, and a leading wind at that. We used it with the trysail, and the Genoa boomed out. The engine missed occasionally but ran better than we had any right to expect. Plunge by plunge the lighthouse was brought abeam, was pushed aft to the starboard quarter.

Ahead we saw a mass of white horses, which we took to be the over-falls represented on the charts of that area. I watched vessels ahead running for shelter, but it was some time before I realised that they were sailing with an east wind while we, although so close to them, still had our sails billowed by a light south-westerly. There was a levante in the Straits.

Prudence seemed to be called for, though at the time I was so obsessed with making progress against the current that I welcomed the prospect of a levante, so long as it proved to be of more reasonable force than the one that had struck us before. Giving Isabel the tiller I went forward and took in the spinnaker boom. Had I not done so the damage might have been awful, for no sooner was the clumsy contraption inboard than the Genoa whipped over to the other side, and we were travelling like the devil with holy disinfectant on his tail, and were making the current and sea against which we had been labouring seem mere nothings. Now we had entered the Straits proper and the sea, like the wind, was from the east. Childishly delighted at being able to dispense with the engine, I revelled in the wind, shouting in the most boisterous manner my silly challenges to fate (it must be remembered that for many hours I had been coaxing the yacht through calms).

A three-masted schooner from Seville, painted white, came storming down on us driven hard by two small headsails. Her crew made signs to us that we should dispense with our Genoa, and I was already con-sidering changing it for the smallest jib, since with the Genoa pulling like a thousand tanks and only the trysail abaft the mast *Serica* was unbalanced. We were travelling so wonderfully, though, that I still delayed. The moment came when I began to worry for the mast, and I went forward, still rejoicing.

Isabel turned off the wind in our usual manner so that I might bring the sail easily and safely to the deck, but when I had begun to lower, a fierce squall hit us, the yacht luffed, and the clew of the Genoa began to strike wickedly this way and that. The sheets struck my head. They were fitted with wire pennants, and I suppose the wire, and possibly the heavy bronze hank to the clew, struck me. For a second or two I must have been unconscious. I recovered in the scuppers and automatically jumped to my feet, since the scuppers then were no place to rest in. I botched the job of getting down the sail, which collapsed partly in the water and under the bows. I had no strength to get it on board. I felt my way aft, blinded with blood, and asked Isabel what damage had been done. She told me, choking, that the wire had apparently lashed me across the eyelids, the brow, and just above the bridge of the nose. I found that I could with some effort open my eyes, so judged that I had been extremely lucky (which was the case), but I was obviously in no condition for hard sailing, and without the mainsail we could have made little progress beating up the Straits against both current and levante. Accordingly, under trysail alone, we turned tail, and hurtled back to a small cove known as Cala Spartel, somewhat in the lee of the Cape.

When we had dropped anchor I bathed my injuries until the sting of the salt had gone from them. I was famished, and took heart from my hunger, for if a horse will eat there is still work in him. I also had a tremendous thirst, one that called, nay bellowed, for WINE. I thought that during the night I had finished the last of our wine, but Isabel reminded me of a bottle stowed for safety in the forecastle. The day before we left the Tagus Tony Reynolds, of Barreiro, had come alongside us in his yacht, *Gannet*, and had presented me with the bottle. This red wine, of his own making, proved to be magnificent. After lunch I rolled on to a settee and collapsed in a semi-coma of fatigue and drunkenness that in ordinary circumstances it would have taken three bottles of Burgundy to induce. But I did not collapse before we had worked out the tides in the Straits, and had decided to move on again at 3 a.m.

\*         \*         \*         \*

Waking, I felt my way to the basin and bathed my eyelids with warm water and boracic. After this treatment I was able to pull each lid up with my fingers. The time was thirty-five minutes after midnight. The levante still howled down the Straits and we were rolling in the sea that swept round Cape Spartel. I woke again at 3.30 a.m., and, after the same agonising process with my eyes, saw and heard that the levante had dropped. We hoisted trysail and Genoa and motored round the cape. The sails did nothing to help, but a strong tide now bore us along.

Spartel, the point of Africa, smelled of thyme and rosemary, and we heard the three-syllabled language of quails seeking their food while the moon touched the mysterious heights. Many big ships, hieroglyphs of illumination, were on the move farther out, and once we were round the cape, still keeping on the spine of the tidal stream and making fast progress, we saw the lights of a hundred fishing-boats and heard the cadenced singing of their crews. Our engine would run correctly for a period varying from 90 to 300 seconds and then would miss for a few beats, only to pick up and perform as well as before. Water oozed from the cylinder head, and I reasoned (probably incorrectly) that the periodic missing was caused by slight leakage of cooling water into one or two cylinders. With each half-failure and subsequent resumption our spirits rose. Malabar light led us to the entry of Tangier harbour, where, immediately within the breakwater, the engine consumed the last drop of petrol and expired. We slid inch by inch into the harbour through a clear and exquisite dawn, the peppery smell of the town strong over the water. The street lights still burned above us as we anchored off the entry to the inner port.

A bum-boat was soon alongside. It contained a Moor, who rowed, and an efficient young Jew, his fruity face shown off delightfully by a tarbush, who introduced himself as Frenchy and who advised me to "hang up doctor flag". I gave him two Jerricans, asking him to buy us some petrol. I told the doctor's launch, which was soon with us, that we should not be landing at Tangier. (I had been advised that to land in that amusing port might prejudice our receptions in Gibraltar and later in Spain, since most of the Mediterranean smugglers were believed to be supplied from Tangier.) Several more bum-boats were soon floating in our vicinity. Their occupants, questioned about the weather, forecast another levante, and advised us either to make tracks immediately for Gibraltar or to shelter where we were. Frenchy came back with the petrol, for which he did not outrageously overcharge, and we were off.

Using the large-scale chart of the Straits, we had carefully worked out the currents, and we steered to take full advantage of them. Our first objective was to make sufficient easting so that if the levante came strongly (and suspect puffs of cloud were gathering on the summits on both sides of the Straits) we could beat into the shelter of Tarifa point. This meant putting ten miles between us and Tangier, and when that had been accomplished I half-hoped the levante would replace the calm, for the battlemented Moorish walls of Tarifa looked inviting, away over the swelling channel. But by now we could see the outline of the Rock of Gibraltar, a heavy cloud impaled on its summit.

Early in the afternoon, with the engine still missing, but the yacht as clean and neat as we could make her, we hove-to off the southern entry to Gibraltar harbour, twenty-five days after sailing from the Tagus. A smart launch hooked itself to one of our handrail stanchions (which instantly broke in half). The naval officer who came aboard told us that we had long been expected, and directed us to No. 21 buoy, near the Royal Gibraltar Yacht Club. A police launch garish with red and aluminium paint and filled with elongated constables in London helmets and blue tropical shirts shadowed us across the harbour. Isabel asked them if they would take our chain to the buoy, and this they did. It was amusing to see the fresh faces and tall, loose-jointed frames. It soon transpired that they, being the progeny of the unions of British soldiers and sailors with women indigenous to the Rock, were bilingual in Spanish and English, and the latter they spoke with the convincing accents of say, Bermondsey or Dorset, Manchester, Glasgow, Cardiff or Connemara. Two of them came aboard and presented us with numerous security documents. When we landed from that berth (though not from others we later occupied) I had to make out passes for Isabel and myself:

> "Please allow I. B. Millar (seaman) to go
> ashore on leave.
> Signed: G. MILLAR,
> Master."

Complying with all the formalities, we hurried ashore, and made our way to the Rock Hotel. Isabel (usually a small and choosy eater) was violently hungry. Alas! we were no longer in Spain (though many Spaniards, if not all, would have it otherwise) and the hotel had fixed, English hours for meals. All they could give us was tea with ham sandwiches, and the sandwiches were a gracious dispensation of the Spanish waiter from La Linea. Never did tea and ham sandwiches taste better. We felt that in arriving at Gibraltar intact, or nearly so, we had achieved something, and were in a mood to love everything and everybody we saw. Whether others felt the same about us I do not know. My face was liberally scarred and mauled (though it soon regained its normal state of bestial innocence) and Isabel's plastered arm, irked by salt-water sores under the plaster, was carried like a rifle at the port, though in an unintentionally aggressive manner. Like a twin-engined human plough we descended through the heat to the old town, and the people parted watchfully to let us through. The imported fruit in Gibraltar was luscious and varied. We bought quantities of magnificent strawberries, peaches, figs, and greengages, and thus laden we repaired to the yacht, where, despite the levante which had begun to rage again and which gave *Serica* an excuse for rubbing her aristocratic nose against the buoy, we ate a meal that few ashore could have bettered, since the Gibraltarian has been Anglicised out of any gastronomic qualities he may once have possessed (and surely he possessed some, because, after all, the English seized the fortress from the French).

Next day I had a hair-cut and went to see the Flag Officer, Admiral Brooking, who proved to be immeasurably kind. He took me to the spartan office of Mr. Watson, the chief constructional engineer, who looked at *Serica's* lines on the blue-print I carried in my pocket and said that he did not think they had ever slipped a boat like that before, but that they were quite capable of slipping any boat (though the work would be thorough, not cheap). We moved *Serica* from the buoy to the torpedo camber, where we lay near *Diotima*, Admiral Goldsmith's twelve-ton cutter that had preceded us at Milfontes. Whenever the yacht was secure there we climbed to the Rock Hotel, where we stayed for two nights and a day. Isabel was restless away from the yacht, and I suppose I was too, for on our last evening at the hotel I became embroiled in a sulphuric argument with some English people who were talking loudly in a public part of the building about the second German war, saying that "we" had won it, and that "we" had "stood alone", over-simplified, ungenerous statements that I can never tolerate (and ones rarely made by those who had anything to do with the actual fighting). After my outburst I felt that I was suspect among those travellers, and I was as glad as Isabel to get back to the more cramped quarters on *Serica*.

# CHAPTER 19

## SUN ON THE ROCK

A NAVAL tug lashed us to its side and, a black ox bearing off an osprey, moved us to the destroyer camber where a line of slips is set. Two important men of Mr. Watson's department, Messrs. Stevens and Shearer, stood on the quay waiting for us. Beside them was a mob of workers armed with ropes, hooks, fenders, saws. Stevens and Shearer . . . we were to owe much to those two planners and supervisors, to whom we merely constituted a minute addition to the work schedules of a few days in June. Stevens, burly and clear-skinned, worked in a white shirt, khaki shorts of the army pattern, stockings and brown shoes. He spoke without accent in a deep, quiet, slow voice that had a sort of west- or north-country weight to it. He was something of a god to the Spanish workers and their Spanish foremen, an Old Testament god whom they worshipped and also, for no reason that we could perceive, feared. Shearer, despite the heat, was always dressed in the English fashion, very neat and spry. From daily contact with him while we were in the grip of his department we came to know him fairly well and to admire him for his technical proficiency and for his deftness in handling the temperamental Spaniards who worked to his directions. For every situation that slight, mild, whimsical man could draw the right weapon or reward, were it rebuke, sharp order, flattery, or just a tendency to disagree. Always busy, always on the move, he was always calm and soothingly efficient. I learned a deal of good about my own race from those two. They and their Spanish workers made a combination that it would surely be hard to better anywhere in the world, for while the supervision was (without obtrusiveness) detailed, and skilled in all questions of quantities, materials, and technique, the work was done nervously, speedily, and with tremendous gusto. We soon understood that both Englishmen thought highly of the Spanish labour, and were quick to leap to its defence. And so do I, for almost everything that was done to our boat by the employees of the Naval Dockyard was well, even beautifully, done.

The Spaniards beside Stevens and Shearer transferred themselves to our deck, thirty-two men all told. While the two bosses stood silent on the quay each of the men on board loudly advised on the operation. As Captain Slocum would say, it was a howling success. All these men were riggers, and there were more riggers ashore, manning the windlass and cable. Those aboard made *Serica* fast to the cradle, resting her on a substructure of wooden blocks specially built to receive the outline of her racy form. The riggers were under the immediate control of a stout but nervous-seeming foreman with whom I was later, in the Police Club behind the North Gates, to enjoy many a pint of Messrs. Flowers' bitter. He controlled them by yell and by whistle. With every precaution we were hauled out until our deck was twenty-five feet above the concrete and our underwater form was revealed. The yacht had been antifouled (the reader may remember) in January, and had lain for five months in the teredo-suspect water of Belém Dock before we moved her. We were therefore in a hurry to get down the ladder to inspect her bottom. There was no call for shame. She was perfectly clean; not a vestige of weed, not a sign of worm. When we had grounded at Larache, however, we had torn the brass plate that comes forward over the after end of the bottom of the lead, and a lump of oak the size of a man's fist had been gouged out aft of the lead. The propeller shaft obviously needed rebushing. When the supervisors had agreed that we were safe and solid (extra safe and solid, you may be sure) it was time for the men to stop work, their five-day week ended. The filth on our deck was already indescribable. Astern of us the oily waters lapped, hideous with the stinking corpses of bonitos that had been trapped when the dry dock was emptied.

That week-end, the yacht being free of workmen, we cleared all the spaces below decks, and began scraping, sand-papering, painting, varnishing. On the Saturday morning I chartered a lorry and went in search of the three packing-cases of gear and stores that we had sent from Lymington. I found the cases in the King's Store (I think it was called that), and after a great deal of fuss I was allowed to cart them off. One case was full of paints and varnish, and this case, being "dangerous" cargo with a "flash point", should have been shipped on deck, while the other two travelled in a hold, but the notice to that effect had been affixed in error to the case containing China tea, strawberry jam, and other household necessities or luxuries, and as a result the eatables had been soaked with both fresh and salt water while the paint tins had travelled dry. It was hot and heavy work hacking open the cases (which had been constructed by boat-builders to withstand any amount of rough usage) and carrying the contents up the ladder to the limited stowage space in the yacht.

Meanwhile Isabel, walking through the crowds in John Mackintosh Square, heard a woman behind her calling: "Señorita Isabeluca, Señorita Isabeluca!" Turning, she met Rosa, who, as a Spanish girl had been a maid in my mother-in-law's households. During the war Rosa, a young woman of startling beauty, had left this service to marry a man who had been evacuated from Gibraltar. (When Gibraltar was bombed the population was evacuated for its safety to London, where the bombing was more severe.) Most touchingly affectionate was the re-union in John Mackintosh Square, with warm gushes of Spanish on either side and floods of compliments. Nothing would satisfy Rosa but that Isabel should return with her forthwith to her new flat in Victoria House, and as they walked she poured out her welcome news. . . . Her husband would be at home that morning, since it was Saturday. He was employed in one of the offices in the Naval Dockyard, and was clever, handsome, and amiable. They had one daughter, aged four. Rosa's mother-in-law lived with them. They had one of the new flats that the Government had built. It was a lovely flat, Isabel would see, and they had been able to furnish it as it deserved because, the year before, Rosa had won many hundreds of pounds in the weekly Gibraltar lottery. The money had been "useful". They had bought a car, new clothes for everybody, furniture, a shop. They had made a trip to Madrid. Rosa had run the shop for some time, but it was hard work, and recently the Government had instituted a tax on commercial profits. "Who wants to work for the Government's benefit?" Rosa asked.

So they came at last to the flat, which was all that Rosa had promised. "And at a most reasonable rent."

The husband, mother-in-law, and daughter were introduced. All were charming. "And where is *your* husband?" Rosa asked.

"That's our boat," Isabel said, taking them to their balcony, and pointing at *Serica*, far below, perched beside the others on the slip, harbour tugs, torpedo boats, R.A.S.C. launches, pinnaces.

"You came here on that tiny thing?" the husband said.

"And that's my husband."

They searched the wide space of the dockyard below them, looking into the corners of shadow, skimming the blank surfaces of concrete.

The only figure in view was that of a man struggling with a huge packing-case, some poor devil who had to work in the sun on that hot holiday. They could hear the bangs of his hammer and the echoes from the serrated faces of the great blocks of new flats. They could even hear his far from gentlemanly expletives as he ran a sliver of wood up under a finger-nail.

"Yes, that's him. Isn't he *dirty*?"

The family looked at Isabel, not sure whether to laugh or be serious. It would never do to hurt her feelings. Rosa pulled out an album and showed pictures of my mother-in-law, sister-in-law, and Isabel, dressed for garden parties or stepping into motor-cars. The last photograph represented my late esteemed father-in-law togged out in absurd full dress, silk stockings, sword, cocked hat, and all. The pictures only seemed to emphasise the filthiness of the figure below on the concrete, and Isabel knew it would be hopeless to begin to explain to Rosa and her family circle that she was glad, positively glad, to have escaped from the life in the photograph album and to be married to a tramp.

"Come down and see our boat," she said. "I'm afraid she isn't looking her best—you'll have to use your imaginations—but she's lovely, and she sails like the wind. . . ."

"No tiene motor?" the husband asked.

"Si pero. . . ."

Having unloaded the last case, I was painting the bilges when I heard footsteps on board and many voices talking Spanish. A dapper man, thoroughly neat from polished hair to shoes of brown lattice-work leather and white socks, came doubtfully in my direction (the floor-boards were up, and the table was perched on one settee).

"Mr. Millar," he said, holding out an immaculate hand, "I am Rosa's husband."

"Rosa's?"

Fortunately Isabel was close behind him. The party sat on ugly cushions (the covers had been sent, like every other washable thing on board, to Ambrose's Laundry), their feet dangling over the open bilges. They looked around them politely, having remarkable success in concealing their astonishment. The husband drank a glass of sherry and smoked a few cigarettes, and there was much talk from Rosa of the glorious days before she and Isabel had been married.

"Where do you sleep?" she asked Isabel, returning to the present and switching her sparkling eyes on the berth under the doghouse. "And where does your maid sleep?"

We were all shining with heat as though we had been greased. I expect they were relieved when they felt that they had stayed long enough to satisfy etiquette after a fortuitous encounter with a beloved figure and the man who had dragged her down to such discomfort. The bonitos were at the peak of their stench-producing form, and there was still the oily ladder to negotiate. I was asked to help the little girl. She was a trump. Though she was dressed in ribbons and white frills, it was a case of a wolf in sheep's clothing, for she stepped down the rungs, her short legs only encompassing one at a time and that with a giant stretch, yet scorning the height and my assistance.

When Rosa and her family had gone, Admiral Goldsmith appeared with his camera to take pictures of *Serica* (I supposed to have them by him as a reminder of his idea of what a cruising yacht should *not* look like). Dressed in his khaki-drill Seville hat, a blue shirt, khaki-drill trousers, and brown sandals, yet contriving somehow to look very much like an admiral, he paced over the black hawsers and other obstacles as though they were not there.

"I say, what a beautiful craft, my dear," he began. "A slippery customer no doubt. But I can't say I like her shape."

"What's wrong with it?" I asked, hoping to learn something, but he merely growled that he personally neither needed nor wanted a yacht that handled like a racing dinghy.

"Will she selfsteer?" he asked.

"Yes, she will."

"But not off the wind?"

"No."

"Ah well, there are two of you. And I must say I'm a little worried about *Diotima* in that respect, though the old haystack was designed to stumble along on her own—poor thing, poor old thing. Perhaps she will one day. We shall see."

This was only his way of talking, I had better explain. Far from being old, *Diotima* was newly built at Dartmouth, and we had no doubt at all but that she sailed herself most excellently, the wheel locked with the admiral's patent device.

"It's a question of compromise, isn't it?" he continued. "You doubt-less travel very fast, but then I should be worrying all the time about that great mast. *A damnable thing*! well stayed of course, but can you be sure? can you be sure?"

Mr. Ambrose now hailed us from the ground to ask Isabel some question.

"Who's that?" the admiral asked with every appearance of mistrust.

"He's Mr. Ambrose of Ambrose's Laundry."

"Laundry!" The admiral, determined (even in port) to be self-sufficient, liked to do his own laundry, ironing on a small table specially devised in the saloon and hanging wet garments on neat lines forward of the main rigging. "Steam- or motor-driven?" he asked, however.

"Women-driven," Isabel said. "I didn't want to give our things to a laundry—who would who's had any experience of the mechanical dissolvers-cum-pulverisers known as laundries nowadays?—but Ambrose's is all right. No mechanisation at all; just five or six nice Spanish women from La Linea."

"Hmph!" was all he would say. (A few days later we saw him in conference with Mr. Ambrose.)

"What are you doing there, my dear?"

"Lighting the Primus, Admiral, to make you some tea."

"How very kind of you, but I can't stop now. I haven't got my pipe." (He smoked one pipe of tobacco after each of the day's meals; otherwise, and this was significant, he did not smoke at all.) He took us to *Diotima* and gave us a better tea than we could have encompassed on *Serica*.

Indeed the admiral was good to us when we were grilling on the malodorous slip and later, when we were berthed near him in the torpedo camber. In a hundred ways he helped and entertained us, most of all by giving us his company. Without his kindnesses, without his distinguished past, his accomplishments as a worthy officer of the greatest of all navies, we would still have loved him. One day as I was dodging my way down the pavement of Main Street, unable to take to the roadway for the constant press of motor-cars (Gibraltar was said to have more cars in proportion to its population than any other place on earth), I met him, shopping-bag in hand, the Seville hat well down over the humorous eyes set in a face that some would call grim.

"Well, my dear," he said in his resonant, crackling naval voice, and the whole crowded street seemed to light up for me. The passers-by glanced curiously at our two rum figures. I was proud to know him and to walk with him past the Indian bazaars to the market, where he made a few careful and ascetic purchases of vegetables, fruit, and bread. He is an ascetic, having in him, though I doubt if he would approve of my saying so, many of the qualities of the great hermits. I can imagine him sitting at the mouth of a cave high up on some dangerous crag, laughing at those who crawled up to his presence to be cured of this or that. A very few years earlier this man with the shopping-bag and his questions about price, determined to live simply and retiringly (though adventurously), had been in command of big convoys arriving at that port. The Flag Officer's pinnace had fussed out to fetch him ashore and a car flying the White Ensign had waited by the waterside to drive him quickly to the comforts befitting his rank and responsibilities. A great man; one of the men who, however eagerly they seek obscurity, tower above those around them.

\*     \*     \*     \*

On the Monday the workers clustered on, in, and under *Serica*. There were: two elderly caulkers; two middle-aged painters (I think the best I have seen anywhere); an engineer and his apprentice and another engineer who worked for the department dealing with stern glands and propellers; three antifoulers; two carpenters; and a rigger, a burly great Spaniard with a round, shaven skull, who might have stalked off an Armada galleon. Our mainsail was wheeled away on a trolley to the dockyard's sail loft, our anchor chain was wheeled in another direction to the galvanising tank. The reader may recall that we had lost our C.Q.R. anchor at Sines. I was anxious to get another exactly similar to fit the chocks on deck aft of the cockpit. I tried the civilian ships' chandlers in Gibraltar, and then turned with little hope to Mr. Jenkins, the "Hardware Officer" at the dockyard.

"Yes," he said, looking into the pages of a catalogue, "yes, we can do you that." He gave me a form which had to be signed over a Gibraltar stamp. One of his clerks guided me through a maze of costing and other departments and finally a storeman led us to a series of pigeon-holes that appeared to contain all sizes of that particular type of anchor. Later I availed myself of the same efficient machine to buy such small articles as sail needles and a mop.

A naval surgeon removed the plaster from Isabel's arm which, covered with salt-water sores and fantastically emaciated, reminded us gruesomely of the poor inmates of Belsen Concentration Camp. She had suffered so much with the arm that we hoped for immediate improvement when the casing was taken off, but the effect at first seemed to be the opposite; some weeks were to pass before she regained her normal health, and some months before she could use her left hand comfortably.

*Serica* spent one week on the slip, and by the end of the week of extreme heat, work, and hospital, we were little more than two skeletons encased in brown skin. We should never have got through the work below decks had it not been for a 3,000-horse-power steam tug called *Nimbus*. The Navy had been in a quandary about the problem of Isabel's living on the slip until Lieutenant-Commander Imrie, the berthing officer, conceived the notion that she and I might (with the captain's permission) use the officers' bathroom on *Nimbus*. The biggest ocean-going tug in the dockyard, *Nimbus* was normally berthed some distance astern of us. She would go out once or twice in the day and occasionally at night, and we watched her movements with close attention, for many times a day we visited her to wash or take showers. Her interior was a quaking steel envelope smelling of fuel oil and carbolic. The metal floor of the bathroom was so hot that we could not stand on it with bare feet, the alleyways were quivering ducts of heat, yet during the hours of work thoughts of *Nimbus* constantly flickered through our brains, thoughts of her clean bath and glorious shower. I used to look forward to the hour when the Spanish workmen, each with his canvas bag in which to carry white bread and other British goods across the frontier to La Linea, would begin to flood toward the North Gate. Then I would drag my tired, dry body through a silent dockyard that was resting peacefully until the morrow. Twenty minutes later I would come off *Nimbus*, the steel revivifier, feeling ready to make a forty-mile forced march over the bare rock spines of southern Spain.

Usually, according to my limited experience, boats are launched from slipways at high speed, almost flung into the sea, but *Serica* was apparently thought to be too precious for such cavalier treatment. Heavily laden with riggers, we creaked down the slip so slowly that when we were neither in nor out of the water we stuck, and the riggers ashore had to organise blocks and tackles to haul us down. This was a slow business, and the many Spaniards on board began to cry out. At first I listened to their plaint merely as a noise, thinking that they were missing the exaltation of a speedy launching. But then, divorcing the words from the noise, I learned that the hour for the midday meal was approaching, and that they feared they would not be ashore on the stroke of twelve. Their fears were justified, and our deck became an octopus of whirling arms as all but the owners clamoured to get ashore. Even the engineers, who had been remarkably patient and thorough in taking the engine to pieces and reassembling it, and who had frequently told us how eager they were to test it when we were once more in the water, joined their voices to the general lament. The moment *Serica* floated she was whisked out of the cradle and all the men were clear of us in a flash. The Spaniards working in the dockyard had assimilated certain British habits (naturally not the best of them). They worked like boxers to the split second of the bell, and they took time off now and then to swill tea from tins.

Not sorry to be alone, we started the engine, and picking up our pilot (regulations), motored round to the torpedo camber, where we made fast in the berth normally occupied by the fire float.

After the slip the camber was a paradise. Although we were snugly berthed without danger to our newly-painted topsides and waterline, we could step ashore at will. There was a fresh-water tap at the end of the pontoon to which we were made fast, and a series of agreeable police-men (most of them by now well known to me) from their cubby-hole at the corner kept watch on *Serica* when we were absent ashore. It was the most convenient berth imaginable. We had Admiral Goldsmith near us, a mine of interest and pleasure. Now he would be reading the *Iliad*, now designing a new derrick for lifting his dinghy to the deck, now cooking, now writing a letter to Deadly Nightshade. (When the admiral moved with his family to the beautiful little town of Lymington he found—I can only suppose—that many of his neighbours' houses were named after flowers. Noting such names as The Ferns, Rose Cottage, and The Lilacs, he named his own house Deadly Nightshade.)

A man's little foibles bring him to life in the hearts of those he pleases, and so individual a character as Admiral Goldsmith is not without idiosyncrasy. As befitted a deep-water sailor he had what some might term a fixation concerning his fresh-water supply. As Piloto Eugenio had advised us, *Diotima* carried her fresh-water tank (I believe it held 100 gallons or more) under the saloon table. (*Serica's* forty-five-gallon tank was amply big enough to give us a fortnight's supply, and we are what most yachtsmen regard as water squanderers, for we wash several times a day in fresh water and also use it for cooking, washing dishes, and cleaning the brightwork on deck.) The admiral seldom went ashore without a container that he filled at the tap and emptied into his water tank when he returned to the yacht, and as a result—so frugal with water was he by the habit gained on many a long passage in a small boat —his replenishment outstripped consumption. . . . One day when we went to have tea with him Isabel asked if she might wash her hands. The wash-room on *Diotima* is much more spacious and better fitted than that on *Serica*. The basin, however, contained soapy water when Isabel went in. She emptied it. I saw Admiral Goldsmith's look not of disapproval but of astonishment as the noise of pumping penetrated the bulkhead.

"Good *heavens!*" he cried in his loudest voice. "Do you need *clean* water to wash your hands? Good heavens!"

The same careful habits seemed to extend to his use of electricity. I noticed his surprise one evening when he was in *Serica's* saloon and I switched on a couple of electric lights. *Diotima* was fitted with electric (and almost every other type of) light but he used a variety of oil pressure lamps—even in that heat—and "saved" his batteries. I could not help saying to him that he would benefit them if he used them more, since batteries, like (we are told) some human beings, rot in idleness.

"I know, my dear," he answered. "But I cannot bring myself to use the current unnecessarily. I just like to feel that it's there, the foul thing."

He had considered the possibility of charging batteries by using wind or water power. I believe that either of those methods might work. On *Serica* we sailed so many miles without using an engine other than for charging that I often wondered why no firm (so far as I know) has put on the market a charging device worked by the sea's passage. When I worked as a saboteur in France during the war, and had to have charging sets to keep my batteries going even while we were hidden in the woods, at least half a dozen ingenious methods were put at my disposal by the inventors in London. There was a charging set worked off the back wheel of a jacked-up pedal cycle; another (made by toy locomotive manufacturers) worked admirably on steam when a wood fire had been kindled under the boiler; another worked with a water wheel. It is time that the man who goes sailing in a boat that really sails can have his electricity without the onus of a charging motor. . . . The admiral while we lay near him had his navigation lights (very large and powerful ones) changed from paraffin to electricity.

"I shall switch them on when I see a ship," he said. "And switch them off when the sea has resumed its most pleasant state of emptiness."

\*　　\*　　\*　　\*

*Serica* was beginning to look herself again, but much remained to be done. The decks had to be cleaned off, though I left the caulkers' mess on them for as long as we could endure it. The spars and all the teak except the deck had to have two coats of varnish and the coach-roof two coats of paint. The dinghy was scraped and varnished and a new fender made. Sails were overhauled, rigging renewed, the mainsail (beautifully repaired by the dockyard sailmakers) bent on, the anchor chain marked off. Below decks the yacht was as good as, or better than, new, for she is built of woods that improve with age and care. Many of these things I had intended to have done by the dockyard, but when the Costing Department had convinced us that work there was as expensive as in England we decided to do everything possible ourselves.

We had dreaded Gibraltar, anticipating that time spent there would be a penance. Yet we enjoyed it almost more than any other place we visited. I had passed through Gibraltar in 1944 and then, desperately anxious to return to England after twenty months in prison camps and four months of avoiding recapture, had longed to get away from the place, and had grudged every moment spent there. But this time, on the yacht, I had no wish to leave, and had no intention of leaving before we were completely ready and had a favourable slant of wind. When I passed the Bristol Hotel, where I had been quartered as a junior officer waiting for a seat in an aeroplane, I found it amusing to recall how I had then fretted, hurrying to offices where I hoped to get my departure from the Rock expedited.

The levante playing round the angles of the Rock sent down williwaws that freshened the hot air in the torpedo camber. After breakfast we would rub down varnish or paint, and when the sun lapped up the dew we could get out our brushes and pots, secure in the prospect of a rainless day. There were days when we had to rig awnings, for varnish might boil on any surface flatly shown to the sun. At midday we would wash and change, and stroll along the shady side of the street to the Royal Gibraltar Yacht Club, which kindly offered us its hospitality. Like many of the amenities of Gibraltar the yacht club is built of wood in an almost temporary manner, but it seems to gain from its unassuming exterior, and the interior reveals a comfortable and thriving club and one with a large proportion of its membership devoted to sailing, which is trickier there, owing to the wind conditions, than in most places. As may readily be imagined, Isabel and I did no boating at Gibraltar. But we ate at the yacht club every day, and enjoyed the excellent fountains of ginger beer (for Isabel) and other potions (for me) that gushed in profusion from its bar. Alcohol is cheap and strong in Gibraltar, and many of the inhabitants, temporary and otherwise, are aware of their good fortune in this respect and do not deny the gifts showered on them by the combination of strange circumstances that make the fortress what it is. After lunch I would buy milk chocolate to keep me going through the afternoon's labours. Perhaps in the evening we would have tea with the admiral, or he with us, and when the sun went down we would go to the yacht club or to the equally hospitable Naval Officers' Pavilion to have showers, and sometimes dinner. I never felt better physically than I did in that place, for the heat and the sun suit me and I was hard from much work. I could walk in the streets feeling under light and comfortable clothing the joy of muscles in harmony so that each step was a springy adventure. There were times when I envied Admiral Goldsmith his long sail to the West Indies, and wished that we had some equally ambitious project in view. If only one could sail from Europe to the other side of the world and find Europe there when one arrived! I should like to sail across the Atlantic from England; but it would be an anticlimax to arrive in America.

For eight days our simple existence in the torpedo camber continued with only two breaks. One night we crossed the frontier and visited the fiesta at Algeciras. We dined in an open-air restaurant, the fireworks shrieking upward, the crowds padding past our table; a scene remarkable for the quality of the light diffused by the electric bulbs strung overhead against the sky and the trees and for the variety of the playing or singing beggars who came to our table that was weighed down with meat and wine. Another day we crossed the frontier to Jaime Russo's villa at el Campamento. After lunch Jaime and I rode two of his horses out along the beach at the head of Gibraltar Bay. The horses, glistening from hard food, strapping, and exercise, cantered along knee-deep in the water, shying now and then as we came on a pig that had walked down from the outlying houses of the village and had nosed out a watery hole to sleep in through the afternoon. In England you never see pigs on the seashore, but in Spain, Portugal, and Africa pigs love beaches as exaggeratedly as holiday-making Londoners, and perhaps it

might be a good idea for our pig-breeders to give their charges an annual
holiday with pay; I am convinced that most pigs would make for the
seaside. Jaime and I turned inland over the stony fields leading up to
San Roque. When we got back and had seen the horses rubbed down
we had a late tea on the terrace with mulberries and cream. (This was
June 23rd, and Jaime's mulberries were falling from the tree; in
September, when we had returned to Dorset, the mulberries were
*nearly* ripe on the glorious old tree in the orchard at Bingham's
Melcombe.

*      *      *      *

  Each morning and evening I would (by courtesy of the Commander
of the dockyard) telephone the Main Signal Office and have the weather
report read over to me. At 6 a.m. on Sunday, June 25th, the man read:
"Light southerly or south-westerly winds (ten to twelve knots) with
haze on the coast and weather generally good."
  *Diotima* was now on the slip. We hastened there to say good-bye to
Admiral Goldsmith. She perched where *Serica* had been, but how
different, how much more solid with her long, straight keel and more
stumpy, heavier, gaff rig. I took a last look at the details that I liked
(such as the twin spinnaker booms, the huge, ingenious hatches that
could be opened wide in hot ports but when shut left no weakness or
leakage in the deck). Her copper was being renewed at the waterline, and strips of copper and brown paper littered the ground.
  "*Diotima!*" we hailed. "*Diotima!*"
  No reply. But placing my ear against the hull, I heard the clink of a
spoon against china. I climbed the ladder, and there he was, seated at
the table eating an excellent breakfast.
  "I had absolutely no idea it was you, my dear fellow," he said on
seeing my head upside down in the companionway. "I thought it was
merely some scoundrel who intended to disturb me before I had done
my housework." He rose and came on deck. "Did you ever see such a
mess?" When he learned that we were leaving he said: "Well, that's
how it is with us . . . we stop for a little and then we move on, don't
we? I shall miss you both. Come back to Gibraltar in the summer of
1951; I may be here." So we left him there on the slip overlooked by the
blinking faces of the new buildings and with the decomposing fishes
sending waves of stench over yacht and admiral. We wished that the
Main Signal Office could have forecast unfavourable winds for another

month so that we could have remained near him. He intended to wait in Gibraltar until the late autumn (in order to avoid arriving in the West Indies before the end of the hurricane season).

"And can you believe it?" he said to us once, "I was talking to that ass R. . . . in Lisbon, and he told me he intended sailing for Jamaica in *August*. 'What about the hurricanes?' I asked. 'Oh,' he bravely replied, 'in a big lump of a ketch like this we've nothing to fear. Heave-to, you know, with plenty of sea-room. . . .' Balderdash! When a hurricane really strikes, the crews of yachts in harbour sometimes saw off their masts."

I recall that when Isabel had described our crossing the bar to enter the Rio Mira he said firmly: "I'd never have done it, *never*."

"Why not?"

"I'd have been afraid of making an ass of myself and losing my ship. . . ."

Every time that I visited him on *Diotima* I saw something that showed afresh how thorough he is, the care and science that he, all in the day's work, puts into ensuring that he will not lose his ship. It would have to be a peculiarly fierce and crafty turn of weather that caused that, and I pray that Admiral Goldsmith's ship may sail for another half century at least, though his demands are not excessive in that respect; I remember his summing them up in the words: "Just one more passage before the North-East Trades, oh Lord."

"Watching a man clearing a piece of rough land . . ."
A landscape up the RIO MIRA a few miles from MILFONTES (see page 169)

"'That's our boat,' Isabel said, taking them to their balcony"
(see page 201)

# CHAPTER 20

## THE HEATS BEGIN

WHEN we pushed our bows, once more glistening with white enamel and gold leaf, out of the moles we realised that the weather forecast had betrayed us, since such airs as prevailed (and they were insufficient to propel us) were from the east. We motored round Europa Point and set course across the wide bay for Punta de Calaburras. To the north-east the summits of the banked Sierras broke the upper surface of the mist. We busied ourselves about the boat. Not a breath of wind all that hot day except for ten minutes in the afternoon when we had a brief taste of the delight of sailing. In the early evening we rounded Calaburras and anchored off the pretty village of Fuengirola after a day's run of fifty-three miles. We wanted to visit the place with its wattle shelters on the beach and the doors of the houses opening directly to the sand, but the water is shoal there, and it would have meant a long pull in the dinghy. This did not deter the chief of police, who had himself rowed out to us, but he proved to be amiable, and we enjoyed his visit.

All next day we alternately ghosted with the spinnaker or travelled on the engine. We were experiencing the beginning of the real heats, and using the engine did nothing to improve the temperature below decks. The coast was obscured by haze. In the evening the sea became glassy and the yacht seemed to thrust through it with difficulty. Even breathing was an effort. We put into the big harbour of Motril and anchored in the middle near a few coasters and some fishing craft. Flinging the dinghy overboard, we jumped in with two Jerricans, for the evening was advancing, we were afraid the petrol pumps might close down, and we had to have more fuel if we were to continue without wind the following day. The dinghy tried very hard to sink. (I had not liked to leave it, freshly-varnished, in the somewhat oily waters at Gibraltar, and its timbers had dried out.) During the pull to the shore the little boat was filling faster than Isabel could bail. We did sink, but near the edge and in only two feet of water.

A delightful Customs official, thin, soft-voiced, his eyes invisible behind black lenses, came to us with the police and after steering us

through their somewhat rude questioning he accompanied us in a taxi
to the town of Motril to buy petrol at the scandalous "uncontrolled"
price of nine pesetas the litre. While the Customs man led Isabel off to
find fresh vegetables, fruit, and bread, I wandered round the grey town,
which was filled with a horde of dusty men in from the hills. More
stared upon than staring, I drifted in the press, looking into grey faces
with furrowed, almost empty, eye-sockets. Among the rabble moved
cavaliers wearing shining black hats and silver spurs. Mounted on barb
stallions, they rode with hollowed backs, pinched waists, their leathers
very long, their hands held high. . . . A night of stifling heat.

Motoring out of the harbour at 5.30 a.m. in the hope of an offshore breeze we encountered a steep head swell from the south-east
(roused presumably by bad weather elsewhere in the Mediterranean).
Off the first cape, Sacratif, we might have been battling in one of the
dangerous races of the English Channel. The seas were breaking,
although the morning was then windless. The currents, which according
to the Sailing Directions should have been in our favour, set strongly
against us, and the engine had to work hard.

In the afternoon a head wind came suddenly. We sailed fast and
splashily into it with mainsail and No. 3 jib. Isabel, still feeling the
effects of her bad arm, was violently ill, so ill that she coughed blood.
(These terrible spasms proved to be a blessing; we were later to con-
clude that they in some mysterious way altered her, because in all our
voyaging that summer subsequent to this painful experience she was
immune from seasickness.)

It may sound callous, but *Serica* sailed so beautifully into the sharp
wind that on the whole I enjoyed the afternoon. . . . I was working the
bilge pump, the yacht sailing herself, when a big wave knocked her
bows off, she tried to go about and got caught in stays. When I had her
sailing again I found that the log line had entangled itself in the free-
wheeling propeller. It would therefore be impossible to use the engine
for entering the port of Adra, and this perplexed me, for the Sailing
Directions were doubtful about this "port under construction", and our
friend Henry Denham, who had cruised that way in his fine cutter
*Korby* the year before, had informed us of shoal water and a sandy spit
immediately inside the harbour entrance.

We beat well past the port (which that evening was difficult to distinguish), then downed the mainsail to run back under small jib alone.
We travelled too fast for my liking. I streamed our heaviest warp

astern, forty fathoms of it, and it tautened as though it were mackerel line. A youth on the end of the mole signed to us to turn hard astarboard after entering. This we did, anxiously watching the bottom, and carried our way to a comfortable anchorage in the shelter of the east mole. We were pleased with ourselves; full of animal vigour, I dived in to cut the log line clear. Neither rotator nor propeller was damaged.

A security policeman was soon alongside in a dirty boat that temporarily scarred our topsides. A handsome and intelligent young man, he had taught himself French and some words of English. His local title was el cabo (corporal). He was very friendly, and sat for a long time in the hot saloon. El cabo wanted us to go to one of the quays but we resisted, preferring, as always, to lie at anchor.

"Wednesday, June 28th: *Diotima* is due to leave the slip today," my diary written at Adra records. "I wonder what the admiral is doing at this moment? I shall remember a Gibraltar enriched by his presence; when I think of the Royal Navy I shall think of it as his cradle and a large part at least of his frame, and when I think of England my love tinged with exasperation will be deepened by memories of him, of his strangely (and I must say, unintentionally) heroic flavour.

"Grilling hot on board, hotter still when we land. The town wavers in heat rising from the thin earth and a smell like that of a hen-run rises with it. There is no tree. Dusty roads channelled where electric wiring is dug in, low buildings reflecting the sun. Give a man the Jerrican and ask him to get it filled. We buy a loaf of repulsive bread and then, energy expended, move back to the waterfront to look for el cabo, who soon wears in sight, unbuttoned uniform flapping, trousers flapping, dark glasses steamy. He says there's a restaurant at the end of the shipyard, under the stern of a fifty-tonner just being ribbed. A bold girl, square, strong, with a mane of tight black curls, unlocks a shed the size of a foaling box. The walls are of almost fossilised driftwood, the roof of withered palm fronds. The interior is one-third kitchen, two-thirds restaurant. She cooks, looking at us through a sort of stable half-door. We sit damply, drinking red wine with water. The cook occasionally makes sorties to joke with us or the handsome corporal. Children come begging to the door, hair and skin encrusted with years of dry dirt. A linguistic meal, the corporal insisting on trying his English, then falling back on his more varied French, then galloping on in his own tongue. The food is passable by any standard. Interesting to note how superior

are the small red mullets of the Mediterranean to their big brothers of
the Atlantic, even those magnificent ones we ate under the bulls at
Larache and in the Restaurante Naval Setubalense. I stagger back
through the heat to the dinghy, carrying a gallon of wine and five
gallons of petrol. El cabo flaps along beside us, his pistol holster
weighing down his belt, but doesn't offer to carry anything. Dignity?
or does he suspect that our petrol is purchased on the black market?
I curse him as I toil along. . . . Returned at last to the yacht, and
wondering why we had ever left its awninged cockpit, I make a bathing
ladder of rope with wooden rungs covered in canvas. (Am getting more
handy with a sail needle.) Then we bathe. The water is warm enough
even for me. We swim and float, swim and float round *Serica* until we
find that we have been in the sea for an hour."

*    *    *    *

Next morning was again windless. To go or not? We argued this out
in the cockpit and then, treading water, in the sea. We had not enough
petrol to motor far, yet if we could creep round Cabo de Gata ("Cabo
de Gata—mind your hat-a!" as Admiral Goldsmith had warned us) we
might expect more wind. We decided that this would be worth heavy
expenditure of pesetas, and I accordingly landed with another petrol
can. While we were still conferring in the water I had had words with a
score of small boys. The boys of Adra are aquatic. They had made
their way out to *Serica* like a school of porpoises, and showed that, with
or without permission, they intended to clamber all over the yacht. I
warned Isabel to hold them severely at bay, yet as I rowed for the shore
I saw three boys climb the anchor chain and reach the deck.

When I had beached the dinghy I chose the most agreeable of the
boys surrounding me and asked him to lead me to a petrol pump. He
took me up the shaded side of the main street, past scores of grocers'
shops filled with indeterminate and unattractive foodstuffs, past cafés
filled with yawning men. The proprietor of the first petrol pump took
me to task for seeking to buy black-market petrol.

"How can I be expected to have petrol coupons?" I asked him.
"They are obtainable only from the Bank of Spain, and we have not
been in any town of sufficient importance to boast a branch of the Bank
of Spain."

"The fact remains that by attempting to buy petrol without coupons
you are upholding an exaggerated price that all cannot afford to pay."

"Will you be gracious enough to tell me where I may thus break the law?"

"At the next corner."

The small boy and I took turns in carrying the full Jerrican. He tossed it up to his shoulder and carried it more easily than I did, its side leaning against his ear. He was sixteen, but looked more like ten. We met el cabo and a friend, a Guardia Civil. They took me to a small bar on the waterfront and bought me wine. We ate olives, tomato salad, and chorizo. El cabo's friend was very tired after four days and three nights of operations against bandits (or political dissenters), in the hills.

"Not one shot fired," he told us. "Not a smell of them, not a sign, after all those hours of scrambling and marching and jolting in lorries. It was enough to make a man throw his rifle away."

As I rowed back to the yacht I heard Isabel warn the young ruffians who swarmed on deck that I might be hostile, and that they had better leave. They left like a plague of water-rats, with one concerted splash and then a fan of wet heads moving for the shore.

We were glad to leave the frying-pan of Adra, and soon after we cleared the harbour found a light onshore breeze with which we made good progress. When we had sailed past the impressive coastguard station on Cape Sabinal the wind backed to the east, coming at us from Gata, the other point of the deep bay in which Almeria lies. Accordingly we sailed into the bay, setting our bows on the mottled blue smudge that represented, from a distance of fourteen miles, the city of Almeria. We enjoyed an idyllic sail on a smooth sea. We took turns of diving over from the bows and catching the rope ladder as it rushed past in a cloud of bubbles. When we climbed out of the water steam instantly rose from our bodies. We bathed naked, free from the restrictions of watchers, and were so invigorated by sun and salt water that off Almeria we decided to put about and try to beat round Gata. But the wind (as though saying "Oh no you don't") immediately died, so we motored into a splendid harbour unencumbered by shipping. Our engine ran poorly, showing by coughs and splutters that the Spanish petrol was as impure as it was expensive. I wondered how many of the litres I had bought for such an outlay of pesetas had been adulterated with water. In the centre of the harbour the engine expired, but we were travelling at nearly seven knots, and carried ample way to choose a good anchorage and get to it. We dropped fairly near a quay backed by tall trees. Lying at the quay were a number of small craft, including a captured smuggler, a former British M.L., that flew the Red Ensign. We were therefore not surprised to be boarded by a squad of four policemen representing four different branches of security. They asked us numerous questions about "cargo", and although they were too polite to search the yacht, they stayed on board for what seemed an eternity. When they had gone we did not use our lights (fearing that they might attract more policemen), but went straight to bed. At 3 a.m. I became so worried about the carburettor (I had never previously had occasion to take the thing to pieces) that I got out of bed and by the light of a powerful torch dismantled and cleaned the whole petrol system, finding water in carburettor and filters. This took me nearly three hours (practice gained in Spanish waters later made me much quicker at the work), and we had just breakfasted when two more policemen came on board. In our dealings with them we stated (as with other Spanish officials) that we had come from England, and were going to Majorca. We were careful not to mention Gibraltar or France, since either name might have annoyed them. We soon rid ourselves of those two, because a breeze from the south-east had jumped the moles and rippled the wide harbour. We hoisted mainsail and Genoa, sailed the anchor out of the mud, and darted away. Was this breeze my reward for the early hours of mechanical labour? It seemed so, and I could have asked for none better. Sailing in the Mediterranean—a sea that does not get its fair share of wind—is made up of a few exquisite hours set in many hours of chafe, idleness, or sail-changing. How lightly we skipped out of the hollow of that great bay! How easily we rounded Cabo de Gata, the windshed about which we had been so assiduously warned! The sunlight on its snubness, the very blue swell, gave Gata an air of morbid good-humour. But capes are swinish features always eager to spring surprises on those who seek only to pass them in peace, and when we were round Gata and I had expended my forces to get the spinnaker out and ready for a useful airing, the wind disappeared. Our high spirits were nearly quashed, but not quite, for we had never anticipated the dividend of our fast sail from Almeria. The engine was started and we travelled with it for fifteen miles up the ferociously rocky coast to a small bay known as Fondeadero de San Pedro. "Fondeadero" sounded rather grand for what was no more than a sandy cove; behind the beach (Playa de las Negras) a coastguard building, a half-ruined castle (Castillo de San Pedro) groggily rearing its rust-red keep from the cliffs, and the few cottages of the village called Nijar.

The place seemed to us—thinking in terms of shelter—to be insufficiently isolated from the sea and extraordinarily isolated from communication with the land. How did any supplies penetrate that fierce girdle of precipice?

The water in the bay was crystalline. Within a moment of dropping anchor in three fathoms, sand, we were overboard and swimming for the shore. We were dissuaded from continuing in that direction by the jerky behaviour of uniformed men who kept running in and out of the coastguards' building. They made much play, though not in a threatening manner, with rifles and a telescope, and we judged it unwise to test them too severely by appearing from the water incorrectly dressed (according to the Spanish law which, like the Portuguese, ordained that woman must not show her midriff, nor man his chest). We had not been long back on board when we saw three coastguards clumsily launching a small boat that lay moored off the beach, where the swell was considerable.

Marooned by their duty in that queer corner of the European continent their eyes, their bare feet, the strangely animal growth on faces and heads, even their worn Spanish uniforms, combined to give them the "isolated" appearance you might expect to find in three men who had spent a twelvemonth on a desert island. This impression was strengthened by their wild excitement at seeing us. They asked at once whence we came, and then exclaimed, still too excited to climb up to our deck: "All the way from England! Did you come to see the baby?"

"What baby?" Isabel asked gravely.

"Our child. The son of 'Chacha' Rojas. Will you come with us now to see it?"

"We have work to do on the boat, but tomorrow we shall come to see it, tomorrow. . . ."

"Mañana. We'll tell 'Chacha' to have him clean for your visit. We'll say that a white boat from England has come so that the fame of our child may go out into the world."

"News of it has already been in the newspapers of Almeria Province," another said. "Now that the weather is improving we shall have many visitors from beyond the cliffs."

"Is there a road over the cliffs?" Isabel asked.

"A track," one of them said, stretching out his arm to point at the almost indistinguishable line creeping round this precipice and up that ravine. "Usually, however, we do our travelling in this poor boat or in the boat of Juanito Rojas, the father. Round Punta de las Negras, there, we land by the roadside, and on that road there are buses for Almeria. One of us makes that journey every two weeks, and a heavy load there is for the way home. All our bread is supplied from Almeria just now and it is ten days since we had the last load. Then there is no certainty about when the next journey can be made, for Juanito Rojas is beginning to think himself too important. 'Chacha' has more sense in some things, though she is unspiritual, that must be said. All she wants to do is feed the child and persuade it to sleep. But then 'Chacha' always went her own way and thus she took long to find a husband. Ah, but she is a good woman, and look what she has done for us. We must say nothing against 'Chacha' nor yet against Juanito.''

One of the coastguards began to feel seasick as they sat in the cockpit. He accepted a cigarette, but thrust it into his hat "to smoke ashore". Soon the others took pity on him, and bundled him into the miserable boat, a coracle of unseasoned timber. I never saw people so dangerously inept with a boat.

This also applied to our next visitors, who arrived an hour later, five females ranging in ages from young-marrieds to schoolgirls (who tended goats instead of going to school). They were all dressed in black and their feet were bare. The men had been timid with us, but the women and girls were quite un-shy and took great pleasure in examining the interior of the boat, which seemed more extravagant to them than anything they could have imagined. We were drinking a scented brand of China tea when they arrived, and this they smelled at and sipped, bursting into ear-splitting screams of infectious laughter. Their curiosity had been only partially assuaged when seasickness drove them ashore. Only one of them was at her ease in the boat; a tall girl more lissom and muscular than the others, she was Maria, the oldest daughter of the fisherman Rojas. The others, puffy and unhealthy, were so clumsy that they ran great risk of watery extinction, the more so because, although most of them had been born there on that sandy cove beside water that was perfection for bathing, not one of them knew how to swim.

These were only the first of many visitations. All the inhabitants of the place came out to *Serica* in the short time we stayed in the cove, and they were so enthralled by the peculiar ménage that had suddenly floated into their ken that we could not but welcome them with all the warmth in our natures. But that first night darkness and the swell protected us from more visitors.

# CHAPTER 21

## THE CHILD

A STRONG east wind blew fiercely for a day and a night, confining us in Fondeadero de San Pedro. Although that anchorage give; an impression of complete exposure to sea and elements it affords shelter from easterly or onshore winds, since all the wind that ought by rights to catch one broadside is sucked in by peaks and gorges and funnelled down the dry watercourse lying north of the village. Nijar must be one of the loneliest places on earth, set in a narrow isosceles triangle, the base formed by the sea, the sides by immense cliffs. To make it the more sad, Nijar was once a bigger community. We saw this when we landed. The larger proportion of the cottages had been robbed of doors, window-frames, and rafters, to provide for the repair of cottages still inhabited. We walked up the cultivated space behind the village, stumbling on the quartz that came through the soil. There was water, strangely enough, in abundance. We came on a blindfolded she-ass, bulbous with pregnancy, ambling round and round tethered to a water-wheel that scooped the surface of a spring and sent water flowing down wooden runnels to a reservoir, whence there were other runnels and little water gates so that the life-bringing fluid could be sent at human discretion to a score of different levels and plots of cultivation. The ass was blindfolded in case her task should make her collapse from giddiness. Round and round she stepped, her ears wagging, her belly swaying, and only us foreigners to watch her with pity and love.

Farther up the rockgirt triangle we came on a spring that gushed from a rock (requiring no donkey to cause the ultimate stage of its liberation). While we were admiring this exuberant sight an old woman supporting herself on a crooked stick waxed with years of usage came hobbling to us. The crowd that followed in her train stopped at a distance of some twenty yards while she took charge of us.

"There is little that is good in this water except that it is wet," she said at once. "Between the castle and my house we have a spring of pure water. You must not drink this; but the water up above is our pride, and before the birth of my grandson Agustin Rojas, whose name will one day resound through the world, we used to say of our village:

'We have sweet water, though little else remains to us.' Now all is different, everything is changed. . . ." Murmurs of approval from the others, edging nearer. "But that is no reason to neglect our water, for it could not be bettered. I wish I could say the same for all of us." She fixed what seemed to be a malignant eye on another old woman. "We have been in need of good influences," she continued. "When I was born here some seventy years ago there were eight Holy Fathers in this place; now there is none. And the one who came to see our beloved child the other day is—unsatisfactory. . . ." Noises of approval. "He would not remain to see the manifestations. No, before darkness came he must mount his mule and hurry away over the cliffs to seek his supper elsewhere. Ah! that is the nature of man . . . and there will be much jealousy inland, yes and in Almeria and even in Valencia when news of our child has been substantiated by honourable persons."

She led us back down the crumbling paths. She opened the door of the roofless and windowless church, which was used as a goat pen, and the door of the neighbouring dovecote, which had no doves in it but was still whitewashed, clean, and in good repair, for it was used as a fodder store.

"When most of the people went away, leaving me with these few families and the coastguards, they took their pigeons with them," the old woman said. "The birds that remained wearied. Some flew out to sea, and the others had to be eaten, for their presence was a sadness to us, who had been so proud of our pigeons. Why did our people go away? Have you not heard of the disaster of San Pedro? . . . The anchorage (as you should know) is very dangerous. Now, with the wind from the hills, it is a safe anchorage, but the wind will sometimes change with fatal suddenness to the south, and then it is death to be floating near this shore. Last summer a strong ship was wrecked here. The wind changed to the south and they could not make the engine start. Slowly, despite their anchors, they were driven toward us until the ship was lying on its side in the surf. In 1929 the wind so changed when all our boats, and they were many and strong, were launched. Only three boats, including that of my son, Juanito Rojas, survived by stretching their sails and running clear of the isleta, there. With the boats gone and a quarter of the able-bodied men dead this was a sad village. So most of the community dispersed to other places. Only a few of us would not leave, too few for the work that the place demands; and sad we were until the birth of my grandson. . . ."

She climbed the hill to the castle, and we followed, slowing our steps
to avoid hurrying her, for although she moved easily enough, her
breathing was painfully irregular. Turning the weathered base of the
fortifications, we came to a round pool with ilexes and junipers shading
the smooth clay parapet. The water shimmered over a bottom of
golden rock, and fresh water curved in from a tiny runnel fashioned by
man in another rock above. The old woman stepped forward and,
damming one side of the gushet with her hand (the habit of a long lifetime) drank from the jet. She caused a tumbler to be brought and made
us both drink deeply of the celebrated water. She dismissed the
attendants, and invited us to go with her to her own house. It was a low
white cottage standing on a terrace with an outlook over the rest of the
tight valley and the anchorage beyond. More than half the cottage was
a stable for donkeys, and the remainder formed the one room (about
twelve feet square) in which she lived, ate, prayed, and slept. The floor
was of beaten earth, the walls of whitened cement. It was an extraordinarily neat interior, the solid envelope of a methodical life. There
was little furniture: a high bed, the puffy bedding covered with crochet
work in the blues and whites of Staffordshire ware, a table half the size
of a card table, two small, rush-seated chairs, and a rocking-chair. A
few shelves had been hollowed out of the walls. They held Seville
pottery, a vase from Valencia, a broken china coffee-pot with a gilded
spout, three plates and, leaning against the wall and crossed like clay-
mores on the walls of Blair Castle, a table knife and an eating utensil
that was spoon one end, fork the other. All other ornamentation had
been put on the walls. Looking round the several objects fixed with
brass wire and nails to the white surfaces at varying heights but grouped
in patterns, I saw a collection of empty scent bottles, castanets bought
in Granada, a fan from Seville, a copper bed-warmer, a silver bell, two
or three small holy pictures, and a colonic irrigator. It was cool in
there. The old woman asked me to sit in the rocking-chair. She sat by
the open door, holding a whip consisting of a well-polished bamboo
handle and a lash of plaited corn fibre. With this she struck at any
chicken that dared to bow its inquisitive way through the door. She
then told us the story of the child, weaving it into her own story. . . .

"I was born in this house, and was promised to Juan Rojas, who
entered the coastguard service, went to other places and then for many
years was in the Americas. When he returned to our village I was in my

twenty-ninth year, and I had not expected to see him again. But he was
still in the service, and he needed a wife; also, he said, he was a man of
his word, though he had tarried so long away. We were married in the
church down there, and I gave him four sons and three others who died,
all sons. We lived then in the coastguard house. When my husband
died I came back up here where I had been born and took my own place
and beasts and soil from the man who lived here when I was elsewhere.
. . . Yes, I work the soil and tend the beasts, helped by my grand-
daughter Maria, who told me of her journey to your boat and of your
great kindness to her and your hospitality, which I wish I could return,
but we are poor—it was not always so—and have barely enough for
ourselves." She pointed to the rafters where one brown loaf, flat and
round, was lodged (all that remained of her ration from Almeria).
"Other houses I have too. Some are paid for in work, or grain, or flesh,
and some in money. In one of them, to which I shall presently take you,
lives the child, the son of my only son remaining here, Juanito Rojas, a
good fisherman, the one fisherman still working from our village where
once were so many and so strong and clever. From the earliest age
Juanito was supposed to have married a certain Nicolasa Rodriguez,
but when the time for marriage drew near (mark this well) Nicolasa was
afraid. One day she walked over the cliffs there, and did not return. It
was years before we had news of her, and then we learned that she had
gone to Madrid, and from Madrid to England, and from England to
America, from America to Japan, then back to Madrid—all this covering a period of years, and all in the same employ with a family of rich
Madrileños. She looked after the children of the house, by whom she
was called 'Chacha', the name by which she is now known. While
'Chacha' was on her travels my son Juanito had taken another wife who
gave him five daughters of whom the oldest is that same Maria, and a
fine girl, too. I hope you will agree. Maria will not run from her
marriage; no! she will more likely run to it. . . ." A pause for laughter
and a sip of water from a jug. "In giving birth to the fifth baby my
daughter-in-law caught fever and died. She had not been two years in
the grave (and two years is the period of mourning here as everywhere
else), when a little woman arrived in the village with her basket, a
woman whom only my son Juanito knew to be Nicolasa Rodriguez.
Now listen, for this is important: I will put the questions, and I will
answer them in one sense if not in the other. . . . Why did Nicolasa
Rodriguez (or 'Chacha') happen to come back at the end of Juanito's

mourning and before he had time to take another wife? Because,
'Chacha' says, the war in Spain had broken up her employers' household, and the children whom she had cherished as though they were her
own had aged into men and women and had gone to their own places.
. . . I repeat, why did she return at the end of his mourning? She says
she did not know his wife was dead, let alone that his mourning was
nearly ended. . . .

"I was against the marriage of Nicolasa and my son, for I was blind,
failing to see the meaning of all those happenings that from now will be
plain to everybody: how my husband had travelled far and had come
back; how Nicolasa also had travelled and come back; how I had borne
eight sons, rearing five, and how Juanito's first wife had borne only
daughters; how if a son were granted to Juanito and Nicolasa all those
far countries and people might be somehow mingled in the tissue and the
blood of one small Spanish boy; how (and this is clearly the most
important) Nicolasa had left our village at the age of sixteen, a virgin,
and how she returned to it at the age of thirty-six, still untouched by
man.

"Although Juanito is in many respects a good son, my false counsel
did not, could not, prevail. They were married and Nicolasa gave birth
to a boy child. He it is, my grandson, on whom our wonder centres.
Although he is very small for his age of ten months he can already speak
the language, and there are manifestations in Juanito's house, for the
room in which the child lies is, since his birth, illuminated by a glow that
was never there before. You can stand outside the door or the window
at night and see the delicate light that shines within. This sight is a cure
for the cataract, or other forms of partial blindness. But that is not
all. . . . Juanito, his father, had long had a running sore on his hand
that would never heal, but on the day the child was born the sore
instantly dried, nor has it run since, nor will it unless the child be taken
from us. Further to this, the corporal's wife had a baby girl who was
dying of the cough as many babies have died in this place. She laid her
baby beside the child. From that night the cough was better, nor was
Agustin any the worse. And sometimes, not often, the child will croon
to himself in the night; on these occasions his father always returns
before the dawn with a catch of fish so heavy that the sea almost enters
the boat and sinks it. Sometimes in the night the child weeps or screams.
On such nights Juanito finds the nets empty, and search though he may
he comes to believe that all fishes have left this sea. What if the child

both sings and weeps on the same night? Then Juanito will find some
nets filled with fish almost to burst them, but others, perhaps better set,
will be empty altogether. . . . And I could tell you more besides, but
come with me, and you shall see for yourselves . . . and remember, his
name is Agustin Rojas."

Before we stepped into the sunlight Isabel complimented the old
woman on the great beauty of her house. Señora Rojas nodded slowly
and picked up her stick.

"It is a fine house," she said. "There is none better."

The house to which she guided us was, though less well situated,
somewhat larger, as indeed it had to be to house Rojas, his five
daughters, "Chacha", and the baby. In her wonderfully commanding
way the old woman made those who stood on the threshold move back
while we entered. Rojas himself was down on the beach attending to his
nets and his boat with Maria, who helped him in such work. "Chacha",
a small woman delicately built and the only woman in that place who
did not wear black clothes, rose and offered Isabel and the mother-in-
law crystallised cherries from a pink china jar, while to me she handed a
glass containing some fiery liquid in which shrivelled morsels of fruit
floated. Isabel took one cherry in her tapered fingers, but the old
woman, who probably did not often have such an opportunity, seized a
handful and crammed the sticky things into her mouth, thus stifling the
initial introductions.

"I hear you want to see my child?" the mother said. "They say that
you came from England to see him, but I told them it was more likely
the east wind that brought you here than any workings of the higher
world."

"Possibly the east wind and the higher world are connected," Isabel
said. "At any rate we have heard so much of the baby that we should
be very interested to see him."

"They make such a fuss of him. It's bad for the baby. I'll take him
away from here if they go on like that. . . . My husband's too easy
with them, and takes their part against me. It suits his vanity to imagine
that he has fathered something remarkable, even something super-
natural. They accuse me of jealousy, but it is not so. . . . I'm thinking
for my child, for I can have no more, and I've spent my life with
children, though never before with one that belonged to me. I tell my
husband that even Our Lord was brought up simply, with plenty of

nourishing food and probably only His own family's adulation, and was not called upon to fulfil His mission on earth until He had developed His strength. It has been so with all great men and all the saints. . . . As for my baby being holy, all babies are holy: it is later that they cease to be so. When I was in Rio de Janeiro there was a boy pianist of great brilliance who stabbed an admirer in the eye with a lead pencil because no boy can stand the continued adulation of grown-ups. . . . But I'd like you to look at our child, for he's a dear thing, really exceptionally good and clever. Of course he's thin, but it's very difficult to feed him in this hot, dusty place, and only goats' milk. I abominate goats' milk. It makes me sick. . . . *Mother!* it frets him when you do that. Please put him back on the bed. . . . "

The old woman, laying aside her stick, had picked up the baby and, having gulped down the last of the cherries, unmasticated, was kissing it and crooning to it. Four stepsisters had crowded around the pair, pinching, stroking, kissing the poor child. "Chacha" soon had her way. The baby was put back on the double bed, where he lay quite still and immediately fixed his magnificent eyes on Isabel, gazing, gazing at the corn-coloured hair that swung round her brown little face and blue eyes, a colour combination that he was probably seeing for the first time. Whether I was in some way influenced in that isolated place by the belief of other people I do not know, but certainly I had been prepared to be bored by the baby, yet I found myself staring at him with a good deal of wonder and almost, yes, almost love. He was no bigger than a doll. Thin, too, with hands that looked big and clever on stalk-like arms. He was naked, and there were bites on his otherwise smooth, very pale skin. It struck me, and Isabel too, that his nose was unusually long and straight in proportion to the unformed cheeks and chin, and it struck us (though this sounds banal, it is the truth) that the child's eyes were wonderfully knowing. Large and black, set in the usual blue-white of the pure in body, they seemed to ripple with change, now sultry, now humorous, now calmly inquisitive. At any rate I had no wish to possess it or one like it, for although it is conceivable that I might envy another man his horse, his pictures, or even his wife, I could never covet his baby. . . . On the way out I stopped beside "Chacha" and, forgetting to be self-conscious about my Spanish, said: "And the room, Señora? Is it true what they say about the room?"

"Yes," she answered. "Yes, the room seems to glow when all else is dark. It *seems* to glow, but very, very faintly, you understand. This light doesn't come from the baby, not at least in my opinion. Though it's true that when I carry him outside the glow seems to fade from the room. Please come and see it tonight, if you happen to feel so inclined."

On our way down to the beach we were stopped by a young woman who wanted to sell us a pig. We were at first under the impression that the pig was dead, but . . .

"He eats little for his size and will eat anything," she said. "He's a strong, red pig, six months old and well-grown for his age."

"What would we do with a live pig?"

"All the boats that come here carry a pig. The pig eats the scraps, and I can sell some straw. When you need fresh meat you kill the pig. Then you sell the manure and buy another pig. . . . Where do you come from, then?"

"From England."

"Is England outside Spain—somewhere else?"

That night I sat on deck with the binoculars, watching the window of the fisherman's house. The yacht was rolling, and dew gathered on the lenses. It was difficult to see and there was some moon, but I imagined (only imagined?) that the interior of that house looked lighter than any other interior. . . . But I felt that I was spying, and had no business to watch the place. I have never paid to see the Siamese Twins or the Bearded Lady, and am never likely to.

"What were you doing?" Isabel asked when I went below.

"Looking at the weather."

# CHAPTER 22

## THE SWIMMING PILOT

THE first warm breath of morning came from the south-east. Spreading our sails to it, we were carried away from San Pedro, round the Punta de la Isleta, round the Punta de Media Naranja at the seaward end of la Mesa de Roldan, a mountain with the upper half sawn off and thrown into the sea. This is an interesting stretch of country, but one that plays queer tricks with the wind, and from the deck of a small boat we did not like the look of it at all. We were glad to strike off from the land, thinking we might find a truer wind over the open sea and that if we could but get a good slant we might sail for the Balearics. When the sun grew strong the wind died. With our light canvas we managed to creep on, bathing every hour or so. A beautiful day. At 10 p.m. we lost steerage way. We furled the sails and lay down on deck to sleep. The interior of the yacht would have served as the hottest dry-heat room of a Turkish bath. Much shipping passed us, and I had nightmares that we were being rammed. What an infernal noise ships make in the night!

At 3 a.m. I hoisted the mainsail and the Genoa and we slowly moved north, using light airs from the east. Isabel was still asleep on the fore-deck, sleeping more easily, for the yacht was steady now.

In twenty-four hours we had sailed seventy miles, slow progress, but achieved without any effort, for we had been satisfied to rest and bathe and wait for wind. Gradually during the morning we closed the coast-line where Cartagena tucks itself into the hills. When it seemed that we were going to clear Cabo Palos, a dangerous corner some miles east of Cartagena, the sea became glassy, and we rolled and wallowed, sails flapping. The barometer was falling and the sky was dark over the land. *Serica's* rolling was fierce enough to make me feel irritable, and I was surprised to see Isabel in good spirits. It was I who wanted to turn on the engine and motor to one of the anchorages in Cartagena Bay. She insisted that we should stop where we were to see what wind came, if any. We went below, where the rolling was less severe than in the cock-pit, and ate an excellent meal, which I recommend to yachtsmen in very hot weather: smoked ham with (one tin of) baked beans, both very cold from the refrigerator and eaten with a salad (green pimentos, cucumbers, one small onion, parsley, and chervil); red wine with ice in the glasses; iced chocolate.

In the late afternoon the wind came suddenly from the south-west, catching us both asleep. Soon we were bowling along the coast for Cabo Palos. We had an exciting gybe off the cape, then dashed north in a white, breaking sea that seemed the whiter by contrast with the darkness of the evening. We could not take our eyes off the startling sight of the land to windward lashed by rain squalls and crossed by a high network of lightning. We decided to make for Fondeadero del Estacio, and soon after rounding Cabo Palos we made out the yellow light-tower at the head of that anchorage. *Serica* seemed to know where she was heading for, and that we were in a hurry to beat the weather, which loomed more and more threatening. She bounded on. One finger touching the tiller was enough to fix her on the objective. Nearing the anchorage in the semi-darkness I furled the mainsail. The smallest jib pulling madly, we surged through the narrow opening. The bay is formed by a small peninsula, somewhat hooked in shape, with the light at the outer end, and from that end a sandy spit runs northward parallel to the coast. It is an underwater spit so grown with tangled weed that it serves to keep out the seas even with an onshore wind. That night the wind, half a gale, was offshore, but the shore is formed only by a low sandy barrier separating the sea from the huge salt-water lagoon known as Mar Menor. So all the shelter round us consisted of sand ridges and the submerged spit. The wind tore at the rigging. The burgee stood out as though forged of Toledo steel, yet the hull was in shelter, and the water was flat though fretted. A most powerful, salty, weedy atmosphere created by the rotting edges of the lagoon, an old boat lying deserted on the steep sandy shore, the yellow lighthouse with its friendly automatic glimmer . . . those completed the frame of that lonely anchorage. Why does it jump back so clearly to my memory? why do I see it and smell it now as though it had been the home of all my desires?

Early in the morning we both awoke, knowing from the sound of the dinghy's bouncing that a change of wind had come. The wind was now from the north-west, and was blowing down the anchorage, raising a sharp sea in the shallow water. While we breakfasted we watched the flags through the skylight, seeking to gauge the strength of the wind. As the immediate prospect was a beat to windward we decided to be brave and hoist the mainsail unreefed. It was a very stiff blow. Before I had the chain properly in, *Serica* had darted from the anchorage and was snorting out to sea. The sea, building swiftly off the shore, was so fierce that we sailed a point or two nearer the wind, and gradually closed the land. Then we sailed up the coast, scorching along less than half a mile from the beach in smooth water and with the sheets right in. This was wonderful and comfortable sailing, for with a boat of that class nothing is more invigorating than travelling close-hauled in smooth water (I think this was the only time we ever had that pleasure). For amusement, I checked our speed by taking compass bearings on the hamlets and landmarks we passed so easily: Punta del Pudrimel, Torre de la Encañizada, the coastguard hut at Mojón, Torre de la Horadada, Cabo Roig, Torrevieja, Punta de la Cornuda, Cabo Cervera, the shimmering strip of Playa de la Mata backed by vegetation coloured silver-green and yellow, the foaming mouth of the Rio Segura, Santa Pola, she flung them behind her, travelling always at eight knots. By some trick of evaporation from the sea the small houses on the low island of Tabarca stood up like skyscrapers. As we approached the island, slanting out to pass to seaward of it, the wind was suddenly sucked up into the sky. We lay there, puzzled, listening to the silence that followed the wind. The sun struck down with blistering heat, and we were soon resting in the cool folds of the brilliant water. Lying on my back, and occasionally finning luxuriously with foot or hand, I had floated some distance (perhaps 150 yards) ahead of *Serica* when I heard a cry from Isabel. A sudden lereche (south-east wind), the opposite to the north-wester that had carried us at such speed from Estacio, had flipped the yacht forward, and there she was, sailing north on her own, and both of us floundering in the sea, at least a mile from the nearest land and wearing only our skins. I swam as hard as I could to intercept, but she passed me like a knife, with a clean cutting noise and an occasional "wonshhh!" as she dipped her bows in a roller. Isabel, a wet head and two curving arms, was away over on my left hand. We drew nearer each other and watched the yacht growing smaller, exchanging guilty remarks and (in my case at any rate) experiencing numbness rather than exasperation or fear. Fairly sensible men will go out with machine-guns and try to kill each other or be killed (there is supposed to be nothing ridiculous about *that*), but how many sensible men would have become embroiled in our present adventure? Yet when I had had time to reason the matter out and discuss it with my partner, I began to feel more hopeful. The jib was still sheeted as for the north-west wind, while the mainsail had swung over to the other side. It could surely only be a matter of time before the yacht's head was pushed round and she came back in our direction. The lereche was so fickle, however, that *Serica* must have covered nearly a mile before we saw her fall away, her sails aflap. She took an age to come round. Then she began to sweep back more or less toward us in short segments. She carries weather helm, and she would sail up into the wind and then fall off until her sails filled again. Even so, she travelled at what seemed to us a terrible speed. I thought it wisest to split forces for the interception, and swam some two hundred yards inshore of Isabel. Alas for our plans! *Serica* as she approached us held longer to the wind than usual and gathered so much speed that when she lost the wind she shot up into it for a long way, then the jib filled almost immediately, and she frothed on, passing well to seaward of Isabel. Our situation was beginning to look worse than absurd. The water was warm enough, but if we exhausted ourselves in attempting to catch the yacht, and failed, we should not be able to swim to the shore.

Isabel was swimming after *Serica*. I wanted to shout to her that her chase was useless. But as I watched and steadily followed I saw the dot of her head creeping nearer, nearer to the nervous white boat that lay wondering how to adapt itself to the wind. In an agony, I watched the jib sheet tauten, then relax, tauten, relax, tauten. The jib had filled, in an instant the mainsail would fill and the yacht would be at least 300 yards farther from us. But there came a cry of triumph, and I saw that even as the yacht gathered way Isabel reached out a despairing hand and just grabbed the last rung of the bathing ladder. It had been a matter of inches, nay less, of an inch. So exhausted was she by her ardent swim in pursuit that she had no strength to pull herself up the ladder until the yacht had once more sailed into the wind—and it takes considerable effort even to hang on to the ladder while *Serica* is travelling at three or four knots. But at the first luff Isabel climbed on deck and held *Serica* safely hove-to until I climbed out of the sea. I arrived in a state of strangled laughter, for now that all was well I could not help wondering what they would have made of us on that lion-coloured coast had *Serica* sailed herself over the horizon and had we landed naked from the deep. It would plainly have been a situation calling for drastic official punishment.

We hoisted the Genoa, and soon were making great speed. But the lereche became very strong. I was in the galley, preparing a pungent

risotto, when I noticed by the angle of heel and the noise of our movement that we were over-canvased. Isabel had not wanted to disturb
me during one of my rare spells of cooking. I hastened on deck and
handed the mainsail.

Search though we would for the light-and-whistle buoy off Tabarca
"painted black and exhibiting a *green flashing* light about *every half-
second*", we could not see it, so we had to sail out far beyond the island
before turning into the Bay of Alicante. The bay, wide open to the sea
then running, was an inspiring tumble of waves rushing at the mountainous land and the distant city that shone like a jewelled scimitar.
The Genoa had to be replaced by No. 3 jib. We ate our meal singly in
the cockpit, for the sea was high and toppling and the wind (about force
six) called for exact helmsmanship. Alicante has an outer and an inner
harbour. Judging that there would be plenty of room inside, we let the
yacht race on round the outer mole, against which several big freighters
were lying, down the length of that basin, then a turn to port through the
entry to the inner harbour, a large expanse of water. Many yachts were
moored in front of a pseudo-Moorish building. We sailed in very fast,
described a great semi-circle, downed the jib, shot fifty yards into the eye
of the wind, dropped the anchor in four fathoms of water clean enough
to let me see the flukes bite the sand, and fell back on the flank of the
other yachts. Isabel had been alone in the cockpit during this silent and
enjoyable manœuvring and many people on the terraces of the yacht
club clapped their hands in approval when they saw that we were
anchored. (They took me for Isabel's yacht hand.) We at once rowed
ashore to the club, the Real Club de Regattas, passing on the way an old
Fyfe twelve-metre converted to ketch rig and looking like a half-tamed
shark.

As we passed up the steps leading straight from the water to the
interior of the club the members, chiefly young men, raised their eyes
from the dominoes with which they were playing. A page boy took us
to the secretary's office, and that gentleman bade us welcome to his club
and his city as only a Spaniard can. "We hope," he ended, "that you
will honour us with a long stay."

We told him that we should have to leave the following morning,
weather permitting.

"Weather?" he said contemptuously (though ours had appeared
to be the only boat out of the harbour), "this is only the lereche; when
the sun goes down the wind will drop."

He showed us the club's ante-rooms, ballrooms, card-room, and the long hall where rowing eights and fours and "funnies" and "whiffs" were kept on racks. He showed us silver and gold trophies presented to the club by Kings and Queens of Spain. Then he said: "You have not registered with the police? I must telephone them at once, and I'll send Hercules, the page boy, to show you where the police office is."

The yacht club was expanding its premises and building, among other amenities, a gymnasium; Hercules told us, as he led us through the town, that he was looking forward to improving his physique with the rings, "horses", and parallel bars.

Three policemen in civilian clothes were seated behind desks. We made the initial mistake of walking towards the jefe, seated at the central and largest desk, and were rudely called back by the junior assistant at the small desk by the door. We showed him the boat's papers, and he asked for our passports. We said we had left the passports on board.

"Then get them at once."

His manner was insufferable. I told him he had no authority to demand our passports, since we were not sleeping ashore; I was master of the vessel, and Isabel the crew. We were entitled to travel thus all over the world, without passports. This was the law in our own and foreign countries.

"You are not in 'a foreign country'," he replied angrily. "This is Spain. What law did you say?"

"International Law."

"Here it is la ley español, and you'd better conform to it or things will go very badly for you. . . . *International* Law!" he exclaimed, turning to his colleagues, "*International* Law! did you ever hear such nonsense?"

The others laughed gently, and the jefe asked if we carried any passengers. We thought he had some idea that we were in the right; but he was going to support his assistant no matter what line that disagreeable young man might take. Hercules stood behind us with a stony face. I had no idea what *he* thought of the argument, which Isabel now developed. The Spanish words roared and rumbled round the office, for, as Spanish arguments will, this one became hotter and louder the longer it progressed. The assistant swore that he would not only see our passports immediately (and the more inconvenient it might be for us to produce them the better), he would keep them until he was convinced that we were on the point of leaving Alicante—and a good riddance that would be. . . .

"Leave our passports in *your* hands!" Isabel said. "We might as well burn them. We should never see them again once *you* laid hands on them."

"Bring your passports here at once or we'll come out to your miserable little boat and take the passports and the pair of you too," he shouted, following this order with a stream of foul personal adjectives (which I could not understand).

"You allow your lackey to use such language to a woman?" Isabel asked the jefe, who murmured that she had got on the wrong side of his colleague. We left the office with the negotiations in a state of dead-lock, the junior assistant swearing that a posse would visit *Serica* if the passports were not in the office within half an hour.

At the Real Club we told the secretary of our tiff at the police office. Hercules stood by, glumly nodding. The secretary was upset. He went into his office and shut the door. We waited while his telephone rang again and again. He came out shaking his head.

"I'll come with you now to the yacht and wait on board to see what happens," he said. "I've told them, in order to straighten things out a little, that, weather permitting, you'll leave Alicante tonight. And remember, whatever emissary or emissaries come to the yacht from the chief of police, we must all remain calm, *extremely* calm. You won't permit me to send the passports with a note to the chief of police, Señora?"

"I'm very sorry. No."

"In that case we'd better go to the yacht at once, and wait."

I brought out a bottle of whisky, and as the half-hours crept by the secretary kept saying that the situation was improving, since the police had not come. It was stiflingly hot below decks; he said it was wiser to wait down there, for he feared that our appearance on deck might be thought provocative. At last a policeman whom we had not seen before arrived. He was a tall, tired-looking person, and as charming as a man could be. He accepted iced whisky, and was very friendly. He panted in the heat (for he wore a dark suit and a high collar) and when he had written down the numbers of our passports he was glad to go. Then the secretary said that we might go on deck. When I showed him round the yacht he looked into the paint locker, and seeing the not insignificant array of British tins he offered to do an exchange for the lot—five gallons of brandy or sherry for every gallon of British varnish, paint, or antifouling. At that time the yacht's cellar (after considerable purchases in Gibraltar and Algeciras) was better stocked than at any other period of our ownership, and I could not accept his generous (but not over-generous) offer. The secretary was rowed away through the reflected bars of light from the shore (Alicante was brilliantly lit up) and a few minutes later his sailor came back with a present, a bottle of fine sherry and a delightful note of thanks for our hospitality.

He had advised us to move to Calpe, which he said was the best jumping-off place for the Balearics, so with the first whiff of an offshore breeze we made sail. But the anchor and chain fouled certain of the underwater connections of a moored rowing-boat from which the occupants, a fisherman and an elderly socio of the Real Club de Regattas, had let down two grapnels and nine deep-sea fishing lines. After about an hour that was passed good-humouredly on both sides the cobwebby lines of nylon were disentangled, and we were able to sail on.

We had not long left the harbour when a head wind came (from the north-east). We beat out to sea, and were in luck, for when we were twelve miles offshore the breeze was accommodating enough to veer, allowing us to sail direct for Calpe.

Knowing from the Sailing Directions that Ifach, the rock at the northern end of Calpe Bay, is supposed to resemble Gibraltar, we sailed inland too soon, mistaking for Ifach the precipitous coral heights of Sierra Helada, an extraordinary ridge sharp to the sea and sloping gently inland. Within a mile and a half of the Sierra we were becalmed though near us, and all around, we saw wind on the sea. We read that: "Sailing vessels should give this stretch of coast a wide berth, for during onshore winds they may be becalmed under the cliffs, and with offshore winds heavy squalls are experienced." Without an engine we should have had to kedge to await a change of wind. A current was setting us in under the precipices, where the water reflected red and the sea cackled against the red stone. Once clear of the windless zone we sailed comfortably across Calpe Bay.

Our friend in Alicante had drawn the new harbour of Calpe on our chart, but not a sign of the vast harbour he had marked so blackly could we see until we came under the baby Rock of Gibraltar, when we made out that the harbour was about one-hundredth part of the size he had estimated. Two small (and uncompleted) moles had been built to shelter a space in the lee of the rock.

We sailed in. At the entry I began to spy the wormcasts on the sandy bottom under our bows. I dropped anchor in a hurry, and even so as the yacht swung she gently grazed the sand. A patrol vessel—a fishing-boat with a gun, a searchlight, and awnings—was anchored near-by and its commander, a rubicund, grey-haired Friar Tuck, for there was something jovially priestlike in him, came aboard to help us moor.

"Ah!" he said. "Here comes el practico."

A most extraordinary craft was forging across the harbour, sending up fierce bow waves. It seemed to have been made out of two soap-boxes and was five feet in length and three feet in beam. The floor was flat, and the powerful man who was rowing so lustily, with two oars shaped like wooden spoons, sat on the wet floor. As this miniature dreadnought approached it began to develop a wobble, and in no time it was bottom up, and we could see the practico totally submerged yet swimming smoothly. He soon climbed to our deck, rather the better for his dip since it was a day of baking heat, and he wore only a thin shirt and thin trousers, no shoes. He and the petty officer skilfully helped us to moor in the only possible berth for *Serica*—anchored off and with stern warps to the seaward mole. So cheerful were those two that they entirely coloured our first and subsequent impressions of Calpe, and these were in no way spoiled by the first policeman who came to question us, a hobbledehoy unusually stupid even for one of his calling.

"Motivo de la entrada?" he asked, thumping his rifle butt on the cock-pit gratings.

"El viento."

"Cuando salen?"

"Depende del viento."

"No tiene motor?"

Since the practico and the petty officer were still with us, Isabel explained politely to the policeman that travel with the engine was less agreeable and economical than travel with the sails; that we used the engine to enter or leave places where it seemed dangerous to use sail alone, to help us through calms, to keep the boom from slatting and reduce chafe when the sea was big and the wind inadequate, and occasionally to break out the anchor. The policeman left, muttering to himself doubts of the sanity of a woman who said she admired those who navigated without engines. We heard later from the practico (who also disliked engines) that when he rejoined his comrades at the station the young policeman reported: "There's a mad Englishwoman in the harbour: her head's full of wind."

After 8 p.m., when the heat began to go out of the air, we rowed across the harbour, beaching the dinghy beside the practico's home-made gun-boat. He had told us that he owned a bar, built underneath one of the villas set on an overhanging cliff. It was a tumbledown bar with a straw roof over the few tables outside the door. In the earthy cavern of an interior he kept his casks of red, black, and white wines, his bottles of anis, brandy, and lemonade (gaseosa), his tins of crayfish, sardines, noodles, and corned beef. He had not changed his clothes since his immersion.

He was a gaunt man with a stringy muscularity apparent from his shoulders to the tips of his splayed fingers. His features were in a vulpine manner handsome, and the eyes and mouth were gentle. Although he was an uneducated man who had lived in crude places he was sure of himself and so courteous that we were at ease in his company. We sat under the straw roof, glasses of red, black, and white wines before us (for we needed wine, and were sampling) through the gloaming and long into the velvet darkness that seemed to draw our own country nearer to us and to make our surroundings the more strange. . . . The swimming pilot told us some of his story. . . .

"For twenty-six years I worked; and now I'm back here where I cut my milk teeth. Content? What man is content? But it might be worse.

"I worked as a stoker on American ships, stoker or fireman, prefer-ably the latter, usually the former. I know what you mean, Señora, about marine engines. Devils, that's what they are, devils.

"Every voyage I saved half of my dollars, and of the rest I spent half on myself (for a man following that line of work must look to himself or he goes drifting up through the funnel in the form of hot steam or slops down to the bilges in the form of boiling alcohol) and half on my family back here in Calpe. The dollars that I saved I kept always in my ebony sea chest, a possession I inherited from my grandfather, who had had it off a Chinaman. The chest I would deposit with the captain or the purser at the beginning of each voyage, and when I left that ship or signed on for another trip (which wasn't often, for you soon tire of any engine if it's you who has to feed the infernal thing), I'd add dollars to my chest. Sometimes I'd get back here to my wife, and always when I came back my family would grow and I'd say to them: 'Never worry.

One day there'll be money to buy a vineyard up here by the village and to rig up a bar down near Ifach where the new villas are building.' But I didn't intend them to have the money, you understand, not till I was back here permanently, to see to the spending of it. It was too hard-earned to let others have the spending.

"Twenty-six long years on American ships; yes, and I bless them, for they kept me away from the fishing. Only two months at the fishing did I do in all those years, and that was when I couldn't find an American ship. Twenty-six good years? Well so-so. Over and done with now, thank God! and I'm back at Calpe for good. . . . Soy español, and to prove it I tell you that in twenty-six years I didn't learn to speak twenty words of English, though I learned to piece together the meaning of the easier words.

"My last voyage ended at San Francisco. Yes, I came home from there a passenger, and I'll tell you why. . . . At San Francisco I went to the captain to get my chest, but the captain was nowhere to be found. For two days I waited by the ship and still no sign of the captain. I went to the Spanish Consul and said to him: 'My sea chest. . . . It's in that captain's safe—at least I hope it is.' My soul quaked with fear for my dollars, for although I'd told the captain it held only curios and family papers how did I know that he hadn't opened it and taken the money to buy an automobile? The consul sent for me, and told me: 'Your captain is dead. I've been to the owners and they say the captain killed himself by falling or jumping off the high bridge. Now they've read all his papers and they say there's no mention of your chest. Did he give you a signed document in exchange for the chest?'

"He'd given me no document, and I'd asked for none. The consul told me that he'd go with the owners when the safe was opened, and would do his best to get my property for me. They hadn't found the key of the safe, but the next day or the day after they were going to have it opened by a locksmith. The consul arranged lodgings for me, and was sympathetic.

"You'll understand my feelings? For me twenty-six years of furnaces and boilers, to say nothing of a vineyard, and a bar, were in that chest. I couldn't live till I held it in my hands. And if the owners found it would they believe my story? would they even believe that the contents were honest money?

"There are many Spaniards in San Francisco, as you'd expect, for it's a Spanish town, or should be; one of them, a felon, was the man I chose to help me. On the second night, having heard nothing more from the consul, I led my chap to the captain's cabin. He opened the safe after two hours' work. It was empty, bare.

"I came out from the cabin. The other slipped away down the deck in the darkness, and I stood there, caring nothing for the night watchman who screamed at me. I climbed to a little place high in the ship, monkey's island it's called, and with only the stars above me I considered the advantages of killing myself. I looked at the great bridge with the water boiling round its piers and high, high above was the roadway of light where the automobiles crossed. How could I go back to Calpe without my dollars? Nobody at home would believe that I'd ever had dollars but I'd spent them foolishly. Already, indeed, my dollars were something of a joke in the pueblo. But it had been a joke sweet to me when they had said: 'Alvaro, lend us a few thousand dollars, we want to buy a sardiner,' or when they called me the dollar millionaire. How could I go back? And I wanted to go back.

"I walked on the great bridge. I stopped in the middle of the centre span. Very distant were the two shores, and I said to myself: 'Jump, coward, for bitter now is your life.' But a voice answered me, a deep, foreign voice that seemed to resemble that of the dead captain, and it said: 'No need to give up hope yet, my man. . . . Time enough to jump when you *know* your money's gone. . . . Besides, you've got your pay for the last voyage and you're hungry. Go and eat. You can always jump tomorrow—that's a comforting thought. . . .'

"I ate, and went to my lodgings. Morning found me asleep and dreaming. When I woke the consul stood by the bed—and he had my ebony sea chest in his hands. . . . It was like the answer to a prayer, though I confess (not for the first time either) that I hadn't prayed for my chest.

" 'Well, here you are, here's your old box,' he said.

" 'Where did you get it from?'

" 'From the owners. They had the safe opened yesterday afternoon.'

" 'And did they look inside my chest?'

" 'How could they? It's locked. Presumably you have a key?'

" 'Yes,' I said, taking the key from my neck, 'and have you got a gold watch that chimes the hours?'

"That afternoon I bought the consul a gold watch, a heavy one that cost eighty-three dollars; and every year from that date, on his Saint's Day, he's received from me a box of carne de membrillo. . . ."

The practico told us many other things. I have forgotten much of it, but the impression remains in me of a lively and interesting man.

"You saw my boat turn over, and it often does that if I drive it above a certain speed," he said. "I think it's a question of the mathematical relation of the length to the beam. The boat was built for the children to play with. But once I'd made it I was inclined to use it myself. The children won't trust themselves in it."

His dislike of fishing to earn a living was only equalled by his sympathy for fishermen. "Poor devils. Their work's all worry. The fish have swum away to Africa and the Government's forbidden fishing by night in the hope that if men kill less here the shoals will return. The fish they catch are still the best, though, the fish of Calpe being renowned for their lack of size and their remarkable tastiness. Fish, like women, should not be big, and ours are seldom longer than bananas (remark too that the best bananas are the small ones from the Canaries). Our fish are succulent, and so full of fat that when you lay them on the grill—look out for your eyes."

Sailing into the harbour we had noticed on a near-by promontory an hotel, the Parador de Ifach. The paradores were a new idea, state-sponsored hotels to attract tourists to Spain by giving them at reasonable prices the type of comfort they might be expected to desire. When we asked the swimming pilot about the hotel he said: 'It wouldn't suit me, but don't go by that, for if you take a thousand lentils and examine the lot with sufficient care you'll find that each lentil is different from all the others."

We walked up the road. The air was scented by tobacco plants, their white flowers opening now that the sun's torment had gone at last. It had been a long day. Dark faces and white clothes against the lemon-coloured wall of a farm. The open, yellow-lighted door of a shop giving a glimpse of the waxy sheen on tiers of oranges, tomatoes, and artichokes. The new hotel was clean. It made an effort to be bright and gay. Stiff flowers, compressed into vases, one vase to each table; waitresses in frills and high-heeled shoes; food detasted for tourist consumption (no garlic—the English don't like *that*). At one table was a Belgian honeymoon couple, rather stiff, and extremely warmly clad for the Spanish climate. At another table was a young Englishman, all alone and too shy even to look around him, poor fellow. We thought the place would at least be cheap. But it was not. The following morning I saw the young Englishman and the Belgian couple lying on the hotel beach waiting for lunch-time to crawl round. Such holidays and honeymoons set grisly dependence on the stomach.

Isabel made up a parcel of margarine and China tea for despatch to a friend in Madrid. Margarine seemed a poor present, but Isabel had received a letter in Gibraltar saying: "What we should really like would be some British margarine." We walked through searing heat up the neck of the isthmus, past flooded rice fields and then through orange groves to the walled village of Calpe. The post office refused to take our parcel, firstly because it was not sewn up in canvas and dotted with lead seals; secondly because it weighed over two kilograms, and no parcel weighing more than one kilo was acceptable to the authorities. Our parcel was spurned in a sour manner that we found thoroughly disagreeable. However, when we came out of the post office we were mobbed by friendly women, whose excitement arose from a glut of tomatoes which had suddenly brought cheap profusion to the market place. While we were buying there from the food laid out on the cobbles a funeral passed. Two priests in black and gold with a shuffling black tail of mourners, sixty or seventy of them. Up and down the streets and in the market place we saw genuine tears. The funeral was that of a young girl whom all had known and (apparently) esteemed. Even the rubicund butcher seen behind the scraggy cadaver of a chicken and with a porker, some turkeys, and a bullock hanging on steel hooks behind him, wept unaffectedly for the dead (girl).

In Spanish centres of population the various departments of the post office are dispersed as though to lessen the pulverising effect on communications of aerial bombardment, fire, or sabotage. You buy stamps at one side of the town, send parcels from another, telephone from here, telegraph from there. The telegraph office at Calpe was up a steep staircase of polished maple. The office presented a complicated interior with bead curtains on all sides giving entry and egress to the rooms of a spotless house, with mats lying on tiled floors and small ornaments in their hundreds. A pug was lying by the grilled counter. He allowed us to proceed with our business, but when another man came in, none other than one of the officials who had scorned Isabel's parcel, the animal barked himself into a red-eyed passion.

"No need to bark at *me*," the official shouted at the pug. "Soy español."

Until he had gone the barking continued. Then the pug lay down against the counter. It was agreeably cool in the telegraph office with its tinkling curtains and cunningly encouraged draughts. (It amused me to recollect how my grandparents in Scotland fought a never-ending action at great expense of money, energy, coal, coke, and electricity, against the smallest lance of draught-air that might penetrate their centrally-heated, double-windowed fortresses of warmth, whereas here in Calpe every house was a draught trap, every possible unmechanical means was taken to entice those airy wandering coolmen who might, if properly entertained and cosseted, thin out the wedged battalions of heatmen. How terrified our Victorian grandparents were of draughts! Yet somehow they never succeeded in conveying their terror to us, their grandchildren, or even to our fathers and mothers, their children. I remember in my young days that my parents were apt to rage against the "stuffy" rooms in which they thought that germs might multiply and corrupt. So, from the child's point of view, there was a constant and interesting struggle afoot between parents and grandparents, the haters of "stuffiness" and the haters of draughts.)

Any country would be proud of such a village as Calpe, though no other could encompass it. In England the roads, drains, and social services would be better; in France the food would be better; in Italy, at any rate the northern half of Italy, the people and places might be a little gayer; but Calpe could only be Spanish because the Spaniard is the tidiest, the cleanest, of the world's villagers. . . . The doors of the houses, high double doors of oak or other hardwood fashioned, it seemed, with a dash of Austrian baroque in the design and the counterpoise of panel and carved ornament, were wide open from the streets to give long vistas through the impeccable, tiled, draught-patrolled houses to the gardens behind. The interiors full of soft darkness that took the edge off their possibly excessive neatness were the enlargements, the cool branches, of the narrow, hot, white streets running in spirals from the top of the cone to the outer perimeter of walls.

Returning to the boat, still carrying the melting margarine, we were able to forget the hot kilometres by talking with a cultivator going in the same direction with his mule cart. Was the mule old? Isabel asked. No, young, he answered, no older than seventeen. He preferred to talk of money, and began with the words: "La peseta no vale nada. . . . Nothing in Spain is worth a damn. D'you know what I'm doing? I set aside a portion of my profits. With this money I buy gold, and with the gold thus obtained I buy American dollars."

The vines nodded their green heads as though to say: "Is that what you grow us for, then? But what *are* dollars?"

We were so hot when we arrived at the harbour that we stopped without previous agreement at the swimming pilot's bar. "Why?" I asked him when he brought out the wine and water, "why do you keep a bar down here, and not in Calpe where you have your home and your family?"

"One day in Valparaiso," he answered with typical obliqueness, "another stoker, a Catalan, but a decent enough man none the less, said to me: 'Look here, Alvaro, it's a queer thing about me—the farther I'm away from my family and the longer I'm away from them the more I love them. If they didn't live in Barcelona, Alvaro, I don't know that I'd bother to see much of them. Indeed it might be better so, for then I could do two things I desire—live in Barcelona and keep on loving my family.' Sensible enough. . . . And there's another point of view. It's easier for the family to esteem paterfamilias if he's often absent. Fond as I am of my wife and my children, there are nights when I think: 'They'll like me all the better if they don't see me before tomorrow.' Then I can doss down on the bar and be independent. It's no use going home if it's only hunger that takes you there. . . .'"

Next day, the wind remaining unfavourable for the crossing to the Balearics, we decided on a change of scene, and sailed up the coast to Morayra. Ensenada de Morayra is protected from northerly and (to some extent) easterly winds by the beak of Cabo de Morayra, a grim lump of rock. The anchorage (which proved to be disappointingly shallow) resembles in shape that of Fondeadero de San Pedro, although in no other way, for the country at Morayra is fertile, lovely, and closely inhabited, and on the sandy beach at the head of the bay sits the prettiest little holiday resort, a collection of cottages owned mainly by burghers of Valencia rich from exploitation of the orange, the onion, the vine, and (as nobody who has eaten arroz à la Valenciana can forget) that wonderful annual, the rice plant.

As it was now July 8th, many of the Valencians were in holiday residence and, when we arrived after midday, were rising from their beds for the morning bathe and booming frolic on beach and water. We were abashed by those sleek, seal-like bodies and the (also strangely reminiscent of the circus) small American caps they wore as decoration or to shade their eyes. When I had set the awning we hurried below. They buzzed round us in boats with outboard engines, and as we ate we

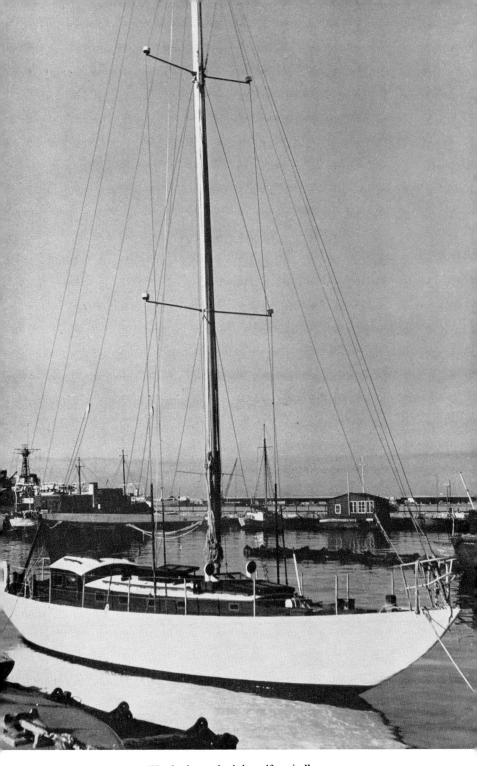

"Beginning to look herself again."
*SERICA* in the Torpedo Camber (see page 209)

"Will she selfsteer?"
*SERICA* on the slip at GIBRALTAR (see page 203)

listened to their remarks. They decided, since no seams were visible on our topsides, that *Serica* was built of steel and was worth a good deal of money. They were sure that, hidden beneath all that surface gloss of mast and rigging, the yacht had an extremely powerful engine: guesses of 80 or 100 horse power were hazarded. When they had all gone in to eat at 3.30 p.m., we landed to stretch our legs in the orange groves, and to bathe from the surfy beaches lower down the coast.

# CHAPTER 23

## THE BALEARICS

GLISTENING rollers came sneaking round Cabo de Morayra to thunder as they shoaled in the ensenada, and *Serica* lay to them (the cow) broadside on. We motored round the cape and headed out to sea, taking the tiller in hourly spells. The half of the crew not steering had the choice of baking in the saloon or grilling on deck. After pushing us ten miles from the coast the engine stopped. Dirty petrol. Sweat dripping from my finger-ends to the hot metal, I began to dismount the carburettor. While I was thus engaged a blessed tongue of air licked out of the south. We stood on deck enjoying its coolness and praying that it would strengthen. Then we hoisted mainsail and Genoa, prepared lunch, and had a splendid bathe, letting the yacht tow us and rolling over and over in the frothy water that slid from her counter. When we were on board again she did not seem to be moving, and her boom clattered to the swell while we ate. But soon a steady breeze from the south sent us flying on a broad reach. An hour of such progress and the bold outlines of the island of Iviza rose from the sea on the port bow. Now it was fresh on deck, and the tiller was alive in the hand. All afternoon we raced on, and in the dusk we sailed along the south-western coast of Iviza, a warmer landscape than any we had seen since Portugal, greener, more treed. To starboard was the lower island of Formentera. Iviza and Formentera are almost joined by a string of islets, and between those there is a narrow channel marked by tall light-houses. A treacherous place it must be in dirty weather from west or east, but we passed through serenely with the last of the daylight and of the south wind that had served us so magnificently. Once through the jaws we dipped our bows into a high easterly swell. After a few puffs from the east we held a fresh breeze, a westerly blowing down off the highlands of Iviza, where the villages showed garters of light on the dark thighs of the hills. Gunwale under, steady, though rising and falling on the contrary swell, we hissed through the hot darkness toward the many navigational lights marking the dangers off Puerto de Iviza. The Sailing Directions say that the inner harbour of Iviza is "small" and that

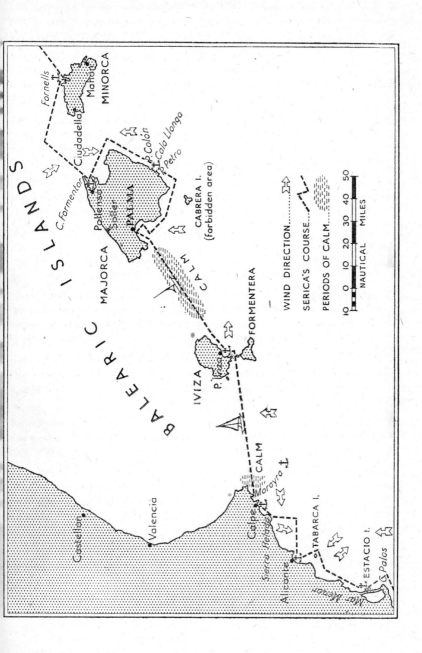

"vessels must either make fast to the landing place or secure head and
stern according to draught", but we had a large-scale chart of the
harbour and we found courage to sail in with the mainsail, downing the
Genoa as we rounded the mole, and dropping anchor in the middle of a
dark purple pool of water splashed with gold from the dazzling quay-
sides. All other vessels *were* secured to the quays. But Puerto de Iviza
was in a turmoil of fiesta and we judged that we should be undisturbed.
Below decks the thermometer registered 97 (F). We ate fruit and
drank wine in the cockpit, and then lay down to sleep on deck. The
yacht played her usual tricks at anchor, darting about restlessly in the
gusts. Ashore the mob paced the streets, a black, noisy, shifting mass,
feet stirring dust that rose like smoke through the yellow light stained
scarlet or blue here and there by the coloured signs of cafés and bars.
Music fought music from every open door, and this many-sided engage-
ment was dominated by a brass band that played in the open near the
waterfront.

Iviza looked even more interesting at dawn, with the cats prowling the
simple streets while the dogs lay asleep in the litter of the fiesta. Now
we could see the castle, the steep alleys of the old town, the deserted ice-
cream barrow, the chestnut-roasting stand, the accumulation of white
coasters—a spinney of solid masts—the yacht club with a line of
pleasure boats and one up on the slip. But the westerly was still there,
though sadly weakened, and thinking that our impression of the port
was already good enough (and perhaps would only spoil from closer
contact) we sailed from the harbour.

We sailed in company with a local fishing-boat, cutter-rigged and with
a long bowsprit and a boom stretching far aft of the counter. This boat,
well handled and setting three voluminous headsails, topsail, and mainsail, all of some flimsy material suited to the light airs, held her own
with us round the island. But when we had set course for Palma,
Majorca, and saw that the westerly predominated on the open sea we
hoisted our huge parachute spinnaker, and that sail lifted our bows and
hauled us away from our engaging rival, who had taken the keenest
enjoyment in the race. The light airs persisted till midday, when we lay
becalmed, half-way from Iviza to Majorca and with both islands well
down below the horizon.

Late that night the engine pushed us into Palma harbour.

Although I should have been warned by the praises of Palma sung by

Spaniards around the coasts from Corunna to Alicante, I had expected
to find an unspoiled and simple port like Iviza. . . . We entered under
the spangled bosoms of new hotels, and the windmill of a night-club, its
sails studded with red lights, revolved unnaturally on that night of airless
heat. Outside the entrance we had met three Spanish submarines
running on the surface in line ahead, and these had covered the water of
the port with oil. We anchored off the imposing though bald frontage
of the new yacht club and two sailors put out in a dinghy to take our
stern warps. We were drawn back to the quay between a top-heavy
motor-sailer from Valencia and a trim little blue sloop from Barcelona.
We set our stern gang-plank in position for the first time on the voyage.
On either hand the "afterguards" were dining in the awninged cock-
pits while hands ran aft from the cooking stoves (the yacht from Valencia
had a collapsible coal range of almost country-house-kitchen dimensions
set on deck) with dishes and more dishes for the tables. Neither vessel
approached the beauty, or even the tonnage, of *Serica*. We ate biscuits
and cheese, and tumbled off to sleep in the superheated interior. We
could not sleep on deck, watched by the crews of the neighbouring
yachts and by the crowd that had gathered on the balustraded quay
astern.

    In the morning we were alone, for those around us were still treading
the mazes of sleep. There was oil on the water, and in the oil floated
many dead fishes, but Palma took on its true form. We saw that the big
hotels were grouped in the suburb of El Terreno, flanking the harbour,
and astern the old town rose, red and brown and (important embellish-
ment) served by a tramway network.
    We went ashore that morning to the yacht club to leave my card and
formally acknowledge the club's hospitality. The acknowledgment was
received, in the absence of president and secretary, by the steward, a
lithe and intelligent Spaniard showing under the open throat of his shirt
a strong chest crossed by a white singlet (confirming my correct impression that he was ex-Navy). This man went by the name of Ismael.
He had soon organised everything material that we wanted from Palma.
The accommodation ladder repaired with teak? he would send a
carpenter on board that morning. Laundry? he would send a woman
that afternoon. Eighty litres of petrol? good petrol did not exist, but he
would send a boy with a handcart immediately if we could supply the
bidones. Ten litres of ultra-refined paraffin? one of the members was

a director of the firm of Shell; he, Ismael, would see what could be done. . . . He spoke rapidly, leaning his head well back, with all the authority of the man around whom one of the biggest yacht clubs in the world revolved, a club with about eight thousand members and five hundred boats on its register. When he was not busy Ismael sat just inside the outer porch, watching the comings-and-goings, the pulse of the organisation he tended with ardent efficiency. He showed us round the various bars and public rooms, the dining-room, the ballroom, the patio with its outdoor dancing floor. That afternoon, he told us, there was to be a thé dansant. The following evening a soprano from La Scala would give a recital in the ballroom (all members and their friends cordially invited—collection for the orphans of St. Fatima). And the following night in the club there would be fiesta, yes, all night till four, five, six in the morning. Music! Ismael said. Champagne! The prettiest girls in Palma and many from the mainland.

Inland from the club stretch the water garages holding the members' boats. If few of these were individually impressive or even interesting, the mass was impressive in the extreme. Perhaps six or seven cruising yachts, a score or two of small-class boats, and hundreds of boats of the local type, white, half-decked, with engines and lateen sails, excellent little boats, economical, serviceable.

During the three days that we lay in Palma the yacht club was of the greatest use to us. We took advantage of its bathrooms, its excellent restaurant, its bars, and we could always find relief from the blinding light of the Balearics in the sitting-rooms which, though anything but intimate, though unpossessed of the cloisteral charm that we in England are apt to associate with clubs, were well suited to place, climate, and function.

In the mornings we would take a tram up through the town to a market. The stalls were arranged tightly under a dark canopy. One stall supplied, according to its banner, "le vrai pastis de Marseille", a beverage for which, in hot weather, I can always discover a liking (and which, during the war, I used to manufacture without difficulty by buying a litre of alcohol from a pharmacist and adding to it the contents of an aromatic packet). Vegetables were superabundant and of supreme quality, fruits abundant but mediocre, and the butter—this was the first Spanish port we had visited where fresh butter was readily obtainable— was up to French standards. In a burrow off the side of the market a specialist and his boy assistant were always making ensaimadas. The ensaimada should be eaten with coffee (and dipped in it) like the croissant, but it is superior to the croissant, being lighter and more delicate, less greasy. The ensaimada is round in shape, and is made in all dimensions, from those of a five-shilling piece to those of a round dining-table. Ensaimadas are baked by men who do not sully their talents by producing ordinary bread. Perhaps I had better add that the man in the market told me he was making his ensaimadas from imported American flour.

If you enjoy the Giant Racer the tram-cars in Palma will please you, for they are always rushing down a hill or rushing at a hill. There are notices in the trams forbidding smoking; the drivers and conductors smoke constantly, and the passengers who stand beside the driver in the front cab (forbidden) conversing with him (also forbidden) ply him with cigarettes. We made one trip from the Banco Hispano Americano at the top of the old town, through the suburb of Terreno with its hotels and bungaloid growths to the terminus at Puerto Pi, and all the way the driver and the conductor, supporting each other in the rocking cab, sang duets from unknown operas, the driver a tenor, the conductor a falsetto mezzo-soprano. Most passengers left the tram without paying, though one or two pressed forward to the cab and thrust money into the hand of the singing conductor. Everybody was laughing. It was an exciting ride, and many were the stations we passed where we should have stopped and the stations at which we stopped when there was no need. . . . There is one narrow street (near the Palma railway station) that is just wide enough to take the tram, and nothing else besides. Before the entry to this gulch the tram halts nervously, clanging its bell. You would expect it to crawl through then. But no! The electric motor thrums, the brass lever is swung right over, the bell increases its tempo, and the car plunges into the street like a piston down a cylinder, its cow-catcher outstretched to pick up a lapdog, to snatch at the skirts of a girl who may have jumped too late for the safety of a doorway. The shops and their wares fly past, each with its own hollow groan, the sound varying if the contents happen to be mantillas, racks of newspapers, or bottles.

One hot night I was strolling back to the yacht from the Café Formentor. In the shadow under a plane tree in the handsome Avenida a man spoke to me in English from an invalid's chair. What was more— and I was startled—he addressed me by name,

"I should like you to come to my house for a talk," he said. "That is, if you can spare thirty minutes. Where did you buy these cigarettes?"

"Gibraltar."

"They are very good."

"They are yours since they please you."

"Why do you ride so much on our street railways?" he asked, pushing a lever on his wheel-chair (which was propelled by electricity). "My house is not far away, and I can adjust my pace to yours, so walk as it suits you, please."

"Would it be indiscreet to ask how you know that I ride on the tram-cars?"

"Anything that you might ask I would surely answer were an honest answer within my diminishing powers. . . . It is well known in Palma that you ride on the street railways, for eccentricity is quickly noted in our island, a place where eccentricity is valued. . . . You like it? You like Palma? . . . Ah yes, I knew you would appreciate this town, for it is the most beautiful on earth without a doubt, and the most aristocratic." The last words were spoken in a manner that seemed almost challenging, and he moved the lever so that his chair crept suddenly ahead of me while I walked.

"What is eccentric about travel on a tramway?" I called after him.

"You came here on a yacht, without servants. An anachronism. All right, everybody says, he has probably had a row with the servants and thrown them overboard. Your wife speaks Castilian with faultless accent, so she has been well educated, that is certain. You speak good French, so you are a man of education, that is probable. But what do you do? Instead of going in the Lincoln motor-car of the American who hastens down to see you from the Hotel Victoria you walk past the fish market, sniffing at it and examining the fish; you take the street railway to the old town and to the most stinking parts of it. You go diving into the market among all the cooks of Palma, and you drink coffee or alcohol there when you could choose from a hundred agreeable bars with electric fans. Even your wife dives in among the cooks, and she buys vegetables and puts them in a bag. Is that not eccentric? You take another street train and go to Puerto Pi. It is thought you are going to the restaurant there, but no! You take another street train back to Terreno. Ah! it is thought, now Señor and Señora Millar will visit the American at the Hotel Victoria or their friend the admirably-connected Spanish lady who is also staying in that comfortable place. But no!

You enter a restaurant, the Patio, at this moment perhaps the best in all Palma, and there you spend a ransom on food and wine. This sum would have procured you taxis for a week, two weeks. But when you have feasted (good appetites, eh?), when you have feasted you take the street train back to the fish market. You walk to the yacht, and on the yacht, instead of taking a siesta, you sit in the sun *and sew sails*! My dear sir, if you were not English we should pronounce you mad, and possibly dangerous. Though," he added, "a man does not have to be mad to be dangerous."

"We never supposed that we were followed or our conduct might have seemed still more outrageous."

When we had crossed a street he said: "I take an interest in all that happens in Palma. I could tell you many things about any house of consequence, yes, I think, any house. I used to be everywhere myself in Palma, everywhere. Now that I have lost my legs I am the more consumed with curiosity. Then I have faithful servants, men bred into the veins of my family so that their blood is almost my blood. . . . I am particularly curious about the English because—forgive me, but I say it with no personal intent as between us two—I hate them."

"That is understandable."

"Broad-minded!" he snarled at me. "The English have ruined me, that's why . . . here is my house. If you will be good enough to pull that bell . . ."

"How have we ruined you?" I asked when one manservant had shown us across a wide patio and another had helped to lift the wheeled chair up three steps leading to the salon, a polished vastness hung with tapestries and set with inlaid furnishings.

"Before the war," he answered, "I refer to the Spanish War, and not to your affair with the Hitlerians, I had factories on this island and on the mainland. I imported from England and its Dominions immense quantities of raw or processed materials. My factories made many things from these, and the trade was good for Majorca, for Spain, and for me. But since the war it is forbidden by the Spanish Government for me to import from England at all—so I am ruined. My factories are closed. Some of the workers go out with the maquis and rob the innocent and the good. . . ."

When he had questioned me closely about the ports we had visited and especially, again and again, about our motives for making such a journey, he decided to take me on a tour round part of his house. We

1*

entered room after room and a servant would switch on lights to shine
upon leather, tapestry, mother-of-pearl, gilded picture-frames, and pale
mats on dark floors. Passing through his library he opened a cupboard
and chose a box of cigars. Before handing it to me he broke the seals
and examined each cigar on the top layer. "They are too much for me
since I lost my legs and take no exercise," he said. "Too heavy. . . .
Don't keep them long, now. Smoke them furiously, smoke them all the
time. That's the only way to treat cigars. Smoke them till your head
whirls and the fire brigade arrives at your yacht. . . . Ah! be grateful
for your straight legs, young man. . . . Which reminds me that I have
not shown the museum."

The museum, whitewashed with a groined ceiling, was in the base-
ment, and the majority of the exhibits were from his collection of
weapons, which included an English longbow said to have been fired at
Agincourt. "*This*," he said, "is a more personal exhibit." The leg,
naked, slightly bent at the knee, lay on a black velvet cushion inside a
complicated airtight glass case. It had been embalmed and shaved, and
was of a curious colour rather like that of an unsmoked meerschaum.
It had been severed on the thigh, and that part was covered with a
velvet pad. Two-thirds of the foot were hidden in a light slipper of pale
blue morocco.

"See that mark below the knee?" he asked. "Done when I fell from
my pony on my father's estate near Córdoba sixty years ago. Poor old
leg. Though it's younger than I am, a lot younger too. Its brother is in
the railway museum of Palma. I will give you the address and you must
go to see it—Room D., downstairs. This one here is fatter. Public
museums are poor places, I fear. But I should tell you why I sent it to
the railway museum. . . . In the month of May thirty-one years ago
when a friend of mine—a young man of unimpeachable character—and
I were in wine we had a great quarrel by the roadside. The subject of the
quarrel was of no subsequent importance. Suffice it to say that I struck
my friend and he returned the blow at an unfortunate moment. I fell in
front of a street train. The wheels of such vehicles (you declare that
you actually *like* the things?) are made of steel, and fit into the steel
grooves we call rails. The two together might have been designed as
nutcrackers or scissors."

The following day when I was working on deck one of the legless
gentleman's servants appeared among the small crowd standing on the

quay astern. After a while, becoming uncomfortable under my scrutiny
(for I frequently lifted my eyes from the splice between my fingers to
stare at him) the man strolled away, stopping to speak with Ismael, who
was sitting, keenly resting, in the porch of the yacht club. Then the man
wandered still farther away. When I saw him talking to some fishermen
from Alicante who were marooned in Palma because of a damaged
propeller, I laid aside my work and went over to Ismael.

"Do you know the employer of the man who has just spoken to you?"
I asked.

Ismael smiled. "Of course I do. That fellow is employed by one of
our greatest philanthropists, a noble soul. . . ."

"In an invalid chair?"

"Just so. He lost his legs in an accident. . . . There are many kinds
of philanthropist," Ismael said, "but the man in the chair is the best we
know. He claims no reward for his goodness. He helps those who can't
help themselves and who can do nothing to repay his bounty and his
thoughtfulness. What's even more astonishing, he helps, where he can,
anonymously. Frequently when some poor person (and there are many
such) receives money or food or both he's no idea who's the donor; he
had had no idea that anybody, let alone a wealthy man, was aware that
he and his family were in desperate need. The philanthropist in question
is an eccentric, there can be no doubt about that. He does good by
stealth. And I pity anybody who goes to thank him for his generosity,
for on such occasions his tongue is swift and bitter, since he doesn't care
for thanks, or so it would seem. . . . You look surprised. You've
met him I suppose?"

"Last night."

"He's known all about you since the morning after you arrived. Each
day, sometimes twice a day, one of his servants came to ask on his behalf
if there's anything we can think of that you might need for your comfort
and that of the Señora. . . . Did you by any chance last night receive a
present? Some cigars? Ah! Ismael is not so stupid. You see, yesterday
morning I heard one of the stewards telling a certain man's servant that
he had seen you accept a cigar from your friend the American of the
Hotel Victoria. . . ."

*　　*　　*　　*

Two French yachts met by appointment in Palma harbour on our last
morning there. One came direct from Algiers with a crew of three men.

The other came from Barcelona with two men, a woman, and a child on board. This yacht was an old friend, the somewhat ponderous little cutter *Winnibelle* in which Marin-Marie had crossed the Atlantic single-handed. We had last seen *Winnibelle* lying in Monte Carlo harbour in the early autumn of 1946. She had been in bad condition, and we were glad now to see her refurbished and once more trundling the seas. The other yacht was an old eight-metre re-rigged as a Bermudian yawl. The three men on her were experts, and the owner, the oldest of the three, had had the good sense not to weigh down so fast a craft with heavy gear. Their travel was swift and spartan, nothing done for appearances, and little for comfort. Both sailed in soon after dawn, and their crews as they hauled the craft astern to the quay near us had the drawn, dusty look of people who have spent several nights at sea. It warmed my heart to see the sharply-featured French faces and to hear the precise and delicate music of spoken French after so many torrents of Spanish, lovely though that language can be. How quizzical French people can look when abroad! this intimidates me in England, but it amused me in Spain. . . . They were full of Gallic remarks such as: "En Espagne on mange affreusement mal".

While we were listening to them our passenger, M.T., arrived from her hotel. Of Spanish birth, she is the widow of an Englishman. She has exceptional strength of character and a tough constitution which appears to thrive on a citified life in Madrid or London. Her experiences on *Serica* may serve as a warning to femmes-du-monde who might consider a short cruise in the Mediterranean on a small boat.

There is plenty of sea-room in Palma harbour, and we beat out of it easily without recourse to the engine. Clear of the mole, we found a lively breeze and one of the flattest seas of that summer. We were delighted that M.T., of whom we are both inordinately fond, was seeing the yacht and the sea at their sparkling best. But her voice, normally resonant and set deep on the Spanish model, was a little faint as she asked questions regarding the speed of the boat. Impeccably and coolly dressed by land standards, she could endure neither the heat in the saloon nor the glare on deck. We arranged a cushioned seat for her on the lee side level with the shrouds, where there was some shade from the mainsail (though the deck was steeply sloping and the sea flicked past within inches of her little feet). She was surprised at the amount of work involved in sailing a boat, and insisted that we must allow her to help. Isabel carried forward pimentos, cucumbers, and white cabbage,

thinking that cutting up the salad might take M.T.'s mind off the
unusual movement. Our guest managed to eat an early lunch, and then
she had to plunge into the infernal heat below decks, where she took to
her bed, missing a day of glorious sailing with enough wind to make
conditions on deck tolerable, at any rate for us, accustomed to the heat
and to wearing a minimum of clothing.

We had a long reach to Punta de las Salinas, the easternmost point of
Majorca's south coast, and then we rushed north-east with a series of
gybes, each of which would draw some query from below: "What are
you doing?" "Why all that noise?" "Is anything wrong?" "What is a
gybe?" "How far is it now?"

The island was beautiful from the sea. It was splendid to stand in
toward so friendly a coast with its wide ranges of grazing country, its
many trees. After Spain, it was a richly earthy scene.

Within four miles of the entrance to Puerto Petro the wind did a
disturbing volte-face. We were sailing with the sheets right out, the
south wind on our quarter, and suddenly, with no vestige of a lull, the
same weight of wind headed us from the north. The northerly grew
stronger. We feared a real blow, and feared even more for the comfort
of our passenger. Fortunately we were able to lay the harbour close-
hauled. The entrance, less than one cable wide between two low rocky
points, was hard to identify. I made haste to get sail off her between the
points, and we slid into one of the most satisfying small-boat anchorages
we had ever seen—the place one often pictures from the chart and
seldom finds in reality. Turning to starboard we soon closed the
entrance and anchored one hundred yards from the shore, the chain
streaming brightly out through water nearly as clear as the air. The
anchorage has about ten fathoms at the entrance but is shoal in places
farther in. It is composed of a series of small bays but the shape of the
whole appeared to be an almost landlocked circle. Opposite the
entrance there is a well-built mole sheltering a fishing-boat harbour with
depths of no more than five feet (according to our observations).
Behind this harbour stands an astonishingly beautiful village, pinkish in
colour with white boats beached before it. Where we lay we were half a
mile from the village by water. The anchorage is surrounded by trees
and is remarkably green for that climate. Overlooking our own little
bay was a stone-and-concrete machine-gun post; but no police or
military bothered us in that place. M.T., showing the resilience that we
expected from her, bathed with us from the yacht, and bathing could not

have been more perfect. After dinner, she said that she began to have *some* idea why we were so attached to that ridiculous means of travel. We all slept on deck, and she told us before saying good-night that she had never experienced such peace. The yacht lay still on the glassy water. The dew came down so lightly that no touch was sensed. Not a sound was there beyond the ripple of a fish breaking the surface.

\*         \*         \*         \*

I woke in the morning with wind all round me, a lively blow from the north-east. The blanket-shrouded form of M.T. was moving restlessly, though she still slept.

"What are you doing?" Isabel asked.

"Getting out No. 2 jib. There's a good breeze."

"But this is a head wind. We can't take M.T. out in it. We should have to beat all day. The poor thing would be desperately uncomfortable."

The swell entering the harbour mouth and turning into our sheltered bay was unpleasant for our guest, and when she had drunk her coffee I ferried her ashore with books, a thermos of iced tea, and a long air cushion. We landed on a small beach no more than twelve feet long between red rocks. I felt very badly about settling M.T. on the air cushion under a pine tree, but she lay down with every sign of relief and enjoyment. The flies were her only annoyance.

As for me, I spent most of the morning swimming round the yacht rubbing off (with cotton waste soaked in paraffin) the dirt of Palma harbour from the waterline and from under the long counter. When that was done there were other tasks on board. Before leaving England I had envisaged a quiet and peaceful spell on *Serica*, reading, writing, and no arithmetic, but plenty of sailing. . . . In three months I had scarcely had five minutes leisure without being stirred by thoughts of ropes' ends to be served, sails to be sewn, engines to be attended to, varnishing or painting to do, the refrigerator to fuel and clean, water-tanks to fill. Work for two people on a sixteen-ton sailing-yacht is never-ending unless the crew make up their minds to live in one or two places as on a houseboat, or to tolerate dirt and unseaworthiness. When we went to Greece on *Truant* in 1946 I had found such work irritating. But now I can honestly say that I enjoy it, all of it, for with gradually increasing competence comes interest in the work. My next boat (if I have another) may be the type that Admiral Goldsmith called "a haystack". There is a *little* less maintenance to do on a haystack, particularly on one with canvased deck and no brightwork. British varnish is said (and not only by the makers) to be the best in the world, and according to the makers' advertisements a thorough varnishing of several coats at fitting-out time should last through the season. This may be true for yachts sailing in the British climate. But in those burning suns we found we had to varnish carefully all round at least every six weeks, even though the varnished surfaces were wiped over each morning while the dew was still on them. (I do not include the mast and the booms; two coats of varnish put on them at Gibraltar were as good as new at the end of the season.)

In the early afternoon Isabel and I landed and walked with M.T. to the village. The grove in which our guest had spent the morning was part of the grounds of a private house, low, shuttered, and uninhabited. A thicket near the house was studded with what appeared to be concrete sentry-boxes, all of them befouled by hens. We learned later that the owner of the property had organised a poultry farm, and had designed hen-houses of that shape believing that the extra height would keep the inmates cool. The chickens had not thrived; instead of manufacturing eggs they had passed their days and nights challenging each other and presenting arms.

A few of the small houses of Puerto Petro had been bought by middle-class people living in the interior of the island; those exteriors were preserved although the interiors were gutted and "improved". None of the absentee landlords was in Puerto Petro while we were there. The superior windows of the improved cottages blinked emptily over the creeks and bays, while from their still backward neighbours came shouting, singing, the cries of babies, all the bubble, squawl, and sudden calms of human life. We had to walk round a sandy creek to get to the village. Boys were out, ankle- to knee-deep, in the water digging up bait for their fathers' hooks. One of the buildings by the water had a pergola supporting a heavy vine; under the pergola two café tables and a few chairs. Pushing aside the bead curtain, we entered a spacious room with a bar at one end and a door open to the street behind. Cool air passed through the tiled expanse and after the heat outside the interior struck almost chill. There was little enough to eat. When we asked the elderly woman who cooked and waited if there was no fish to be had she answered contemptuously that the fishermen in the port were no more than "pescadores de agua fresca" (meaning, we gathered, that they fished only near the coast and by day). M.T. was astounded by this disparagement, for she had watched the fishermen leaving the anchorage in their lateen-sailed boats, and the sight of them balancing on the seas outside had moved her to admiration-cum-vertigo. However poor the meal, the restaurant was an agreeable place, and the welcome was delightfully warm and unembarrassed.

That afternoon, playing about in the water, I swam over a spike of rock sticking up from the depths, its peak just submerged. Kicking myself free I thrust my left foot down on a sea-urchin, and knew, not for the first time, the agony that that animal can cause with its defensive "spines". My foot was pouring blood when I returned to the yacht. I had been told that the best cure was to hold the wounded part in the flames of a wood fire, but I preferred to hold it in hot water and dig out with a needle such of the thorns as were excavatable. The ball of my foot and the three biggest toes were riddled. But the pain died away remarkably quickly.

The next morning was calm, and we had M.T. out of her sheets by 5 a.m., for we judged that it would be a day of light and fluky airs in which we should have to work hard to sail the sixty-odd miles to Formentor, at the north-eastern corner of Majorca. Once out of the harbour I set the vast spinnaker; it and the mainsail in the first two hours of sailing managed to draw us four miles, passing the narrow mouths of two anchorages somewhat similar to Puerto Petro and equally agreeable, judging from the chart, Cala Llonga and Puerto Colom. But when the sun rose the breeze freshened from the south and the spinnaker drew out ahead until we were travelling on top of the sea at great speed. Between 11 a.m. and noon we covered twelve sea miles (reckoned by the patent log and by crossbearings on the coast only two miles away on the port hand). She flew, light as a withered leaf in a gale. She would perch herself on the seas running up under her counter and surge forward on them. The main sheet was right out and the mainsail full of wind; the spinnaker sheets twanged like tuning-forks. It was glorious. The bows were lifted and she ran on with not a roll in her, as though her speed held her steady, slightly heeled to port. These were moments worth any discomforts, any toil, moments of an exhilaration strong enough to kill doubts for the gear.

M.T. and Isabel sat on deck preparing our lunch, which later we ate comfortably in the cockpit, though Isabel and I had to take turns at the tiller. I cannot pretend that the steering was easy, for if the hand on the tiller was not responsive she would yaw off as she finished her rush on one wave before picking up again on another. The coastline, growing more mountainous, fairly streamed past us until Cabo Pera, the eastern point of the island, was abeam. I was considering the problem of handing the spinnaker and gybing to alter course when M.T., who was enchanted at the wonderful surge of the sea beneath our flying hull, claimed prematurely that she had gained her sea legs. Ten minutes later she was lying on her back in a berth while I struggled to get the spin-naker in—a task that called for more crew than we could muster. The wind, now stronger, was coming flukily off the cape, and the sea was growing confused. At length I got the big sail in (rather wet) and stowed its boom. We gybed, and thrashed away north-east, crossing the wide bay of Alcudia with the mainsail and No. 3 jib. Hearing a moan from below I left Isabel at the tiller and found that M.T. was in agony from sunburn and seasickness. Fortunately she had worn a wide-brimmed hat and dark glasses all the time she was on deck, but her widely-admired arms had been exposed, and they were blistered and scarlet from wrists to shoulders. We dressed them as best we could, though unfortunately our medicaments on board were scanty. She is a brave woman, and her gruff voice was firm as she made a few sardonic remarks about her own apperance in those moments of stress.

Two capes with a bight between them, Cabo Menorca and Cabo del Pinar, divide Bania de Alcudia from Bahia de Pollensa. When we were off this area the wind suddenly changed through 180 degrees, as it had done when we were approaching Puerto Petro, but with even more violence. We carried the right sails for beating, and with only a few more miles to go we settled down to enjoy ourselves. But as the yacht heeled and began to slam into the quickly-rising head sea there came insistent cries and queries from below. At last, judging her remarks to be insufficiently appreciated, M.T. rose from her berth and, forgetting her burning arms, staggered aft. What on earth were we playing at? She seemed suddenly mistrustful of our competence. Where did we imagine we were going? . . . I pointed out our selected anchorage, Cala del Pino de la Posada, about two miles away on the starboard bow.

"Why aren't we pointing at it?" she asked.

"Because we can't sail straight into the wind."

"Of course you can't. Then what are you going to *do*?"

"Beat up to it . . . zigzag . . ."

"Zigzag! Please stop zigzagging at once, and go straight for a change. *This is awful.*"

As proof of my regard for her I started the engine; we headed into the wind, and Isabel and I got down the flapping sails. If it was painful for us to waste so good a breeze, M.T.'s pain was surely the greater, and we must not prolong it. At least we should have time to get the decks cleared before we entered the anchorage, which at that time was hidden from us by the Isla Formentor. But when we rounded the island we regretted our sympathetic compliance with the passenger's wishes, for a big motor yacht flying the Red Ensign was lying at anchor together with a fine Spanish ketch and a small but very workmanlike and up-to-date French ketch. Isabel was as upset as I that we should approach this gathering under power in a good, though very gusty, breeze. We went in carefully, and anchored with plenty of scope, the holding ground being only fine sand.

We fell back close to the Spaniard, and were at once approached by the owners or charterers, extremely beefy men from Barcelona, who told us they were having a fiesta on board that night and hoped that we would attend it in order to drown our sorrows and forget the menace (as they put it) that communism offered to the civilised world. Isabel and M.T. made some excuse about having to meet friends ashore. "Excellent!" the fattest of them replied in effect. "The more the merrier. There will be plenty to eat and drink. Bring your friends." On board his ketch electricians were fitting up strings of lights. The charging motor was running at highest revolutions. A panatrope was spouting the usual rhymes, stars-guitars, moon-June, blue-you.

No sooner had the men from Barcelona gone than I drew Isabel's attention to a smart dinghy that was approaching rowed by a tall, very lean man whose back looked familiar. It was that member of the Ponsonby family of Lymington whom we had had the good fortune to meet at Benodet the previous summer. He told us that he had taken summer employment as captain of the motor yacht, a tubby, somewhat top-heavy vessel, which was chartered to a wealthy Frenchwoman. The Frenchwoman came swimming round us as we spoke to him, and said "Good afternoon" with a faultless English accent. Ponsonby was in good spirits, and said he was well pleased with his holiday employment.

"The fat of the land, old boy! Everything paid for by Madame down to one's postage stamps and American cigarettes. First-class chef, cellar, stewards. . . ."

"Where have you come from?"

"I joined at Antibes. Cleaned up the barge a bit. Steamed down to Barcelona. Picked up Madame, the Duke, and the Duchess. Waited for a good old mistral to blow us down here, and made a fast passage. She rolls, of course, but the engines are very good. It's devilish hard work, but I thrive on that, as you know. . . . The Duke's mad about fishing. He has me out in the motor-boat at 0500 to draw a b. great net. Yes, we go out and set it the night before. Have to get out early because the local fishermen are devilish hot stuff. They'd have the lot if you left it till 0700. What fish? Rouget mostly. That's what the Duke's after. Then back aboard, and he goes to his bed while I chivvy the crew and get on with the old astiquage. You ought to see my varnish. It isn't ordinary. It glistens. I go over the whole barge with a chamois before the dews are off. Madame says she's never seen her boat so clean. Must be off now. See you at the fiesta on the ketch?"

Our next visitor, the Frenchman from the smaller ketch, came paddling round us in a rubber dinghy.

"Your sloop was designed by Robert Clark?" he asked. "I thought so. She is a dream of beauty. . . ." He came aboard and looked round. then took me back to see his boat, designed and partly built by himself, finished that year. He had been a champion in Stars, and his ketch reflected the dinghy or small-class sailor, except that she seemed under-canvased to me. Her spars and gear were too light for my liking. The blocks on her main sheets were the kind carried on a twelve-foot dinghy, and the sheets themselves were of thinner rope than we had in our jib downhaul purchases, a rope with a dark thread running through it.

"That is the rope used by Alpine guides," the owner told me. "It is *very* strong." The design of the ketch was extremely interesting, with a cabin aft of the cockpit, and two forward of it. But the cockpit was not self-draining, and to get at the engine you had to lift up the cockpit floorboards. Her lines were wide but easy.

"Don't you sometimes ship water over the engine?" I asked.

"Yes, but it doesn't matter because it's a Diesel."

I reflected that if we had not had a self-draining cockpit we should not have reached Formentor, but would have foundered somewhere west of the Straits of Gibraltar. The Frenchman, part artist, part writer, part sailing enthusiast, struck me as being a very admirable man, and not at all untypical of his race, which throws up that type more often than some might suppose. He lived very hard on his ketch. He seldom wore

more than a loincloth, and was burned to leather by the sun. It seems
to me from much observation of French yachts that they generally err
in providing too little comfort or too much. It is a mistake to have less
comfort than is reasonably possible on a small yacht, because the most
dangerous enemy of those who sail such vessels is fatigue. On the other
hand it is a greater mistake to sacrifice performance for unwieldy
comforts, but, after all, the French boats that are so fitted seldom move
very far from Cannes, and are generally used as mobile apartments or
restaurants.

Before we left *Serica* to go ashore we looked over to the motor yacht.
Owner and passengers were drinking champagne under the awning that
covered the whole of the afterdeck. Ponsonby, sitting in the wheelhouse with his feet up, was considering charts and smoking his cigarette
with explosive little puffs. The ports were all fitted with air scoops. Gas
cylinders (spares for the galley and the stewards' pantry) were carried
on the foredeck. The engineer was tinkering with the motor tender. He
was a dark, curly-haired young man from the Midi, full of song and love
for pistons and his wife.

In the pinewoods above the cove stands an immense hotel. We found
it and its gardens full of French visitors, many of them honeymooners
and the majority extraordinarily vulgar. France too had her war-time
profiteers and these were not confined to the producers of food and the
factory owners. On the terrace overlooking the cove almost-naked
women danced rhumbas with their husbands or attendant swains. The
most popular drink with the French seemed to be orange juice. English
couples, made rather shy by the French who so greatly outnumbered
them in that Spanish resort, drank sherry, and an American party were
drinking rum imported from the American base at Puerto Rico. Here at
Formentor we said good-bye to M.T., who probably was not sorry to
leave *Serica*, and who did not understand that she had been fortunate in
her weather, since while she was with us we had enjoyed two of our
most comfortable sailing days. Comfort in such circumstances is firstly
a matter of inclination and secondly of acclimatisation. She returned to
Palma by road.

We slept on deck. At 4 a.m. I woke and judged that the party on the
Barcelona ketch was breaking up. There was a cluster of people at the
accommodation ladder, and much shouting for the motor-boat that was
ferrying to the shore. The voice of the energetic Mr. Bing Crosby
(certain sections of the Spanish, Italian, and French populations, the

more flashy elements, have been even more Americanised than the
English or the Americans) came four times magnified from the panatrope. "When you're lonely and blue," he advised the morning scene,
". . . Wrap your troubles in dreams, And dream your troubles
away . . ." We were only protected from the open sea by the headland
of Formentor, high and wooded, but quite narrow. I thought for a
while of Mr. Crosby's advice and then of the sea outside, incalculable
and mysterious. I thought I heard Mr. Crosby singing under the sea, and
that strange, bubbling noise sent me to sleep.

When strong winds blow out of the Gulf of Lions (as they frequently
do blow) alarming gusts stab down from the Formentor ridge. On the
day following the fiesta such a wind blew force seven, and heavier in the
gusts. We let out another ten fathoms of chain and took anchor
watches for two hours. The Spanish ketch dragged right past us at a
speed of half a knot. All that day she dragged about the anchorage, now
this way, now that, depending on the direction from which the hills
funnelled the wind. Crew and "afterguard", stupefied by their fiesta,
were asleep on board or ashore in the hotel bar. I watched them pick up
their anchor the following morning when they motored to Pollensa at
the head of the bay. They had no more than seven fathoms of chain out,
and only a light stockless anchor at the end of it.

Ponsonby also moved up to Pollensa that morning to take water—a
recurrent necessity, since the motor yacht did not have an exceptionally
large fresh-water tank, and this was soon drained by the bath taps of
Madame and her guests. Madame and the Duke and Duchess were still
sleeping when Ponsonby (always an early bird) got the anchor with the
help of the one Breton deck-hand. Then he walked aft to the wheelhouse and the plump vessel made for the point, twin exhausts burbling
on the waterline—she had a squat yellow funnel, but it was used for
stowing cheeses.

Whatever the cove's faults, and we considered it to be overdominated
by the hotel, it has a most glorious bathing beach of sand backed by pine
trees. The sun was so hot that, except in the early morning or the
evening, bathers could not lie very long on the beach. We stayed so
long there that day that we both felt dizzy, and I contracted a sore
throat which I wondered whether to attribute to the effects of the sun or
to the sea-urchin poison in my foot.

The hotel at Formentor is isolated, and sends a motor-boat to fetch

its provisions from the market at Pollensa, but the manager kindly
agreed to accommodate us with stores. We took our baskets and wine-
flasks to the kitchen wing, and in a dark vault beside the main kitchen, a
place filled with openwork wooden shelves holding most things from
pepper to sides of beef, we were sold all that we needed at reasonable
prices. The manager explained to us that it gave the management
pleasure when yachts came to the Cala del Pino de la Posada. "Our
clients notice them there," he said.

We intended to sail from Formentor direct to the Anse de Port Man,
set on the inner side of the island of Port Cros, near Toulon, a distance
of some 300 miles. The Frenchman on the ketch advised us that this
was a bad plan, as we were likely to have foul weather out of the Gulf of
Lions. The majority of yachts leaving the Balearics for the south of
France make for the Costa Brava and Barcelona (one of the dirtiest of
harbours), and then they closely hug the coast of the Gulf all the way
round to Marseilles. That route did not appeal to us, and Ponsonby
was not in agreement with the Frenchman. "If you've any luck at all
you'll get a strong mistral," he said. "Set your trysail and jog along
comfortably. It'll be a fair wind even if it does blow a bit ragged."

When morning came our departure was postponed by an alarming
experience.

## CHAPTER 24

### "THE BOTTLE"

It was a quieter morning, with some wind shaking the tree-tops on the hills, but only a ripple on the water. Among the trees a fire was burning and rapidly spreading. The offshore airs carried the smoke over us. Around the fire stood square miles of woodland with here and there a house in the woods, and down by the shore a line of villas, their gardens and walls enmeshed in the trees. The fire was moving west, in the direction of the villa where we had dined the previous night with a delightful English family. True, the Murrays' villa was still some distance from the fire, and even had they been surrounded by flames they could have plunged off their terrace and swum or waded to safety. We searched their windows with our binoculars. No sign that anybody was awake; this did not surprise us as the household was on holiday, and the time was 6.45. We jumped into the dinghy and hurried ashore, scrambled through the undergrowth behind the beach, and found ourselves on the road leading to the big hotel. We ran in the direction of the fire. The smoke grew thicker, the noise of crackling louder, the smell of burning resin rich and ticklish. Somewhere a bell began to ring and a peasant galloped past us on a donkey, which he belaboured with the limb of a thorn tree.

We followed man and donkey up the hill, leaving the road. The track was steep, and carpeted with slippery pine-needles still damp with the night's heavy dew. The smoke was thick enough to make us cough one moment, but the next some fluke would clear the air. Five peasants ran past us, unsuitably dressed for firefighting in their rope-soled shoes, cotton trousers, and straw hats. They were blowing heavily and were expending as much wind on shouting as on running uphill. A Citroën car stopped with a shudder at the foot of the hill and a party from the hotel, four men with four women, undressed for the early morning bathe, jumped out and climbed after us. The track twisted into a circular space before a small house, very spick and span, with lemon trees in yellow tubs lining the front. An old lady in a high-throated dress, white with small black spots, sat on a garden chair beside the door of the house.

Her hands and ears glittered with diamonds. A blind whippet crouched at her feet, quivering and growling. The lady's eyes, brown and large in a thin face, watched the hurrying people and the smoke clouds. Her hands rested on the arms of her chair. Her feet rested together, shoe pressing against shoe. A woodman with a sharp axe was slicing branches from the trees near the house and was handing a branch to each newcomer. We went on up the hill. The young men from the hotel, Frenchmen, were waving their clubs. They saw a patch of smouldering undergrowth and flung themselves on it, beating. The four women, laughing, joined them until one of them, caught by a cinder, screamed lustily and flung herself to the ground. I was joined by Isabel, holding a stick rather bigger than herself. We climbed higher up and followed three peasants along a path. Ahead we heard shouting. We came to another clearing stretching diagonally up the hill. Near us some twenty men were gathered round a wooden shed that was already smouldering. We hurried in that direction, but one of the peasants held us back. "Tengan cuidado," he said. "The man is not here and he has the key. But when they break in the door . . ." As he spoke the door splintered and six mules came out like bullets. I have seen kicking horses, but surely animals never kicked like those brutes. They seemed to be kicking with all four legs at once, and at the same time they galloped. First they scattered in a fan, then they swerved together and came for our group. We rushed for the trees and flung ourselves among them, careless of scratches, while the thundering band of madness shrieked past. A cloud of smoke hid them. Then they came back and galloped right up the clearing until they were dots on the hill-top. We emerged cautiously. From the wood ahead a tongue of flame would reach high up and subside, followed by a mass of pale smoke tinged red. What an awesome thing is fire, our servant! Now and then came the crash of a falling tree accompanied by a volcano of sparks. A line of men were already passing buckets of water through the wood to the mule-shed. The buckets arrived slowly. There were enough men but too few buckets. It was increasingly difficult to see for smoke. Nobody seemed to be doing much more than defending himself, beating at the sparks round him, watching his own clothes, watching where he set his feet. I was very thirsty. I longed to taste the water they threw to the flames.

At length a man in some kind of grey uniform, open at the collar and down the chest, filthy, and black with burns in places, came at us waving his stick and ordered us to go farther up the hill. He accused us bitterly of cowardice. All of us were glad to have leadership. I know that I personally was quite flustered, and I felt that I could do little, for my voice had gone, not from shouting but as a result of my sunstroke of the previous day or of my poisoned foot. The scene was even more confused than in a battle. The uniformed man posted us along the edge of another wide clearing. It happened that through a break in the trees I could see *Serica*, and as I worked with my stick I kept clearing my aching throat and thinking of the whisky in the saloon cupboard and the iced water in the refrigerator. When we saw flame we set upon it madly, pounding it to death, but the more serious enemies were the sparks, which flew invisibly around us. We were so hot that we all deluded ourselves into thinking that we were doing useful work. Sometimes the little flowers of flame sprouted ahead of us in the rectangle of wood that evidently held the core of the fire; sometimes, like a skilful enemy, they appeared behind us. I supposed that elsewhere the battle was more bitter, more important. Isabel was thrashing away on my left hand and seemed quite happy. The man on my right annoyed me by catching me a back-handed swipe across the shin. Everybody shouted at everybody else. We all looked behind us as much as ahead, for we were obsessed by the fear of encirclement. We imagined (as one does in war) the enemy to be everywhere, omnipotent.

Suddenly I noticed that a few of the men were sitting down and lighting cigarettes with the friendly fire they pulled from their pockets.

The man in uniform came down the clearing and stationed himself in the middle of our line. "The wind has fallen," he shouted. "The fire is surrounded on all sides and is dying. It must be finished off before the wind comes again. I call on you for a great effort. We will advance until we meet other beaters coming from the left and the right and ahead. Advance in line. . . . Advance!"

Very careful where we stepped and what we touched, we shambled into the wood, beating here and there. From several directions came the sound of sawing. They were cutting down big trees whose upper branches had caught the hot leprosy. Before we met the cohorts from our left, our right and our front we were ordered to withdraw. No explanation was given. It had been extraordinarily like a battle. Men began to tell each other of their deeds and their burns.

Down at the house the old lady still sat in her chair; the blind whippet was still quivering at her feet. The woodman and another servant were filling glasses with manzanilla poured from a wood-and-copper jug that went frequently to the house for replenishment. We drank the manzanilla like water. As the woodman filled our glasses he said: "Garcia, over there, is badly scorched. We're waiting for the doctor from Pollensa."

Garcia lay on a bank under a black woollen blanket. Only his face showed, for he still wore his hat, which was made of some velvety substance. He smoked cigarettes given him by the crowd that surrounded him, cigarettes made in loose paper bags. The dusty burning Rubio fell from his face to the blanket, and those watching him brushed away the sparks.

"Garcia is starting another conflagration," they joked in gentle voices.

Garcia appeared to be trembling violently beneath the blanket. Small pearls of moisture broke from the skin on his temples and ran down his face, streaking the dust that coated him. Being the only casualty, he was the man of the moment. And he was a man, for he seemed to be rather bored by his situation. His black eye, very bloodshot, rested for a long time on me in the most embarrassing stare.

We returned to the yacht, whence we could see the wound made by the fire, a long, grey, still-smoking wound. The Murrays were arriving on the beach to bathe. They were waving to us. How absurd our fears of the early morning now seemed! When I had drunk my iced whisky we made sail and left Cala del Pino de la Posada.

*       *       *       *

"Sudden squalls are experienced," the Sailing Directions warn, "especially under the high land on the northern side of the bay of Pollensa, and great care is necessary in boats when under sail." This information is correct: the wind was northerly and light but as we sailed along under the cliffy headland there were gusts that laid us flat and soundly tested the gear. The French ketch had left the anchorage half an hour earlier, bound for the town of Ciudadela, on the west coast of Minorca. I was interested to see how she sailed, and was half-disappointed when we overhauled her rapidly.

Having cleared the high point of Formentor with its lighthouse we set a north-easterly course for France and I streamed the log, watching the little ketch. Although we were close-hauled and she was reaching we were sailing three feet to her one; but she was a pretty sight with her very pointed mainsail and mizzen, and it gives a feeling of warm comradeship to watch another familiar small boat sailing the wide sea on a different course from your own.

When we were ten miles out the wind began to turn easterly and head us. He who would sail in the Mediterranean should possess elasticity of plan and temperament. Although we had both been looking forward to the long sea crossing, we had an equally attractive alternative in mind, and now, being headed from France, we changed course, making for a port we had often considered on the chart of the Balearics, Puerto de Fornells in the northern coast of Minorca, a place that we always (because of its extraordinary shape) called the Bottle.

We had a hard day's sailing, for the wind was playful and did not come from any direction for long enough to allow us to settle down. We had difficulty (the engine was going through a period of gloom) in coaxing the boat in light airs and a heavy swell round Cabo Fornells, a jagged place clustered with submerged horrors that forms one side of the bay from which Puerto de Fornells is entered. At last we beat round it and with slightly eased sheets slid on for the mouth of the harbour. The mouth is about two hundred yards wide, and looks less. The channel through it is dead central. Once through, an expanse of smooth water confronted us. To starboard (on the neck of the bottle) was the white village of Fornells with its shallow harbour. The lagoon stretched on, a mile wide and three long, into folds of green, rolling country sloping up gradually to a wild dark ridge, some twenty miles to the south. Farther down the lagoon were the three islands, Sargantana, Rabells, and Porros, uninhabited now that men seldom shut themselves in fortresses. There was only one disappointment; the Bottle was shallower than it looked. After much sounding we anchored near Sargantana, and more than a mile from the village. While I was sorting the sails on deck and paying attention to the agreeable sounds and smells rising from the galley, a naval petty officer came chugging out to us in a motor fishing-boat chartered for the occasion. The handsome man in his pretty white uniform wondered why we had penetrated so deeply into the lagoon, and had anchored so far from the village.

"Granted that Fornells is a poor place," he said. "But there's nothing *else* to be seen for miles."

"Fornells is beautiful."

"Mahón, the capital, is beautiful," he said. "That's my town. Apart from Mahón there's nothing to be seen in Minorca."

"The mules are superb," I said, pointing at the glossy monsters that were being led through the gloaming to bathe their limbs in the lagoon.

"Yes, the mules are about as good as mules can be, which isn't saying much, and the horses do well too . . . but why should I bother with such creatures? I'm a sailor."

"The cows look good," Isabel said.

"The cows? They do well here and give milk and calves as cows do in other places, but then the fresh water is the trouble, not at Mahón, in this crude little corner."

"Yet the fields are green."

"Green enough, and they produce good grain and fodder. . . . But look at this," he said, picking up one end of our main sheet. "Nowhere in Minorca or even in Spain would a man find such rope as this, not if he were Commander-in-Chief, not if he were a millionaire. Your excellencies' boat is a good boat, and if you take my advice you'll leave here tomorrow morning early for Mahón, where you'll see *something*. You've no engine? I saw you come in with the sails alone. Sail is the only way to travel on the sea. Travel with engines is burdensome by comparison. I was in a Spanish cadet ship. We went under sail to all the countries of Latin America. Hard work, but interesting. . . . Then I was in submarines. Little work, but a liverish life. Now I am shore-based, and that is the best place for a sailor. Only I have been two whole years in Fornells. . . ."

"Will you be moved?"

"Yes, when I get promotion, and that may happen in six or seven years, perhaps in twenty . . . it all depends how many people die off in the higher grades. . . . Ah! I mustn't say too much against Fornells. The fishermen are a good lot, and they've a deal to contend with around that accursed cape outside the entrance. The inhabitants are, generally speaking, agreeable enough. I'm my own master here. But Fornells is too small, too small. The Navy doesn't inquire about personal inclinations. For example the Admiral is coming here to-morrow for a short inspection and lunch in the big house up there (very rich people, fantastic!), and if he's in a good humour he'll ask me if everything's going well with me. I'll answer, 'Yes, sir.' What else is there to say? If I spoke to him as I've spoken to you, frankly that is, I might find myself back on submarines within ten days. And I don't want to leave my home. . . ."

"You have many children?"

"None, worse luck, but my wife is beautiful, far too beautiful to leave unguarded. If you come ashore tomorrow I'll show her to you."

We passed an ideally peaceful night, bathing, eating in the cockpit, sleeping on deck, waking early and bathing again. There was a fair breeze for France, but I refused to leave the Bottle so soon. We hoisted a headsail and moved up the lagoon, anchoring in one and three-quarter fathoms near the harbour. The water we rowed across was full of great wooden cages for live lobsters.

The petty officer was waiting to take the dinghy painter. We ordered lunch at the restaurant and walked with him round the town. He showed us where to buy melons (little bigger than cricket balls, but succulent and sweet), bread, lettuce, pimentos, tomatoes, plums, and wine. The cobbled streets were immaculate. Horses and mules drawing the farm-carts were shining with healthy fat but were plagued by the heat and by the strange, clawed horse-flies that are so amazingly tenacious of life. Fling them down and stamp on them, burn them with a cigarette, they live; cut off their heads, the headless bodies claw and sting. The sun was blinding and the semi-darkness inside the shops seemed the only desirable kind of light. Five or six shops all sold the same things: a little bread (extremely bad, and as expensive as lobster); potatoes, beans, lentils, and onions; dirty paraffin and watery methylated spirit; toothpaste from Barcelona, razor blades (that would only fit Spanish razors) from Toledo; cooking utensils of cheap quality and chamber-pots with serrated edges (to discourage the ruminant baby); Japanese plums, Seville lemons, condensed milk; corned beef, sausages, particularly chorizo and the less good sobreasada; thread stockings for women, artificial silk socks for men; washing soap that neither looked like, nor smelled like, nor performed the duties of, soap; alpargatas and other shoes; needles, but no thread; barrels of cheap wine and expensive oil; buckets of spaghetti and other doughy abominations; Spanish cigarettes and cigars. I bought a few cigars, thinking that they would while away the hot hours of our crossing to France. The petty officer took us to his house, which was empty.

"I know where she is," he said. "She spends most of her time there." He seemed disgruntled. "The villagers say she doesn't feel happy in her home, but that's not true."

We followed him out of the village to a rocky point, down a few steps and into a deep trench. The trench curled round, we could hear the booming of the sea, and before us was a heavy door marked, *Propriedad del Almirantazgo . . . Prohibida la Entrada.*

She was gathering together several big sheets of paper as we walked in, and she looked thoroughly startled. The husband introduced us and clambered through the rectangular aperture to lay, in one of the rock pools below, the bottles of beer he had carried from the café. The gun post had been hollowed out of the rock and was of irregular shape. Only the aperture was smooth, for it had been faced with concrete. She had been sitting on an ammunition chest, and working on a rough wooden table made from pieces of driftwood. There was no other furniture. She nervously held the papers behind her while she spoke to us and asked Isabel to sit on the chest, but I knew at once what she had been at because coloured crayons and drawing charcoal were scattered on the table, and her hands, square with short fingers, were smudged. She was, as he had claimed, a beautiful young woman, shy, trembling, and wild-looking, with sad dark eyes and fair hair drawn back and tied behind her neck. Her voice was higher than one would expect to hear in Spain, and she spoke somewhat jerkily, forgetting to end her sentences, or perhaps losing patience with them.

"Let me see," he said, climbing back into the little cave.

"No," she answered. "No."

"Come on, let me see." He forced her, quite gently, to give up the papers and looked at each one with mock attentiveness. "Baby!" he said, not unkindly. She snatched the papers from him, crumpled them, and flung them into the sea. When she turned back to the cave her face was stony.

She would hardly speak to any of us. When we left the place she locked the door, and put the heavy key into her skirt pocket. They walked back with us as far as their house in the village, and she hurried in. The husband came on to the café restaurant. Lowering his voice (so that the waitress would not hear) he discussed his wife's "weakness".

"She gets a craving to draw something and nothing I can say or do will stop her. For a time it was donkeys, and that was not so bad because she was always out of the village when she had these moods on. Then it was human faces. I allowed her to draw me in the privacy of our house, but after a time I began to feel it was wrong to humour her. Besides, the faces on the paper were nothing like mine. Then there was a scene, for she was found drawing the policeman's young sister, and she had made the girl let down her blouse and lay bare shoulders and breast. You can imagine what the policeman thought about that? There was talk of a prosecution. So now my dear one goes every day and sometimes twice a day to the place where we found her. She struggles, poor soul, struggles and struggles to put the waves on her sheets of paper. Sometimes, however, she will take something with her for a model, some fruit, a bottle, a plate, and the other day I had a mess to clean up, for she had a baby porker and as it would not stand still she had tied it to the table. It's a worrying business. But I know it will come right for us in the end. If only we could be blessed with a child of our own! If she started to bear children she would have no time for foolishnesses. . . ."

Three palm trees in front of the café restaurant dropped a wedge of shade over the tables. It was a good place to sit. Everything outside that shady refuge was saturated and dazed by the sun. Around the harbour small palms, protected by cages made from wire-netting and wood from Italian packing-cases, had been set in a hopeful ring. The petty officer, questioned about the new trees, explained that the leaders of the community hoped to exploit Fornells as a tourist centre ("being jealous of Mahón, you see"). The attraction, the leaders had agreed, would lie in the proximity of some truly remarkable caves (the people of the Balearics, if not cave-worshippers, are strangely obsessed with the importance of caves), and they also agreed that Fornells should be made to look more like a tourist centre, and the dust-sheathed baby palms were the first step in that direction. I asked the corporal why palms had not also been planted in the streets, and he answered that while in summer there was no water, in winter such torrents of rainwater poured down the streets that no palms would be likely to prosper there.

"Besides," he said, "we don't want palm trees in the streets. Plane trees, yes; palms would be unlucky."

"Why?"

But he pointed to a cloud of yellow dust advancing swiftly on Fornells down the road from Puerto Mahón. "The Admiral," he said, and left us.

As we sat back happily in our dark shade, listening to the noises of the bar and the kitchen, an excursion party arrived in two engagingly period American motor-cars of the pre-four-wheel-brakes era. Both radiators spouted steam. Four middle-aged married couples and their children alighted. They had taken the taxis from Mahón to enjoy a fish luncheon at Fornells. Fish soup, fried fishes, and grilled lobsters with rice had been ordered in advance, and they unloaded from the taxis such extras as they did not expect to find in the small village—cakes and sweetmeats, fruits and cheeses.

The men with their open-necked white shirts and jaunty familial airs were very like English townsmen on the spree at Whitstable or Margate. One of them got his amusement from a pair of binoculars (every member of the party had to study the yacht through them). Another had a rubber ball that he kicked about with several of the boys. (Spain was in the throes of a football mania.) Another couple whiled away the time before lunch with fishing rods hanging hopefully over the edge of the quay and parasols shading the fishermen's heads. The wives sat at the table beside us, contemplating the scene, each admiring her children, and spurning the blandishments of the waitress, who wanted to sell drinks. The children, unhealthily nourished, kept up till all hours, cosseted and worshipped, eroticised by constant fondling and by too many opportunities for observing the behaviour of their elders, were pasty-faced, obtrusive, and self-satisfied.

We ate extremely well. The lobsters were all that the locals claimed them to be.

That evening we sailed down the lagoon, anchoring near the inner end, the bottom of the Bottle. The landscape was less depopulated than the previous evening, for this was a Sunday and many bathers had come by mule- or donkey-cart or bicycle from villages and farms inland. When we had set the charging motor going in the cockpit we rowed ashore. Near the edge the water was only a few inches deep, and the mud bottom was studded with sea urchins, the very look of which made me quiver, for my foot was troubling me. (Some of the spikes were still in one toe nine months later.) We found a jetty, and made our way inland through squashy meadows and then up to firmer ground where (Sunday or no) men were cutting corn with sickles. On our right hand was the house where the admiral had gone to lunch, a splendid building of red brick with white stone facings, three floors high and dormered, a skilful and satisfying architectural composition worthily set in its avenues, its lawns, and its well-arranged series of buildings and fields. From the stables a groom was leading three blood horses to the lagoon for their evening bathe.

I had often wondered at my father's affection for mules, but I understood it when I saw the mules around the Fornells' anchorage. Glossy, short-backed, with straight, clean legs, good pasterns, and small feet, they obviously stood the climate better than the horses, and had I had the choice of a mount it would have fallen on a certain liver-chestnut mule with quarters on him like a Grand National entry. He was regularly ridden, for he carried no loose flesh but only firm muscle, and we saw the saddle mark on him. When we entered his field he came galloping in great fashion, stopping before us with a deep snort. The roads were rough; cyclists kept to smooth dust paths at either edge and shouted at us as they approached, asking us to walk in the middle of the road, but the mules, trotting along pulling two-wheeled hooded carts, moved sinuously, the shoulders rippling, the delicate forefeet floating out, the long, but by no means ridiculous, ears pricked and swivelling to any untoward noise or suspected danger. By comparison horses, fretted by the uneven going, were clumsy.

The fields were walled with large stones built to a height of four feet and topped with a smooth cement coating. This band along the top of every wall was whitewashed. I never saw a more satisfying agricultural landscape, the fine houses and farms, the woods and orchards, the green fields picked out by the grey and white lines of the immaculate walls. We did not see any gates, and it appeared to be the strange local custom to build up a gap in the wall when the animals were put through and pull it down again in the evening when they were driven to the farm to be watered. There was no sign of water in any of the fields, but these were all prudently ditched against the winter rains, and the ditches, often as deep as eight feet, were sometimes paved with closely-fitting flat stones, like garden paths in English suburbia.

All whom we met made us very welcome. A farmer's wife, leading us to her dairy, gave us a present of a crusty cheese so heavy that it made my arms ache, and filled us bumpers of fresh milk. The dairy was spacious. A monumental churn stood in the middle, its oak polished black with age, its six legs curving out and down and ending in iron feet shaped like dahlias' heads. Floor, walls, shelves were of unmortared stones all scrubbed nearly white. Our hostess wanted to load us with fresh butter as well, and she took a hardwood knife to cut some from a glossy hunk big enough to satisfy a German battalion (and I have seen German soldiers cramming butter into their mouths with their fists). We told her that our refrigerator was still half full of butter from Gibraltar, and that the cheese was almost more than we could carry. Her husband had gone up to the hill to look at the herd of goats which was tended night and day in relays by three of their four sons. Their daughter, a sunburned baby, she carried on her strong hip. The woman was a picture in her black dress cut low and square at the neck. Her face and forearms and brown spatulate feet were the colour of old

17                                                                    K

unpainted pinewood, the brown tinged with the blood coursing in mad abundance below it. . . . Inside the farmhouse, strongly built as a castle, a maid was sweeping and singing, but we did not see her; we saw a cloud of dust and heard a flamenco song.

We returned to the yacht in the moonlight. A speckled baby gull that had taken a fancy to us from our arrival was sitting (unperturbed by the charging motor's roar) on the rail. He clumsily took to the air as we approached, but flopped into the water near the companion ladder. Though he had not respected our teak deck we fed him with bread and cheese until he would accept no more and sat himself on the dinghy to digest.

# CHAPTER 25

## RIVIERA LANDFALL

AT dawn we ran aground. It was my fault, for when I had got the anchor I failed to turn the yacht's bows by holding the headsail aback. I signalled to Isabel to gybe and, although she rightly complained, she obeyed, and *Serica* bowed stiffly as her keel slid into the soft mud. The water became opaque around her. We ran about the deck, galvanised, though a moment before we had been sailing away sleepily, going through movements that we had too often rehearsed. After half an hour's manœuvring with the engine and the long boat-hook we got clear and sailed for the harbour mouth, somewhat hot (the temperature was already eighty-eight [F] in the doghouse). There was a very light following breeze. We set the big spinnaker before we had cleared the neck of the Bottle. The sounds of Fornells, waking to a fine day, came over the quiet water as crisply as Japanese glasses tinkling in a window. A mile offshore we found ourselves in the middle of the Fornells fleet of fishing-boats. The men were hauling in lobster creels. Wine-coloured creatures squirmed inside pale yellow creels made from the husks of maize.

"Where are you going?" the men asked.

The airs were chancy all morning. We sailed now with the spinnaker set normally, now set as a Yankee, its sheet led to the end of the main boom. We took half-hourly spells at the tiller and we swam three times before lunch at 1 p.m. The coast of Minorca was then twenty-three miles away, low, but still clear. After lunch I settled in the cockpit with a book and a black Spanish cigar while Isabel slept for two hours in the shadow of the mainsail. She relieved me and I slept. The day wore peacefully on until, with the going down of the sun at 9 p.m., the light airs ceased. We took in sail, hung up the anchor light, and went to bed on deck. Our day's run was the creditable one of sixty-five miles.

*Serica* rolled a good deal, but we slept well, and did not wake till dawn came with a light breeze from the north-east, a head wind. We had three agreeable hours of beating, then a lull when we bathed and breakfasted, then a light reaching breeze from the east, then the previous day's spinnaker airs from the south.

279

In the middle of the day we were plagued by a heavy swell rolling out of the Gulf of Lions to the north-west, and we thought we were in for a mistral. I had got as far as shackling on the trysail sheets when the black clouds dispersed, the glass, which had suddenly dropped two points, came back to its original position, and the swell eased. By 8 p.m. we had covered 140 miles—extremely good going considering the calms (and our average speed for the daylight run of seventy-five miles was 5.2 knots). We held on to the spinnaker until half-way through the night, when the breeze turned easterly and we set the Genoa instead. It was a splendid night for sailing, though the wind was usually only force one or two. We were alone, outside any steamer lane, and the stars glittered madly on the black sea.

During the night we did three-hourly spells at the tiller, the one off-duty sleeping below in the quarter berth (for we were sailing north and the air was already cooler).

Just before daybreak there was a quick shift of wind from the east to the north-west, and we knew we should easily make the coast of France that third day, and in a mistral. The sky was thickly clouded, the wind chilly, the air leaden. No dew had fallen on our deck. By breakfast time a fair lump of a sea had built up. We thrashed along, carrying the mainsail and No. 3 jib.

I was hoisting the Tricolor at the yardarm when I was terrified by an immense blast on a ship's siren. Isabel darted up from the galley. The yacht was sailing herself, the tiller lashed, and a French tanker, the *Hammamet* from Tunis, had come up in our lee to have a look at us. The officers on her bridge had seen our consternation and appeared to be vastly amused. The captain himself, through a loud-hailer, asked us where we were from and whither bound. He offered to give us our position, but I told him that we knew it, not to impress him but because I felt that to be given it would spoil the interest of our landfall. He next offered to supply us with any stores we might need, adding: "We have about a hundred tons of petrol to spare, but we can see you don't need any of that. My first officer tells me that you are sailing at seven and a half knots." He then dropped politely astern, worked round our counter, and plunged off on his course for Marseilles. A fine ship, and well kept. . . . It may seem odd to the reader that he had been able to stalk us, but sailing the wide sea on a small boat one ceases to look around very often, and when one does look it is generally to wind-ward.

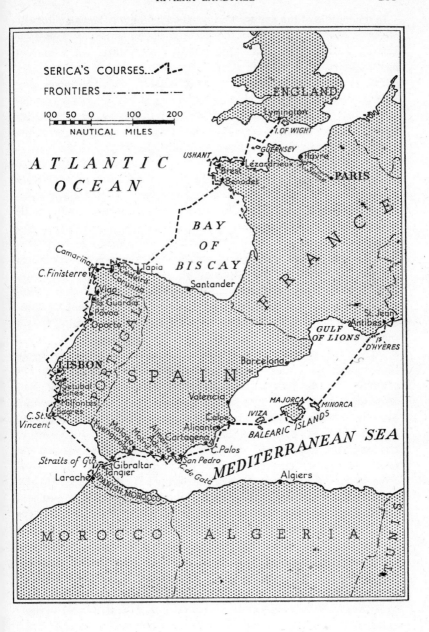

SERICA'S COURSES...
FRONTIERS

100 50 0    100    200
NAUTICAL MILES

*ATLANTIC OCEAN*

ENGLAND
Lymington
I. OF WIGHT

USHANT    GUERNSEY    Havre
Lézardrieux
Brest    PARIS
Benodet

*BAY OF BISCAY*
Santander

Camariñas
C.Finisterre    Tapia
Cedeira
Corunna
Vigo
La Guardia
Povoa
Oporto

*FRANCE*

St.Jean
Antibes
GULF OF LIONS    Is D'HYÈRES

LISBON    *SPAIN*
Setubal    Barcelona
Sines
Milfontes
Sagres    Valencia
C.St.    MAJORCA    MINORCA
Vincent    IVIZA
Cabo    BALEARIC ISLANDS
Malaga    Alicante
Almeria    Cartagena
C.Palos
Straits of Gib.    San Pedro    *MEDITERRANEAN SEA*
Larache    Gibraltar    C. de Gata
Tangier    Algiers
SPANISH MOROCCO

*MOROCCO    ALGERIA    TUNIS*

*Serica* beat on all morning, the tiller lashed, flinging the spray in grey-white whiskers from her bows and sometimes taking the very top of the top of a wave on deck. She was so steady, though, that I was able to sit below and type a long letter.

The wind became more gusty towards midday, when I supposed that we were nearing land. By my dead reckoning we were within four miles of the channel between the islands of Port Cros and Levant when we first sighted them in the mist. We were so jubilant at the correctness of the landfall that we decided to approach yet faster, and set the Genoa. The patent log registered 218 miles from Minorca. We entered the channel at top speed. In the lee of the high maquis of Port Cros we got calms and squalls, and fell in with an English yacht of some sixty tons flying the Blue Ensign. Our fears that she was making for the same anchorage as ourselves were justified, but we drew comfort from the thought that there was ample room for both of us in the Anse de Port Man. Since she did not depend on the wind, she took a more direct course. We watched her bulbous cruiser stern swing round the point. A little later we opened the cove, and discovered that five other British yachts, all motor-boats, were anchored there, and three French yachts. At the very head of the cove, in water no deeper than three feet, four more French yachts lay fast to the jetty. Around the rocky edges dolled-up fishing-boats were moored. Parties picnicked in the scrub, their fires smoking, their voices shrilling above the mating hum of the crickets. The water round the rocky points squiggled with the bodies of swimming archers or gunmen, faces immersed, lungs filling and emptying damply through tubes of aluminium or yellow plastic sticking up from the sea like mutilated tulip stalks. It would have been a brave big fish that cruised there, and we wondered that the hunters did not take (as is man's custom) to shooting each other.

We had last anchored in the Anse de Port Man in the summer of 1946, when we had found the cove, set in wooded hills, to be the one peaceful anchorage in the South of France. But its peace had disintegrated in the four intervening years. After the rural beauty of the Bottle this Riviera anchorage seemed worse than tawdry. We felt like putting about and sailing back to Minorca. Seeking to avoid the other yachts, we sailed close to the western shore, and dropped anchor in water that was still as clear as ever—though this was no longer an advantage, for now when we looked at the bottom (sand and weed) we read "Bovril", "Ovaltine", "New Zealand Lambs' Tongues", "Yellow Cling Peaches", "Nescafé", and "Condensed Milk (Sweetened)", on the tins that fraternised rustily with dark bottles.

The strengthening mistral sent prolonged gusts into the cove from all directions, and we soon found ourselves in difficulties because we had anchored too close inshore and we were dragging in the gusts. Try as I would, I could not start the engine. The spark was weak, and I suspected that we needed a new coil. We attempted to sail off the shore, but the gusts were so strong and so varied in direction that we were having an anxious time of it. I was considering kedging when I gave the engine another chance, and it started. This time we anchored in the middle of the bay, and the English came from the wombs of their motor-boats to look at us. All of them looked very intently, and I can only suppose that we seemed rather peculiar to them (I know that they seemed fat, juicy, and noisy to us). We were certainly the reverse, for my voice had now gone so completely that I could not even emulate the clicking noises of José at Larache, and neither of us carried any spare flesh.

The mistral played merry hell with the yachts all night, buffeting them about, now roaring, now shrieking, now retreating to allow a period of unsettling calm. We slept below and only fitfully, though we were both tired.

When we had washed down in the morning we fitted the trysail, watched by the yacht hands around us. Some of them looked at us enviously, we thought, for although they enjoyed the ease of motor-boats most of them had probably tasted the delights and memorable torments of sail. The skipper of one yacht was good enough to warn us that a mistral was blowing, and that we should remain in the anchorage until the skies cleared. The "afterguards" were breakfasting under wind-shaken awnings when we moved out.

A majestic sea ran up under our counter in the channel between the islands and the mainland, but its appearance belied the wind, which was fierce only in gusts. We made fair headway with trysail and small jib, being bounced on like a ping-pong ball by the waves. When we had crossed the bay of Cavalaire and were approaching Cap Camarat the mistral suddenly dropped, so we headed for the land, intending to have lunch and a bathe in one of the coves. But no sooner were we anchored than the mistral was at us again, shaking us, worrying at us, while we lunched on deck. Coming from the Balearics represented a great change in light: it was like stepping from the glare of the stage to the comparative gloom of the auditorium. We enjoyed the change, and from then on took all our meals on a table in the cockpit. The temperature was also several degrees cooler, although at this time the inhabitants of the Côte d'Azur were complaining (they are by no means uncomplaining people) of a heat wave.

We made off with the same sails as before, and this time the mistral was blowing very hard. Of all the thousands of yachts on that coast we seemed to be the only one at sea. Yet the sailing was superb until we were a mile or two past the Gulf of St. Tropez, when the wind changed (as it frequently does about that place) from mistral to vent d'est. Up went the mainsail and No. 2 jib. We settled down to a long beat. Far out to sea we sighted the black schooner *Valdora*, probably on her way back to Monte Carlo from Corsica. A fine old boat, clipper-bowed and full of quality, she presented a sorry sight, for she was motoring in a good reaching breeze, not a stitch of canvas set. Doubtless she was on charter.

Now, with the clear afternoon and the steady breeze, the white yachts spread their dragonfly wings and flew out of Cannes harbour to sail round the Îles des Lérins and then dart back again to the capacious lair where they slept in huddled rows.

Another long beat took us into Golfe Juan at the hour when our compatriots in the Hôtel du Cap, gleaming above us, were sitting down to dinner. Two more boards took us round Cap d'Antibes, rustling its pine trees and much darker than the rest of that glowing shore. We sailed for the fort until the light on the end of the mole at Antibes changed from red to green, and then gybed so smartly that we nearly ran down the buoy off the entrance. This sailing was done without charts, for we remembered those waters. Antibes harbour was packed with yachts, fishing-boats, and smuggling craft of British origin. The only berth we could find was near the entrance with the dredger to starboard and the sunken wreck of a once-comfortable motor yacht close to port. This latter, mussel-hung, was a good neighbour. It was enchanting to watch the fishes slink from one dark cabin to another, and in the morning, when the sun came burning through, flying-fishes shining palest blue swam round and round the hulk as though seeking to dazzle its shy inhabitants with their loveliness.

## CHAPTER 26

## SMUGGLERS AND OTHERS

EVERYTHING was delightful about our first meal on French soil (eaten Chez Félix au Port, looking through the Roman archway into Antibes harbour) except the bill. This was not the fault of Félix but of French inflation and of a low rate of exchange for the pound sterling. After Spain the costs of food and drink in France seemed outrageous. I had never before (certainly not during the German occupation) eaten so badly in France as our purses now commanded us to eat, nor had I ever before (so far as I can recall) eaten prix fixe meals in France. But now we had not enough money to eat à la carte and we sloped round the restaurants, studying the menus and balancing the prospects of a poor or merely indifferent meal at 250, 350, or 450 francs. Under these circumstances we soon tired of restaurants and I thought of my old friend, Hartley Dane, who always kept an excellent cook. . . . Hartley had his detractors, but I was never one of them, for provided a man treats me fairly and to some extent courteously I do not require him to be amusing, or a saint. He had not lived very long in Antibes, having moved there shortly before the 1939–45 war to convert a fisherman's tenement in the old part of the town to his own uses. I never feel that those conversions by the rich are successful, and I had liked less visiting him there than in his villa on another part of the coast or at his château near Paris.

Hartley always had a certain talent for making himself comfortable, though in this respect, considering his age and his nationality, he was less of an old woman than he might have been. Broad, heavy, with American footballer's shoulders, a rasping voice, an oblong, disbelieving, sardonic face and an extremely crude sense of humour, he had lived as much in France as he could and, since he was wealthy, I suppose that was most of his life. One of the most fascinating of his characteristics was his habit (common enough among rich Americans) of taking a sudden, tottering plunge into snobbery. One instant he would be a snob of pantomime dimensions—and the next a satyr. I don't think he and I had much in common, but I had known him for many, many years and had liked his little berets, his strange, ugly, old face, his table, and his habit of employing odd servants and of having long public discussions with them in French. He once told me that he had been trained in America to practise an estimable profession. But he had just come to France to live. To live? At any rate we both looked forward to seeing him, though we climbed the ramparts somewhat nervously, for the last time we had been there he was enduring a painful and humiliating disease, a disease that was bound to kill even Hartley in the end.

Old women were sitting on their doorsteps complaining of the heat and dragging in each breath with a rustle of effort. I asked two of them if the American still lived at the corner.

"You will see his name on the door," one said.

When we rang the bell a woman thrust her head from the window above the door.

"Whom do you want?" she asked.

"Monsieur Dane. He is not at home?"

"Il est mort."

"Le pauvre!"

"I don't know so much about that. He suffered physical torment at the end, and the goings-on here were pretty extravagant. Shocking it was. . . ."

"Probably you were more polite when Monsieur Dane was alive."

"Here! What's this?" she shouted. "Don't you come wasting my time and your own by giving me a bad name. . . . The house? Hasn't been sold nor yet rented. The family in America hasn't agreed about it yet. Plenty'll want it, Americans I mean. . . . The body's been carried off to America. I suppose they never liked him living in France the way he carried on. . . ."

"If I were you I'd be afraid."

"Of a little squirt like you!"

"No; Monsieur Dane's ghost might take reprisals against you for speaking of him like that to one of his friends."

"So you were one? I don't wonder. . . ."

The two old women were still sitting gasping on the step.

"Why didn't you tell me he was dead?" I asked.

"We feared you might be one of the family," the older answered, squinting up at me. "It was better you should have the news from the house where all is officially known. A nice man, Monsieur Dane, and generous to Antibes. Yet his body has gone to America. It's surely not there he'd choose to lie, but in France." Then she tried to question us as to our relationship with Hartley. All this poking and prying and complaining, his image hanging in the dark lane, these were painfully unsatisfactory substitutes for the presence of the man himself.

He had often smelled this atmosphere of eau-de-Javel and olive oil in a frying-pan and chervil and Gauloises and fresh-planed pine, coming, the last, from the chair-mender's establishment at the corner. For those were the sort of things, I believe, that he had noticed in France. Those and a million small and apparently unimportant flavours and sounds and sights made him love France as I love it for ever and always better than any country except my own. This is a love that is only increased should the beloved be humiliated in battle, that survives should she be clamorously victorious. This was what Hartley and I had in common.

We both missed him very much, and hoped that he knew we were thinking of him affectionately, for the space, the void, we create when we leave the earth matters as much as our mark on it.

*          *          *          *

With the shortage of new engines in France at that time mechanics were greatly sought after, and I had to woo young Auguste Guidobaldi of Antibes as a newspaper correspondent woos a Chef de Cabinet. Guidobaldi appeared one morning in his own car, darted at our engine, dismounted almost everything dismountable and carried it away in his car. That afternoon he reappeared and fitted the engine together again. This took him, with adjustments to the timing and the carburetion, about ninety minutes. He started the engine with a half twist of the handle, and pronounced it to be in good order. At the end of this speedy work he drank a citron pressé and named a high price for his skill. I was glad to pay it, for he was the first mechanical near-genius who had assisted us, and the first in whose promises I had absolute faith. The Spanish mechanics in Gibraltar had been thorough but had lacked the touch of inspiration and luck that were so clearly in the fingers and eyes of this young Frenchman, a married man with two children. From then on we seemed to have a new engine, and the confidence in the engine that had seeped away in Larache soon returned to us.

*          *          *          *

*Serica's* small windlass of agreeable and convenient shape was a fitting that drew much unsolicited admiration from French yachtsmen. But although it had been satisfactory in open anchorages I found it too delicate for the harbour work of the South of France, where one is likely to foul something each time one drops an anchor. The ideal windlass for such work, even on a small boat, is a powerful one with a low and a high gear. When we had decided to leave Antibes harbour late one evening I found that I could not move the anchor. We bounced the bow. We tightened on the chain until the windlass handle bent, the counter was in the air, and the mast tilted forward. Faced with the alternative of slipping the cable and making the end fast to the quay or of staying the night in Antibes, we decided on the latter course, for we did not care to risk losing forty-five fathoms of good chain and a good anchor. We hauled our stern back to the quay. In the morning we had consultations with various friends in the harbour including the elderly harbour-master, a charming fellow with whom I daily discussed running ulcers (his particular cross), and with whom I remained on affectionate terms, for I frequently gave him packets of the small and potent French cheroots known as Voltigeurs. He was of the opinion that our anchor was hooked in one of the wrecks that the Germans had sunk in the middle of the harbour. Others advised us to seek assistance from Mr. Loel Guinness, whose immaculate Diesel yacht, *Sea Huntress*, was lying in the port. Stepping past the supercharged Alfa Romeo at the end of *Sea Huntress's* gangway, I met the owner, a well-built man in swimming trunks, and told him of our trouble. Shortly afterwards Guinness came aboard *Serica*. Adjusting a fishing mask over eyes and nose, suspending from his person an apparatus enabling him to breathe compressed air from a bottle, and squeezing his feet into rubber flippers, this un-usually adventurous man took stock of the situation from *Serica's* bows, and without more ado dived neatly into the oily water. We watched with gratitude and dismay the trail of bubbles that marked his submarine progress along 180 feet of our anchor chain. For some considerable time the bubbles and clouds of oozy mud appeared in the centre of the harbour, where our anchor lay in three fathoms. Then the diver surfaced and swam back to us. He had not been able to dislodge the anchor or to discover how it was held because any movement of the stock, which was standing upright, had stirred up underwater ex-plosions of filth. He thereupon arranged to get his own yacht out of her berth to haul on our chain with her powerful hydraulic windlass. In a few moments we had moved until our chain was up and down, *Sea*

ned toward us.  A south-west breeze blowing across the basin made
manœuvring difficult for us, and more so for *Sea Huntress* despite her
powerful engines and twin screws, for she only had a few yards to play
with between the dredger and the broken masonry at the other side of
the harbour.  She was imperturbably handled, but as she began to haul
on our cable *Serica* surged forward and, dodging the fenders with which
*Sea Huntress's* crew sought to ward off the attack, took a long gouge
out of the white paintwork.  The Danforth came away from the bottom
with a jerk, and soon I had it and the chain on deck.  Both vessels
extricated themselves from the harbour, *Serica* whisking round and
going out full speed ahead to make room for her big saviour, which
came out gingerly stern first.  We had to thank her owner and crew for a
most Christian and skilful action, which preserved to us two in-
dispensable servants, anchor and cable.  Other yachts then lying at
Antibes belonged to Sir Alexander Korda, Sir Oswald Mosley, Lord
Stanley of Alderley, and the Hon. Neville Berry.

We sailed west and anchored for the night off Théoule, where there is
shelter from westerlies and the water is deep right up to the sandy shore.
I lost a leadline there, for we were confused by the reflections of the shore
lights in the smooth, blue-black water, and I took so many soundings
without finding bottom that my right hand began to lose feeling and I
allowed the whole line to slip through my wet fingers.  It was good to
see the anchor go down through clean water to a bottom most unlikely
to be fouled.  Our earlier cruise in those waters with the ketch *Truant*
had been our first experience of managing a boat on the sea, and except
for the excellent anchorages of the island of Port Cros we had concentrated on the man-made harbours, going from Marseilles to Bandol,
Bandol to St. Tropez, St. Tropez to Antibes, Nice, Monte Carlo, San
Remo.  This time we knew enough to realise that we were more secure,
infinitely cleaner, and likely to get better rest outside the harbours than
in them.  From Théoule we called for some friends at la Napoule.  That
night the heat wave had broken and we woke in torrents of rain (for
we had slept on deck).  This was the first rain we had seen since
Gibraltar.  The yacht was perfectly tight.  Not a drop came through
deck or hatches.

We motored through the rain (thoroughly enjoying its novelty) to the

Îles des Lérins. These small wooded islands are the haunt of most of the yachtsmen on the coast. They repair to the Îles in shoals to bathe and have lunch either on board or ashore. But it was still raining when we dropped anchor in the channel between the islands and near the small harbour of the monastery on the outer island, the Île St. Honorat. No other boat was near. We set the cockpit awning to protect us from the rain. While we ate, more boats, two-thirds of them British motor yachts, arrived from the mainland. We had not expected to like this fashionable anchorage, but that day we were delighted with it. The water was so transparent that we might have been floating on air, and the bottom, spotless sand and weed, said much for the cleanly habits of those who often anchor there. We were very close inshore; when the rain stopped the sun came out bringing to us the good smells of the shrubs and pines. The crickets buzz there as they do at Port Cros. With the evening breeze we sailed fast round the inner island, Ste Marguerite, and back to la Napoule. A mistral was gathering strength when we moved on to Théoule, where we anchored close inshore and landed to buy provisions. The village was full of English people, plainer and more lively than those that crowded Cannes. Entering a tabac to buy *Nice-Matin* and a drink, I found Englishmen clustered round the zinc bar and sitting confabulating at the big table. They were good specimens from the north of England, thoroughly enjoying themselves, their faces burned brick colour over their white, open-necked shirts. When we got back to the yacht the mistral was increasing, and we gave the cable more scope.

The *Héron Blanc*, an old stager belonging to Monsieur Auniac, director of the shipyard at Antibes, came into our bay for shelter. She was a motor yacht of, I suppose, some forty tons, Thames measurement. She presented a top-heavy appearance, and yet her owner was envied, for she was widely regarded as the perfect yacht for those waters, since she had a good turn of speed, all the necessary gadgets, could be handled by a professional crew of two and a female cook, and provided maximum comfort for as many guests as her hospitable owner cared to take with him for a day on the water. Her galley (a part of the deck accommodation, and both roomy and airy) was a sight to see with its many pots and pans hanging on hooks and its picturesque cook hard at work on a full-size cooker. *Héron Blanc's* awnings were stoutly fixed, and threw shade all along the deck. In this respect almost any of the British yachts were inferior, because in Britain, a country enjoying only filtered and intermittent sunshine, awnings are not properly understood. No motor-boat should travel to the Mediterranean unless it can be covered with well-secured awnings from stem to stern, and there should also be canvas flaps to let down in harbour from the edge of the awning to deck level to protect the side that is exposed to the sun. This is the only way to keep the temperature below decks from becoming intolerable in anything approaching hot weather. . . . On sailing-craft the problem of shade is more complex. A modern sailing-yacht carries so much bulky canvas that it is hard to find stowage for awnings, and the latter must be easily dismountable or the temptation to leave them up and use the auxiliary engine is too strong in waters where breezes are light and fitful. The engineer of a big British ketch lying in Antibes told me that the mainsail had not been used between Lisbon and Gibraltar, although they had held the Portuguese Trades all the way down the coast. "To hoist the mainsail we'd have had to strike the main awning," he explained.

On *Truant* our awnings had been so bulky that we had often been too tired to put them up, so for *Serica* I had had made a small cockpit awning (which stretched forward over the doghouse) with four wooden battens fitting into pockets. (Each batten folded on a central hinge for easier stowage.) I would have done well to have had another similar awning to go forward to the mast, another for the space from mast to pulpit, and a side awning interchangeable from one side to the other. On my next boat (if I have one) I shall also fit a cockpit awning stretching from a permanent horse for the main boom to two stanchions set in slots at the forward corners of the cockpit. Such an awning would have been most useful to us, but unfortunately *Serica* has a teak crutch of the scissors type that is unshipped when the mainsail is hoisted.

The cause of the above digression, the *Héron Blanc*, woke me at 5 a.m. when she drew in her chain. She thrummed away rapidly, aiming to reach her home port during the mistral's early-morning lull. We moved some three hours later, and carrying the Genoa alone romped down the coast to Cannes. The mistral was blowing full blast, and although I did not bother to check our speed (except by the patent log, which gave us over nine knots) we thought we were travelling almost as fast as we had with mainsail and spinnaker off the east coast of Majorca. In an astonishingly brief time I had to hand the Genoa, and we entered Cannes harbour under power. The harbour was packed with yachts of many types, sizes, and nationalities, and with the craft of smugglers lying like dogfish among goldfish. The yachts were two-deep round the quays in several places. We anchored off the Quai St. Pierre and, thanks to the good offices of a delightful Welshman (a smuggler), we were able to get a line out and haul ourselves astern against the weight of the mistral. We lay in the lee of a former Admiralty craft into whose tall bows, do what I would with our warps and chain, we bumped our shrouds at intervals throughout the day. We had seldom occupied a more hellish berth. The mistral, howling across roads, beaches, and gardens, turned the wide basin into a swirling inferno of dirt, sand, and small stones. Within an hour the yacht, like all those around it (though the mistral had done little to alter the condition of some of *them*), was a floating dust-heap. On deck our feet sank into layers of grit and below decks dust-pyramids began to form under the Dorade ventilators.

If the stockbroker, the ballet dancer, the oil magnate, the bank clerk, the deposed monarch, the successful artist, the gambler, the book-maker, and the pawnbroker like to live on the Côte d'Azur, why not the smuggler? Anyway, there he was in his hundreds. Sometimes he looked poor, sometimes rich, sometimes costive, sometimes genial—it was impossible to generalise about him, except that we always seemed to know who was a smuggler and who was not. About his boat, yes, you could generalise: it was of British origin (having been bought when the Admiralty disposed of shoals of fast craft at the end of the second German war); it always seemed to fly the Red Ensign (sometimes in the wrong place—for example, one smuggler we met on the coast flew the Ensign at the yardarm, but then her captain was German); and it was extraordinarily dirty and ill-maintained, though doubtless this did not apply to the engines. Strange indeed, we thought, to see so many of those rough boats among the yachts and on a coast that we so well remembered with never a smuggler, at any rate of that commercialised type. At one end of the coast smugglers had always crossed the Pyrenees with rucksacks on their shoulders. (Two such men had smuggled me from France into Spain during the war.) At the other end smugglers had crossed the Alps into Italy, or had sailed round the frontier in small boats. Smuggling will always exist so long as nations divide themselves into separate trade boxes and in varying degrees levy governmental incomes by taxing easily marketable luxuries. But here was smuggling on a big scale. What did they smuggle? . . . I asked them if they carried rice or flour or hashish or women or Nazis or Communists.

They answered (if they answered at all) that they carried that vulgar, uninteresting, comparatively harmless, dirty, little opiate—the cigarette. This too was the local theory, or at least such of it as was explained to us (and of course I cannot vouch for its truth). We were told that the centre for Mediterranean smuggling was the "free" port of Tangier. From there ships went into the Mediterranean carrying cargoes of American cigarettes. Fast motor craft came out from their shore bases, loaded up far out at sea with the cargo, and ran it to points on the coast whence it was distributed over Italy, France, or Spain.

British yachtsmen sometimes told us that although the smugglers' craft flew our flag the ownership was only technically British; they thought that not an Englishman, a Scotsman, or a Welshman would you find among the crews. We soon disproved that. The crews were made up of all European nationalities, it seemed, and a fair number of them were British men and women. In harbour the smugglers, being simpler people and more natural than the yachtsmen, led a more openly domestic existence. One of our neighbours, a former M.L., had its quarter-deck piled high with cases of empty beer and wine bottles and among the cases a woman with bleached hair was washing a heap of men's clothing. She said she was a Lithuanian. After a time a big man came out to help her. He worked at the tub while she hung up the washing. He said he was an Alsatian. Three men sat forward, smoking and intently playing cards; they were Spaniards (from Perpignan, the woman said). When the washing was done and steaming on the lines she took a worn broom and began to sweep up the litter in the wheelhouse. She was employed "to cook and keep the boat clean".

"That must be hard work," Isabel suggested.

"Oh no. There are three of us girls . . ." (she was a woman in her thirties), "and we take turns at everything. Lili's cooking today and I'm doing the tidying. My other pal's ashore with her cousin, the engineer."

"And do you go to sea?"

"Oh yes. The cooking has to be done just the same then. But I don't like that part of it. Last time we were all three sick as dogs. The lads weren't much better, some of them. It blew a mistral."

"Where were you then?"

"I don't know."

"Is your old boat fast?"

"I can't say. . . . All I know is she leaks all over us if it rains—and I'd better get on with my work."

There were certain risks entailed in the smugglers' work, and we knew from observing them that there were long hours of boredom. They had little regular work to keep them on fair terms with each other, and there was friction and bad temper, though outwardly they were well behaved. They were probably relieved when they got an order to put to sea, if only for a change of air and a breath of excitement. Two smuggling craft, very fast ones, had been destroyed by gunfire from an Italian patrol vessel a day or two before we arrived at Antibes.

What was our reaction to the smugglers? At first we were priggish as you would expect people to be who had never had occasion to sail but with clear consciences. We objected to seeing so many obvious and un-punished breakers of one of the important laws of the sea. We hated seeing the Red Ensign on so many disreputable, even disgustingly sordid, vessels. Yet the smugglers themselves were interesting, much more so than most of the yachtsmen prinking about in their pretty Florida or Cannes clothing. Since the smugglers were not on holiday, and many of them were unhappy or embarrassed in this way or that, their attitude to life was sympathetic. They were always ready to give us a helping hand.

"I've got just the thing here for your throat," the gentlemanly Welshman said, and he gave me a bottle of penicillin tablets. "Suck one of those every two hours and you'll have your voice back in a day or two. You've caught some streptococcal infection, that's what's the matter with you. . . ."

I was embarrassed. He saw my bewilderment, and understood it.

"Perhaps you'd be happier to know that you can buy these tablets in any French chemist's," he said. "At home you can't get penicillin without a doctor's prescription. The stuff is a cure for a certain disease, and the British authorities insist on knowing exactly how that disease is going. But the French, as you might expect, take another line; so far as they're concerned, the more people who cure themselves without bothering doctors or hospitals the better—so the sale of the drug is free."

I asked him to advise us where to eat in Cannes.

"Personally I can never afford to go to a restaurant unless I'm invited," he said. "I always eat on board. But they tell me they give good value for money at a place called la Crémerie Provençale; it's in one of the streets behind the Croisette. You should get there before midday because the French simply pack it out."

Already the small restaurant was so crowded that we were directed to the last two empty seats at a table for six. The tables, perhaps twenty of them, were tightly spaced, and the two hefty maids had to twist about with apologies and frantic extrications from narrow corners. Here for as little as 450 francs each (nine shillings) we had an excellent meal with some choice (and we might have eaten less copiously but as well for 350). Isabel, who had of course been marketing for our meals on the boat, could not understand how the patronne had managed to get together so much food at such reasonable prices. But the prices were obviously achieved by running the place at top speed and taking a large number of very small profits. I had never (even in England) been so hustled through a meal, and before we had been many minutes at the table I saw what I had never seen from a French restaurant, a queue of French people forming outside the doors. They stood two and three deep on the hot pavement. So eager were they to get in and eat that family parties would split up, mother going to one table, father to another, son and daughter to another. How were the mighty fallen! This in a town probably boasting hundreds of restaurants.

* * * *

That night the mistral died away and the moon came out. There was an offshore breeze. It was impossible to resist so welcome a change of weather. We loosed the many ropes that held us to the shore and to our unlawful but kind-hearted neighbours. Our anchor, we were delighted to discover, was not fouled. We floated out of Cannes harbour, the moon-light glistening on our sails, the Genoa goose-winging. Less than an hour later we dropped anchor in the lee of the Île Ste Marguerite. Bucket after bucket of phosphorescent water we sent cascading over deck and coach-roof, and when *Serica* was clean we plunged into the sea. It was after midnight when we landed to bake lobsters and potatoes in the ashes of a fire smothered with kelp. We walked about the woods while our meal was cooking, and, returning to the beach, drank white wine from Cassis with the hot smoky food.

Next morning we did not wake till the sun was warming our faces. The passengers on a steamer passing toward Cannes grinned at the sight of us half asleep on deck. We sailed up the coast, that day, wondering where to go. . . . The end of July had come and it was time to find a berth where *Serica* could be safely left while we returned to England. But where? Some people advised la Ciotat, back down the coast near Marseilles, many said Cannes, others Antibes, others Nice, others Villefranche, where the Frères Voisin have a dry dock for yachts.

Five motor cruisers flying our Ensign bobbed under the well-populated Mappin Terraces of Eden Roc, where men and women lay on red cushions cooking themselves with oil, and where a turbaned specialist, whom we had seen daily catching the bus from Antibes, told fortunes in dulcet French or English. The yachts were rolling and all their awnings were too skimpy for the climate, but I suppose the people on board thought they were suffering discomfort for a worth-while purpose.

In the afternoon we sailed across the wide Baie des Anges. Forest fires were burning on the mountains behind Nice. Several boat-loads of tourists lay off the stubby end of Cap Ferrat. They were fishing, and enjoying themselves. To port of the lighthouse, which was being rebuilt, Mr. Somerset Maugham's white villa showed through the trees, its gardens rising on the terraced hill. We turned into Villefranche Bay and that evening dropped anchor in the bigger of Villefranche's two harbours. We found an excellent berth, though the water was foul with oily scum from the engines of the thirty smuggling vessels gathered in the port. Monsieur Voisin, a giant with curly hair, was working torse-nue at a drawing-board in his cave of an office. Villefranche is a good place. I like it, but it can be damnably hot and airless, and the mosquitoes there can be infernal. We were called from Voisin's office by the harbour-master, who, just roused from his siesta, his eyes hot with sleep, was in a rage because I had berthed without his permission. Such official wrath is rare in a French harbour. I listened to it for a long time without making reply, and Isabel went calmly off into the town to do some shopping. We would have to move that evening, the official said. The berth was reserved for a bigger boat which might arrive that night or again might not arrive for a week; it was coming from Italy. Small boats, he said with a contemptuous gesture at *Serica* (by far the handsomest boat in the harbour) were not allowed at that quay. If I was determined to inflict myself on his harbour he would have to find me another berth.

"Do you see this?" I said to him, lifting one corner of our Blue Ensign. "To you it is only a foreign flag, but it belongs to me, I belong to it, and I strive to bring nothing but honour to it."

"Bravo!" exclaimed three filthy men, Polish smugglers, who were listening to us, and, "Bravo!" echoed the harbour-master.

"You tolerate in your harbour many other vessels flying my flag."

"Comme de bien entendu," he agreed, looking round at the hugger-mugger collection.

"So you must just put up with us."

"Is that your last word?"

"It is."

"Then stay here tonight, but no longer—and no more arguments, mind, flag or no flag."

"Bravo!" repeated the one Pole who remained. "The commandant appreciates direct speech. At any rate he gets nothing else from our crowd."

The harbour-master made off and the Pole brought out from behind his back some large object wrapped in damp newspapers. "Will you dine with me?" he asked.

"With the greatest pleasure."

"I am so glad. For two years I was in England and then I came here as a contrebandier. Rotten job. Too much competition. You have a cooking stove? You'll let me cook the dinner on your stove?"

"I'll cook it," I said, thinking that safest.

"Good!" he said, handing me the parcel. "Here is the dinner. I'll be back in one hour."

"Wait a minute." I unwound the newspapers and found a huge chicken, the feathers still on. "You pluck it down there," I said, "and I'll cook it, but I warn you I've no oven."

"Stew, that's best," he answered, squatting on the quay and making the feathers fly. "Boil him good."

"Give me ninety minutes." I cut the chicken into pieces and fried it in butter. I fried onions. I fried tomatoes. I made stock with the remains of the chicken, and herbs and wine. I simmered the lot with young carrots, potatoes, button mushrooms from a tin, and green pimento. I also cooked rice. Isabel, returning from the town, said that she had noticed steam rising from the galley when she was a mile away and commented that my cooking had sent the temperature below decks up to ninety-four (F). She laid the table in the cockpit, and when the Pole arrived we had a fine meal. I watched him carefully, for I had been determined that he would not find the chicken stew as he would expect to find it in England. He ate swiftly, without any visible attempt at mastication, and his manner was a little peculiar—as though he were waiting for something unpleasant to happen. We finished the stew (he playing his full part), two bottles of Macon, one kilo of green figs with cream, the contents of a coffee-pot, and one-third of a bottle of whisky (as a liqueur). At last, his eyes watering and his frame shaken by hiccups, he said good-night.

Two hours later another Pole came into the saloon.

"What have you done to my friend?" he asked.

"He was all right when he left us."

"All right! He's dying. . . . The doctor's with him now, pumping him out. Did you give him any matières grasses? He has an ulcerated stomach. The doctor does not allow him to eat fats. He is supposed to subsist on the jelly of beef or the boiled flesh of fowls. He insists that all he ate here was boiled chicken, but the doctor is not disposed to believe him. You understand that if my friend dies the police may be called, and they might require details from you. So if you would not mind telling me what he had for dinner . . ."

I brought out a saucepan with chicken bones in it. The Pole took off the lid and sniffed. "Chicken, as he truthfully said. And a bay leaf and a little wine would not have hurt the poor fellow. Did he drink much?"

"Only a little wine, and some of this . . ."

"Whisky!" he said so movingly that I filled two small glasses and handed him one. "The King of England!" he said, and emptied his glass.

"The President of the Republic!" he said.

"Poland!" I said, refilling.

"The Royal Air Force!"

"Warsaw!"

"Damnation to all blacklegs!"

"Good-night . . . good-night . . ."

When he had gone we hauled out from the quay, switched on the navigation lights and hoisted the mainsail before winding in the last four fathoms of chain. It was a perfect night with a light south-westerly breeze. We rippled smoothly out of Villefranche Bay, rounded Cap Ferrat, and anchored in a small bay set in the eastern side of the cape.

Bathers were splashing in the moonlit shallows. La Paloma, a beach bar, was still illuminated and a few couples were dancing with the jerky energy of French dancers. In the garden of the big Gothic villa footmen were clearing a dinner table. The silver and glass in their hands spat gleaming light into the darkness as though wanting to be rid of it before resting the night away in baize-lined repositories. When we had stowed the sails La Paloma was closing down, the last fines-à-l'eau and coupes-de-champagne were gurgling in the throats of the last clients; and the soft artificial turf lapping the Gothic walls of the villa was untrodden and drinking the dew. *Serica* sat the water like a painted swan and the scent of night-breathing flowers came out to her from the sleeping coast. High up in the hills behind the bay fans of moving light swept down the bends from the Château de Madrid, and further east Monte Carlo, hidden by the promontory with the aquarium, sent a broken column of light into the soft, clear air. We slept on deck.

In the morning all was peaceful, for the Côte d'Azur is no early riser. A six-metre called *Hope* came sailing out of the small harbour of St. Jean, about half a mile away. A lovely sight, well handled by her Swiss crew, she slid past us so near that we heard the bubble under her counter.

"What do you think she draws?" Isabel asked.

"About the same as *Serica*."

"Then there must be a berth free now in St. Jean. Let's go in at once."

Before the anchor was down she said: "It's lovely here. Not a smuggler and clear, clear water. *This* is the place to leave *Serica* tucked up for the winter."

To enter the harbour we had had to round the bows of two big motor yachts both flying the Blue Ensign and one going by the refeshing name —yacht names are apt to be somewhat Pre-Raphaelite—of *Mome Rath*. The entry channel had looked almost dangerously shallow, and as we hauled our stern to the quay, between *Mome Rath* and a pretty French six-metre, a thoroughly feminine craft, the bottom, waving with green weed, seemed to spring up at us. Lying with our counter close in, we had about two feet of water under the after end of the keel. Sterns to the same mole lay the two (comparative) Leviathans and six or seven yachts of *Serica's* size or smaller; on the shallow landward side of the basin Stars and sailing dinghies were moored.

We were discussing our luck in finding what seemed to be the last berth in so delightful a harbour when another yacht came in, an old Camper & Nicholson cutter, painted black and so battered that the name on her counter was unreadable. Slightly longer than *Serica* and much beamier, she was crewed by four married couples who had been at sea for some time and in heavy weather, for their handsome faces were a dusty brown, and bruises showed on their arms and legs. Her saloon was piled so high with wet sails that canvas (how sordid wet canvas can look!) exuded from the skylight. Noting these sights, Isabel stirred me to help her make room for the black cutter. We hauled still closer to the glossy side of *Mome Rath*, and moved the six-metre away from us by adjusting her stern lines. The Bretons, for such they were, waved acknowledgments and came astern until they lay touching our fenders. Their eyes were startlingly bright in their dark, tired faces, their voices gruff. The women were already bringing everything up from below to dry in the sun, sweaters, blankets, mattresses, cushions, books. They pronounced *Serica* "impeccable", which was far from the truth by Cowes standards, but not so far by comparison with their own agreeable vessel, which, from rusty anchor chain to rusty charging motor lashed on deck, showed evidence of that kind of insouciance that I admire in other yachtsmen yet fail to accomplish myself. Their yacht had been built in Victoria's reign. They had left her at St. Jean the previous winter in the charge of an elderly fisherman to whom they paid 5,000 francs a month. They had arrived thirty days before our meeting, had found the condition of their yacht to be satisfactory and had sailed that evening for the Bay of Naples. Returning to St. Jean via Corsica, they had run into a fierce mistral, and had spent five days at sea. Now they were back in St. Jean harbour, their holiday over, their boat, they cheerfully admitted, in a terrible tangle and with scarcely a shred of paint left on the hull. They were departing in three hours on a train for Paris (after having a chat with the fisherman-caretaker). They produced five bottles of vintage champagne (no point in leaving any of *that* on board) and invited us to join them, bringing the ice from our refrigerator. They were a delightful group of people, virile and natural, overjoyed with their holiday, yet glad to be returning to the north, some to Paris, others to the coast of Brittany. (One couple lived at Benodet.) An hour later they were gone.

I kept an eye on the black cutter, for I thought we might rely on the same fisherman to look after *Serica*. But in three days following the owners' departure the decks were unwashed, the sails were still piled in the saloon, the charging motor and the mattresses still lay on deck. I mentioned these things to the captain of *Mome Rath*.

"When some of the initial 5,000 francs has been digested the man will begin to do some work," he said. "That's how they are in the Midi."

That's how they are. But generalisations are always untrue, and while we lay in that place I watched the work of one of the French hands on

*Mome Rath*, a thin, scrupulously neat individual called, I soon learned, Alphonse, and known in the harbour as Phonphon. *Mome Rath*, a converted Admiralty motor launch with powerful twin Diesel engines, new pitch-pine decks, stainless-steel guard-rail stanchions, and a large deck saloon including in its permanent furnishings a bar and a stucco statuette of Mr. Winston Churchill making the V sign, did not attract us as a vessel; but thanks to Phonphon she was immaculate. Early each morning I watched him at his astiquage. How he washed and polished, polished and washed! Then he would beat out the mats and lay them along the port side of the deck lest some stranger should step on the clean wood. Once I saw him stalk his owner down the length of the deck, wiping with a chamois leather at places where that jolly man had rested his perfectly clean hand. When Phonphon had no other astiquage to do he would set to work cleaning and polishing his owner's Rolls-Royce. I was not surprised when the owner, without prompting, told me that Phonphon was the best man he had ever employed.

Phonphon took a grave delight, a serious interest, in *Serica*, for he had been a yacht hand most of his life (he had served in the Gaulliste navy during the war) and yachts were in his blood. He helped to persuade me to leave the boat for the winter at St. Jean.

"Ici on est tranquil, l'hiver," he would say. "I've a mooring (un corps mort), and you're most welcome to it if you decide to leave the yacht here. St. Jean's the cleanest harbour on the coast, and the most honest because it's so small that everyone knows all about everyone else. Last year there was a man who stole, but now he's gone to prison for eighteen months. . . ."

There was little water traffic to set up uncomfortable washes, and, since the mole astern was a cul-de-sac, no wheeled traffic passed to raise dust except for the van of that useful citizen, the ice man, who arrived every morning at seven. There was excellent bathing within a yard or two of our counter, for we had only to cross the Mole to dive off the bathing ladder into the open sea. There was a fresh-water tap on the mole (water provided free to yachtsmen) for washing and watering the boat and for hosing each other after bathing. An admirable baker's shop sent its odours across the harbour, and at six each morning one of us would stroll round to it to buy warm croissants for breakfast. Milk, cream, butter, and eggs, all of the freshest, were available from a farm set among the small villas off the road behind the bakery. These products were dear, but, as the farmer's wife explained, property being

what it is on that coast, there was no room on the farm for more than a
dairy, a byre, a chicken-run, and a barn; fodder had to be bought from
the north of France, and the transport of a ton of hay cost twice as much
as the hay itself. Monsieur Jean Cappa, the leading restaurateur of the
place, offered to give us a dry room under one of his restaurants in which
to store all our gear, while Monsieur Antoine the garagiste of Beaulieu,
an old friend, promised to take care of our engines and batteries for the
winter.

While our thoughts turned to the winter delights of England we
also looked beyond the winter to the pleasure of returning to St. Jean
Cap Ferrat in the early spring and beginning again the round of the
paint-pot and the varnish-pot, the scraper and the scrubber.

NOTE: It is only fair to point out that we met the smugglers in July and
August of 1950. When we returned to that coast in April, 1951, the smugglers
had vanished, though a few of their boats mouldered in dead corners of certain
harbours while many others had been converted into bona fide yachts. The
reason for this disappearance, we were told, was the launching and operating by
the French and Italian authorities of fast well-armed vedettes.

## CHAPTER 27

## "A WHITE BOAT FROM ENGLAND"

WE were sitting in the bows on a hot night at the beginning of August.
Our bedding lay beside us on the deck. We looked across the harbour
to the lights of St. Jean clustered above the port, thinning out as they
climbed the hills with here and there a tree outlined against a light.
The harbour was asleep, and we were about to sleep, for we had spent a
tiring day stripping the engine and carrying gear to the store-room.

Gentle splashing drew our eyes to the water below us. We saw a man
in an inflated rubber dinghy. The paddler shone with wetness, face,
hair, clothing. His appearance was dejected yet full of urgency.

"This is your boat?" he asked in thick French. "There has been an
accident, and my friend is in the water far out, wounded and bleeding.
It was an explosion. He and I found ourselves alone among the wreck-
age. This rubber boat would hold only one of us and he was not fit to
paddle. I put him in a lifebuoy. Then I came for help. It was all I could
do to reach the shore against the wind. Had the wind been stronger—
*adieu!*"

"How far out was your accident?"

"One, two miles beyond the cape, Cap Ferrat. . . . This is your
boat? It has an engine?"

"No, we dismantled the engine today. You had better look for a
motor-boat."

He paddled away to the head of the harbour, but in a few minutes he
came walking along the quay.

"There's no other boat but yours," he said.

"You said there was a breeze *against* you as you came in?"

"Yes, yes, a land breeze, but too light for a sailing-boat."

"Then free the stern warps, come aboard, and pull the gangway after
you. Will you know where to find your friend?"

"Yes, I will," he grunted, hauling on a warp. "I remember how the
light on Cap Ferrat looked when I left him, and there is a floating
emergency light attached to his lifebuoy—pray God it still burns. . . .
You're sure your motor won't work?"

303

"Carburettor, coil, distributor, and batteries are all at a garage in Beaulieu."

"Beaulieu's not far."

"It would be by the time we'd found a taxi; and then we'd have to look for the garagiste, since the garage will be locked up now. If there's still a breeze we'll travel fast enough with the sails, you'll see."

We had to push *Serica* out of the harbour with the long boat-hook, prodding wherever we could touch the other yachts. An agonised yell came from the interior of *Mome Rath* as our boat-hook probed at Phonphon's paintwork. Once outside we gave our passenger the tiller while Isabel helped me to hoist the spinnaker. The land breeze was, as he had said, very light, but we soon picked up speed and moved steadily out past the point. The sea was calm, with a slow, inky heave to it.

"You carry no lights?" he asked.

"We put them ashore today, but we've a battery lamp. You'd better go forward and shine it ahead so that your friend may see it and answer if he can."

"I won't be able to see under that huge sail."

"Yes you will, if you go right forward into the bows. And keep an eye aft to get your bearing on the lighthouse. You can signal aft to us with the lamp: one flash to ask us to steer to starboard, two for port, and three for dead ahead."

"I'm very cold," he said.

"Hungry?"

"No, but I could do with some cognac and a thick coat."

Isabel took him below. I had streamed the log when we were level with the end of the cape. When we were three miles out I went forward and told him of the distance.

"Should we put about?" I asked.

"I don't think we've gone far enough yet. He'd probably drift out with the wind like this."

"Better try hailing him."

"All right. But I don't suppose the poor devil still has his hearing. . . . *Pierre*! . . . *Pierre*! . . . *Pierre*! . . ."

"You're certain he has a light? Did you test it before you left him?"

"Yes, yes, it burned automatically as soon as it reached the water, but it was faint and yellow. It wouldn't show up well, especially from this low level and with the roll of the sea."

"One of us should go up the mast. Will you go? I'll haul you up in the bosun's chair."

"Up there?" he said. "Not I! I feel sick enough at this level."

"Would you be too weak to haul me up? My wife will help."

"Go ahead," he answered. 1 took the torch from him and dropped down into the forecastle to look for the bosun's chair. I made it fast to the jib halyards. Isabel came forward and took a turn with the rope round the drum of the windlass. They began to haul me up, and 1 had to ask the man to heave less lustily. Since the mainsail was set and drawing I had to climb facing aft and I had difficulty in getting handholds. The higher I went the more the yacht seemed to plunge and sway. At last I had my feet on the top spreader. I wriggled out of the chair and climbed another eight feet until I could see over the spinnaker. When I felt myself secure I looked down on the sea. First ahead; nothing there. To port, nothing. But far out on the starboard beam I saw a flickering, yellow light. I shouted to Isabel to make fast the jib halyard and go aft to the tiller. When she had swung the yacht to head for the light she took a bearing. The spinnaker was now hanging in ghostly folds round the forestays, and one corner was in the sea. The strength was ebbing from my arms. I slid down to the chair. The man lowered me and did his best in the dark to help me take in the spinnaker and set the Genoa. We moved steadily on. The man kept shouting. But only the sea answered with its wet whispers and chuckles. We sailed on for what seemed an age. I had found the strain of looking forward too great for my nerves, had gone aft and was suggesting to Isabel in the cockpit that I ought to go aloft again when there was a shout from the bows.

"La lumière! tribord un peu, Madame, tribord. Ça-y-est."

We hove-to, looking down on that piece of human driftwood. His eyes were closed. He was as slimy as an eel. The lifebuoy, coloured blue and red, was tied under his arms. As we shone our light down on him we saw shoals of fish under him. The sight frightened me, thinking of the helpless, perhaps wounded, legs dangling below. I turned off the lamp. The man had flung himself on the deck, head and shoulders overboard, under the rail. He caught hold of the thick dark hair and lifted up a pallid face.

"Pierre! Eh, Pierre, it's Franz. You're saved mon petit."

Isabel had put the companion ladder over the side and opened the rails. I went down the ladder and tried to lift him, but he weighed a ton. The man on deck, Franz, he had called himself, got a noose round the lifebuoy, but still the three of us could not lift him up those high topsides until we took down the mainsail and got the main halyard to him. Then he came up. As I slacked on the halyard the water sluiced off him, rattling on the deck. When we had him safe Isabel hurried below. She lit our anthracite stove (the first time, this, that we had seen it burning). She collected a pile of blankets and made up a bed in the saloon. There was a damp nip in the air, but down there with the Primus, the oil lamp, and the stove going, it became very warm.

"Leave the wounds," Franz said. "A doctor can see to them if we get him ashore alive. The first thing's to make him warm, but mind that arm—it's broken, see? the bone's come through the skin, poor devil!"

We opened his teeth (strong but tobacco-stained) and poured a mixture of brandy, warm milk and sugar through them.

"Now, Madame," Franz said, "it would be best if you left us to work on him."

"Yes," she said. "I'll start beating back. I expect we should make for Villefranche."

"That's right," Franz said, pulling gently at the unconscious man's shirt. "Your knife, please, Monsieur. . . . Yes, we've friends at Villefranche and can get him at once to a doctor. I was trying to paddle there in the rubber boat but the wind pushed me away."

I heard her hoisting the sails. The saloon leaned gently over and the water began to bubble past the skin of the yacht. When we had stripped him we began to rub him with warm olive oil. The skin was gritty with salt. The heart was beating but the flesh was pulpy and cold. We turned him and rubbed his back. Franz became nervous and turned him again to listen at the chest.

"Still beating."

"A Frenchman?" I asked, looking down into the square, grey face. A deep cut ran down one side of the temple, passing near the outer corner of the eye to the cheek-bone.

"Yes, French. . . . I wonder if we're doing right. He must have lost the hell of a lot of blood. And the salt in those wounds'll drive him crazy if he comes to."

"Did he go under, d'you think. He may be full of water."

"We'll soon see. He probably swallowed a bit." Franz seized the shoulders and turned the body over, springing on to the back. "Any water coming out of his mouth?"

"Very little."

"Try some more brandy. That's right."

"Was there anybody else on board?"

"Only the engineer, an Egyptian. He must have been blown to bits. He was below beside the petrol tanks. Babazoun we called him. A decent soul. There was no trace of him. Not so much as a finger or a toe."

"Have you any idea what caused the explosion?"

"Yes," he said with a short laugh. "Pierre and I had a damned good idea what caused it—but the less said about that the better."

"You were bound for Villefranche?"

"Yes."

"From?"

"From the Italian coast. . . . A big cargo too. We obey orders, you see. We sometimes don't know where we're from or where we're bound. . . . Did you hear that?"

We both stared down at the man on the settee. He moaned again more loudly. A bubble expanded and broke on his lips. My companion leaned over him. Two dark eyes opened, wounded eyes, and Pierre cried out.

"Ah, God!" he shouted. "My arm!"

"Lie still now, little one, and soon we'll be in Villefranche and the doctor will make you comfortable. Your arm's only broken, and that's nothing to worry a tough customer. . . ."

"Where am I?"

"A white boat from England, a sailing-yacht. . . . All right, Monsieur. I can look after him now. I'll hang his clothes round the stove and they'll be dry enough when we get to Villefranche. Madame has made good speed," he added, looking through the glass in the coach-roof. "There's the lighthouse, and not so far away either."

Pierre gave a terrible cry, and lost consciousness.

Two men carried him ashore on an improvised stretcher. He was moaning. Franz stopped to thank us. "He's only twenty-two," he said. "You've saved the best part of a life, you and your good little boat." He patted the doghouse, and turned to hurry after the others.

We worked *Serica* slowly out of Villefranche harbour and sailed round the cape for St. Jean.  Had all our meanderings in *Serica* been to some purpose then?

We entered the harbour the first fingers of the day were stretching into the night.  We picked up the mooring and hauled *Serica* astern to her peaceful winter quarters.  The baker was already working, and the smell of new bread came over the water.

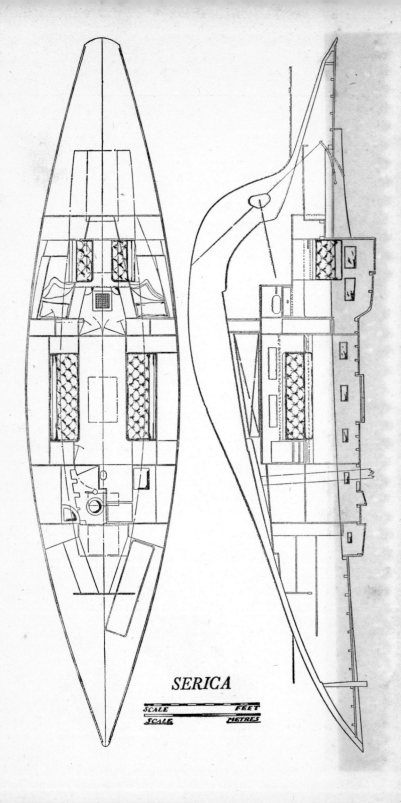

SERICA

SCALE           FEET

SCALE           METRES